Demands of the Dead

EXECUTIONS, STORYTELLING, AND

ACTIVISM IN THE UNITED STATES

EDITED BY KATY RYAN

UNIVERSITY OF IOWA PRESS, IOWA CITY

University of Iowa Press, Iowa City 52242

Copyright © 2012 by the University of Iowa Press

www.uiowapress.org

Printed in the United States of America

Design by Richard Hendel

The University of Iowa Press is a member of Green Press Initiative
and is committed to preserving natural resources.

Printed on acid-free paper

Library of Congress Cataloging-in-Publication Data
Demands of the dead: executions, storytelling, and activism in the
United States / edited by Katy Ryan.
p. cm.
Includes bibliographical references and index.
ISBN-13: 978-1-60938-088-5 (pbk)
ISBN-10: 1-60938-088-6 (pbk)
1. Prisoners' writings, American. 2. Capital punishment in literature.
3. Executions and executioners in literature. 4. Capital punishment—
Moral and ethical aspects—United States. I. Ryan, Katy, 1968–
PS508.P7D46 2012
810.8′09206927—dc23 2011042124

for my parents

It is the dead, not the living, who make the greatest demands.
—Sophocles

The Sunday before my mother passed, that Sunday and Saturday, she was out in the neighborhood, canvassing, out at the mall, at the stores, getting petitions signed. Even that Sunday she was at church, getting her petitions signed. She had her petitions in her bag. When she went to the doctor's office that Monday morning, she had her petitions and she was getting her petitions signed. And someone asked my sister . . . would it be offensive to have petitions signed at the funeral? And my sister said, "That's what my mother died doing, getting petitions signed. It would be something glorious for my mother for someone to carry on the legacy."
—Kimberly Davis, sister of Troy Anthony Davis
    who was killed by the state of Georgia on September 21, 2011

Contents

My dad put *The Autobiography of Malcolm X* into my hands at an early age and taught me, by example, to distrust the barbed wire, not the people inside. My mom always encouraged me to write, to think, to love. My first thanks to my parents, Bill and Mary Ryan, for whom justice is a matter of everyday struggle.

To Renaldo Hudson and William X for sharing their lives and letters with me. They should be free.

It has been a great pleasure to work with the contributors to this book. I owe special thanks to Bruce Franklin for his guidance and scholarly example. To Anthony Ross and Steve Champion, who trusted their words to a stranger. To Jason Stupp, who sent me a copy of Willie Francis's "My Trip to the Chair"—and this collection found its opening. To Delbert Tibbs, who visited West Virginia University in 2004 and shared with students his experience on death row. I watched his words and spirit change minds.

Karen Cardozo understood this project before I did and provided generous feedback on the introduction. Paul Wright offered detailed advice and extensive knowledge from his work at *Prison Legal News*. At every step I relied on Tony Christini for perspective and clearheadedness.

For countless conversations over the years, I am joyfully in debt to Molly Ryan, Catherine John, and Jen Pepi. Many thanks to my friends at the Appalachian Prison Book Project and my wonderful colleagues in the English Department at West Virginia University, especially John Ernest, Mark Brazaitis, Cari Carpenter, and Gwen Bergner.

I gratefully acknowledge support from the West Virginia University Eberly College of Arts and Sciences as well as research fellowships from the Tanner Humanities Center at the University of Utah and the Harry Ransom Center at the University of Texas–Austin. In Utah, I had the good fortune of canyon walks with Melanie Rae Thon. Joe Parsons at the University of Iowa Press responded with enthusiasm to this manuscript, and I will always be thankful to him. For his patience and good humor—invaluable traits in a copyeditor—praise and thanks to Jonathan Haas. The same to Charlotte Wright.

When my son Vincent saw a photograph of people carrying signs of an electric chair with a line through it, he asked me, "Why are those people against chairs?" I hesitated and stammered and interrupted myself to say, "You are only six. I don't want to dump all the meanness of the world on you." Vincent responded, "I want to know everything." Here's to you, Vincent. To justice, to peace.

Some of the material in this collection has appeared in print previously. Steve Champion's essay is drawn from a chapter in his memoir, Dead to Deliverance (2010), reprinted by permission of Split Oak Press. An earlier version of H. Bruce Franklin's essay was published as "Billy Budd and Capital Punishment: A Tale of Three Centuries" in American Literature 69 (June 1997): 337–59. Jill McDonough's poems are reprinted from Habeas Corpus (2008), by permission of Salt Publishing. A different form of John Barton's essay was published as "Liberty Ltd.: Civil Rights, Civil Liberties, and Literature," in REAL 22 (Yearbook of Research in English and American Literature), ed. Brook Thomas, 2006: 145–78. "Capital Punishment" is reprinted from The Summer of Black Widows (1996) by Sherman Alexie, by permission of Hanging Loose Press. David Kieran's essay substantially expands "Remembering Lynching and Representing Contemporary Violence in Black Arts Poetry" in M/MLA: Journal of the Midwest Modern Language Association 41.1 (Spring 2008): 34–45. A longer version of Katy Ryan's essay, under the same title, appeared in American Literature 83.1 (March 2011): 121–51. Delbert L. Tibbs's poems appeared in Selected Poems and Other Words/Works (self-published).

The United States has puzzled for centuries over the most humane and least offensive way (to spectators) to kill people—hanging, gunfire, gas, electricity, or lethal injection. Willie Francis, a teenager whose narrative opens this collection, dispensed with such concerns in the middle of the twentieth century: "I wasn't worried at all whether it would hurt me," Francis explains about Louisiana's portable electric chair. "I was more worried about the fact it was going to kill me."

Executions in the United States take place in a prison chamber, usually late at night, before a limited number of witnesses. Afterward, the state announces that justice has been served, an illusory line drawn between justifiable and unjustifiable homicide. *Demands of the Dead: Executions, Storytelling, and Activism in the United States* is a study of that line and that lie. The collection features a pamphlet written by Willie Francis, who survived, temporarily, the electric chair; essays by imprisoned writers, antiprison activists, a former correctional officer, and a coeditor of Jacques Derrida's lectures on capital punishment; as well as performance scripts and poems. From these diverse locations and modes of writing, contributors explore the appeal, administration, and atrocity of executions.

The death penalty is often imagined as a matter of simple calculus—a life for a life. Politicians and prosecutors who support state killing perform an allegiance to law and to grieving citizens, crafting a story of necessity and somber judgment. David Dow, who has represented over one hundred capital defendants in Texas, knows the importance of storytelling in the legal system: "The facts matter, but the story matters more."[1] If capital punishment depends on oversimplified narratives of personal responsibility,[2] *Demands of the Dead* works to provide more full and unsettling narratives about individual and political violence. A government employee inserting a needle filled with fatal chemicals into a person's body is not an act of God or justice but the culmination of a series of deliberate calculations and very human actions, and the repetition of a race-based history of violence.

The United States has the highest rate of imprisonment in the world. A vast penal system is woven into culture much like slavery once was: over two million people live in cages under the force of laws and guns, consigned to civil death, with captive labor producing an increasing number of goods and services.[3] This network is intimately connected with children who catch predawn buses to make visiting hours; with parents who write letters every week; with victims of violent crime who fear release dates; with stock options in private prison corporations; with ongoing and exported torture.[4] H. Bruce Franklin argues that "if we teach modern American literature without reference to the American prison and its literature, we are behaving like those who failed to see, hear, or speak about slavery and its literature."[5]

Writers are a vital part of death penalty history, contributing broadsides, pamphlets, essays, poems, novels, songs, autobiographies, and plays to the national debate.[6] On the day that the federal government killed Ethel and Julius Rosenberg in 1953, Sylvia Plath wrote in her journal, "There is no yelling, no horror, no great rebellion. That is the appalling thing. . . . Two real people being executed. No matter. The largest emotional reaction over the United States will be a rather large, democratic, infinitely bored and casual and complacent yawn."[7] There was more than a yawn—protests took place nationally and internationally—but Plath recognized a cultural complacency about state killing and connected it to American democracy. *Demands of the Dead* recalls and contributes to a literary record that has not responded with bored resignation to state killing.

Novelists have created well-known fictions about capital cases (Nathanial Hawthorne's *The Scarlet Letter*, Richard Wright's *Native Son*, Harper Lee's *To Kill a Mockingbird*) and have drawn from actual executions.[8] In his 1928 novel *Boston*, Upton Sinclair tells the story of a widow turned activist, Cornelia Thornwell, who joins the struggle to save the lives of Nicola Sacco and Bartolomeo Vanzetti. In the hours before the executions, Cornelia feels as if "she had taken Dante's place, in a journey through the various stages of hell: all this elaborate display of killing power, a thousand intricate and ingenious inventions, all the arts and sciences which civilization had contrived, applied to the wholesale and instantaneous wiping out of human life."[9] Especially unforgiving of academics, Cornelia considers the wealth and resources of Harvard: "So many hundreds of professors, of every kind of subject on earth, and they couldn't teach anything worth while!"[10]

The abolitionist literary record makes a broad appeal to principle and to social justice, often dramatizing familiar arguments about the immorality of state killing, the dubious claim of deterrence, the evidence of class and race bias, and the vulnerability of people with mental disabilities. Writers express empathy (Elizabeth Cady Stanton: "As to the gallows, it is the torture of my life");[11] concern for social responsibility (Ralph Waldo Emerson: "The money we spend for courts and prisons is very ill laid out. We make, by distrust, the thief and burglar and incendiary, and by our court and jail we keep him so");[12] commitment to human rights (Frederick Douglass: "Life is the great, primary and most precious and comprehensive of all human rights");[13] the need to expose the professional brutality of the state (George Jackson: "Anyone who passed the civil service examination yesterday can kill me today with immunity");[14] and folk realism (Johnny Cash: "I'm waitin for the pardon gonna set me free / With nine more minutes to go / But this ain't the movies so forget about me").[15] Literature, music, and criticism that chart the struggle to end state killing do not deny the devastation of individual acts of violence but urge a more careful response to the worst that humans do to one another.

To understand how and why the United States persists with a practice that has been abandoned by most countries in the world and all other Western democracies,[16] I look in the following sections to the cultural performance of state killing, to the legacy of slavery, and to the carceral system. Slavery and lynching distinguish the cultural force of capital punishment in the United States from its use in other countries.[17] The adamant historical directedness of capital punishment toward black men and deference to states' rights create the social force and capacious legal space that can and do pronounce death in multiple directions. More than half the people on death row today are white; ten of the twelve women executed since 1976 were white; Latino/as have a more difficult time securing relief from death sentences than do white or black people; and Los Angeles County sentenced more people to death in 2009 than any other county in the country, with Latino men constituting a third of those sentenced.[18]

Demands of the Dead also recognizes the human costs of the prison system writ large and moves, to lift William Brennan's memorable phrasing, in the direction of "too much justice."[19] Anthony Amsterdam, who successfully argued *Furman v. Georgia* (1972)—the U.S. Supreme Court decision that rendered capital punishment, as practiced, unconstitutional for four years—suggests that the penalty of death "extends the boundaries of permissible inhumanity so far that every lesser violation of humane values seems inoffensive by comparison, leading us to tolerate inhumanity in non-capital matters relatively easily."[20] The end of judicial murder could have a transformative impact on the prison system and larger culture. Franklin Zimring believes that the end of capital punishment in this country "will require greater effort (and achieve more good) than the standard abolition in a Western developed nation."[21] But this greater good is contingent on the scope and meaning of abolition.

After four of the Haymarket Anarchists were executed in 1887, W. D. Howells decried in the *New York Tribune* "those spasms of paroxysmal righteousness to which our Anglo-Saxon race is peculiarly subject" and argued that the men would be alive "if one thousandth of the means employed to compass their death had been used by the people to inquire into the question of their guilt"[22]—an observation that remains apt given the 138 people exonerated from death row since 1973.[23] In 2009, the American Law Institute concluded that the government does not provide "a minimally adequate system for administering capital punishment."[24] The New York Supreme Court ruled the state death penalty unconstitutional in 2004. New Jersey abolished the death penalty in 2007, New Mexico followed in 2009, and Illinois in 2011. Thirty-four states and the federal government retain state killing. The Supreme Court declared unconstitutional the execution of people under eighteen at the time of the crime (2005) and people with mental retardation (2002).[25] The court also found that juries, not judges, must decide sentencing (2002), and in a case involving a challenge to Kentucky's use of a three-drug protocol, the judges ruled that this method of lethal injection does not constitute cruel and unusual punishment—but indicated that more challenges are likely to arise (2008).

As the death penalty abolition movement gathers strength, it is worth remembering a few more numbers. According to the Department of Justice, in the five-year period between 2001 and 2006, over twenty-five thousand people died in state prisons and county jails, easily surpassing the total number of people executed during the country's four-hundred-year history.[26] The demands of the dead, in other words, are not restricted to those who have been legally sentenced to die.

Death Theatre

Since the colonial period, over fifteen thousand people have been legally executed.[27] The gallows once drew crowds of thousands to witness the righteous authority of the government and the wretched status of the condemned. With the movement away from public executions, beginning in the North in the 1830s and continuing through the early part of the twentieth century in the South, and accelerated in the South by the use of the electric chair, the state consolidated its control over killing scenes. Often described as barbaric, the death penalty is also an essentially modern and adaptable instrument of state power.[28]

The removal of state killing from public view coincided with other changes in criminal punishment. Starting in the late eighteenth century, European and U.S. reformers recommended an alternative to corporal punishment. No longer would the captive body (unless enslaved, unless condemned to death, unless under colonial rule) be subjected to overt state violence, no longer screwed to the rack, drawn and quartered. The soul would become the site of corrections. Isolated in a cell, chastened by silence, disciplined by labor, the prisoner would reflect and become penitent, journey through death to rejoin the human family, reborn, rehabilitated.[29]

Or so the story went. There has long been a disjunction, as Jason Haslam writes, between the "supposedly humanist intentions of the prison project and its actual brutalizing effects."[30] With the rise of the modern penitentiary, executions persisted, and punishment "remained, at a deep level, what punishment had already been in the earlier age of the scaffold and the pillory: a theatre for the performance of society's founding political myths."[31] *Demands of the Dead* asks whether the tale we tell ourselves about U.S. democracy and human rights conflicts with imprisonment or depends upon it—a variation on Toni Morrison's observation that the "concept of freedom did not emerge in a vacuum. Nothing highlighted freedom— if it did not in fact create it—like slavery."[32] Caleb Smith similarly finds in the history of the U.S. prison a struggle over "the very idea of modern humanity"[33]—a struggle also made visible by photographs taken at Abu Ghraib.

Enclosed within prison walls, state killing minimizes the chance of disturbance from unruly masses whose enthusiasm for blood might reflect poorly on the state or whose sympathies might be dangerously aroused for the condemned. In general, executions elicit scant news coverage and modest, if any, protest.[34] The execution of Troy Anthony Davis on September 21, 2011, was a striking exception. Hundreds of people gathered outside the Georgia Diagnostic and Classification Prison in support of Davis, and more than half a million, convinced of his innocence, signed petitions calling for clemency.[35]

Louis Masur reminds us that Benjamin Rush and other early prison reformers "would have found the idea of private executions disturbing—a form of private revenge suitable for monarchy but never a republic."[36] Most states require a few members from the press and general public to attend.

Some states allow family members of the person to be killed to be present as well as relatives of the murder victim.[37] Zimring emphasizes that the idea of state killing "as a personalized matter of victims' rights has been important only on the American side of the Atlantic Ocean and only in very recent history."[38] State and federal courts have grappled with whether the press has the right to televise state killing; the Supreme Court has decided it does not.[39] State killing is to be seen but not too much. Willie Francis describes how it felt to have eyes on him: "It was the realest misery I ever knew, to see them watching me."

Execution protocols outline a careful script to ensure the cooperation of correctional officers and the person to be killed. The prison administration indulges in a sudden show of regard for the prisoner—extended visiting hours, last meals, final statements. Sr. Helen Prejean recounts Warden Burl Cain's advice to Dobie Williams, a man about to be killed in Louisiana, and his family in 1999: "We're all in this and have to do our part. It's best for Dobie if you're strong and not crying and broken up. He's strong. See? God's with him. It's like Shakespeare says, all the world's a stage, and each of us has a role to play, which is in God's hands, and I'm playing my role and you're playing yours."[40]

Kenneth Dean, who participated in over one hundred executions in Huntsville, Texas, also suggests dramatic staging when he details how a person to be killed is restrained:

> Each supervisor is assigned a different portion—like we have a head person, a right arm, left arm, right leg, left leg. And the right leg man will tell him, "I need you to hop up onto the gurney. Lay your head on this end, put your feet on this end." Simultaneously while he's laying down the straps are being put across him. . . . Usually within about twenty seconds he's completely strapped down. Twenty to thirty seconds. I mean, it's down to a fine art.[41]

In California, once the man or woman is tied down, a drape opens, allowing witnesses to see the chamber. Barbara Becnel, a friend of Stanley Tookie Williams, described his execution as "Death Theater. They even had a curtain. Macabre. Worse than anything I've seen in my whole life."[42] San Quentin officials inform witnesses that there can be no loud sobbing: "You will be removed immediately and without discussion."[43] The Texas Department of Justice requires the audience to "refrain from verbal outbursts or any inappropriate action during the execution process."[44]

Such regulations mean little to people who are watching a nightmare.

Reporter Michael Graczyk has seen a mother who "collapsed, hit the floor, went into hyperventilation, almost convulsions." Another reporter, Leigh-anne Gideon, has seen family members "scream and wail. I've seen them beat the glass." News director Wayne Sorge has witnessed people fall on the floor and "totally lose control," but how, he asks, "do you tell a mother that she can't be there in the last moments of her son's life?"[45] Witnesses at San Quentin are told how to act after the murder: "We will stand there approximately thirty seconds and watch the motionless remains."[46] San Quentin Operational Procedure Number 0-770 (2007) specifies that the "body shall be removed with care and dignity and placed in a post-mortem bag pending removal as pre-arranged with the contract mortuary."[47] An earlier version of the manual used the phrase "body bag" instead of "post-mortem bag"; this adjustment veers attention away from the warlike violence.

In 2000, Shaka Sankofa (Gary Graham) refused to abide by the prepared script. Guards used mace to force him out of his cell. Other men and women are too frightened to walk or speak. Dwight Conquergood explains, "Either response—defiant resistance or terrified hysteria—rips off the mask of civility, the illusion of order, inevitability, procedure, due process."[48] One purpose of ritual, Conquergood stresses, is to make sense of contradictions, to provide a symbolic vision that can withstand the eruptive power of paradox.[49] Botched executions and certain people (female, elderly, disabled) especially threaten the frame of responsible state action. In 2009, technicians tried for over two hours to insert a needle into Romell Broom's arm before the execution was halted. Broom recounts in an affidavit how six nurses poked at him, how he tried to help them locate a vein, how he was encouraged to relax.[50] The medicalized performance of lethal injections exemplifies what Noam Chomsky calls the "new humanism," practices that purport to prioritize human life while furthering state violence against overwhelmingly poor people.[51] In the coerced performance of state killing, in the grotesque intimacy of the death chamber, the state reveals a social order.

Patterns of Injustice, or White Lightning

As TV commentators declared that everything looked different during the 2008 inauguration of President Barack Obama, I imagined a photostream of Cook County Jail, Angola, Parchman, Huntsville, SCI-Greene, the Tombs, Baltimore City Detention Center, prisons and death rows across the country where things don't look that different. During the inaugural month, Curtis Moore, Frank Moore, Reginald Perkins, Virgil Martinez, Ricardo Ortiz, James Callahan, and Darwin Brown were executed in the United States. Four of these men were black, two Latino, one white.

The growth of the prison system post-Emancipation resulted from policies designed to incarcerate and disenfranchise the newly freed and extract again unpaid labor in the South. Assisted by the exclusion clause of the Thirteenth Amendment and the Black Codes,[52] the new penitentiary morphed into a site of penal servitude, changing from a mostly white to mostly black population. The continuities between slavery and penal practices—well-documented by W. E. B. Du Bois's *Black Reconstruction* (1935); Matthew Mancini's *One Dies, Get Another* (1996); David Oshinsky's "*Worse than Slavery*" (1997); Angela Davis's *Are Prisons Obsolete?* (2003); Austin Sarat and Charles Ogletree's *From the Lynch Mob to the Killing State* (2006); Douglas Blackmon's *Slavery by Another Name* (2008)—encourage a broad definition of the death penalty. No one, David Oshinsky reports, survived a ten-year sentence of convict labor in late nineteenth-century Mississippi.[53]

Since 1976, 80 percent of executions have taken place in the South. "Of equal noteworthiness," writes Zimring, "those areas of the United States where lynchings were rare a century ago are much less likely now to have a death penalty or to execute."[54] He analyzes a wealth of data, a time span of a hundred years, and regional variations to demonstrate the predictive value of vigilante traditions. He recognizes that the capital system conflicts with other U.S. legal traditions—due process and a commitment to individual rights—but he argues that this conflict is resolved for many people when executions are seen not as the work of a hostile government but as the expression of communal values.[55] Charles Ogletree remarks that the "application of the death penalty may be fairer than the vigilante justice that characterized the Jim Crow era, but not by much."[56] (There is little moral high ground with regard to retaliatory and, for private companies, profitable punishment, which extends to INS detention centers.[57] The Northeast and Midwest imprison black and Latino/a Americans at higher rates than the South.)[58]

In addition to geographical location, legal executions and lynchings share ideological and practical elements. White mobs mimicked legal hangings by drawing an audience, incorporating coerced confessions, and staging photographs.[59] Law enforcement often looked the other way or actively participated. ("Above all," writes Robyn Weigman, "lynching is about the law.")[60] In turn, some courtrooms ceded to the mob, going through motions for a preordained outcome.[61] As lynchings declined in the 1920s and 1930s, state executions increased. Scholars debate whether, on local or regional levels, state killings began to substitute for lynchings. James W. Clarke stresses that these killing practices "worked in tandem for nearly three decades" and credits the willingness of courts to do white suprema-cist bidding as the most significant reason for lynching's decline.[62] David Garland suggests that the lynching model is critical for understanding col-lective violence, including "the ways in which the right to kill and the asser-tion of sovereignty are bound up with regional conflicts and power struc-tures."[63] There is no question that both forms of killing convey a terrorizing message to African American communities and create, in Angela Davis's phrasing, an "ideological enemy."[64]

In a 1931 trial that came to define a Southern town, nine black teen-agers were convicted of raping two young white women. Thousands of white people gathered outside the Scottsboro courthouse, some armed with guns, others with ropes. One of the defendants, Haywood Patterson, assumed that the National Guard was "part of the lynching bee."[65] The charges called upon a tested rhetoric of rapacious black men and South-ern white womanhood. Despite the lack of evidence and improbable testi-mony from the alleged victims, eight of the defendants were sentenced to death, and the youngest, thirteen-year-old Leroy Wright, was sentenced to life. In historian Dan Carter's words, guilt or innocence "was, at most, a peripheral question."[66] The real question was whether white people could continue to kidnap and kill black people. (Ruby Bates, one of the accusers, later recanted her testimony and worked for the defendants' release.) The resistance of the imprisoned, their families and supporters, the Commu-nist Party, the International Labor Defense, and the NAACP generated sus-tained public pressure on the state of Alabama. The case became a rally-ing point for other popular front concerns, including antipoverty, workers' rights, the end to capitalist corruption, and antilynching activism.

In his neglected autobiography Scottsboro Boy (1950), cowritten with Earl Conrad, Patterson remembers the sorrow that he felt on a visit with his mother. She tried to reassure him: " 'Son,' she cheered, 'white lightning struck us, that's all.' "[67] U.S. Supreme Court Justice Potter Stewart reached for a similar metaphor in Furman v. Georgia: "These death sentences are cruel and unusual in the same way that being struck by lightning is cruel and un-usual."[68] While there is something random about the death penalty (less than 1 percent of all homicides in the country will lead to a capital con-viction), there is much that is calculated in the selection process with re-gard to race, income, and geography. In other words, Stewart left the white part out of his metaphor, the historical relationship of the case to political power. Janie Patterson knew the force that had taken her son away was shocking, predictable, and white.

On the one hand, racism in the contemporary justice system is more subtle than during Jim Crow. The murder of white people, for instance, more often results in death sentences than the murder of black people. Nearly 80 percent of those executed since 1976 have been convicted of killing a white person, though black Americans constitute more than half of all murder victims—52 percent from 1976 to 2005.[69] In a U.S. Supreme Court decision from the Scottsboro case, the court agreed with the defense that black Americans had been excluded from jury pools in Jackson County, Alabama. Eighty years later, a 2010 study by the Equal Justice Initiative found racial discrimination in jury selection in eight Southern states. In some counties, 75 percent of black jury pools in capital cases had been excluded. (Mostly black juries tend not to impose the death penalty, and racially diverse juries take longer to deliberate and "make fewer factual errors than all-white ones.")[70] On the other hand, in 1974, a juror in William Andrew's capital case in Utah wrote on a napkin "Hang the Nigger's" [sic]. The judge refused to order a mistrial, and Andrew was executed in 1992.[71]

The goal, of course, is not a system that metes out lethal punishment more equitably but a refusal of what Herman Melville called "ruthless democracy."[72] The 2010 racial breakdown of the thirty-two hundred people on state death rows—44 percent black (who make up 12 percent of the overall population), 41 percent white (66 percent of overall), 12 percent Latino/a (15 percent of overall), and 2 percent "other"—confirms that black Americans remain disproportionately sentenced to death and that the repercussions of state killing extend across racial lines.[73] As Davis notes, when discriminatory practices become institutionalized, "white bodies can also bear the brunt of the racist violence."[74]

The importance of Scottsboro to national memory has generally been confined to the stark lesson it provides of unequal justice in death cases, but Scottsboro is also the story of long-term imprisonment. Collectively the nine defendants spent over 130 years in prison for a crime that never happened,[75] beaten, sexually abused, and often denied visits and information. After a dozen trials and two Supreme Court decisions, Alabama agreed in 1937 to release the two youngest, Eugene Williams and Leroy Wright, and the two with the most severe medical problems, Olen Montgomery and

Willie Roberson. (Patterson wryly notes, "The state said they weren't guilty of rape, so they had been punished enough" [80].) The remaining five were re-sentenced: Patterson and Weems to seventy-five years; Andy Wright to ninety-nine years; the rape charge against Powell was dropped but he was sentenced to twenty years for stabbing a guard. Clarence Norris was again sentenced to die. During World War II, the state released everyone except Patterson, who escaped from Atmore farm in 1948. All nine were dogged by the ordeal. "Freedom," Andy Wright once said, "don't mean a thing to me."[76]

The Cage

The expansion of the prison industrial complex in the past thirty years, accomplished through drug laws and unequal sentencing, constitutes part of the backlash against another freedom struggle, the civil rights and black liberation movements. Most prisoners have been convicted of nonviolent crimes, and the fastest-growing prison populations are black women and undocumented people.[77] George Jackson understood that "the ultimate expression of law is not order—it's prison. There are hundreds upon hundreds of prisons, and thousands upon thousands of laws, yet there is no social order, no social peace."[78] Dylan Rodriguez offers the term "prison regime" to shift the conversation from a law-and-order presumption to a structural analysis of the inequalities that prepare certain populations for prison.[79]

Prison studies insist on the shaping pressure of public policies on social well-being, on the ways, in Stephen Hartnett's words, that "the stunning failure of the democratic process—including our collective inability to think compassionately about schools, health care, immigration, and human services—also fuel the desperation, cynicism, and drop-out mentality that lead to crime and violence."[80] *Demands of the Dead* positions state killing within this larger unfreedom and alongside other modes of violence, such as torture, isolation, and routine prison conditions.

Prisons are designed to isolate and to bury. Manhattan's jail complex, built between 1835 and 1838 and called the Tombs, was modeled on an Egyptian mausoleum, and although the facility and official name have changed over time, the Tombs remains its popular designation. (The Tombs appears in several literary works, including Melville's *Bartleby, the Scrivener* and Manuel Piñero's *Short Eyes*.) The point of imprisonment, writes John Wideman, is "to create the fiction" that the imprisoned do not exist:

"Prison is an experience of death by inches, minutes, hours, days."[81] Or, in Dylan Rodriguez's words, the "fundamental logic of the punitive carceral is the institutionalized killing of the subject."[82] Imprisonment confers social death and often hopelessness. Felony laws deny even former prisoners voting rights and equal access to employment. (In certain states, the spouse of a prisoner was once legally considered a widow.)[83] While some death statutes have been rejected by the courts as insupportably metaphysical, prison continues to exert a killing force. Censorship and the confiscation of writing and reading materials further isolate, "criminalizing critical literacy," in Steve Champion's words.[84]

Administrative segregation units and supermaximum cells add another dimension to the isolation of imprisonment. These units usually have no windows or bars; a slot in the door allows in mail and food. As many as one hundred thousand people are subjected to isolation, confined with no human contact generally twenty-three hours a day. In this collection, a former correctional officer, Rick Stetter, describes solitary confinement in 2006: "I spent many nights working alone in the sweat box that was the Luther Unit Ad Seg. The temperature at midnight remained above the century mark, and the inmates sprawled naked on the concrete floors of their tiny cells in a vain attempt to escape the heat. As I did the half-hour cell checks I dragged along behind me a large plastic ice cooler meant to hold the lunches and sodas of officers, throwing leftover ice on the nude bodies and talking to anyone who had the need and energy." While Stetter admits to ambivalent feelings about the death penalty, he does not hesitate to call these conditions torturous. Atul Gawande refers to the experience of U.S. prisoners in prolonged isolation as "no different" from that of prisoners of war or hostages: severe depression, mental disintegration, debilitating anger, at times catatonia, set in.[85] (Neither the use of isolation nor resistance to it is new in the United States. In 1868, Elizabeth Cady Stanton criticized "needless cruelty in solitude," insisting that "our jails, our prisons, our whole idea of punishment is wrong, and will be until the mother soul is represented in our criminal legislation.")[86]

While solitary and death chambers are vivid examples of state aggression, there are less visible signs as well. The suicide rate in prisons is particularly high, most dramatically in small jails (those with under fifty people) where the rate is 169 per 100,000. In the general U.S. population, the rate is 11 per 100,000.[87] Jessica Mitford's candid assessment from 1974 remains apt: "The jails have no apologists, they are universally recognized to be hellish places."[88] The United States is the only country that allows children, those seventeen years old or younger, to be sentenced to life without parole—a punishment in violation of the Convention on the Rights of the Child, which the United States has not signed, and the International Covenant on Civil and Political Rights, which the United States has signed. In 2007, the Equal Justice Initiative reported 2,225 such cases; seventy-three cases involved thirteen- and fourteen-year-olds who had been sentenced to die in prison. Of these, almost half (49 percent) were African American. Most of these children serving life without parole were victims of sustained abuse that, for many, began when they were infants and toddlers.[89]

Abuse—physical, sexual, mental—often continues inside prison. According to the Justice Department, in 2008 at least 216,000 people were sexually abused in domestic prisons, mostly by guards.[90] Michael Hames-García rightly argues that bodily violence "is a central disciplinary technique of the penal system, whether that violence is carried out by guards or by prisoners."[91] These "known consequences" are no less part of the punishment system because corporal punishment has not been officially ordered.

Death penalty abolition efforts that do not call for life without parole take the more difficult road in terms of mainstream politics; it is far more palatable to argue for long-term sentences than to ask why we want to throw away a key and what happens when we do. The Prison Education Advocacy Project's 1976 handbook defines abolitionism as the struggle for "economic and social justice for all, concern for all victims, and reconciliation within a caring community."[92] The restorative justice movement offers an alternative to the adversary model of the criminal justice system, and family members of murder victims continue to organize to end capital punishment.[93] Amnesty International, Human Rights Watch, and the Southern Center for Human Rights oppose state killing without exception.[94] Following W. E. B. Du Bois, Angela Davis (who faced the death penalty) advocates for "abolition democracy," the dismantling of prisons, and the creation of truly democratic institutions.[95] At Chicago's Cook County Jail in 1902, Clarence Darrow declared, "There should be no jails. They do not accomplish what they pretend to accomplish."[96] Edward Mendiata offers this straightforward assessment: "So long as the prison-industrial-complex remains, American democracy will continue to be a false one."[97] Only a refusal of death sentences and the prison regime enables us to address fully the responsibility of the state, the nefarious operations of prisons and jails, the role of responsive communities, and the best ways to create the conditions for meaningful freedom.

Demands of the Dead

The three parts of this collection critique a "national fantasy" of crime and punishment, and create a dialogue between life-writing, fiction, poetry, and critical scholarship.[98] As interdisciplinary study strengthens, English departments internally hew to fairly strict borders between genres: the creative, the critical, the technical/professional. Scholar-versus-artist divisions in performance and theater studies have emerged from complex institutional and disciplinary developments.[99] A multigenre collection like this one encourages a diverse readership[100] and offers, I hope, an alternative to the specialized and often exclusionary writing that has become dominant in literary studies.

Toward the end of his memoir *The Autobiography of an Execution*, David Dow admits to an uneasiness he felt as his book neared publication: "I realized what's missing: all the other cases."[101] He could not possibly describe all his capital cases or tell all the necessary stories. The abolitionist literary record also includes far more stories than are represented in this collection. Lesbians, gay men, and transgendered people are disproportionately sentenced to death. Women, who make up 2 percent of people executed since 1976, are often prosecuted for failing to abide by gender norms, and their experiences at trial and in prison warrant specific attention.[102] Work remains to be done on early American periods and Latino/a literature, and a great reservoir of writing about state killing, incarceration, and prisoner revolts has yet to be organized into a literary record.[103] My hope is that *Demands of the Dead* compels more research and affirms the political and artistic vitality of U.S. literature.

Part 1 — Words through Walls

Part 1 features writing between and within prison walls, a call and response to the terror of state executions. The contributors document personal and creative efforts to prevent further injustice and to ensure dialogue and transformation—on all sides of prison walls. Against considerable odds, composing from, in Mumia Abu-Jamal's words, "the razor's edge between half-life and certain death,"[104] death row prisoners have moved their voices and artwork outside.

In 1946, Willie Francis, a black sixteen-year-old, was convicted of murdering a Cajun pharmacist, Andrew Thomas, in Louisiana. During the two-day trial, the defense called no witnesses and conducted no cross-examinations. A confession obtained without counsel served as the only evidence against Francis. The all-white jury quickly returned a guilty verdict. Eight months later, in the electric chair, Francis felt voltage going through his body, a "razor" cutting into his leg, and assumed he was dead. When it became clear that he was not, the executioner applied another surge of electricity. Francis remained alive and the execution was called off. From a prison cell, Francis narrated his experience to a local resident, Samuel Montgomery, who published the pamphlet "My Trip to the Chair" (1947).

Part 1 opens with this complex, double-voiced pamphlet distributed to raise funds for Francis's appeal.[105] Francis also hoped to "help other people to understand each other." Of the seconds after the electrocution, Francis recalls, "I thought it was funny how you can feel hands the same way when you're dead as when you're alive. I thought it was funny you could think a little, too, because I wondered why they didn't just leave me alone." The state did not leave him alone. In a 5–4 decision, the U.S. Supreme Court refused the argument that a second execution would violate the Eighth Amendment. In his dissent, Judge Harold Burton referred to the first attempt as torture and asked, "How many deliberate and intentional reapplications of electric current does it take to produce a cruel, unusual and unconstitutional punishment?" The majority decision, *State of Louisiana ex rel. Francis v. Resweber* (1947), continues to be cited by the court, including in a ruling on lethal injection, *Baze v. Rees* (2008).[106] Francis was again tortured and electrocuted to death at midnight on May 9, 1947.

Demands of the Dead is in part an attempt to grasp its opening, to generate, or at least imagine generating, the contexts and methods needed to understand the words of Willie Francis, who knew "how real it was to die." Jason Stupp helps considerably in this direction by analyzing Ernest Gaines's popular novel, *A Lesson before Dying*, alongside "My Trip to the Chair." Stupp pursues an inquiry at the heart of this collection: what might be strengthened or created by alliances—across genre, across town, across prison walls?

Literary collaborations also develop behind prison walls. In the 1990s, Anthony Ross (aka Ajani Addae Kamara), Stanley Tookie Williams (aka Ajamu Kamara), and Steve Champion (aka Adisa Akanni Kamara) embarked on a spiritual and intellectual project at San Quentin. Champion details this disciplined and joyful effort. "In the midst of war," he recalls, "we were becoming writers." Tom Kerr, a writing professor at Ithaca College, met Champion through the most common form of writing in prison, the letter, and reflects in his essay on their working and personal relationship and on the possibilities for restorative justice through writing.

Before writing the screenplay *Leaving Death Row* (2005), Elizabeth Stein visited Peckerwood Hill, a twenty-two-acre cemetery where the state of Texas buries people who die in prison and whose bodies are not claimed. Stein's script explores the high stakes of a pen-pal relationship between a man on death row and a woman from Bulgaria, and culminates with the uncertainty created by every execution: what will happen to the body?[107] Huntsville, Texas, the site of the most executions in the country and in the western hemisphere, is also the setting and source for Rick Stetter's essay. An officer with the Brazos County Sheriff's Department and a former correctional officer, Stetter recalls a day of training at Huntsville, reflecting on what separates and connects him to those on the other side of the bars.

Part 2—History and State Power

Part 2 defines the penalty of death as a particularly frank expression of state power, an instrument of slavery, racism, war, expansion, and empire. Death chambers concentrate (but do not exhaust) the state's claim to absolute power over life and death. In a landmark essay, H. Bruce Franklin changed the way critics talk about Melville's *Billy Budd*, a novel set in 1797, completed in 1891, and relevant to twenty-first-century military "necessity." To contextualize death penalty debates in a story that casts state killing as an abandonment of the "rights of man," Franklin returns to the American Revolution and the "Bloody Code" of King George III as well as the bloody code of U.S. slavery.

The title of Jill McDonough's book of poems, *Habeas Corpus* (2008), comes from the Latin phrase, "you have the body." Legally, the term presses upon the state the need to defend its capture of a person. McDonough's sonnets move through four hundred years, devoting each of sixty sonnets to people executed (including Willie Francis, Nicola Sacco, and Aileen Wuornos). The poem "December 26, 1862: Chaska" recalls the largest mass execution in U.S. history and again connects war and state killing: thirty-eight members of the Dakota Nation were hanged in Mankato, Minnesota, on that date, after being convicted of killing white settlers.

We-Chank-Wash-ta-don-pee, a man known as Chaska, was one of 265 people whom Abraham Lincoln pardoned after the convictions. Yet, Chaska

EXECUTION OF THIRTY-EIGHT INDIAN MURDERERS AT MANKATO, MINNESOTA.—FROM A SKETCH BY MR. HEENAN, OF ST. PAUL.—[SEE PAGE 29.]

1. Page from *Harper's Weekly*, February 17, 1863.

was hanged either because of mistaken identification or intentional re-taliation. He had allegedly taken a white woman and her children as pris-oners, but the woman, Sarah Wakefield, defended Chaska at the tribunals, saying he had saved her from certain death. Wakefield believed that Chaska was targeted for a presumed sexual relationship between them. A month after the mass execution, *Harper's Weekly* reproduced this report:

> The gallows stood upon the high street close in front of the levee. It is estimated that not less than four thousand people, exclusive of the mili-tary, were in attendance. The gallows was erected in the form of a dia-mond, twenty-four feet on each angle, sufficient to execute ten on each side. A square was formed around the gallows by the military, and the citizens occupied the sand bar on the river. The ceremony was brief, and the whole number of savages were sent at the same moment before the Great Spirit to answer for their inhuman barbarities.[108]

The article described the Dakota singing and dancing on the platform "as if pandemonium had broken loose. It had a wonderful effect of keeping up their courage." According to another report, prisoners called out their names and those of friends, and several held one another's hands during the drop.[109]

In his well-known *On Crimes and Punishments* (1764), Cesare di Beccaria argued that the death penalty is not a "right" but "a war of the nation against a citizen," or as the executions of native and black people indicate, also a war of the nation against those refused citizenship. John Cyril Barton highlights Beccaria's influence and, through a survey of the extensive literary engagement with legal murder in the early part of the nineteenth century, the paradox of executions in the new democratic republic. Jennifer Leigh Lieberman turns to the uneasy alliance between science and state killing. Responding to a forgotten novel by Gertrude Atherton, *Patience Sparhawk* (1897), Lieberman analyzes late nineteenth-century discourse about the electric chair and the ongoing role of journalism and the power of technology in executions.

"Don't forget history, history made today," announces Nat Turner in Kia Corthron's *Life by Asphyxiation* (1999). Nat Turner, leader of a slave uprising in 1831 Virginia, and Crazy Horse, a Lakota who fought U.S. aggression, are on death row next to JoJo, a black man in his fifties who raped and killed a sixteen-year-old white girl named Katie. Occasionally Katie appears onstage and talks with JoJo. From these tense conversations, we learn that Katie does not want to hear an apology: "I can't hear 'I'm sorry.' 'I'm sorry' I'm deaf to." Corthron rivets attention on liberation struggles and state violence (Crazy Horse was killed by a military guard in a Nebraska prison in 1877; Nat Turner was executed in 1831—his body beaten, quartered, and decapitated), on a man regretful of his past and frightened to die, and on a girl who loved to play basketball. *Life by Asphyxiation* answers, as well as any critical work, Meg Sweeney's call for "theories of crime and punishment that better attend to the intersections among individual, structural, and historical forces."[110] In a signal line for the collection, Katie reflects, "Murder . . . once you been through it, you never wish it on nobody else."

Anthony Ross, who has been imprisoned for a quarter of a century in San Quentin, knows a great deal about power. He describes routines on death row—chaotic, meditative, horrific—before imagining his own possible death on a gurney. Ross anticipates the state's attempt to wrest even the truth of death from the dead. If prison officials ever ask for a final statement, Ross will shake his head: "I'm not big on monologue." He rejects the official story of humane killing. "Death comes in less than fifteen minutes," he writes. "There will be nothing peaceful about it."

Part 3—Voices and Bodies in Resistance

In 1996, Jacques Derrida sent an open letter to President Bill Clinton, asking for a new trial for Mumia Abu-Jamal. It was not his first attempt to intervene in a U.S. death case. As Derrida explained, "Nearly twenty-five years ago—this memory causes me anguish and despair—we came together, alas in vain, in an attempt to pull from an infernal juridical-prison machination someone who at that time in the United States, in those years, represented an exemplary figure for the young Mumia Abu-Jamal."[111] Derrida referred to George Jackson, fatally shot at San Quentin in 1971.

Derrida cautioned against turning the death penalty into discourse and expressed hope that his final lectures would not be "merely a seminar on the death penalty." Derrida did not want to add "one more discourse, and a discourse of good conscience to boot" among people who feel themselves disconnected from executions: "One must do everything to get as close as possible, in one's own body, to those for whom the death penalty is really the death penalty." To unravel the "right to punish," to grasp the illogic of death *as* punishment, Derrida recommended that we "follow the thread of what there is here to think, starting from what one so tranquilly calls literature. Or theatre."[112]

The writing in part 3 grapples with the necessity and difficulty of getting "as close as possible" to state killing. Thomas Dutoit, a coeditor and translator of Derrida's death penalty lectures, explains how Derrida deconstructs philosophical justifications for executions (and philosophy itself) through readings of Immanuel Kant and Franz Kafka. Sherman Alexie's poem, "Capital Punishment," offers another way into the death chamber. The speaker of the poem is a prison cook sitting alone in the prison kitchen, trying to avoid the clock. He has prepared a last meal for an American Indian and, getting close, tasted the food with the prisoner's fork: "Maybe a little piece of me / lodged in his mouth." The repeated line, "I am not a witness," slowly undoes itself, and we know he is, like us, a witness.

The next three essays turn to performative writing and art. David Kieran discusses how African American poets continue to draw from the cultural memory of lynching to give shape and force to descriptions of contemporary state violence. My essay reviews the production history of *The Exonerated*, a documentary play based on interviews with people who were sentenced to die for crimes they did not commit. While acknowledging the power of the voices and the political work of the performance, I criticize the timid coordination of the innocence argument and sentimentality that drives the script. Working from Walter Benjamin's *Critique of Violence* and the 1992 gangsta rap album *Guerrillas in tha Mist* by Da Lench Mob, Matthew Stratton elaborates further on the shared logic of terrorism and state killing. Stratton also importantly argues that statistics, unlike art, will never liberate.

The collection closes with the voice of Delbert Tibbs, a peace activist, poet, and musician. In the 1970s, while hitchhiking across the country, Tibbs was wrongfully convicted of the murder of a white man and the rape of a white woman, and was sentenced to die. An international defense committee, which included Pete Seeger and Angela Davis, worked for his release. On appeal, the conviction was overturned, and Tibbs was released in January 1977. From this poet who mourns "for the whole world because it's such a horrible place so often,"[113] we also hear praise—for beauty, for children and ancestors, for sun and stars. For justice.

A simple public list tells us who is likely to be killed in the coming months: how and when and where. It is a peculiar knowledge, and it connects us to more violent death, unfathomable grief. *Demands of the Dead* joins efforts to create a more just and sane culture—the work, to borrow from Gwendolyn Brooks, "to be done to be done to be done."[114]

Notes

1. David R. Dow, *The Autobiography of an Execution* (New York: Twelve, 2010), 101.

2. See, for instance, Austin Sarat, *When the State Kills: Capital Punishment and the American Condition* (Princeton Univ. Press, 2001), 14; Gregg Crane, "Reasonable Doubts: Crime and Punishment," *American Literary History* 18.4 (2006): 797–813.

3. For labor and prison, see Asatar P. Bair, *Prison Labor in the United States* (New York: Routledge, 2008); Ruth Wilson Gilmore, *Golden Gulag: Prisons, Surplus, Crisis and Opposition in Globalizing California* (Berkeley: Univ. of California Press, 2007); Tara Herivel and Paul Wright, eds., *Prison Nation: The Warehousing of America's Poor* (New York: Routledge, 2003), 112–37; Barbara Esposito and Lee Wood, *Prison Slavery* (Silver Spring, MD: Wood and Esposito, 1982). For race and prison, see Michelle Alexander, *The New Jim Crow: Mass Incarceration in the Age of Colorblindness* (New York: New Press, 2010); Loïc Wacquant, "The Great Leap Backward: Imprisonment in America from Nixon to Clinton," in *The New Punitiveness: Trends, Theories, Perspectives*, eds. John Pratt et al. (London: Willan, 2005), 3–26; Angela Davis, *Abolition Democracy: Beyond Empire, Prisons, and Torture* (New York: Seven Stories, 2005) and *Are Prisons Obsolete?* (New York: Seven Stories, 2003); Christian Parenti, *Lockdown America: Police and Prisons in the Age of Crisis* (New York: Verso, 2000); Marc Mauer, *Race to Incarcerate* (New York: New Press, 1999); Jerome G. Miller, *Search and Destroy: African-American Males*

in the *Criminal Justice System* (New York: Cambridge Univ. Press, 1996); Mumia Abu-Jamal, *Live from Death Row* (New York: Harper, 1996).

4. For torture, see the archives of *Prison Legal News*; H. Bruce Franklin, "The Inside Stories of the Global American Prison," *Texas Studies in Literature and Language* 50.3 (2008): 235–42; Avery Gordon, "Abu Ghraib: Imprisonment and the War on Terror," *Race and Class* 48.1 (2006): 42–59, and "Methodologies of Imprisonment," *PMLA* 123.3 (2008): 651–57; Benjamin Whitmer, " 'Torture Chambers and Rape Rooms': What Abu Ghraib Can Tell Us about the American Carceral System," *New Centennial Review* 6.1 (2006): 171–94; Jared Sexton, "Racial Profiling and the Societies of Control," *Warfare in the American Homeland: Policing and Prison in a Penal Democracy*, ed. Joy James (Durham, NC: Duke Univ. Press, 2007), 197–218; William F. Pinar, "Cultures of Torture," *Warfare in the American Homeland*, 290–304; Angela Davis, *Abolition Democracy*, 49–76.

5. H. Bruce Franklin, "From Plantation to Penitentiary to the Prison-Industrial Complex: Literature of the American Prison," *Modern Language Association Conference* (December 2000), http://andromeda.rutgers.edu/~hbf/MLABLACK.htm.

6. See Paul Christian Jones, *Against the Gallows: Antebellum American Writers and the Movement to Abolish Capital Punishment* (Iowa City: Univ. of Iowa Press, 2011); Caleb Smith, *The Prison and the American Imagination* (New Haven: Yale Univ. Press, 2009); Kristin Boudreau, *The Spectacle of Death: Populist Literary Responses to American Capital Cases* (New York: Prometheus Books, 2006); Daniel A. Cohen, *Pillars of Salt, Monuments of Grace: New England Crime Literature and the Origins of American Pop Culture, 1674–1860* (Amherst: Univ. of Massachusetts Press, 2006); Dylan Rodriguez, *Forced Passages: Imprisoned Radical Intellectuals and the U.S. Prison Regime* (Minneapolis: Univ. of Minnesota Press, 2006); Michael Hames-García, *Fugitive Justice: Prison Movements, Race, and the Meaning of Justice* (Minneapolis: Univ. of Minnesota Press, 2004); Austin Sarat, *When the State Kills: Capital Punishment and the American Condition* (Princeton: Princeton Univ. Press, 2001); Theo Hamm, *Rebel and a Cause: Caryl Chessman and the Politics of the Death Penalty in Postwar California, 1948–1974* (Berkeley: Univ. of California Press, 2001); David Guest, *Sentenced to Death: The American Novel and Capital Punishment* (Jackson: Univ. Press of Mississippi, 1997); Ann M. Algeo, *Courtroom as Forum: Homicide Trials by Dreiser, Wright, Capote, and Mailer* (New York: Peter Lang, 1996); and Louis P. Masur, *Rites of Execution: Capital Punishment and the Transformation of American Culture, 1776–1865* (New York: Oxford Univ. Press, 1991).

Autobiographical works include Steve Champion, *Dead to Deliverance: A Death Row Memoir* (Vestal, NY: Split Oak Press, 2010); Wilbert Rideau, *In the Place of Justice: A Story of Punishment and Deliverance* (New York: Knopf, 2010); Jarvis Jay Master, *That Bird Has My Wings: The Autobiography of an Innocent Man on Death Row* (New York:

HarperOne, 2009) and *Finding Freedom: Writings from Death Row* (Junction City, CA: Padma, 1997); Reginald Sinclair Lewis, *Where I'm Writing From* (Lewis 2005); Ernie López and Rafael Pérez-Torres, *To Alcatraz, Death Row, and Back* (Austin: Univ. of Texas Press, 2005); Haywood Patterson and Earl Conrad, *Scottsboro Boy* (Garden City, NY: Doubleday, 1950); Clarence Norris and Sybil D. Washington, *The Last of the Scottsboro Boys: An Autobiography* (New York: G. P. Putnam's Sons, 1979); Caryl Chessman, *Cell 2455, Death Row: A Condemned Man's Own Story* (New York: Prentice-Hall, 1954). For letters, see "Ray" and S. O'Riain, *Condemned: Letters from Death Row* (Dublin, UK: Liberties, 2008); Marion Denman Frankfurter and Gardner Jackson, eds., *The Letters of Sacco and Vanzetti* (New York: Penguin, 1997); Michael Meeropol, ed., *The Rosenberg Letters* (New York: Routledge, 1994); Philip S. Foner, *Autobiographies of the Haymarket Anarchists* (New York: Humanities Press, 1969); John Howard Lawson and Wesley Robert Wells, *Letters from the Death House* (Los Angeles: Civil Rights Congress, 1953). Also see Marie Mulvey-Roberts, ed., *Writing for Their Lives: Death Row U.S.A.* (Urbana: Univ. of Illinois Press, 2007); Bell Gale Chevigny, ed., *Doing Time: 25 Years of Prison Writing* (New York: Arcade, 2000); Franklin, H. Bruce, ed. *Prison Writing in 20th-Century America* (New York: Penguin, 1998); Mumia Abu-Jamal, *Live from Death Row* (New York: Harper, 1996).

7. Sylvia Plath, *The Unabridged Journals of Sylvia Plath, 1950–1961*, ed. Karen V. Kukil (New York: Anchor Books, 2000), 541–42.

8. For literary responses to the Haymarket anarchists, Leo Frank, Emmett Till, Gary Gilmore, and Karla Faye Tucker, see Boudreau, *Spectacle*. For Scottsboro, see James A. Miller, *Remembering Scottsboro: The Legacy of an Infamous Trial* (Princeton: Princeton Univ. Press, 2009); Hugh Murray, "Changing America and the Changing Image of Scottsboro," *Phylon* 38.1 (1977): 82–92. For Chester Gillette's case in *An American Tragedy*, see Guest, *Sentenced*; Algeo, *Courtroom*; and Donald Pizer, "Crime and Punishment in Dreiser's *An American Tragedy*," *Studies in the Novel* 41.4 (Winter 2009): 435–50. For Nat Turner, see Mary Kemp Davis, *Nat Turner before the Bar of Judgment: Fictional Treatments of the Southampton Slave Insurrection* (Baton Rouge: Louisiana State Univ. Press, 1999).

9. Upton Sinclair, *Boston*, vol. 2 (Long Beach, CA: Station B, 1928), 719–20. See Jennifer Lieberman in this collection for the rhetoric of "instantaneous" death by electrocution.

10. Ibid., 747.

11. Elizabeth Cady Stanton, "There Will Be No Gallows When Mothers Make the Laws," in *Voices Against Death: American Opposition to Capital Punishment, 1787–1975*, ed. Philip English Mackey (New York: Burt Franklin, 1976), 121.

12. Ralph Waldo Emerson, *Emerson: Essays and Lectures* (New York: Literary Classics, 1983), 148.

13. Frederick Douglass, "Resolutions Proposed for Anti-Capital Punishment Meeting, Rochester, New York, October 7, 1858," in *The Life and Writings of Frederick Douglass*, vol. 5, ed. Philip S. Foner (New York: International Publishers, 1975), 418.

14. George Jackson, *Blood in My Eye* (Baltimore: Black Classic Press, 1990), 7.

15. Johnny Cash recorded Shel Silverstein's "25 Minutes to Go" on the album *Sings the Ballads of the True West* (1965).

16. Amnesty International, "Figures on the Death Penalty," http://www.amnesty .org/en/death-penalty/numbers.

17. Across the slave South, legislation defined punishment according to the race of the convicted person. See Banner, *Death Penalty*, 137–43; W. E. B. Du Bois, *Black Reconstruction in America, 1860–1880* (New York: Free Press, 1962); Watt Espy, "American Gothic," in *A Punishment in Search of a Crime: Americans Speak Out against the Death Penalty* (New York: Avon, 1989), 47–53; Zimring, *Contradictions*, 134–35; and Franklin in this collection.

18. Elizabeth Rappaport, "Staying Alive: Equal Protection, Re-election, and the Execution of Women," *Buffalo Criminal Law Review* 4.2 (2001): 979; ACLU of Northern California, "Death in Decline '09," http://www.aclunc.org/docs/criminal_justice/ death_penalty/death_in_decline_executive_summary.pdf.

19. In *McCleskey v. Kemp* (1987), the U.S. Supreme Court accepted findings of racial disparity in Georgia death cases but upheld the conviction of Warren McCleskey, arguing that a level of racism was "inevitable" in the system and that to reverse the conviction would throw into question judicial functioning at every level. William Brennan wrote in his dissent that the court seemed to fear "too much justice."

20. Anthony G. Amsterdam, "Remarks at the Southern Center for Human Rights," October 2, 2008, http://www.deathpenaltyinfo.org/files/Tony%20Amster dam's%20Remarks%20-%20Oct.%202%202008.pdf.

21. Zimring, *Contradictions*, 136.

22. W. D. Howells, *Selected Letters, 1882–1891*, vol. 3, ed. Robert C. Leitz III (Boston: Twayne, 1980), 201.

23. "Innocence: List of Those Freed from Death Row," *Death Penalty Information Center*, http://www.deathpenaltyinfo.org/innocence-list-those-freed-death-row.

24. Adam Liptak, "Group Gives Up Death Penalty," *New York Times*, January 4, 2010, http://www.nytimes.com/2010/01/05/us/05bar.html.

25. For the limited protection of this ruling, see "Bias and Subjectivity in Diagnosing Mental Retardation in Death Penalty Cases," *Bias in Psychiatric Diagnosis*, eds. Paula J. Caplan and Lisa Cosgrove (Lanham, MD: Rowman and Littlefield, 2004). For more on mental disabilities, see Terry Kupers, *Prison Madness: The Mental Health Crisis behind Bars and What We Must Do about It* (San Francisco: Jossey-Bass, 1999);

Michael Ross, "It's Time for Me to Die: An Inside Look at Death Row," *Writing for Their Lives*, 91–103; Renée Feltz, "Cracked," *Texas Observer*, January 8, 2010: 6–11; Kent S. Miller and Michael L. Radelet, eds., *Executing the Mentally Ill: The Criminal Justice System and the Case of Alvin Ford* (Newbury Park, CA: Sage, 1993).

26. For deaths in jails, see Paul von Zielbauer, "When 10 Hard Days in a County Jail Cell Is a Death Sentence," *New York Times*, February 27, 2005: 1; "Mortality in Local Jails, 2000–2007," *Bureau of Justice Statistics*, http://bjs.ojp.usdoj.gov/index.cfm?ty=pbdetail&iid=2197; "Deaths in Custody Statistical Tables," *Bureau of Justice Statistics*, http://bjs.ojp.usdoj.gov/content/dcrp/dictabs.cfm.

27. ESPY database (1608–2002), http://www.deathpenaltyinfo.org/documents/ESPYyear.pdf. See Stuart Banner, *The Death Penalty: An American History* (Cambridge: Harvard Univ. Press, 2002), 313–14.

28. See David Garland, *Peculiar Institution: America's Death Penalty in an Age of Abolition* (Cambridge: Harvard Univ. Press, 2010), 17–27. For more on the history of executions, see Marie Gottschalk, *The Prison and the Gallows* (New York: Cambridge Univ. Press, 2006); Hugo Bedau, "An Abolitionist's Survey of the Death Penalty in America Today," in *Debating the Death Penalty: Should America Have the Death Penalty*, eds. Hugo Bedau and Paul Cassell (New York: Oxford Univ. Press, 2004), 15–50; Banner, *The Death Penalty*; Franklin E. Zimring, *The Contradictions of Capital Punishment* (Oxford: Oxford Univ. Press, 2003). For the critical 1970s, see David Von Drehle, *Among the Lowest of the Dead: The Culture of Death Row* (New York: Faucet, 1996).

29. Michel Foucault, *Discipline and Punish: The Birth of the Prison*, trans. Alan Sheridan (New York: Vintage, 1995), 16–31, 231–48; Smith, *The Prison*.

30. Jason Haslam, *Fitting Sentences: Identity in Nineteenth- and Twentieth-Century Prison Narratives* (Toronto: Univ. of Toronto Press, 2005), 50.

31. Smith, *The Prison*, 7.

32. Toni Morrison, *Playing in the Dark: Whiteness and the Literary Imagination* (New York: Vintage, 1993), 38.

33. Smith, *The Prison*, 199.

34. See Christopher S. Kudlac, *Public Executions: The Death Penalty and the Media* (Westport, CT: Praeger, 2007); Zimring, *Contradictions*, 199.

35. See William Jelani Cobb, "The Night They Killed Troy Davis," *Atlantic*, September 22, 2011, http://www.theatlantic.com/national/archive/2011/09/the-night-they-killed-troy-davis/245515/; "Troy Davis Execution Sparks Anti-Death Penalty Protests, Backlash," *Washington Post*, September 22, 2011, http://www.washingtonpost.com/national/troy-davis-execution-sparks-anti-death-penalty-backlash-protests/2011/09/22gIQAQawOok_story.html.

36. Masur, *Rites*, 95.

37. See John Bessler, *Death in the Dark: Midnight Executions in America* (Boston: Northeastern Univ. Press, 1997); Robert Johnson, *Death Work: A Study of the Modern Execution Process* (Belmont, CA: Wadsworth, 1997). For families of death row prisoners, see Rachel King, *Capital Consequences: Families of the Condemned Tell Their Stories* (New Brunswick, NJ: Rutgers Univ. Press, 2004); Elizabeth Beck et al., *In the Shadow of Death: Restorative Justice and Death Row Families* (New York: Oxford Univ. Press, 2007).

38. Zimring, *Contradictions*, 49; 42–64. Also see John Paul Stevens, "On the Death Sentence," *New York Review of Books* 23, December 23, 2010, http://www.nybooks .com/articles/archives/2010/dec/23/death-sentence.

39. See Sarat, *When the State Kills*, 187–208.

40. Sr. Helen Prejean, *The Death of Innocents: An Eyewitness Account of Wrongful Convictions* (New York: Random House, 2004), 40.

41. Stacy Abramson and David Isay, prods., *Witness to an Execution*, 2000. http:// soundportraits.org/on-air/witness_to_an_execution/transcript.php.

42. Robert B. Livingston, "Why I Joined the Green Party," *IndyBay*, January 15, 2007, http://www.indybay.org/newsitems/2007/01/15/18347065.php.

43. Brian Rooney, "Eyewitness to an Execution," *ABC Good Morning America*, December 13, 2005, http://abcnews.go.com/GMA/LegalCenter/story?id=1395059.

44. *Texas Department of Criminal Justice—Victim Services Division*, revised February 2005, http://www.tdcj.state.tx.us/PUBLICATIONS/victim.svcs/Execution%20Bro chure%20updated%2012-22-04%20JB.pdf.

45. Abramson and Isay, prods., *Witness to an Execution*.

46. Rooney, "Eyewitness."

47. *State of California San Quentin Operational Procedure Number 0-770, Execution by Lethal Injection*, May 15, 2007, http://www.cdcr.ca.gov/News/docs/RevisedProtocol .pdf.

48. Dwight Conquergood, "Lethal Theatre: Performance, Punishment, and the Death Penalty," *Theatre Journal* (2002), 361.

49. Ibid., 339–67. For more on guards, see Clive Stafford Smith, "An Englishman Abroad," in *A Punishment in Search of a Crime: Americans Speak Out against the Death Penalty*, eds. Ian Gray and Moira Gray (New York: Avon, 1989), 175; Don Hawkins, "The Long Walk," in *Writing for Their Lives*, 144.

50. See legal document at Peter Slevin, "Execution Methods Examined," *Washington Post*, October 12, 2009, http://media.washingtonpost.com/wp-srv/politics/ documents/broomaffidavit.pdf?sid=ST2009101100544.

51. Noam Chomsky, *The New Military Humanism: Lessons from Kosovo* (Monroe, ME: Common Courage Press, 2002).

52. Section One of the Thirteenth Amendment reads, "Neither slavery nor in-

voluntary servitude, except as punishment for crime whereof the party shall have been duly convicted, shall exist within the United States, or any place within their jurisdiction."

53. David M. Oshinsky, *"Worse than Slavery": Parchman Farm and the Ordeal of Jim Crow Justice* (New York: Free Press, 1997), 46. Also see Bruce Jackson, *Wake Up the Dead Man: Hard Labor and Southern Blues* (Athens: Univ. of Georgia Press, 1999); Danny Lyon, *Conversations with the Dead* (New York: Henry Holt, 1971).

54. Zimring, *Contradictions*, 89.

55. Ibid., 111. Also see Margaret Vandiver, *Lethal Punishment: Lynching and Legal Execution in the South* (New Brunswick, NJ: Rutgers Univ. Press, 2006), 9.

56. Charles J. Ogletree Jr., "Black Man's Burden: Race and the Death Penalty in America," *Oregon Law Review* 81.1 (Spring 2002): 23.

57. Laura Sullivan, "Prison Economics Help Drive Arizona Immigration Law," NPR, October 29, 2010, http://www.npr.org/templates/story/story.php?storyId=130833741. Also see Jael Silliman and Anannya Bhattacharjee, eds., *Policing the National Body: Race, Gender, and Criminalization in the United States* (Cambridge: South End Press, 2002).

58. Marc Mauer and Ryan S. King, "Uneven Justice: State Rates of Incarceration by Race and Ethnicity," *The Sentencing Project* (July 2007), 3, http://www.sentencingproject.org/doc/publications/rd_stateratesofincbyraceandethnicity.pdf.

59. See Amy Louise Wood, *Lynching and Spectacle: Witnessing Racial Violence in America, 1890–1940* (Durham: Univ. of North Carolina Press, 2009), 23–25; Vandiver, *Lethal*, 10.

60. Robyn Wiegman, "The Anatomy of Lynching," *Journal of the History of Sexuality* 3.3 (1993), 445.

61. See Vandiver, *Lethal*, 11–12.

62. James W. Clarke, "Without Fear or Shame: Lynching, Capital Punishment and the Subculture of Violence in the American South," *British Journal of Political Science* 28 (1998): 284–85. See Michael J. Pfeifer, *Rough Justice: Lynching and American Society, 1874–1947* (Urbana: Univ. of Illinois Press, 2004); Stewart E. Tolnay and E. M. Beck, *A Festival of Violence: An Analysis of Southern Lynching* (Chicago: Univ. of Chicago Press, 1995).

63. Garland, *Peculiar*, 12–13, 35.

64. Vandiver, *Lethal*, 10–11; Davis, *Abolition*, 54.

65. Patterson and Conrad, *Scottsboro Boy*, 19.

66. Dan Carter, *Scottsboro: A Tragedy of the American South*, rev. ed. (Baton Rouge: Louisiana State Univ. Press, 1979), 242.

67. Ibid., 37.

68. *Furman v. Georgia*, No. 69-5003. U.S. Supreme Court, June 29, 1972, http://

www.law.cornell.edu/supct/. Also see Richard C. Dieter, "Struck by Lightning: The Continuing Arbitrariness of the Death Penalty Thirty-Five Years after Its Reinstatement in 1976," *Death Penalty Information Center*, July 2011, http://www.death penaltyinfo.org/documents/StruckByLightning.pdf.

69. See "National Statistics on the Death Penalty and Race," *Death Penalty Information Center*, www.deathpenaltyinfo.org/race-death-row-inmates-executed-1976; "Racial differentials exist, with blacks disproportionately represented among homicide victims and offenders," *Bureau of Justice Statistics*, www.ojp.usdoj.gov/bjs/homicide/race.htm. Also see Bryan Stevenson, "Crime, Punishment, and Executions in the Twenty-first Century," *Proceedings of the American Philosophical Society* 147 (March 2003), 25.

70. Equal Justice Initiative, *Illegal Racial Discrimination in Jury Selection: A Continuing Legacy*, June 2010, http://www.eji.org/eji/node/397; Shaila Dewan, "Study Finds Blacks Blocked from Southern Juries," *New York Times*, June 1, 2010, http://www.nytimes.com/2010/06/02/us/02jury.html?ref=todayspaper&pagewanted. Also see Ogletree, "Black Man's," 23–27.

71. *William Andrews v. the United States*, No. 11-139. University of Minnesota Human Rights Library, December 6, 1996, http://www1.umn.edu/humanrts/cases/1997/us57-96.html.

72. For this phrase, I am indebted to Timothy B. Powell, *Ruthless Democracy: A Multicultural Interpretation of the American Renaissance* (Princeton: Princeton Univ. Press, 2000).

73. Criminal Justice Project of the NAACP Legal Defense and Educational Fund, "Death Row U.S.A.," Winter 2010, http://naacpldf.org/files/publications/DRUSA_Winter_2010.pdf.

74. Davis, *Abolition*, 54.

75. Miller et al. calculate 130 years. I also count the years spent in prison for parole violations.

76. Carter, *Scottsboro*, 414.

77. Rodriguez, *Forced Passages*, 90; Davis, *Abolition*, 41.

78. Jackson, *Blood*, 99–100.

79. Rodriguez, *Forced Passages*, 41–47.

80. Stephen John Hartnett, "The Annihilating Public Policies of the Prison-Industrial Complex; or, Crime, Violence," *Rhetoric and Public Affairs* 11.3 (2008), 493.

81. John Wideman, *Brothers and Keepers* (New York: Vintage, 1995), 35.

82. "Against the Discipline of Prison Writing," *Genre* 35 (Fall/Winter 2004), 409. For the language of death and prison, see Rodriguez, *Forced Passages*, 185–256.

83. Caleb Smith, "Prisons and the Poetics of Living Death," *Texas Studies in Literature and Language* 50.3 (Fall 2008), 245. For social death, see Sharon Patricia Hol-

land, *Raising the Dead: Readings of Death and (Black) Subjectivity* (Durham: Duke Univ. Press, 2000); Orlando Patterson, *Slavery and Social Death: A Comparative Study* (Cambridge: Harvard Univ. Press, 1982).

84. Steve Champion, "Gang Validation: The New Inquisition," *San Francisco Bay View*, February 18, 2011. Bill Ryan twice sued the Illinois Department of Corrections to ensure delivery of the prison newspaper, *Stateville Speaks*, and *Prison Legal News* has sued multiple states for access. For censorship, see Mumia Abu-Jamal, *All Things Censored* (New York: Seven Stories, 2000); Tom Kerr, "Buried Alive on San Quentin's Death Row," PEN American Center, http://www.pen.org/viewmedia.php/prmMID/1661.

85. Atul Gawande, "Hellhole," *New Yorker*, March 30, 2009, http://www.new yorker.com/reporting/2009/03/30/090330fa_fact_gawande. Also see Joan Dayan, "Legal Slaves and Civil Bodies," *Neplanta: Views from the South* 2.1 (2001): 10; Colin Dayan, *The Story of Cruel and Unusual* (Cambridge: MIT Press, 2007); James Ridgeway and Jean Casella, *Solitary Watch*, http://solitarywatch.com.

86. Stanton, "No Gallows," 121.

87. Margaret Noonan, "Mortality in Local Jails, 2000–2007," *Bureau of Justice Statistics*, July 7, 2010, http://bjs.ojp.usdoj.gov/index.cfm?ty=pbdetail&iid=2197.

88. Jessica Mitford, *Kind and Unusual Punishment* (New York: Vintage, 1974), 5.

89. Equal Justice Initiative, "Cruel and Unusual: Sentencing 13- and 14-year-old Children to Die in Prison," 2007, http://eji.org/eji/files/Cruel%20and%20Un usual%202008_0.pdf. For child abuse and later violence, see Clive Stafford Smith, "Englishman," 173; Dave Mann, "Innocence Lost," *Texas Observer*, April 15, 2010: 16–17; Generation FIVE at http://www.generationfive.org/csa.php; Mikal Gilmore, *Shot in the Heart* (New York: Anchor, 1995).

90. See David Kaiser and Lovisa Stannow, "Prison Rape and the Government," *New York Review of Books*, March 24, 2011, http://www.nybooks.com/articles/ar chives/2011/mar/24/prison-rape-and-government/?pagination=false.

91. Hames-García, *Fugitive*, 148.

92. Critical Resistance republished the pamphlet *Instead of Prisons: Prison Research Education Action Project* (Oakland: Critical Resistance, 2005). For original text, see http://www.prisonpolicy.org/scans/instead_of_prisons/.

93. See Murder Victims' Families for Human Rights, http://www.mvfhr.org; Murder Victims' Families for Reconciliation, http://www.mvfr.org; Brian MacQuarrie, *The Ride: A Shocking Murder and a Bereaved Father's Journey from Rage to Redemption* (Cambridge, MA: Da Capo Press, 2009); Rachel King, *Don't Kill in My Name: Families of Murder Victims Speak Out against the Death Penalty* (New Brunswick, NJ: Rutgers Univ. Press, 2003); Bill Pelke, *Journey of Hope . . . From Violence to Healing* (Pelke, 2003).

94. For the discourse of rights-bearing citizens, see Georgio Agamben, "Beyond Human Rights," in *Cities without Citizens*, eds. Aaron Levy and Eduardo Cadava (Philadelphia: Slought Foundation, 2003); Smith, *Prison*, 201–9.

95. See Davis, *Abolition*, 35; Angela Davis and Dylan Rodriguez, "The Challenge of Prison Abolition," *History Is a Weapon*, http://www.historyisaweapon.com/def con1/davisinterview.html.

96. Quoted in Mitford, *Kind and Unusual Punishment*, 297–98.

97. Edward Mendiata, Introduction, *Abolition Democracy*, 16.

98. With "national fantasy," I refer to Lauren Berlant, *The Anatomy of a National Fantasy: Hawthorne, Utopia, and Everyday Life* (Chicago: Univ. of Chicago Press, 1991) and H. Bruce Franklin, *Vietnam and Other American Fantasies* (Amherst: Univ. of Massachusetts Press, 2000).

99. Susan Harris Smith, *American Drama: The Bastard Art* (Cambridge: Cambridge Univ. Press, 1997); Shannon Jackson, *Professing Performance: Theatre in the Academy from Philology to Performativity* (Cambridge, UK: Cambridge Univ. Press, 2004).

100. See, for instance, Carolyn R. Miller, "Genre as Social Action," *Quarterly Journal of Speech* 70 (1984), 151–67; Frederic Jameson, *Political Unconscious: Narrative as a Socially Symbolic Act* (Ithaca: Cornell Univ. Press, 1982), 106; Elizabeth Ammons, *Brave New Words: How Literature Will Save the Planet* (Iowa City: Univ. of Iowa Press, 2010).

101. Dow, *Autobiography*, 256.

102. See Rickie Solinger et al., eds., *Interrupted Life: Experiences of Incarcerated Women in the United States* (Berkeley: Univ. of California Press, 2010); Robin Lee Row, "Open Letter from Idaho's Only Female Death Row Prisoner," *Writing for Their Lives*, 260–69; Robert A. Ferguson, *The Trial in American Life* (Chicago: Univ. of Chicago Press, 2007), 153–90; Victor L. Streib, *The Fairer Death: Executing Women in Ohio* (Athens: Ohio Univ. Press, 2006); Janet Baus, Dan Hunt, and Reid Williams, dirs., *Cruel and Unusual* (2006); Michael B. Shortnacy, "Sexual Minorities, Criminal Justice, and the Death Penalty," *Fordham Urban Law Journal* 32 (2005); Richard Goldstein, "Queer on Death Row," *Village Voice*, March 13, 2001; Kathryn Ann Farr, "Defeminizing and Dehumanizing Female Murderers," *Women and Criminal Justice* 11.1 (May 2000): 49–66; Kathleen O'Shea, *Women and the Death Penalty, 1900–1998* (Westport, CT: Greenwood, 1999); Victor L. Streib, "Death Penalty for Lesbians," *National Journal of Sexual Orientation Law* 1.1 (1995); Elizabeth Rappaport, "The Death Penalty and Gender Discrimination," *Law and Society Review* 25.2 (June 1991): 367–83 and "Staying Alive," 967–1007.

103. For prison rebellions, see Daniel Burton-Rose, Dan Pens, and Paul Wright, eds., *The Celling of America: An Inside Look at the U.S. Prison Industry* (Monroe, ME: Com-

mon Courage Press, 1998), 217–49; Gary Williams, *Siege in Lucasville* (Bloomington, IN: Rooftop, 2006); Bert Useem and Peter Kimball, *States of Siege: U.S. Prison Riots, 1971–1986* (New York: Oxford Univ. Press, 1991).

104. Abu-Jamal, *Live from Death Row*, 5.

105. Deborah W. Denno, "When Willie Francis Died: The 'Disturbing' Story Behind One of the Eighth Amendment's Most Enduring Standards of Risk," in *Death Penalty Stories*, eds. John H. Blume and Jordan M. Steiker (New York: Foundation Press, 2009), 23. Also see Gilbert King, *The Execution of Willie Francis: Race, Murder, and the Search for Justice in the American South* (New York: Basic Civitas Books, 2008); Allan Durand, dir., *Willie Francis Must Die Again* (2006); Arthur S. Miller and Jeffrey H. Bowman, *Death by Installments: The Ordeal of Willie Francis* (New York: Greenwood Press, 1988).

106. *Louisiana ex. rel. Francis v. Resweber*, No. 142, January 13, 1947, http://www.law.cornell.edu/supct. For the impact of the decision, see Denno, "When Willie Francis Died," esp. 84–93, and Dayan, *Cruel and Unusual*, chapter four.

107. The memoir *To Alcatraz, Death Row, and Back* (2005) opens with a letter from the associate warden of San Quentin to Ernie López's brother. The warden asks if Lawrence López intends to claim his brother's body after the execution: "This will be at your expense and it will be necessary for you to make tentative arrangements with a mortician of your choice" (López and Pérez-Torres). In his final statement, Shaka Sankofa asked Bianca Jaggar, "Bianca, make sure that the state does not get my body" (Elder, *Last Words*, 234). For dissection of executed people's bodies, see Banner, *Death Penalty*, 76–80; Boudreau, *Spectacle*, 184; and Susan F. Sharpe, *Hidden Victims: The Effects of the Death Penalty on the Families of the Accused* (New Brunswick, NJ: Rutgers Univ. Press, 2005), 96.

108. "The Execution of the Minnesota Indians," *Harper's Weekly*, January 17, 1863, 39–40.

109. Robert K. Elder, *Last Words of the Executed* (Chicago: Univ. of Chicago Press, 2010), 40.

110. Megan Sweeney, "Legal Brutality: Prisons and Punishment, the American Way," *American Literary History* 22.3 (Fall 2010), 704.

111. Jacques Derrida, *Negotiations: Interventions and Interviews, 1971–2001*, ed. Elizabeth Rottenberg (Stanford: Stanford Univ. Press, 2002), 125.

112. Qtd. in Dutoit, p. 241.

113. Studs Terkel, *Will the Circle Be Unbroken: Reflections on Death, Rebirth, and Hunger for a Faith* (New York: Ballantine, 2002).

114. Gwendolyn Brooks, "To the Diaspora," *Riot* (Detroit: Broadside Press, 1969), 41.

I decided to become the enemy not of my son's killer
but of the forces that put a young boy on a dark street holding
a handgun. Tony [Hicks] now writes letters from prison that
we use in our programs and that we see having a positive
effect on other kids. Think of how many kids he may save.
That's going to bring me a lot more healing than if he had
gotten the death penalty.

—Azim Khamisa, whose twenty-year-old son Tariq was shot
   and killed by Tony Hicks. At age fourteen, Hicks was tried
   as an adult. He pled guilty and received twenty-five years
   to life.

They tell me that this is the first time anyone ever had a chance to tell the story of how it feels to go to the electric chair and know that you might have to go back there. This is the first time I ever told the whole story and I hope that by at last telling it people will understand what it means to go through what I went through. I hope it will help people to do the right thing and live right. I know how it felt to have them read a death warrant to me, I know how it feels to sit in a cell waiting for the day they will lead me to the chair again. I sure know how it feels to sit in that chair and have them strap me in and put a mask on my eyes. I know how it feels to have the shock go through me and think I am dead but find out I am not. I do not like to talk about it at all, but if it will help other people to understand each other, I want to tell everything.

A lot of people write to me and ask me to tell them something about what I did when I was young. I am only eighteen now, so I guess they mean when I was very young. I was born in St. Martinville, Louisiana. It's just a little town where everybody knows everybody else. We have two sections, one for the white people and the other for the colored, and everybody gets along fine. The white tend to their own business and the colored tend to theirs. It isn't often something exciting happens there and when something does happen like when Mr. Thomas gets killed, everybody gets real excited and wants to know who did it. I don't want to talk about the killing of Mr. Thomas. When they asked me to write this story I said I would only if I didn't have to say anything about that part. I was tried and convicted of the killing, and as far as I think, that's all over. But I will tell you about the electrocution.

I guess from the first minute I was born I gave people something to worry about. Maybe you will think I am superstitious. I guess I am, because I have a lot of reasons to be. I was the thirteenth child of my father, Frederick Francis, and my mother, Louise Francis. And I was convicted of the murder on the thirteenth of September, 1945. Then the United States Supreme Court turned me down on January thirteenth of this year.

We lived in the colored section at 800 Washington Street. It is a little house dull gray in color and faces north. It had thirteen of us kids running through it all the time.

I was baptized Willie Francis. That's what they always called me, anyway. I guess I grew up just like my other colored friends. I belong to the Catholic Church in St. Martinville and my pastor was Father Maurice Roussere. He was there at my electrocution. He comes to see me now and then and tells me how my family is. Every day or whenever he can he goes to see them.

I used to like to play jokes and my friends used to tell me I could make almost anyone laugh when I said or did something. We had a bunch of kids who went around together a lot. We would go swimming in the bayou all day long without telling anyone where we went and when we got back home we got spanked for it. It's something to laugh at now but we didn't like the whipping at the time. Sometimes we went fishing or maybe we would grab some watermelons and go down by the bayou to eat them. It was a lot of fun and we always laughed a lot. More than anything else we like to eat figs. We would snitch them and go sit on the bank and see who could throw them the farthest out into the water. I liked to play marbles, too. I didn't win all the time but when I won it was more often than when I lost. I think I was pretty good at the game. I liked a little baseball now and then if there were enough of us and someone had a ball. Most of the time we used a broomstick for a bat. We didn't have any gloves and I guess we made our own rules, but nobody ever complained.

When you live in a house with that many people in it, things aren't as crowded as you would think. All my brothers and sisters got along fine together because we had to. We knew it wasn't any use fighting or fussing because everybody had to stick together if we were going to all be happy. My father worked in a sugar factory in the cane season and does odd jobs during the rest of the year. He made enough money to keep us all fed and nobody ever starved, that I know of. When things went right and he had a nickel to spare we had a bottle of red pop. For me it was ice-cream.

I don't know how she did it, but my mother kept everything running smooth all the time. The minute she walked out the house something went wrong, and when she came back in, it was all right again. My father made the money but when it came to keeping the house clean and in order, mother did that best. As my older brothers and sisters grew up and could shift for themselves, things got better and mother had more rest. But she still ran everything.

In school I didn't make good grades. Just about what everybody else was making. It wasn't because I wasn't interested; I just couldn't keep my mind on arithmetic when we were thinking of going swimming or having a secret water-melon party that same afternoon.

I used to work in Mr. Thomas' drug store. I didn't work steady for him. I would run around the corners with a package or sweep the floor when he asked me to. Sometimes I would get a dollar or fifty cents for cleaning or raking his yard. He was a very fine fellow Mr. Thomas was.

After they sentenced me on September thirteenth, they drove me to the Parish Prison here in New Iberia, Louisiana. They said I would like it much better here because the death cell is bigger and more comfortable than in St. Martinville. It didn't make much difference. They hadn't said when they were going to kill me, so I didn't care where they put me. The cell where I am now is on the top floor of the Court-House. I have one window to look out over the house-tops of New Iberia in two directions. My walls are painted bright pink. I like the color but I wish the walls weren't behind the paint.

The jailor and the sheriff have always been nice to me. They don't talk rough or cuss me at all. We get along very fine and they are nice men. When they ask me to do something I always do it, and when I ask for something they give it to me. The food here is all right and it's regular.

I stayed up here for a couple of months without anything happening. My family and a few friends would drop in on me now and then. I spent and spend most of the time reading books and magazines my family and other people brought me. When nobody else could come my father did, and brought me little things like tooth-paste. One day he brought me a Bible my mother gave him for me. It's pretty well worn out now.

My pastor, Father Roussere, couldn't come to see me often because he lives in St. Martin, and I didn't have a priest to talk to. One day when I was looking out my cell door window I saw a man walking down the corridor of the jail who was dressed just like a priest. I yelled and waved my arms, and when he looked I asked him to come over to my cell. I guess he thought I was crazy because of the way I acted, but he came in anyway. His name was Father Charles Hannegan and I found out he had been confessor to a lot of men who had to die like I had. From what he told me later I was lucky it was the electric chair and not hanging. About that I don't know; I will just say I think I have been lucky.

At the beginning of April the Sheriff came in to tell me I had to go to the electric chair on the third of May. He said the Governor had written my death warrant. It was funny, the way it was written—real careful, like they thought I might say, "You can't kill me because you have a word wrong on that paper!"

I knew it had to come sometime, so when they told me it was the third it didn't make much difference. Time began to pass by quickly for me. Boy, you sure feel funny when you know you're going to die; almost like you know something only God should know.

The day before I was to go to the electric chair I was plenty scared. Father Hannegan came to see me. He knew I was scared. He told me something funny: He said I was lucky because I knew when I was going to die, and so I could prepare myself in time. I had never thought about dying that way before. All I could see was that I wouldn't be alive any more. What he said made me feel a little better. He said he might fall down the jailhouse steps and break his neck, or maybe he would die between clean sheets in his rectory that night. Anyway, he would never know and I would. He said I had a new life to start when I got up from that chair the next day, and I shouldn't start it like a little cry-baby. Even though I was only sixteen, he said, I had this one big chance to prove I was able to die like a man. It is one of the hardest things to make yourself learn how to die right.

And he told me that the chair would only tickle me for a little while and then it would all be over for me. I didn't have any idea what the chair looked like or what it could do besides that it would kill me, and when I went to sit down in it I was hoping it would tickle me like Father Hannegan said. When it was all over and they asked me how it felt I told them that; that it tickled me. But I'm telling you that chair sure isn't full of feathers. I guess people have the idea it tickled the way you feel when you laugh.

When he left me and I was alone I kept thinking about what he told me. I read in my Bible until the sun went down. Then I thought a lot about dying. I wasn't going to be a cry-baby; I was going to be brave and act like he said was the only way. I was worried about my mother because she was sick in bed at the time. They didn't tell me this—that's why I knew there was something wrong at home.

That night around supper time the Sheriff came in and said: "Willie, this is your last night, so you can have anything you want to eat for supper. What would you like?" I remember how I always liked ice cream so much and thought I would like to have some before I died. The Sheriff laughed a little and said. "Is that all you want, Willie?" I told him I would like something else if it was alright with him. He brought me a very fine steak, which he said was the best one he could find in town . . . and more ice cream than I could eat.

I guess I must have looked worried, because he asked me if I was worried about what was going to happen when I sat in the chair. I told him if I had to die I was ready and wouldn't be a cry-baby. I didn't think anybody wanted to die if he could help it, but since I couldn't do any thing to stop it, I didn't see any point in crying or worrying.

When I was alone that night and everything was dark, I began thinking about what was going to happen to me the next day. I wondered why the chair was called the "hot seat." If it was hot I figured it burned, and if it burned you, I couldn't understand how it could just "tickle" me.

I started thinking about something that bothered me. They say there will be a Day of Judgment, and on that day everybody will be judged. I was wondering about when that day was. I mean, when we die we must all die at the same time. We don't know how long Eternity is and when a man dies we don't know how long he will wait according to time in Eternity until the whole world dies and goes to meet him. What I guess I mean is, when you die it is Judgment Day right away.

I kept thinking that tomorrow I will be dead and they will bury me in a cold cold grave. I wondered what it would look like and I tried to see myself in my mind looking at my own grave-marker. Later on I got on my knees and said my prayers for what I thought would be the last time. I said, "God, tonight is the last time I will sleep in a bed because tomorrow I will have to sit down on that chair and die. Please help me to die."

It's a hard thing to get it into your head, it seemed so unreal.

After I did a lot of thinking I fell asleep way late. I guess I dreamed a lot. When you wake up and try to remember what you dreamed the night before it is very hard, but I didn't have much trouble because I tried to take my mind off the chair that morning by trying to remember what I dreamed the night before. It was something like a bunch of us boys sitting on the bayou banks but I was the only one who wasn't having a good time. While everybody else laughed I just stood on the bank. I was looking to the other side of the Bayou but I couldn't see anything. It was all fuzzy and blurred about in the middle of the Bayou.

When I woke up they gave me some breakfast. When I finished they came and took the dishes away and I just sat around waiting for something to happen. About an hour after, I heard them opening the door again. One of the men who was a prisoner himself in a cell across the corridor from me walked inside. He had a towel and some shaving things in his hands. He looked like he had to do something he didn't want to do. He told me, "Willie, I'm sorry, but I have to get your head shaved, because that's where they're going to make the electricity pass through your body." I sat down and he started clipping me. He talked a little to keep my mind off the chair but I didn't feel much like answering back. When he was finished he stood back to, I guess, admire his work and he smiled, "Well, Willie, I guess that's one hair-cut you won't have to pay for." I guess anybody else would have gotten mad or thought something else. But I could see he was only trying to joke with me and make me laugh so I wouldn't have my mind on dying in the electric chair. I thought it was a very good joke and laughed out loud. Everybody else—those people standing outside and some who came into my cell—started laughing, too. Then everyone started telling me a lot of other funny things. They were all being so nice to me that, for a little while, dying didn't seem such a bad thing.

A little while after eleven o'clock the Sheriff came in with one of his deputies. Everybody got quiet. He asked me if I was ready because it would take us some time to drive over to St. Martinville. I took a look around the cell for the last time and said I was ready. The Sheriff handcuffed me and stood aside. I stopped in the doorway. You get a funny crawling feeling when you walk out of that death cell to go out and die. I tried to think about all the other condemned men who had left this same cell and in cells all over the world to go out and be punished. I wondered what they had thought about, but I could only think about myself and how hard my heart was beating against my chest. I walked outside and started across the hall to where the elevator was. While the jailor was unlocking the door I looked around me. All the other prisoners were staring out from their cell doors. I didn't hear anybody say anything but I could tell by their faces they all felt sorry for me. I saw the man who shaved my head. He was frowning in a funny sort of way, and as I stepped into the elevator and turned around, I saw him wave his little finger at me.

I was dizzy and going down in the elevator seemed to make things worse. Everybody was so quiet and I was thinking about how scared I was so loud I thought they almost heard what I was thinking. They opened the door downstairs and we walked through the lobby to the outside. The sun was real bright and hurt my eyes. There was a black sedan waiting at the curb with the door already open. I tried to walk straight and bravely like Father Hannegan said. The deputy got in and I took a last look up at my window, then got into the car. The Sheriff got on my other side and they started the car. I saw some other policemen around us.

While we drove I kept thinking about not crying or being a baby. I didn't want to die but I wasn't going to say anything about it. They didn't talk to me very much. It wasn't like the joking in my cell at all. I didn't feel much like talking anyway; my tongue was stuck to the top of my mouth, and my ears were ringing. I looked out the windows at all the places we passed. I knew the whole road very well and I couldn't make myself believe I wasn't going to see any of the scenes again. I knew I was going to die, because I was so scared, yet there was something in me that said, Willie, you aren't going to die. About half way to St. Martinville the deputy said to me, "Don't worry, Willie—it won't hurt you very much. You won't even feel it!" I wasn't worried at all whether it would hurt me, I was more worried about the fact it was going to kill me.

I remember looking down at my feet on the floor. My shoes were nice and shiny. I tried to remember just about when I took the first step of the last mile I was supposed to have walked in my life. I couldn't figure it out, but I guessed I would only get to make about fifty more steps in my nice clean shoes and then I would be dead.

The closer I got to St. Martinville the harder my heart beat and the more my knees jumped. When we did get there I noticed the driver turned down into the colored section. I sat up in my seat when I saw we were going to pass my house. I don't know if the driver knew it was my house or not, but it seemed to me he kind of slowed down when we got real near it. But we were still going too fast for me to see anything but the front part of it. I was hoping I would get to see somebody in front—maybe my mother—but nobody was there. It was nice to see it again. I'm glad I didn't see anyone I knew or anyone in my family in front of it. Dying would have been harder if I had, I see now.

When we got closer to the court house the first thing I saw was a large bunch of people gathered around all the doors of the court house. There were both colored and white. And when they saw us pulling up to the curb, they ran up and tried to look into the car. It seemed like everybody in St. Martinville had come out to see me. I upset their way of living so much I guess I was worth a last look.

I got out and looked around the crowd for my father. They had written to me he would be there. Afterward they told me he had to borrow an awful lot of money to rent a hearse and buy a coffin and grave-stone for me. I didn't see him or the hearse, but I saw the truck that had brought the electric chair. As I started to walk forward its motor started and got louder and louder. I could even see some wires leading up to a window where I guessed the chair was. I wished I had seen my father instead. He's a good man, and I know I caused him and the family a whole lot of misery. I tried to hold my shoulders back and walk without anyone helping me like Father Hannegan would have wanted me to. I guess a lot of people thought I was just bragging. We got into the building, and when they closed the door I didn't hear the truck motor or the people's voices any more.

They took me up to the execution room. I never knew so many people could get in a room that small. It was shaped like an "L," and there, almost against the wall was the chair. It was almost like any other chair but a lot heavier looking and it had straps on it. It even scared me to look at it. Nobody said anything and everyone kept looking straight at me. I guessed they wanted me to sit on the chair so I started to sit down on it. But the Sheriff grabbed my arm and pulled me away. I was glad for a minute I had done the wrong thing.

He led me into one of the cells. Father Roussere was inside waiting to talk to me. They closed the door and left us alone. Father started telling me I shouldn't be afraid and asked me if there was any doubt in my mind about dying. He told me a lot of nice things and said he would take care of my family and help them to try and get over my passing away. That seemed to be about all, so I got up and they opened the door. Everybody was watching me as I walked out. I looked at the Sheriff and he nodded, so I walked across the room and sat down in the chair. He took the handcuffs off and the men began strapping me into the chair. They put one strap around my leg and around my waist and tied my arms down, too. I knew then how real it was to have to die. I had it in my mind deep. It was so quiet in there everybody was looking at me so funny. It was the realest misery I ever knew, to see them watching me. It seemed like they would come close to my eyes and then move away from me. I wished they had kept still because I was already dizzy. I was cold and my hands were all wet. I couldn't feel my neck and my head but they say I was soaking with perspiration. They kept on fixing the machine and connecting the wires to my head and to my left leg.

Everything seemed to be finished because everybody looked stranger than before. The Sheriff was looking back of me, and when someone said, "All right," he stepped next to me and asked me if there was something I would like to say before they pulled the switch on me. I was thinking about saying I didn't blame anyone for what they were doing to me, but I couldn't talk. I didn't see my whole life in front of me like they say you are supposed to. When Father Roussere held the Cross out for me to kiss it looked real big. He and the Sheriff stepped back and I relaxed as much as I could. I heard something behind me but before I could turn my head to see what it was, I jumped. They had just touched my head with the hood. It was wet and scared me because I wasn't expecting it. It was a little cap that fitted over my eyes and left my nose free to breathe. Not being able to see made me even more scared. I heard moving around and mumbling around on all sides of me. Then, off to the left side I heard a voice I hadn't heard until then say to me, "Good-Bye, Willie!" It was funny the way he said it—like he was telling me good-bye and I was going off on a trip. I wanted to say good-bye, too, but I was so scared I couldn't talk. My hands were closed tightly. Then—I could almost hear it coming.

The best way I can describe it is: Whamm! Zst!

It felt like a hundred and a thousand needles and pins were pricking in me all over and my left leg felt like somebody was cutting it with a razor blade. I could feel my arms jumping at my sides and I guess my whole body must have jumped straight out. I couldn't stop the jumping. If that was tickling it was sure a funny kind. I thought for a minute I was going to knock the chair over. Then I was all right. I thought I was dead. Father Hannegan had been right, in a little way—it hadn't hurt me too much. Then they did it again! The same feeling all over. I heard a voice say, "Give me some more juice down there!" And in a little while somebody yelled, "I'm giving you all I got now!" I think I must have hollered for them to stop. They say I said, "Take it off! Take it off!" I know that was certainly what I wanted them to do—turn it off. I really thought I was dead then. I could feel hands all over my body. I thought it was funny how you can feel hands the same way when you're dead as when you're alive. I thought it was funny you could think a little, too, because I wondered why they didn't just leave me alone. I was dead and it seemed like they were in an awful hurry to get me out of that chair so they could bury me. They took the blindfold off and I looked around. The straps were off me and I could feel my hands a little bit. Everybody was talking loud and like they were excited. Then I knew I was still alive and wondered if they were going to make me sit down and in a little while try to kill me again. They told me to get up and a man said, "Are you all right?" I was sure glad to be alive and I told him I was all right. The Sheriff took me off into another room and told me to lay down on a cot.

The Coroner came in with his bag and listened to my chest. Then he left. The Sheriff asked me if there was anything I wanted, like water or something to eat and I told him no. Then the other Sheriff came in to tell me they had just called the Governor and I had until the ninth of May—six more days—before they tried to kill me again. I didn't like the idea of going through that all over again, but I was so glad to be just alive I didn't say anything. As we walked out of the room the man who must have thrown the switch yelled at me and said, "I missed you this time, but I'll get you next week if I have to use an iron bar!" He was plenty mad, I guess.

On my way outside to the car they sure looked at me funny. It was my turn to look at them. They looked like they were looking at a ghost. They had expected me to come out feet-first, and I can see why they were surprised. I got into the car and we drove back to New Iberia.

Boy. I was sure glad to see the inside of that death-cell again. It's sort of like being glad you can sit on a gravestone without having the gravestone sit on top of you. The Sheriff asked me if I wanted something to eat. I told him it didn't make much difference and he brought me something.

Father Hannegan came over in a little while. They had sent for him and when they called he didn't believe it was possible I was still alive. His face was funny when he walked in: almost like he was afraid of me. I was glad to see him and I wanted to tell him how I tried to be brave. He said, "Yes, you were brave, Willie. God has been good to you, son." Then I said something he said was the most astounding statement he ever heard. At the time he was so surprised he couldn't say anything, though. He told me later it shocked him because he should have known it better than I did. I just said, "Why Father—God is Always good!"

He's a very good friend of mine and we never had an argument except once and then it wasn't exactly an argument. We just disagreed about something. That is, I corrected him. When he was walking out the door that day I called him back. He asked me what I wanted and I said, "Father, you were right . . . . It did tickle me—but it sure hurt me, too!"

Later on in the day they let the newspaper reporters in to see me. They were excited and talked so much and so fast I got nervous. They took a picture of me reading my Bible.

In the next few days I began getting letters and telegrams from all over the country. I felt just like a movie star, and didn't have any idea I had so many friends. The people who wrote said they were sure the Lord had a hand in what happened and told me to be sure and keep on praying because they were praying, too. They would send me books to read and Bible tracts and wishes for good luck. They were all very nice to me and I tried to answer as many of them as I could. There were so many and I tried to find the time to answer them with the little time I thought I had left.

Nightmares? Yes, I have nightmares. Everybody has, I guess. No, the ghost of Mr. Thomas doesn't come back to sit beside me in my cell at night. I haven't seen him, anyway.

After the electrocution my father went right away to see a lawyer, Mr. Bertrand DeBlanc, and asked him if he would take my case. He told the lawyer he had no money but he would work to repay him. Mr. DeBlanc said it was all right and we didn't have to pay him anything. He said it would be cruel and unusual punishment to kill me.

I had to agree with him on that.

I was all ready to get used to dying again when Mr. DeBlanc came to see me the day before they were going to kill me the second time. He said the Judge had refused to let me go, but I didn't have to die because he got a chance to take my case before the Louisiana Supreme Court the next morning at ten o'clock. He also told me the Lieutenant Governor had granted me a stay of execution for twenty-nine more days. I was glad and very grateful to him. Every time he comes to see me he brings me candy and magazines. I quit smoking and told him so, but I guess he forgets because he brings me cigarettes anyway. About magazines, I guess I like western and romance stories best of all.

I found out the Louisiana Supreme Court said they couldn't do anything to stop me from being killed. But they gave me permission to go to the state Board of Pardons at the end of the month of May. I remember that day well. I was nervous and lonely both. I didn't have anybody to talk to because Father Hannegan had gone with my lawyer to the hearing in New Orleans. Father Hannegan came over the next day and tried to break it to me gently, but I knew by his face before he said anything that they had turned me down. But he said they were going to take my case to the Supreme Court in Washington, D.C.

On the tenth of June they came to me and said, "Willie, the Supreme Court decided not to even listen to your case." Well, I felt pretty bad about it, but after a while I got used to the idea. Then a couple of hours later, they came in laughing and said, "They made a mistake, Willie. Somebody put your papers in the wrong place and they are going to listen to your case in October."

Well, I sure felt glad. When they said I had to die I was disappointed, and when they came in I thought they were going to tell me when. But when they said I didn't have to die at all for a long time I really felt happy.

The strangest letter I got was from a lady in Texas. When I opened it up and read the beginning I could tell she was mixed up. When I read the rest of it I saw I was right. She told me how much she was praying and hoping I would not have to die. Then she said she had a "request" to make. She said she had a brother in her house who had been blind for a long time and wanted to know if I would will him my eyes if I had to die. She wanted to let me know how much she didn't want me to die and felt embarrassed because the request she made depended on my dying. I know it was very hard for her to write that letter so I made it a lot easier for her by writing to her right away to tell her she could have my eyes. I asked Mr. DeBlanc, who had moved to Lafayette, to draw up a will the next time he came. I didn't expect to hear very much from the lady any more except maybe to get a letter thanking me. But she wrote all the time and went all around her state to get up a petition to the Board of Pardons. It has been over a year since her first letter and she keeps on writing me regular. She's a very fine woman, I know, even though I never met her.

That business about the thirteenth child came up again. Just after the first of this year — on January 13th, which was sixteen days before my birthday — I heard that the Supreme Court in Washington gave a decision on my case. Five of the Justices voted against me and four for me. That was pretty close to happiness, I guess. I am not complaining or anything like that, because I know down in my heart everybody has tried to do the right thing for me and for everybody else. It is just that there has never been another case like mine before and I see how hard it is to say what is the right thing in my case.

If I ever get to Heaven I guess I'll get to know.

That is just about all I have to say right now. Mr. Montgomery says that in writing this I may have helped someone, somehow. I hope so. He has written the story of my life and it is much longer than this. I wonder if I will ever get to read the thing.

Note

1. Willie Francis, as told to Samuel Montgomery, "My Trip to the Chair," (Lafayette, LA: self-published, 1947), Afro-American Pamphlets, Part 3 (1827–1948), Rare Book and Special Collections Reading Room, Library of Congress.

Living Death Ernest Gaines's *A Lesson before Dying* and the Execution of Willie Francis

JASON STUPP

Ernest Gaines's *A Lesson before Dying* is, first and foremost, a prison novel. This is worth stating at the beginning because it has not been read primarily as a novel about prison; it has been read as a novel about personal transformation and racial reconciliation. One historical source for *Lesson* is the 1947 execution of Willie Francis, a black sixteen-year-old convicted by an all-white Louisiana jury of murdering a white storeowner, a case Gaines has said shaped some of his decisions while writing the novel.[1] After surviving a first execution in the electric chair, Francis dictated an account of his experience to Samuel Montgomery. Called "My Trip to the Chair," Francis's narrative reflects on the nature of "living death" and the need for communication between those inside and outside of prison. The voice of Willie Francis works against the desire or tendency to remit the incarcerated to the realm of the ghostly or the already-dead. Francis's narrative and *Lesson* testify to the trauma of incarceration and to what Caleb Smith calls an "outcast subjectivity."[2]

The plot of *A Lesson before Dying* is driven by the looming execution of Jefferson, a semiliterate young black man convicted of robbing and murdering a local storeowner in 1940s Bayonne, Louisiana, and the attempts of a schoolteacher, Grant Wiggins, to prepare him for his death. During his trial, Jefferson's lawyer, instead of focusing on the self-proclaimed innocence of his client, appeals to white supremacy, telling the jury of twelve white men that they would be sending not a man but a "cornered animal," a "thing," and a "hog," to the electric chair.[3] Jefferson's aunt, Miss Emma, implores the unwilling Grant to visit her nephew in jail, declaring, "I don't want them to kill no hog. . . . I want a man to go that chair" (L, 13). Scholars typically focus on the relationship between Grant and Jefferson: the former's reluctant yet persistent attempts to persuade Jefferson to recognize his own humanity, and Jefferson's eventual acceptance of his mortality. This scholarship tends to insert Jefferson into a narrative of memorialization and racial uplift.

When acknowledged, the incarcerated are only a secondary presence, a rhetorical device positioned to add context to the novel's principal "heroes"—Jefferson, Grant, and Paul, the white deputy who assists in "reclaiming" Jefferson's humanity and masculinity. Herman Beavers, for instance, claims that Gaines "reprises the jail cell as a site of symbolic action" and gives Jefferson, through Grant, "dignity and purpose."[4] Calling Jefferson's body a "rhetorical implement," Beavers argues that Grant and the benevolent Paul reverse the negative presumptions of whites toward blacks.[5] The novel, he writes, "forces us to confront the necessity of revitalizing those sites of memory which will, in their turn, renew our sense of community."[6] Beavers appears to echo Grant's original objection to the jail visits, namely that Jefferson is "already dead . . . he's gone from us" (L, 14). Since Jefferson is "already dead" when the novel begins, attempts to situate his death into a redemptive tale of suffering focus on the community outside the jail. Caleb Smith argues that the American prison has historically turned inmates into "animated corpses," figures of "exclusion and decay" largely outside public consciousness.[7] Scholarship on *Lesson* contributes to this dynamic by turning Jefferson into an animated corpse—a living symbol on which the anxieties of the Bayonne community are projected.

Memorialization, as the process by which communities form collective histories and memories, risks exalting the dead to a heroic status and undermining the individual in the creation of a symbol. Critical responses to *Lesson* present Jefferson's death as a sacred act of sacrifice for the enduring strength and unity of the outside community. Carlyle Thompson compares Jefferson to a "Christ-figure bound not to a cross but to an electric chair,"[8] a symbol of "redemptive suffering"[9] who "represent[s] the black race . . . with majestic dignity."[10] Arguing that one should view Jefferson's experience as a moral lesson, Thompson places him in a tradition of civil rights activists and other African American leaders.[11] Nowhere in the novel, however, is it suggested that Jefferson wishes to sacrifice himself; his martyrdom is a construction of a community preparing to meet his death with a narrative of suffering and redemption.

The creation of Jefferson's death narrative reflects what Michael Roth sees as two conflicting modes by which we attempt to understand history: the empirical ("correct" history) and the pragmatic ("usable" history).[12] Beavers, by identifying Jefferson as a rhetorical implement, responds to the novel's pragmatic approach to history. There is a communal need to create a usable past from Jefferson's execution, to make his death part of a historical narrative of oppression and uplift. Jefferson's body acts as one of the sites of memory that, once removed from view, is valued in terms of its symbolic capacity; his death, his "legacy," points to the *outside*, to the surrounding community, as does the "symbolic action" of the jail cell. Jefferson's cell, "roughly six by ten, with a metal bunk . . . a toilet without a seat or toilet paper . . . a single light bulb . . . [and] a barred window" (L, 71), signals, oppositely, the *inaction* that suffocates Jefferson as he awaits his death, a stifling barrenness that contributes to his nightmares. These material conditions, if forced to become symbolic of renewal, serve mostly to give insight into the lives of those outside the walls of the jail.

But what if the novel requires us to do what Grant thought impossible—that is, to "raise the dead"? What happens when the dead are allowed to speak? Where do we position the voices of the dead in relation to the nonincarcerated? Again, Roth's distinction between historical modes is instructive, especially his assertion that neither an empirical nor pragmatic approach can satisfy the need for history to be both accurate and narrative-friendly. More constructive might be what Roth identifies as a third approach—piety—that involves "turning oneself so as to be in relation to the past," and, in turn, learning to live with the past instead of simply "moving on."[13] A pious model of history incorporates both public and private memories as well as written histories, locating individuals in a continuum of experience. Instead of situating the bodies of the incarcerated and condemned as symbolic sites of tension that resolve other conflicts—the need for heroic struggle, closure for victims' families—an integrated approach combines literature with lived experience and, in the instance of *Lesson*, brings into focus other sites, such as the courthouse, death row, and the execution chamber.

Private Trauma/Public Knowledge: The Need for Alternative Forms of Remembrance

H. Bruce Franklin has asked if the penitentiary can teach the academy how to read. He argues that literature by those in prison "forces us to view incarceration, social justice, and literacy from the bottom up instead of from the top down."[14] *Lesson*, when read according to an "outcast subjectivity," asks the same question. In *The Ironist's Cage*, Michael Roth describes an ironic distancing used by scholars who lack "criteria of truth or strategies of legitimation" and who continue to write despite "the inability to sustain belief in the possibilities of significant political change."[15] The sizable incarcerated population in the United States that has little to no contact with those on the outside threatens to create a situation such as Roth describes, one in which scholars acknowledge and write about the need for prison reform but offer no tangible means by which such reform might be achieved. *Lesson* explores bottom-up activism and pedagogy, questioning the adequacy of public debate about prisons mediated by those who have never spent time behind bars.

Jefferson struggles within and against two competing mythologies he must embody. He is forced, on the one hand, to be the inhuman black criminal made an example of by a white supremacist culture; on the other, he must symbolize hope and renewal through his suffering for the sake of his community. The community, aside from the older generation of Miss Emma, Tante Lou (Grant's aunt), and their friends, is best represented in the novel by the children of the quarter. Early in the novel, Grant attempts to explain to his pupils what is happening to Jefferson. Telling them that Jefferson once sat in their seats, he explains, " 'They're going to strap him in a chair, they're going to tie him down with straps, they're going to connect wires to his head, to his wrists, to his legs, and they're going to shoot electricity through the wires into his body until he's dead' " (L, 39). In part, Grant uses Jefferson's impending death as a lesson—he tells the students that he will try to make Jefferson an adult, as he tries to do with the school-children, even if they "prefer to play with bugs" (L, 39).

How does one explain to children the process by which someone they know, someone not much older than them, will be killed in a deliberate, gruesome, and painful way? How does one prepare children for such a death, and how does one explain the significance of it or derive meaning from it? Grant's confrontation with his students reflects a conscious pedagogical positioning that, instead of encouraging communication between Jefferson and the children, invokes fear through the comparison of their seats with the death chair Jefferson will occupy.

To both "prepare" Jefferson for his death and to get inside his head, Grant urges him to record his thoughts in a diary, repeatedly encouraging him to adopt a heroic stance. The narrative continuity apparent in such efforts—the young man from simple beginnings who, wronged by an oppressive society, sacrifices himself in an act of restorative martyrdom—prepares the community to *react* to his death. In short, Grant instructs Jefferson how to craft a narrative that will help the community remember Jefferson as an idealized version of himself, just as Francis was asked to write for the outside community, an act which frames the collective remembrance of his death. In writing about how African American communities remembered and redressed the tortured body in relation to slavery—the "history that hurts"—Saidiya Hartman observes that "the significance of the performative lies not in the ability to overcome this condition or provide remedy but in creating a context for the collective enunciation of this pain."[16] In *Lesson* and "My Trip to the Chair," Jefferson and Francis, as sacrificial bodies, are situated in historical memory before their actual deaths; in the novel, however, the "history that hurts" is in many ways displaced by Grant's romanticized contextualization of Jefferson's death.

Paradoxically, some scholarship on the novel treats Jefferson's death as symbolic not just of community strength, unity, and renewal, but also of a sort of racial reconciliation. Ed Piacentino focuses on Paul Bonin, the white deputy who, at the end of the novel, delivers to Grant the diary in which Jefferson recorded his last thoughts. Paul, who is said to come from "good stock," acts as a racial mediator, according to Piacentino; he is a "sensitive, caring, and keenly perceptive young man who celebrates Jefferson's triumph"[17] and "counters racial barriers."[18] Valerie Babb asserts that Gaines's work "transcend[s] mores of race, class, and history"[19] and "transcends African American experience and voices the concerns of humanity."[20] These conclusions can obscure the most revealing and insightful voice in the text—that of Jefferson in his diary.

Providing the voice of a young, semiliterate African American presents novelistic challenges, including how to structure the narrative break that introduces Jefferson's diary as well as how to convey such a voice accurately. Beavers reads Jefferson's poor spelling and grammar as "intended to challenge the reader to elevate substance over form," making Jefferson into a kind of philosopher.[21] He observes, "If Jefferson's life has value . . . it is because there will be men and women, perhaps those sitting in Grant's classroom, who will use that life as the cornerstone of a new society, one which eschews the conventions of the status quo."[22] Jefferson's life is again valued in terms of what he has to offer to the outside community. What is more immediately evident in the writing of Jefferson's diary, however, is exactly what is in danger of being lost—the voice of a human being facing death.

The preservation of Jefferson's voice is central to understanding *Lesson* as a novel about imprisonment. Jefferson's diary, although influenced by others, signals his resistance to the narrative the community fashions to coincide with his death. Encompassing only a single, nine-page chapter, the diary is strategically situated in the novel; it appears immediately after Grant has discussed the execution with Jefferson and immediately before the arrival of the truck carrying the electric chair and generator. The insertion of the diary mediates the experience through Jefferson's eyes, and his words are present as one reads about the townspeople coming out of their homes to watch the truck arrive (L, 235). Throughout the diary, Jefferson struggles to write what he thinks Grant wants to see while at the same time critiquing those who attempt to "save" him. Although Jefferson appreciates the visits from Reverend Ambrose, he concludes that "it look like the lord just work for wite folks" (L, 227). Further, Grant's insistence that Jefferson become a symbolic figure for the community's children confuses Jefferson: "you jus say . . . you can save the chiren and I say I don't kno what you mean an you say I do kno what you mean an you look so tied" (L, 228). In some instances, it seems as if Grant uses Jefferson as a symbol of something that he, as teacher, cannot embody—a redemptive force that will give hope to generations of black children struggling to overcome the forces of racism and poverty.

Jefferson refers to Grant grading his diary or giving him an "A." This evaluative presence throws into question the degree to which Jefferson's thoughts are his own, and in what ways Grant acts as amanuensis. Similarly, Jefferson writes that Sheriff Guidry entered his cell to ask what he had been writing and told Jefferson to make a note of how well the sheriff and deputies had treated him (L, 233). This advice points to the sheriff's (and, to a degree, the white community's) need for a narrative as well. Despite the racism inherent in Jefferson's treatment, the sheriff and the white community, in the creation of their own history and memory, paint Jefferson as a recipient of benevolent white paternalism that erases any guilt associated with his death. By addressing the sheriff's concerns, Jefferson has left a document which condemns white society while defending one of its key representatives. This alternative (white) narrative coexists with the narrative of Bayonne's black community. These considerations place Jefferson's diary in a tradition of writing by some African Americans that reflects the dual nature of their experience in the United States—one marked by a perpetual need to envision a usable past within and against a culture that rejects, whenever possible, their agency to do so.

As an outcast, Jefferson's subjectivity is marked by his longing for and appreciation of human contact. From his description of his grandmother holding him during her last visit (L, 231), to Grant's girlfriend, Vivian, kissing Jefferson on the cheek (L, 232), to the children and the "ole folks" from the quarter coming to see him (L, 230–31), Jefferson longs for human understanding. After the children and the others leave, he writes, "this was the firs time I cry when they lok that door behand me . . . I was cryin cause . . . the peple com to see me cause they hadn never done nothing lik that for me befor" (L, 231). This emotional connection between those inside and outside reveals this very division to be the product of social conditioning, just as the novel ending with Grant crying in front of his class signals his inability to sustain the fabricated memories he attempted to create.

Jefferson's life, as he reflects on it, documents ongoing connections with a community. His assertion that "when I was a litle boy I was a waterboy an rode the cart" and "now I got to be a man an set in a cher" (L, 234) juxtapose life and death while reflecting on his short life in Bayonne. It is this recognition that community is as present in death as it is in life that places the final emphasis of the novel on contingent and fragile human connections. We are made aware of the distinct and irredeemable loss of Jefferson as a person; this recognition is the fundamental "lesson" to be learned from the novel, an important consideration given its enormous popularity in general and in the classroom.

Envisioning Imprisoned Communities

The inclusion in *Lesson* of other criminalized figures in the jail and in communal memory highlights the institutionalization of white supremacy and the disaccumulation of opportunity in the quarter. If Jefferson's death is symbolic of anything, the lesson he imparts is really more of a warning: young black men will continue to be put to death by a state invested in the defense and perpetuation of white power. In a telling scene, Grant watches the children cut firewood for the school and remembers his childhood friends, many of them gone "to the fields, to the small towns, to the cities—where they died" (L, 62). Grant explains, "There was always news coming back to the quarter about someone that had been killed or sent to prison for killing someone else: Snowball, stabbed to death . . . Claudee, killed by a woman in New Orleans . . . Smitty, sent to the state penitentiary at Angola for manslaughter" (L, 62). Grant's memories provide a sense of the violence that accompanies segregation and limited opportunity. He recalls his own teacher telling the children that "most of us would die violently . . . [that] there was no freedom here" (L, 62–63). Later, as Grant remembers reading about another execution, in Florida, he recalls dreaming about it over and over, saying, "As vividly as if I were there, I had seen that cell, heard that boy crying while being dragged to that chair, 'Please Joe Louis, help me. Please help me. Help me'" (L, 91). Grant connects this death to Jefferson's, wondering "if the one in that cell uptown would call on Jackie Robinson as the other one had called on Joe Louis" (L, 91). Jefferson becomes a site of memory, a reminder of an accumulation of black bodies that haunt the community and continue to seek redress.

A sense of community is further fashioned out of the partial erasure of the physical and ideological barriers separating inside and outside. By acknowledging the humanity of the incarcerated and their presence in the community, Grant, who feels imprisoned himself, distinguishes between the person and the criminal act. During Miss Emma's and Grant's first visit to the jail, prisoners "reached their hands out between the bars" as Grant gave them change and Miss Emma stopped to talk with them (L, 71). When leaving, Miss Emma leaves the basket of food she has prepared for Jefferson, asking Paul, "If he don't eat it all, can you give it to the rest of them children?" (L, 74). This sequence of events is repeated each visit; the prisoners stick out their hands, Grant gives them change, and, as Miss Emma leaves crying, she tells "the young deputy to give the food to the other children" (L, 76). Miss Emma identifies *with* the imprisoned through their shared humanity and by acknowledging their youth. The symbolic exchange of money and food inserts the prisoners into public consciousness outside the space of the jail. They become part of the larger community, not just as a rhetorical device. Later, Paul admits, regarding the food, "we've all eaten some of it," adding that the other inmates are "curious" about Jefferson, but "don't bother him at all" (L, 126).

Other interactions include an inmate who cuts Jefferson's hair (L, 127), Jefferson's gift of food to the inmates (L, 128), Reverend Ambrose's repeated prayers for "God to go with those locked up in prison cells" (L, 150, 189), the children's gifts to and visit with Jefferson (L, 186, 230–31), the visit from community members (L, 230–31), and the shock of the townspeople, both black and white, at the arrival of the chair: "My God, the whole town can hear that thing" (L, 242). All of these scenes reveal communities among the incarcerated that are intimately connected to ones outside prison.

Listening to the Condemned: Willie Francis

Directed by Samuel Montgomery, Willie Francis — much like Jefferson — approaches his narrative as an opportunity to "help people." "My Trip to the Chair" was released on Francis's behalf by Montgomery, who served as amanuensis, and has only been available to the public for a short time. After being "lost" for decades, the only known copy was uncovered in the Library of Congress by journalist Gilbert King while researching a book on Francis.[23] Francis's pamphlet, equal parts self-discovery and intervention into the creation of his public image, is a document of history-in-making and a call to understand the needs of those facing death in prison.

On May 3, 1946, in St. Martinville, Louisiana, officials strapped Willie

Francis, a young African American convicted of killing a popular white pharmacist, into a portable electric chair—nicknamed "Gruesome Gertie"—and flipped the switch. When it was discovered after the first attempt that Francis was still breathing, police captain Ephie Foster threw the switch a second time. Francis jumped, twitched, and thrashed, shrieking and suffocating behind the leather mask, and begged for the chair to be turned off. After the switch had been flipped back, Francis gasped for breath while stunned witnesses looked on in disbelief. Francis had survived his own execution—twice. The state of Louisiana decided that another execution attempt would be scheduled within a few days, prompting local lawyer Bertrand DeBlanc to appeal Francis's case. This appeal made its way to the U.S. Supreme Court on the grounds that a second execution constituted cruel and unusual punishment. One year and six days after his miraculous survival, after losing his battle in court, Francis was again strapped in the chair and put to death.

Francis's original trial lasted three days, the jury of twelve white men taking only fifteen minutes to return a guilty verdict. The bulk of the evidence against him consisted of a written confession (most likely coerced) obtained without the presence of counsel, while the murder weapon had disappeared from evidence days before. His defense put forth no opening or closing statements, called no witnesses, and offered no counterevidence, nor did they call him to the stand to testify. His initial arrest, in fact, resulted from his proximity to an unrelated crime—the charge of murder was added during the interrogation.[24] The denial of due process, the inadequate defense, and the sham trial suggest that Francis was sentenced to death the minute he was taken into custody. As with Jefferson in *Lesson*, Francis experienced civil death before his execution, and white supremacy prefigured the outcome of the trial.

Between his executions, Francis dictated his account, which begins with a strategic attempt to take control of the narrative: "They tell me this is the first time anyone ever had a chance to tell the story of how it feels to go to the electric chair and know that you might have to go back there . . . I do not like to talk about it at all, but if it will help other people to understand each other, I want to tell everything."[25] Francis's story is one that cannot be told, yet must be told if, as Francis makes clear, the perceptual divide between those inside and those outside prisons is to be bridged. Francis confronts readers' expectations right away: "I don't want to talk about the killing of Mr. Thomas. When they asked me to write the story I said I would only if I didn't have to say anything about that part" (T, 1). Francis's pamphlet will not add to the sensationalized accounts of the murder of Thomas—there will be no dramatic confession or denial.

The continuity of life that Francis fashions in the narrative is at odds with the justificatory and established discourse of the state and its officials. The prison chaplain, Father Hannegan, tells Francis that he will be starting a "new life" when he gets up from the chair and that he "shouldn't start it like a little cry-baby" (T, 4). He tells Francis that although he is only sixteen years old, he has "one big chance to prove [he] was able to die like a man" (T, 4). Francis's difficulty in imagining how to achieve this transformation—as in Jefferson's plea to Grant to "tell them im strong tell them im a man," although his hands are shaking as he writes (L, 234)—is in part due to his age: at sixteen years old, Francis is asked not only to prepare himself for death but to meet that death "like a man."

For the state, there is a double benefit to this performance. On the one hand, Francis resigns himself to death and is less inclined to be a problem prisoner; on the other, he appears calm, as if he accepts responsibility for his actions, or, to some, as if he is a hardened criminal to whom death means little. Before the first execution, Francis recalls walking to the chair with his "shoulders back" like Father Hannegan asked, concluding that, in the end, "a lot of people thought I was just bragging" (T, 9). To carry a teenager kicking and screaming, crying and begging for his life, to the electric chair would disrupt the orderly process of death that the state has fashioned for the condemned.

Francis's case reveals the process by which state authority seeks to shape representations of the condemned to justify capital punishment. Sensationalized newspaper accounts of the case relied on racial ideology that assumed Francis's guilt from the start. By asserting that he doesn't like to talk about what happened but does so to "help other people to understand each other" (T, 1), Francis hopes that his story will inspire action and dialogue. Francis does not portray himself as a victim, choosing to accept his fate and imagine that, by telling his story, "I may have helped someone, somehow. I hope so" (T, 14). He insists that physical barriers between inside and outside are not and should not be mental or spiritual barriers separating people.

He recalls the community in which he was raised and the one he establishes while awaiting his execution(s). He begins, "I was baptized Willie Francis," and describes childhood memories of family and friends and "secret water-melon [parties]" that distracted him from schoolwork. The narrative then abruptly shifts to his experience in jail: "My walls are painted bright pink. I like the color but I wish the walls weren't behind the paint" (T, 2–3). Similar to Jefferson's coerced entry in his diary, Francis tells how the "jailor and sheriff have always been nice to me" and recounts visits by the sheriff, his pastor, his family, and his friends. His narrative shows the continuity of a life, instead of exhibiting a split between his life outside and inside of jail. Francis underlines the difficulty but also the possibility of communication and community through and within the walls that surround him.

One striking example of these permeable walls is in correspondence between Francis and those who advocated his release. In what he calls the "strangest" letter he received, a Texas woman asked him to will her his eyes so that her blind brother might see again. Francis, sensing her hesitation and embarrassment in the letter (since he would have to die to fulfill her request), responded quickly that she could have his eyes. He asked his lawyer to draw up a will. Francis was surprised to learn that, after reading his letter, the woman traveled throughout Texas gathering signatures on his behalf to send to the board of pardons (T, 13–14).

Francis's sight figures into his narrative in another way that connects inside and out. Concerning his first execution, Francis writes that the surge of electricity that coursed through his body "felt like a hundred and a thousand needles and pins were pricking in me all over and my left leg felt like somebody was cutting it with a razor blade" (T,10). After the initial attempt failed to kill him, recalls Francis, "they did it again! The same feeling all over . . . I thought I was dead then" (T, 10–11). Afterward, as Francis walked out of the building to be taken back to jail, he looked at the crowd and observed that "they sure looked at me funny [but] . . . It was my turn to look at them. They looked like they were looking at a ghost. They had expected me to come out feet-first" (T, 11). Francis's gaze ("my turn to look at them") is directed toward the witnesses in the crowd. Reversing the dynamic of the death procession, Francis walks away from the chair and, as a "ghost," confronts the audience with their own desire to see death. Since the state fashions a narrative with a predetermined end (the death of the condemned), the reversal intervenes into the perceived finality of capital cases. The collective power of ritualized witnessing, disrupted by Francis's survival, revises and distorts the state's narrative of justice—a revision symbolically realized as well when Francis's father, Frederick Francis, after telling his family of Francis's survival, traveled to the segregated cemetery where Francis was to be buried and, with a sledgehammer, destroyed the tombstone he had purchased for his son.[26]

Questions about memorialization and remembrance pervade Francis's narrative as he reflects on his life and legacy. What constitutes an appropriate form of mourning for those condemned to a living death before their actual deaths? When should such mourning begin, and when should it end? Novelist Jane Lazarre, commenting on the merging of her own Jewish heritage with the African American culture of her late husband's family, writes that "there is an old Jewish custom of placing a pebble on the tombstone of loved ones, each small stone marking a visit in obedience to the requirement to remember."[27] Lazarre explains this tradition to her niece, after which they each assemble small stones on the marble marker of her husband's grave. Before Frederick Francis was forced to relive his son's death a second time, he smashed the tombstone to pieces. This action points toward an alternate custom of memorialization for those killed by the state, for it creates a rupture in the ordinary ritual procession of death. The pieces of shattered marble remain a monument to collective inaction and the need for increased activism on behalf of those who waited and wait in cages for their impending deaths—those who, in the words of Francis, "know something only God should know" (T, 4).

A responsible mode of scholarship would combine Lazarre's "requirement to remember" with the active pursuit of justice and the destruction, whenever possible, of discourse that attempts to hide or justify the barbarity of state-sanctioned death. This scholarship would erect new, living monuments that could shape the ways future generations approach capital punishment and larger questions of justice and punishment—a "pious" approach to a painful history and a methodology of reading the lives of the imprisoned and condemned. Such a project is needed to curtail the devastating effects of incarceration on our communities.

The voice of Willie Francis continues to echo in the fight for the rights of the condemned:

> You get a funny crawling feeling when you walk out of that death cell to go out and die. I tried to think about all the other condemned men who had left this same cell and in cells all over the world to go out and be punished. I wondered what they had thought about. . . . All the other prisoners were staring out from their cell doors. I didn't hear anybody say anything but I could tell by their faces they all felt sorry for me. I saw the man who shaved my head. He was frowning in a funny sort of way, and as I stepped into the elevator and turned around, I saw him wave his little finger at me (T, 7).

"Reading" the incarcerated requires that we look to them for guidance. This passage reflects a population comprised of—instead of the hardened, unfeeling, sociopathic individuals of popular accounts—human beings struggling to comprehend the enormity of the deaths (civil, social, literal) that confront them in prison. As in Jefferson's admission the night before his execution that "the place is real quite but nobody sleepin" (L, 233), Francis's experience points to the possibility of a community behind bars—a community that should not be considered apart from those outside who can offer crucial assistance and resistance.

Notes

1. See Ernest J. Gaines, "Writing *A Lesson before Dying*," *Southern Review* 41 (Autumn 2005): 770–77.

2. Caleb Smith, "Detention without Subjects: Prisons and the Poetics of Living Death," *Texas Studies in Literature and Language* 50 (Fall 2008): 245.

3. Ernest J. Gaines, *A Lesson before Dying* (New York: Vintage, 1994), 7–8. Subsequent references to this work will be cited parenthetically in the text as L.

4. Herman Beavers, *Wrestling Angels into Song: The Fictions of Ernest J. Gaines and James Alan McPherson* (Philadelphia: Univ. of Pennsylvania Press, 1995), 31.

5. Ibid., 178.

6. Ibid., 233.

7. Smith, "Detention without Subjects," 244.

8. Carlyle V. Thompson, "From a Hog to a Black Man: Black Male Subjectivity and Ritualistic Lynching in Ernest J. Gaines's *A Lesson before Dying*," *CLA Journal* 45 (March 2002): 298.

9. Ibid., 309.

10. Ibid., 299.

11. Ibid., 303–4.

12. Ibid., 16.

13. Ibid., 16–17.

14. H. Bruce Franklin, "Can the Penitentiary Teach the Academy How to Read?" *PMLA* 123 (May 2004): 648.

15. Michael Roth, *The Ironist's Cage: Memory, Trauma, and the Construction of History* (New York: Columbia Univ. Press, 1995), 148, 172.

16. Saidiya Hartman, *Scenes of Subjection: Terror, Slavery, and Self-Making in Nineteenth-Century America* (New York: Oxford Univ. Press, 1997), 51.

17. Ed Piacentino, "The Common Humanity That Is in Us All: Toward Racial Reconciliation in Gaines's *A Lesson before Dying*," *Southern Quarterly* 42 (Spring 2004): 74.

18. Ibid., 76.

19. Valerie Melissa Babb, "Old-Fashioned Modernism: 'The Changing Same' in *A Lesson before Dying*," in *Critical Reflections on the Fiction of Ernest J. Gaines*, ed. David C. Estes (Athens: Univ. of Georgia Press, 1994), 264.

20. Valerie Melissa Babb, *Ernest Gaines* (Boston: Twayne Publishers, 1991), 138.

21. Beavers, *Wrestling*, 176.

22. Ibid., 178.

23. Gilbert King, *The Execution of Willie Francis: Race, Murder, and the Search for Justice in the American South* (New York: Basic Civitas, 2008), xi.

24. Arthur S. Miller and Jeffrey H. Bowman, *Death by Installments: The Ordeal of Willie Francis* (Santa Barbara, CA: Greenwood Press, 1988), 18–27.

25. Willie Francis, as told to Samuel Montgomery, "My Trip to the Chair," (Lafayette, LA: self-published, 1947), 1. Subsequent references to this work will be cited parenthetically in the text as T. Pages 33–44 of this collection reproduce the entire pamphlet.

26. King, *The Execution of Willie Francis*, 33–34.

27. Jane Lazarre, *Beyond the Whiteness of Whiteness: Memoir of a White Mother of Black Sons* (Durham, NC: Duke Univ. Press, 1996), 124.

San Quentin State Prison was a violent inferno when my codefendant Anthony Ross and I arrived in the winter of 1982. Racial wars, stabbings, and murders were as commonplace as the hundreds of feral cats that roamed the prison grounds. By the summer of 1985, San Quentin (SQ) would earn the infamous distinction of being the most dangerous prison in the state and, by some accounts, in the country.

From its thriving black market you could purchase almost anything you wanted: drugs, alcohol, knives, homemade bombs, medicines, food, information, even sex. Prisoners and guards benefited from the trade, and neither wars nor lockdowns could halt commerce. The demarcation lines were clear—race and gang nationalism divided everyone into Balkanized camps poised on the brink of war. It was madness you quickly learned to adapt to—or you ended up dead, broken, or in "protective custody" (PC).

Our first three months were spent in the Adjustment Center (AC)—San Quentin's version of Guantánamo Bay. AC housed gang leaders, revolutionaries, and guys with serious assaults on guards and other prisoners. It also housed the rapidly ballooning death row population, to which we were added. The morning following our arrival we learned from "kites" (brief but detailed notes sent from one prisoner to another, usually smuggled in some manner) that many guys we'd known from the streets, county jail, California Youth Authority, and Juvenile Hall were aware of our presence in AC. Word spread fast through the prison grapevine that Treach and Evil (mine and Anthony's nicknames) were on death row, and a lot of homeboys we hadn't seen in years were eager to see us. Some even managed to send small care packages. It was a bizarre family reunion.

Because we were codefendants, the administration housed us in adjacent cells. They also provided us with "loaner" 12-inch black-and-white TVs, standard California Department of Corrections (CDC) practice back then, like supplying free tobacco. Television functioned as a pacifier. If a prisoner was glued to the TV screen, he would be peaceful. Such was the logic, and for many guys, TV was the drug of choice.

For a while, Evil and I would join their ranks as we settled in for the ninety-day observational period—the time it would take for the administration to determine our "privilege status." Our first thirty days at SQ were spent recklessly. Every day we got high on TV: Kung Fu theater, gangster and horror movies, *Loony Toons*, and whatever unscrambled X-rated channels we could pick up by attaching wire to the antennas and dangling them outside our cells. Like a couple of hyped-up insomniacs, we stayed up transfixed to the tube and reminiscing about the streets.

We were oblivious to the noise we were making and unconcerned about disrupting the programs of men accustomed to regimentation and structure. Evil and I were in our own private world; we felt accountable to no one. We were arrogant and undisciplined young hoodlums with a massive amount of pent-up energy. By daybreak we would have squeezed in an hour of sleep before the breakfast trays came, and then if it was our yard day we'd crawl out of bed and go outside to lift weights, shoot hoops, and shoot the breeze. If it wasn't our yard day, we'd pull the blankets back over our heads and sleep 'til noon. The few books someone sent me on history and politics sat in the corner on the floor collecting dustballs.

The first three weeks passed in a blur, yet we had managed to piss off a lot of people. Though we weren't gangbanging, many considered us bangers who needed to be brought into line. The two prominent black prison groups at the time were the Black Guerilla Family (BGF) and the Vanguards. Both were not thrilled with our lack of respect and our disregard for prison decorum. They started sending kites to a Crip on the tier named Black who had been on the row since 1979 and was considered a veteran. They told him we were fucking up the established program, and it was his responsibility to chastise us.

But since Black regarded us as "OGs" (slang for "original gangster," which at the time meant that a person was of the first, early 1970s, generation of Crips), he forwarded the kites to us. He also felt their writers should have come to us directly instead asking him to play mediator.

After we read the kites, we blurted out for all to hear: "Whoever the fuck wrote these kites, speak up." No one did. Nor did Black receive any more kites about us.

After less than a full month on death row, Evil was shot on the yard, hit in the hip and leg with birdshot from a 12-gauge shotgun. He told me it felt like his skin was on fire. The gunman claimed he mistook Evil for a participant in a fight. Whether or not that was true, we would come to witness enough similar events to suspect dirty politics.

Three days later, as Evil lay in bed recuperating, I got into a yard fight with a racist white guy. It was about not crowding my space and him wanting to prove himself in front of the resident Nazi cadre on the adjacent yard. Several hard blows sent him to the ground dazed, but I couldn't leave well enough alone—feeling a primal compulsion to continue my assault.

The prison's gunman, an ex-Marine everyone called Sharpshooter, fired three times. He was practically hanging over the gun rail to shoot me. I was lucky to have my back to him or I'd be blind now. I caught nearly the full blast of each round that hit the back of my head, shoulders, back, and legs. Evil was right: it felt like my skin was on fire. Now, more than twenty-three years later, the scars from the plump pellets, many entombed beneath my skin, are still visible.

Whether because of such confrontations or because we were growing tired of our aimlessness, Evil and I changed course. I remember telling Evil on the yard that I wanted to read and study subjects that could teach me something. Evil said he wanted to build his vocabulary so he could understand legal terms.

Little did we know that discussion was our first sign of self-reflection. We went back to our cells and, for the first time since our arrest, became introspective. We made a commitment to each other to take our situation seriously. Enlightenment would not occur overnight, but that day we laid the foundation for a rigorous education program. We made a commitment to be responsible and accountable, to never argue unproductively with one another, to be an example for other guys like us, and to study every day.

We started treading our way through books that were alien to us: Plato's *Republic*, Sun Tzu's *Art of War*, Machiavelli's *The Prince*, Mao's *Red Book*, Confucius, Carl Jung, Franz Fanon. There were two older brothers in AC who began to send us books from their personal libraries. I imagine they thought Evil and I needed a crash course in everything. They were the first to notice the change in how we conducted ourselves and the first to give us a list of books to read. The books exposed our minds to countries, continents, and histories, and slowly we began to develop a global picture. We glimpsed links in human history, culture, and religion. In a very real sense, we became each other's student and teacher.

In mid-March of 1983, the SQ bigwigs decided to move the expanding death row. It had taken up the third tier of AC and was threatening to do the same on the second tier. The new destination was C-Section, one of four units in South Block. Death row prisoners would occupy the fifth tier and within a year much of the fourth tier as well. The rest of the tier was for Administration Segregation prisoners, guys doing hole time for any number of infractions.

The racial makeup was the same in AC—predominantly blacks, whites, and Mexicans, with a few American Indians. The main organized groups were Crips, Southern Mexicans, and Aryan Brotherhood. It was possible to be in a cell for years and never speak to guys in the cells on either side of you because of their skin color or because they hung out with the wrong people. Any interaction between groups was strictly political or economic.

Moving to C-Section was like going from a museum to a rock concert. The noise was deafening with more than two hundred TVs, radios, and conversations blaring. We wondered how anyone could sleep or read. But after being there a couple of weeks, I realized the chaos was organized, from the clothing covering cell bars to the dozens of fish lines (strips of sheets or T-shirts used as lines to ferry items from one cell to another) hanging over the tiers. The makeshift screens and communication lines were disrupted only during wars.

C-Section was populated mainly by twenty-year-olds, young guerillas eager to go on "missions." These guys had memorized the locations of all vital organs from anatomy charts, and most of them had life sentences. Everyone seemed to take the daily assaults and stabbings as routine, like changing a flat tire. There was no sense of normality, only a steady ebb and flow of violence that made everyone sick, one way or another.

Once Evil and I settled into C-Section, we put the word out to guys we knew that we were interested in reading material. Soon several books arrived: Mao, Marx, Lenin, Che Guevara—these all came from the BGF brothers. We had no idea who any of these authors were, so we looked them up in the biographical section of our dictionaries. This was the beginning of our learning to research. We also looked up communism, socialism, colonialism, fascism, imperialism, and capitalism. Question after question exploded in our minds: How did capitalism come about? Who started communism? Who controlled colonialism? What are the objectives of imperialism? Why did the African slave trade exist? We wanted answers, and everybody we were asking was simply referring us to this or that book. "Read this book. It's good," they would say.

We began to realize a funny thing: most of the men sending us books didn't know how to articulate the material they had read. Further, their understanding was limited because they did very little comparative study, if any. We learned another lesson. It was one thing to read a book and memorize the contents, but to read it critically and identify its pros and cons was something different. In essence, we realized we were on our own.

In the early 1980s, death row prisoners were allowed out for an hour of tier time, usually two or three prisoners at a time. I would spend most of my time in front of Evil's cell, squatting on one knee with a book in my hand, and when it was his tier time he would do the same. We would discuss basic concepts, theories, and principles. We approached the information through multiple lenses, so we could come away from it with a critical analysis. Often this meant we'd keep people's books for long periods, receiving the occasional kite asking if we were finished.

This problem proved to be a blessing in disguise. We decided to start our own library. The first thing we did was amass the names and addresses of organizations that helped prisoners. Then we got names of independent bookstores and local colleges. We wrote at least ten places a week requesting books on Greek history, ancient Egyptian history, Chinese history, European history, philosophy, political science, sociology, psychology, economics, religion, and military science. It wasn't long before books started pouring in, and within a two-year period we had accumulated close to four hundred books. To circumvent the prison limit—which was fifteen books back then—we'd have other prisoners hold books for us or get books sent to them. Evil and I would write authors we'd heard interviewed on the radio or saw on TV. Some of them sent us their book, some didn't—but we were never discouraged. Minor setbacks strengthened our motivation and resolve.

Studying evolved into a discipline. What became important to us was the real transformative effect books can have. One book that impacted my life dramatically was *The Autobiography of Malcolm X* by Malcolm X and Alex Haley. Many prisoners prided themselves on being experts on Malcolm's life and could quote him verbatim, but when it came to practicing his level of discipline and commitment to personal and social change, they failed miserably. I realized convictions must be demonstrative. It wouldn't matter how much I learned if I could not rid myself of the contradictions that held me back. I could not advocate self-change if I did not start with myself. I began to eliminate my own vices: smoking weed, drinking pruno (prison wine), and my pornography collection. I knew I had to practice what I preached, and this meant setting a high standard for myself.

We outlined an intensive study program and designated specific times for each subject, much like college classes. Whenever one subject overlapped another, however, we merely followed the connection. We didn't know how to stay focused on one or two disciplines; no one told us how to specialize. Thus we delved into multiple fields.

We devised tests that challenged our comprehension and critical, analytical, and problem-solving skills. For instance, when studying geography we took turns scanning a world map for thirty seconds, then from memory drawing as best we could the full outline of whatever country, state, or continent the other called out. Within two minutes we would have to name a landmark and/or the capital (in the case of states and countries). If we provided a false answer or ran out of time, we'd have to do one hundred pushups. When your chest, arms, and shoulders are in pain, your memory can be surprisingly keen.

We called another exercise "negative dialectics," and in this we would state a philosophical hypothesis and see how many ways we could counter or "negate" it. In this way, we strengthened our analytical skills and became familiar with the philosophies of Immanuel Kant, Martin Heidegger, and René Descartes, among others. Stanley Tookie Williams, the Crips co-founder, had joined our intimate study group and was the most competitive of the three of us, and I enjoyed listening to him and Evil argue like two metaphysicians.

As we taught ourselves, we developed a study program that other men could use. Though there were educational classes taught by inmates on the yard, these classes were narrowly focused on political science, military philosophy, and revolutionary theory. Evil and I understood that the majority of black prisoners were high school dropouts, loyal gang members, and criminal opportunists. Giving them revolutionary theory made about as much sense as giving a bushman a toaster. The approach to raising the consciousness of someone from a gang-riddled environment had to be practical. Most of the guys we knew needed some level of therapy, even if it was self-therapy. They didn't need theories. They needed to know how to connect the dots between the pathological behavior that dictated their lives and the conditions that produced it.

A key insight Evil and I gained from our conversations with hundreds of guys over the years is that most are harboring stored-up psychological and emotional traumas. Because Evil and I grew up in the same neighborhood and had known each other since we were ten and seven, respectively, it was far easier for us to talk about issues that would otherwise have been too sensitive to discuss. In this respect we also became each other's therapist, each other's journal. Every day I felt a shift in my perspective and awareness. I was deconstructing myself, redefining who I was.

Two subjects were extremely fun to study: vocabulary and geography. We incorporated them into our lessons early on. The Catholic chaplain had given Evil and I dictionaries and *National Geographic* world maps, which we taped to the wall in our cells. Neither of us knew the names of all fifty states, and we knew absolutely nothing about Asia, Africa, or the rest of the world. We worked our way across the United States, then Central and South America, and Mexico and Canada, and on from there.

As for vocabulary, we started off learning five words a week, choosing them at random from the dictionary, books, or magazines. Eventually we were learning twenty words a week. We had hundreds of pieces of torn paper with words and their meaning taped to our walls. It looked like scattered confetti.

On the yard we would quiz each other as if we were in a spelling bee. Guys would come over and be amazed at how we spelled words and clicked off definitions. Some would even join us. It wouldn't be long before a lot of guys were looking to us for more than just how to spell a word or solve a math equation. They began to seek advice on family and relationships, and guidance on choices they needed to make. This gave us an even greater sense of responsibility, but it also put us on the administration's radar as "Persons of Interest."

In June of 1984, a racial war broke out in San Quentin and spread throughout the prison system. C-Section was ground zero. The war erupted between blacks and Southern Mexicans, and unlike sporadic clashes, this one left a lot of dead bodies in its wake. The CDC declared a state of emergency and we went on lockdown. The prison was searched and everyone was stripped of their property for several weeks. We were in our cells with nothing.

During this period, Evil and I would go over lessons from memory. Our discipline had paid off. We could recall entire chapters and quote authors almost verbatim. When we were able to secure a pen and paper, we started writing things down. Though we weren't attempting to write essays, this is how we first began to translate our thoughts into writing. In the midst of war, we were becoming writers.

When the prison came off lockdown, our property was returned to us. We checked to see if any books were missing. Fortunately, we had about a dozen people holding books for us, so we fared far better than others. We jumped back into our studies. Instead of staying up at night watching TV, we had our faces glued to the pages of books: W. E. B. Du Bois, Dostoevsky, Hemingway, Richard Wright, Emerson, Mark Twain, Lao Tzu, J. A. Rogers, Darwin, Ben Jochannan, Van Sertima, B. F. Skinner, Cheikh Anta Diop—anything we could get our hands on. We had gone from thugs to bookworms. We joked about how on the streets no one could have paid us to read a book. But no matter how much we studied, because we had dropped out of school we always felt a sense of urgency.

Every day when the guard walked past our cells for four o'clock count, he saw us studying. One day he commented on this. Little did we know he was noting it in his daily log report. Soon our cells were being searched while we were on the yard, in the shower, or on a visit. The administration was interested in what we were reading and writing—which apparently identified us to them as leaders.

Despite the daily madness of prison life, racial wars, cell searches, and our death penalty appeals, we remained steadfast in our studies. We ran a fishline between our cells, and any time one of us wanted the other to check something out we just tied it to the line, banged on the wall, and the other would reel it in. What helped us evolve was our brutal honesty with each other and being able to disagree without any resentment. Once we had settled some disagreement or other, it was over; we didn't revisit it. At some point during this process, our egos seemed to disappear, at least as far as our friendship went, and we achieved the purest form of brotherhood. Joseph Campbell, noted scholar of mythology, describes such a connection in this way: "When we quit thinking primarily about ourselves and our own self-preservation we undergo a profound heroic transformation of consciousness."

This consciousness is grounded in altruistic commitment, responsibility, and mutual recognition, and we found ourselves living it and bringing new meaning to the idea of being your "brother's keeper." Not only were we our brother's keeper, we became one with our brother(s), and we felt this bond on emotional and spiritual levels. My relationship with Tookie and Evil helped me understand what Malcolm X meant when he wrote, "In order for someone to be your brother he must first act like your brother." This doesn't happen often, and we understood the significance of our relationship as it related to others: we were modeling transformative brotherhood.

While talking one day on the yard about writing, I suggested that we create a kind of manual modeled after the Freemasons', a guide that moves through different levels of understanding and knowledge. We would revisit this subject many times over the years, but it was Evil who first began to dabble with writing in 1985. I saw his imaginative powers immediately. He wrote short stories, no longer than four or five pages, street tales in which he'd always kill off the main character.

In early 1985 Evil was moved to the first tier right next to Tookie. Though this ended our studying together, we were able to pass books back and forth and keep each other updated on our lessons. Evil started a study program with Tookie who had been primarily focusing on math, art, and vocabulary. Evil introduced him to politics, African history, and Black American history. I used to look out the window and see them walking, engaged in dialogue.

In June of that year, a guard was killed in C-Section. The prison went on emergency lockdown, and once again our property was confiscated for weeks. When we got our property back, most of our books were gone, and the CDC enacted new rules that limited the number of books we could have in our cells—ten per inmate. They also restricted who we could receive books from, such that only bookstores were allowed to send us books. This meant we could no longer get donated books or books sent in from an author, our family, or our lawyers. This incalculable loss of much of our library was a setback only in reading and reference materials; it didn't stagnate our studies. Again, we hadn't realized how much we had absorbed until it was put to the test, so having our books taken was a blessing in disguise. It prompted us to get out of the lab and into the field, to put into practice knowledge and ideas that had reshaped our consciousness. We weren't concerned about what others would think of us. We were concerned with being consistent and true to our new values and convictions.

With Tookie and Evil on the first tier and on a different yard, I bore down even harder on my studies. I noticed the positive effect of my teaching on some prisoners. I often didn't get to sleep until two or three A.M. because I was preparing my next topic for class. I consumed a lot of coffee, hot or cold. I began putting my TV under my bed for weeks at a time, then months, and finally I gave it away.

People looked to Evil, Tookie, and me for guidance, but the prison administration saw it in a much more negative light. In October 1985, and without committing any rule violation, Evil was taken to AC. I would be next, and a new chapter in our studies began.

Shortly before Christmas 1985, I was moved to AC and, as with Evil, the reason was bogus. I hadn't committed any rule violation, but this kind of treatment would become a pattern. In time I was told by several guards with whom I had a rapport that the prison administration didn't want us holding classes on the yard. Moving us from unit to unit was designed to disrupt that.

In the summer of 1986 I was transferred to and from D-Section and the Adjustment Center three times in less than ninety days. Shortly before I arrived in D-Section, Tookie had been moved there. We hadn't seen or talked to each other in more than a year. I was engrossed in learning about anti-imperialist and anticolonial struggles in Africa and Asia, and my writing tended to be angry. Tookie was still focusing on math, English (especially vocabulary), his artwork, and Black history.

My first discussion with Tookie was a prolonged one on Malcolm X and Martin Luther King Jr., and the question of which of these two heroes deserved a national holiday. In the end we agreed they both deserved one. We also talked extensively about Crip history, and Tookie cleared up some misconceptions for me. Tookie never used profanity and possessed a voluminous vocabulary, and we amped up our daily vocabulary work. Our deal was that we both had to pronounce, spell, and use the words in a sentence correctly; failure to do all three resulted in doing twenty-five push-ups on the spot. Unfortunately, I was on the ground more than he was.

I figured with his vocabulary he must be doing some creative writing, but when I asked him he said that he was only writing letters. I was a little stunned and told him, with a vocabulary like his, he should start writing.

A few days elapsed before he slid a manila envelope under my door and asked me to check it out. Enclosed was his first essay, entitled "Peace." I told him to keep on writing. He said he wouldn't mind doing something for children, the ones who need to be reached the most. When we talked about writing, I could hear the enthusiasm in his voice. He began working on another essay, but before he finished it he was transferred to C-Section. We wouldn't meet again for two years.

Tookie, Evil, and I were transferred to the Adjustment Center in 1989. Initially we were housed on different tiers, which made it virtually impossible to communicate. The CDC and San Quentin were going through a major transition. CDC had announced plans for four supermaximum prisons—new Tehachapi, new Folsom, Corcoran, and Pelican Bay—which were to become the prototype for California prisons. San Quentin was in the final stage of lowering its level-four maximum-security status down to minimum security (level two), which meant all high-risk and radical prisoners in SQ were going to be sent to these supermax prisons. Technically, only death row would remain in maximum at San Quentin.

There was an influx of new death row prisoners in the late 80s and early 90s. Most weren't interested in books and self-development, so we saw an even greater need to keep our study and writing groups alive. I started smuggling the flexible ink core (removed from a plastic pen) to the yard along with sheets of paper with shorthand writing so crammed together an untrained eye might misconstrue my writing for a foreign language. On the yard I would transcribe what I had written onto a larger sheet of paper for Evil and Tookie to peruse. Tookie, a whiz with words, would suggest using a different word or two to strengthen my piece. Evil, being the most experienced writer of the three of us, was a much tougher sale. He would scan my work as if looking for land mines. "This is a pretty good piece," he'd say. "But you need to restructure this sentence by shifting this here and moving this down there. And deleting this paragraph." After handing me back my essay, he'd add, "It's still too clinical. You need to tell a story."

The truth was, I didn't know how to write organically, from within me. I was interested in the topical and not the narrative because the latter would force me to look inward while the former kept me removed. After reading poetry by Sonia Sanchez, Amiri Baraka, and Nikki Giovanni, I started taking an interest in poetry. I started scribbling whatever thoughts flashed across my mind and later turned them into poems. Before I went to bed at night, I placed a pen and sheet of paper within arm's reach so that if I woke up in the middle of the night with thoughts, images, or ideas, I could capture them. However, I still couldn't break the habit of writing in relatively disembodied prose because I thought every idea set forth required an analysis or explanation instead of "merely" a story.

Tookie, Evil, and I continued to pursue our studies, using our cells as a laboratory, monastery, and university. The small prison yard was our lecture hall. During our walks on the yard we groomed our ideas, worked out kinks in our philosophy, shared our concerns, and strengthened our brotherhood. It wasn't uncommon in the middle of a discussion for one of us to say, "Hold up," pulling out a two-inch pencil, unfurling a sheet of crumpled paper or a piece of toilet tissue, and asking whoever was talking to repeat that pithy sentence so it could be used in one of his own writings.

Although the bulk of my time was devoted to reading, I wanted to write. I needed an outlet for pent-up emotions. I wanted to find a way to talk about things important to me, what I was learning, and how my consciousness was expanding every day. But I was hamstrung on what exactly to write. While reading an anthology of works by black authors, an idea leaped out at me: we would write our own collection of essays and poems! I presented my idea to Evil and Tookie. They liked it. We already had enough material. What we lacked was someone to type, edit, organize, and find a publisher for it. I contacted the Afrocentric historian Runoko Rashidi, who struck me as someone accessible and down-to-earth. I asked him for assistance and he agreed to help.

After waiting for over a year for Runoko to complete the editing (due to his own busy schedule), we received the manuscript. We titled it *Unchained Voices*. We read it individually and then discussed it on the yard. I thought it very significant that we had produced a coherent manuscript, and Tookie agreed. Evil did not. He was adamant that his name be removed from the manuscript if we went forward with publishing it. He simply said, "We can do better."

He was right. What I had not realized was, in the time it took Runoko to type, edit, and structure the final draft, our writing skills had improved, and our abilities, not to mention our thoughts, feelings, and experiences, would not have been reflected accurately were we to publish the collection. We scrapped the project altogether.

I learned from that experience that mediocrity in writing is unacceptable. I became more conscious of words. Sharpened my voice. Read more fiction. Never allowed any writing with my name on it to exit my cell until I was thoroughly satisfied, no matter how many times I had to rewrite.

Reading had become my mainstay. It was like oxygen to me. Giving it up would be like giving up a lung. Unlike Faulkner, Joyce, and Hemingway, I couldn't globe-trot to exotic places around the world, but I could read about those places and, therefore, write about them. The more knowledgeable I became about the world, the more my creative horizons expanded.

In 1991, Evil, Tookie, and I mapped out concrete things we wanted to do. Our intellectual and spiritual growth and our frank discussions awakened in us a new vision. Shedding the shackles of our preconscious mentality didn't happen overnight. None of us had an epiphany which unfolded and laid out the truth in a singular episode. We were hungry; we ate. The more we ate, the more we grew.

A couple of young brothers had come to death row in the 90s, and one of the main things we wanted to give them was a visual example of what could be accomplished intellectually, spiritually, and physically. Our message was simple: your life isn't over just because you came to death row. There's no pit so deep you can't rise out with genuine effort. The door to redemption and self-transformation is open to anyone courageous enough to walk through it. We told them: "Find your fulcrum. Find your purpose. And let that be the alarm clock that wakes you up every morning." They began to study just as voraciously as we had done in the beginning.

Tookie, after months of prodding from Evil and me, began outlining what would years later become his memoir, *Blue Rage, Black Redemption*. He temporarily deferred writing his memoir to devote his attention to writing a book for children—the idea he had expressed to me in 1986. I continued to make inroads into ancient African history, political science, philosophy, and spirituality. I was fascinated with the world of ideas and irate over the fact that the information I was learning wasn't taught to me when I attended public school. I felt betrayed.

Some modicum of writing success began in the mid-1990s. Tookie started doing news interviews and a video for gang members following the aftermath of the 1992 L.A. riots. Evil had written a powerful short story about a condemned man's last day alive titled "Walker's Requiem," which won First Prize for Best Fiction in the 1996 PEN Prison Writing Contest. (He also received honorable mention for his poetry.) His short story was published in *Doing Time*. At his behest I tried my hand at fiction writing and wrote my first short story, "Escort." Evil loved the story and as he read it he kept saying, "That's how you tell a story." He encouraged me to submit the story in the same PEN contest as "Walker's Requiem." I did. Although I didn't win, I did receive honorable mention and my confidence soared.

I began writing a flurry of essays and poems. I submitted my work to periodicals and magazines. I was rejected at every turn, but I never became dejected. I was waging a one-man campaign to find a venue for my work.

Finally, after eleven years of hole-time, I was released and housed in East Block, where my first order of business was to purchase a typewriter, the first one I ever owned. Tookie was already there and had nearly completed his series of children's books. Evil arrived in East Block a couple months after I did. Together we were able to encourage, support, and critique each other's work. When the three of us met on the East Block yard we reaffirmed the things we wanted to accomplish. We knew getting out of the hole was an opportunity we didn't want to waste. We knew we had to work fast. The bottom line was that we were living on borrowed time. We didn't have a life sentence or a parole date, but a death sentence. We vowed to make every day count.

Tookie hit pay dirt in 1996 by publishing his widely acclaimed series of eight children books entitled *Tookie Speaks*. He followed it up a couple years later with *Life in Prison*, a memoir. Evil had written a nonfiction story, "Little Panthers Don't Roar," which was published in the book *Children of the Dreams* in 1999. I was still honing my writing skills, hammering away at the typewriter, and looking for an outlet. I always felt my break was around the corner.

Gradually, something as unexpected as snow in summer happened to me. I fell in love with writing — the entire process. And as with any relationship, I had to make a sincere commitment to it.

When Evil decided to change his name, it seemed like the most natural thing in the world. Tookie, Evil, and Treach were names from another time and mental state we had long ago transcended. We wanted names rooted in our African heritage, names that reflected our awakened consciousness and inspired dignity. We chose Swahili names. Evil chose the name Ajani: "One who strives for possession." He gave me the name Adisa: "One who makes himself clear." I gave Tookie the name Ajamu: "He who fights for what he wants." We all chose the last name Kamara: "One who teaches from experience."

Eventually my persistence began to pay off. People began to contact me, asking if they could publish my work. In 2004 I won First Prize for Nonfiction in the PEN Prison Writing Contest for my essay "His Spirit Lives On," about my friendship with George Marshal, a death row prisoner who died of cancer in 2001. In 2003 I met Tom Kerr, a writing professor from Ithaca College in New York. He agreed to edit a collection of essays with me, and ultimately we became close friends. With his help I had several essays published, including "One Day Deep," an essay about my first day on death row.

By now, the steady stream of harassment from the administration had let up some, but not completely. There were still the unannounced cell searches by the goon squad (the prison internal gang unit), as well as outlandish lies by so-called "confidential informants," none of which the administration could prove. These lies always made Tookie, Evil, and me out to be mafioso-type gang leaders orchestrating major criminal activity on the street from death row. How we escaped detection by prison investigative units and the FBI remains a mystery! But such tales, despite their ridiculousness, are what certain people wanted to believe. To those people, we would always be gang members no matter what we did. We determined not to waste time endeavoring to change their perception of us; we concentrated on being consistent in our work and our actions.

Becoming a writer has awakened in me a deeper sense of self and even greater responsibility for authenticity. I know each time I place a pen in my hand, press down on a typewriter key, attach language to images, I am learning, growing, and evolving. I write when the spirit calls me. I know writing is a gift and something I must work at to perfect. I am under no illusions. I, like my brother Ajamu, could be executed. But until that day arrives, or does not arrive, I write. I write with all that I have become. And I write with the energy and spirit of my brothers Ajani and Ajamu always flowing through my hand.

Writing with the Condemned On Editing and Publishing the Work of Steve Champion

TOM KERR

Crouched between the wall phone and floor-as-desk so he could hold the phone with one hand and turn pages with the other, Steve Champion read poem after poem to me as I captured them on a digital recorder three thousand miles away. He was out of solitary confinement in the Adjustment Center at San Quentin and able to use the phone only because he was in the Orange County Jail awaiting a court appearance in Los Angeles. Steve's baritone voice shifted as he began each poem, moving from fluid conversational ease to dramatic incantation and rhythmic song. Here is one of his poems:

> TRANSPORTED TO ANOTHER TIME
> I'm seated on the auction block of the courtroom.
> Curious spectators wait to witness a legal lynching.
> The court stenographer chronicles every spoken word—
> History would not forget this day.
>
> Waist chains gird my wrists and waist,
> leg shackles fasten to my ankles.
> I'm transported to another time,
> When men hunted men, cruelly enslaving them,
> not as prisoners of war, but for profit.
>
> I am a commodity, reduced to invisibility,
> and batteries of psychologists and psychiatrists are paid
> thousands of dollars not to testify about my humanity,
> but about my saneness, my fitness to be tried, to be executed.
>
> Every morning the sun rises I chant an African battle hymn;
> Every evening the sun sets I chant a freedom song.
> I am stronger today than I was yesterday,
> but not as strong as I will be tomorrow.
> Victory is mine.

County Jail buses are vessels hostaging black, brown, and white
    bodies.
I am transported to another time,
where slave ships have morphed into slave buses,
where the slave fort is a new prison fort,
where whips, ropes, and chains — utilized to punish, brutalize and
    control —
are updated to tasers, pepper sprays, and stun guns,
And manned by men and women who wear green,
the color of money, the color of greed.

I am transported to another time,
when I'm poked and prodded,
flanked by armed guards,
misdirected and directed to kneel, to be still.
As the shackles come unclamped,
I am not free to walk out of a prison,
but into a cage, another fort,
where I sleep until I am transported to the plantation —
again.

In the background, and especially between poems, I heard the noise of
the jail — distant cries, guards shouting, doors slamming — yet Steve was
crouching by the phone in the dayroom alone, a "high security" prisoner
held apart from everyone else.

In the six years I have known California death row prisoner Steve Champion, he has often explained how important it is for him through correspondence to cultivate and maintain a social world beyond prison. He reminded me in a letter of the existential and practical significance of written
communication for him:

As a prisoner I am deprived of a connection to the social world except through communication with people in society and, to an extent,
studying and so forth. Without that I would be in a bubble and cut off.
Let me give you the latest example. My eldest brother, Lewis, was my
only brother out of three who I could count on financially. He died of a
stroke in April. By the time I received the letter (you know how slow the
mail runs here) informing me of the tragedy, he was dead and buried.
I couldn't even write anything for his memorial 'cause it was too late.

That is why being informed as much as I can, especially when entrusting someone with my work, is important.

Steve's work is his poetry, essays, and books—all of which might be regarded as Steve's correspondence with a world, a society, more precisely, that has condemned him. Certainly, all expressive writing produced with the aim of publication, fiction and nonfiction, is to some degree epistolary, a call for response and recognition, a means of reconciling one's own thoughts and actions with those of fellow human beings. Steve's writing is no different. The context, however, sets his writing life apart from most writing lives. It is not only that he writes in a cell, under brutally depressing and alienating circumstances, subject to censorship and retaliation at every turn, surrounded by people who care little for his welfare, even less for his existence (excepting, of course, his friends), with the certain knowledge that, if the state has its way and he does not succumb first to some natural illness, he will die alone on a gurney with foreknowledge of the time and manner of his death. These circumstances alone make his contributions remarkable.

But even more profoundly, he writes from within and against a retributive criminal justice system premised on a singularly reductive view of human nature and human society. Biologist and social philosopher Mary Clark describes this view:

> [It is assumed] that all breaches of the social code—as inscribed primarily in written laws—are the sole responsibility of the transgressor. . . . Only occasionally are "mitigating" circumstances taken into account—the most successful in the United States being "by reason of insanity," and essentially never "by reason of being poor, oppressed, rejected, humiliated." That society and its institutions could be the causal agent in generating "criminality" is not allowed as a possibility. All members of society are expected somehow to adapt to whatever social milieu they find themselves in, even when they are totally powerless to either change or escape it.[1]

Steve and other writers like him, in their quest for redemption, dignity, and some form of social reconciliation, affirm the possibility of an alternative, restorative form of justice, one that puts a premium on repair of social bonds broken by destructive criminal behavior—which is itself understood as a social phenomenon.

In contrast to retributive justice, restorative justice assumes that society and its institutions are nearly always implicated in criminal behavior and that society has a moral obligation to work with, not against, individual offenders. Emergent drug courts, in which offenders are sentenced to treatment and community service instead of prison, are signs, however faint, of a restorative justice impulse within an overwhelming retributive system. In the drug court, crime is effectively regarded as a cry for help—a symptom rather than a sin. In such a view, criminal justice is about finding solutions to the problems that lead to harmful criminal behavior. It is also about repentance and atonement, about addressing the harm done in ways that are meaningful for victims of crime, even when no direct contact between offender and victim(s) may be possible or desirable. Restorative justice is rooted in dialogue broadly conceived and allows for the possibility of contrition, restitution, forgiveness, and redemption. A collaborative project, it fosters human connections with the potential to transform the social relations that very often—not, of course, always—occasion criminal harm in the first place. For a paradigm shift to occur, restorative justice must be enabled by law and criminal justice policy, but citizens must also actively embrace its principles, which are just beginning to enter popular discourse.[2]

As a death row writer suffering the consequences of retribution most grievously, Steve has an implicit and explicit purpose in writing: to affirm the possibility of collaborative redemption. As a prisoner dedicated to self- and social-transformation via intellectual inquiry, self-reflection, spiritual meditation, and political engagement, Steve is in a good position to report on the many failures of retributive justice as well as to advocate for social justice—that is, for dramatic changes in the social, economic, and political structures.

Ultimately, the Letter from Death Row writ large challenges the very existence of death row and the fundamental values of the society that endorses it. Because constructive, though not uncritical, engagement with society of the kind represented in Steve's writing is anathema to the retributive order, his efforts are discouraged by the system. For this reason, the Letter from Death Row is risky to write and, very often, in the way it reminds law-abiding citizens both of their complicity in criminal behavior and inhumane forms of punishment, unwelcome upon delivery. Steve's writing and our ongoing collaboration illuminate the challenges, the promise, and the necessity of restorative justice.

The Connection

Steve has been on death row at San Quentin State Prison since 1982. That's twenty-seven years as of this writing. Twenty years old when sentenced—eighteen when arrested—Steve was one of the youngest men ever to land on California's death row. I have been teaching writing at various colleges and universities since 1987, or twenty-two years—five less than Steve has spent on the row. In 2003, I sent out a call for imprisoned writers to correspond with members of my Senior Writing Seminar on the Rhetoric of Social Movements, taking the Critical Resistance Movement as our primary case study. Of the dozens of letters my class received from prisoners all around the country, Steve is the only person I have kept in regular contact with, even as I have carried on other class correspondences with other prisoners in other years.[3] For a long-term working relationship to form, the stars must align. In our case, the early letters and essays he sent struck a chord with me, stylistically and politically. I saw Steve as a kindred spirit, even though our life histories and current circumstances would not present that possibility to either of us or to others.

I grew up in Denver; he grew up in Los Angeles. Steve is black. I am white. Steve was raised in a working-class household in East L.A. headed by a single mother; I was raised in an upper-middle-class household headed by a successful, loyal father and stay-at-home mother. Steve spilled into the streets of his neighborhood and L.A. for diversion, while I spent much of my time playing tennis and golf at the Valley Country Club, and playing basketball, shooting pool, bowling, and swimming at the Denver Athletic Club. Quite a few black men and women worked at the Denver Athletic Club, but I can't recall a single black member. The memory of being served lunch with my other ten-year-old white friends by a very kind black woman that my mother "just adored" now fills me with embarrassment. It seemed to me then, more or less unconsciously, that those black employees who were so kind to me and my friends hailed from some mysterious place in the city that I would never really know and which, at the tender age of ten, I vaguely feared.

Steve went to public schools and dropped out of high school. My father shipped me out of my own neighborhood, where busing had begun in 1970, to a private school on seventy-four bucolic acres in the suburbs of Denver. My father wanted me to get a good education, but I suspect he also wanted to "save" me from going to school at a predominantly black junior high school. Private school or no, I was a largely unsupervised teen whose parents lived their own life and trusted me to live mine. While I put on a good face, I should not have been trusted. Because I wanted desperately to be loved and accepted, I was easily influenced by the most spoiled, arrogant "old money" rich kids at my school (talk about a gang!), and they hailed from all parts of town. Well into pot, beer, and liquor by sixteen, I partied all around Denver and the surrounding mountains, migrating from house to house, driving recklessly much of the time, frequently under the influence, high, or both. I raced friends at high speeds on busy streets, weaving in and out of slower traffic, and ran through red lights late at night while crisscrossing Denver and its suburbs. I caused one bad accident (even as the other driver got the ticket) and had many close calls. I was lucky in that period not to have injured or killed someone else or myself, and my potential victims were lucky, too.

More than once, I talked or lucked my way out of trouble with the law. One night, I was pulled over for speeding with three white friends in the car. We were smoking a joint when the cop turned his lights on, and the car was just airing out when the officer approached. Another call came in at the moment, and I was told to slow down and released to go my merry way. In fact, during my teens and early twenties, I had numerous encounters with the police and came away with about a fifty-fifty record of being ticketed or given a warning. When pulled over, I would fall into the role of a nice, earnest, upper-middle-class white kid who just got a little carried away. I respected the law, because in general it protected and respected me, but I would flaunt it when it suited me.

Steve's youthful encounters with the law were never so benign. In his essay "Growin' Up Crip," he explains how his mother didn't know anything about his "relationship" to the police:

Nor did she know about the Rodney King–style terror her eleven-year-old son experienced at the hands of the police. She didn't know the police had taken me to a vacant house, beat me down, put a gun to my temple, and threatened to pull the trigger. She didn't know about the Friday nights my friends and I hid in the alley and waited for police cars to pass on Vermont Avenue so we could hurl rocks and bottles at them. For us, the police were the brutal symbols of oppressive authority. We wanted nothing more than to give them the same mistreatment they gave us, and carpeting their cars with rocks was our way of exacting payback.

Steve's cops were not my cops. As he reveals in his memoir, Steve also became an arrogant, partying teenager—often crisscrossing L.A. with friends—who would flaunt the law when it suited him, but he was flying without a net and without the police tending to give him the benefit of the doubt. I frequently partied in gated communities at the supersized houses of friends. Steve partied mainly in cars and parks. In large measure, I had what I wanted before I wanted it, and Steve learned that he probably wouldn't get what he wanted unless he took it from someone else. He did not have compelling reasons to respect, or obey, the law.

Steve had several brothers, one of whom prodded him into fighting early, cheering him on and showering him with approval for beating up a neighbor kid. I had four older sisters and was terrified of physical violence to the point that I befriended volatile, aggressive kids rather than risk making enemies. I learned to talk fast and shift shapes when necessary, and Steve learned how to respond to aggression and violence in kind. Even now, when editing pieces in which Steve describes violent past encounters, both in and out of prison, I wince, whether in fear or empathy, I'm not sure. And yet, clearly, the reckless disregard for others I expressed behind the wheel of my car was a form of violence every bit as menacing to society as gang violence.[4]

In 1982, at twenty-three, I completed my B.A. in English at Colorado State University and matriculated in the graduate program in English at the University of Washington. Prior to finishing my degree at CSU, I had been bouncing around more or less aimlessly from college to college, moving inexorably toward my undergraduate degree. Steve had been bouncing in and out of California Youth Authority juvenile halls and camps, moving just as inexorably toward incarceration in state prison. Steve was sentenced to die in 1982.

What Steve and I share is a divided, hierarchical society in which ease, security, and opportunity are reserved for upper-middle-class white kids like me, while working-class black kids like Steve very often bear the burden in stress, fear, and frustrated desire. And I did not learn—from my parents, church, school, or culture at large—that we are, as the saying goes, all in this together. On the contrary, I learned to fear the victims of our inequitable, pernicious social system. Had I passed Steve walking down the street in the 70s, I would likely have been terrified of him, and he likely would have ignored me, as I *apparently* had nothing at all to do with his life or concerns. Neither of us, in our youth, could have understood how much our lives depended on the other's, and we certainly could never have imagined forging a creative, productive bond.

The Collaboration

In my possession are many typed and handwritten letters, essays, poems, and articles by Steve. On my computer are my letters and drafts of his essays, all initially transcribed by me onto disk, as well as manuscripts for three books—two published, one in hibernation. There are versions of talks and articles I have written about or with Steve. Then there are the digital recordings of long conversations we have had when he has had phone privileges at San Quentin or while in the Los Angeles County Jail during court appearances. From these recordings of Steve reading poems and, in one case, a message to friends, I have created several CDs.

I have visited Steve three times, once when we could sit in the same cage for nearly four hours and twice for hour-long visits when we were separated by Plexiglas due to his unjust and interminable relegation to the Adjustment Center, the segregated housing unit in San Quentin. The first of the meetings was crucial to our working relationship and friendship. In that face-to-face, we agreed on a writing and editing process that would preserve the integrity of Steve's message and, most importantly, the integrity of his voice. Short of exoneration, clemency, or the grace of God, writing is one of few paths to civil (as distinguished from religious) redemption/ restoration for people on death row. Introspection and meditation might well bring peace of mind but cannot redeem/restore us as social beings: that process requires others, at least *an* other—to hear our story, to understand it, and, if we're lucky, to reaffirm our humanity.

San Quentin's death row does not encourage civil redemption in the form of writing. On the contrary, and because writing is also a form of freedom and political expression, the system actively discourages it, treating all writing from prisoners as potentially subversive—a threat to the carceral and, therefore, to the social order. So even while a prisoner's First Amendment rights are *provisionally* protected[5]—the penal system's overriding preoccupation with security makes conditions ripe both for overt censorship, on one hand, and covert disruption of a writer's work, on the other. Means of suppression range from the petty, mundane, and transient to the cruel, unusual, and enduring. On the petty end of the spectrum: when during our contact visit we asked for writing paper, guards produced a torn piece of brown bathroom paper towel. Mail sent to Steve can, according to him, take up to a month to arrive, with no explanation. On the cruel and unusual end of the spectrum: San Quentin uses several California Department of Corrections and Rehabilitation (CDCR) strategies to damn writers like Steve to solitary confinement, where he has been since December 2005—that is, for nearly four years as of this writing. In the hole, prisoners are deprived of most personal property, including their libraries, prohibited from making or receiving nonlegal phone calls, prevented from contact visits (that is, they are separated from visitors by Plexiglas), and relegated to walk-alone yard time in which their "yard" resembles a chain-link dog run and precludes meaningful interaction with fellow prisoners. The real reasons for isolation are obscured by institutional practices such as "confidential informants," "gang labeling," and "debriefing." Depending on circumstances, each or all of these instruments of control can be used to punish prisoners who find a receptive public audience for their criticism of the prison industrial complex, in general, and of San Quentin, in particular.

While it would require a separate essay to detail the violations of human rights achieved by CDCR methods, the common and galling feature is that none require hard evidence or corroboration for severe sanctions to result. Indeed, Steve was thrown into the hole in early December 2005, just prior to Stanley Tookie Williams's execution, on information provided by a "confidential informant." This informant claimed that Steve and other of Tookie's friends planned to retaliate for the execution by assaulting a guard. According to Steve, no such plan existed, but the uncorroborated claim was enough to hold several men in the hole for many months, and Steve's stay has ballooned into years. In 2007, he and his friend and co-author, Anthony Ross, were written up on suspicion of gang affiliation because of a written reference to "Comrade George Jackson." In "The Paradigm of Abuse: San Quentin's Adjustment Center Revisited," published with my editorial assistance in the *San Francisco Bay View* newspaper and on its website, Steve and Anthony suggested that actions "in AC today [have] ominous echoes of what was occurring in 1971, when Comrade George Jackson was gunned down outside of AC. It also reflects research from the well-known Stanford Prison Experiment (SPE), conducted in 1971 on the psychological dynamics of prison life." A guard subsequently quoted from this section of the article and reported, as follows, to the administration (I have a copy of the CDCR Memo in front of me):

Based on my training and experience I know that members/associates and sympathizers of the Black Guerilla Family Prison Gang who mention GEORGE JACKSON and the term Comrade identify him as a fellow member, associate or companion that shares the same interests, occupation, or actions regarding Prison Gang Activities. Based on this information I believe that ROSS sympathizes with the ideals of the Black Guerilla Family Prison Gang and should be closely monitored for gang activity.

On its face, the claim is absurd—complete bunk—and yet it is sufficient to justify keeping the men under "close monitoring," which can, along with other shady information, keep them in the hole indefinitely. Under such Orwellian conditions, sustained collaboration between death row prisoners and free citizens is almost essential for a prisoner's writing to find an audience. While prison publications, progressive and radical publishers, newspapers, magazines, websites, prison activist organization newsletters all provide venues for prisoner writing, personal connections and collaborations with writers, teachers, and activists are vital to the process of prisoners getting writing published. Without a steady editorial presence and de facto literary agent on the outside, the institution has the better odds.

Steve's work, like the work of talented prison artists, is marked by his long incarceration.[6] His sensibility, his themes, and his style refer ineluctably to the conditions and implications of his confinement. In the first place, his self-education in prison was driven by a powerful desire to understand his position in American society and, more profoundly, on earth. He wanted to know why he and so many other young black men had turned to gangs and crime, had somehow believed that the gang life was their last, best chance to belong, to be accepted, and thereby to enjoy the personal and collective power that came with belonging and acceptance. He wanted to know why and how social, political, and economic power had come to be concentrated in the hands of so few, in the United States and elsewhere. And so like many other U.S. prisoners before him, he took himself to school to learn what the great thinkers and writers of the world, including his African ancestors, had to say about the human condition and about fighting for freedom, justice, and dignity. A passage from his memoir provides a clear indication of his ambition:

> What the *Bhagavad-Gita* did for me was teach me strength in humility and how to temper my ego. It also inspired me to embark upon a spiritual journey. It spurred me to begin a comparative study of various religions. I felt if you were going to do something, you shouldn't do it half-heartedly. I knew this approach would give me a more enlightened view

and deeper respect for all religions because I wouldn't be hampered by bias like many of the religious people I had come in contact with, people who believed their god and religion was the only true one. One of the first things I learned from the book was that no one owns the absolute truth; we all have a piece of it.[7]

Such ambition, which also informed his study of history, economics, and politics, led him to the belief that he, too, had something of value to share with others, some light to shed on his derailed life in the context of our times. He had become a student of history, and he soon realized that writing was the only means through which he could actively join the conversation. Reading, study, and reflection do not complete the circle. As he details in his contribution to this volume, Steve began modestly, with a poem, an essay or two, but soon found himself consumed by the writing life—by the disciplined and regular practice of putting pen to paper—and his writing, as he attests, is one important, if not the *most* important, way he keeps himself sane in an insane environment.

Steve has published in several venues, including inspirational and self-help pamphlets for distribution to other inmates.[8] With Anthony Ross and the late Stanley Tookie Williams, he coauthored a collection of aphorisms, *The Sacred Eye of the Falcon: Lessons in Life from Death Row*. The authors explain in the preface the relevance of their title, which refers to the Egyptian god Horus.

In a great battle with the God Seth (Satan) over the rule of the kingdom, one of Horus' eyes was gouged out. His Eye was eventually restored by Tehuti, the god of wisdom. This act gave Horus divine sight (the all-seeing eye) and he used it to give the people the divine law Maat (truth, justice, righteousness, order, and reciprocity). After years of conflict and imprisonment, our sight has been restored and our lives are governed by Maat.[9]

We see what they mean in chapter 3 in a section called "Life's Lessons":

People learn to hate when they are mistreated. People fight when they are forced. People blossom when they are nurtured. People change when they are shown a way. Be mindful of how your actions may impact others. We all are responsible for what we put into the web of life.[10]

Such is the dominant sentiment in Steve's work, coming directly out of a place that allegedly holds the "worst of the worst."

The Audience

As a writing teacher at Syracuse University in the 90s, I came to realize that the majority of my middle- and upper-middle-class "liberal humanist" students, who were generally open to and even aggressive in questioning authority and systems of belief, took an uncompromising lock-'em-up-and-throw-away-the-key line when it came to criminal justice in America. In this, the majority of students seemed to march in lockstep with received notions of crime and punishment, expressed by one student in the bromide, "Don't do the crime, if you can't do the time." How, I wondered, could the same person advocate passionately for animal rights and the death penalty? How had people in prison come to be so dehumanized, and how might I, in my role as a rhetoric and writer teacher, fight the system?

Frustrated in that first-year writing class with the limits of abstract analysis and argumentation regarding prison, I dedicated two sections of a subsequent research writing class exclusively to the topic, and I made a concentrated effort to bring my students into closer proximity to prisons and imprisoned people. Before students embarked on research focused on an aspect of prison that correlated to their majors—art in prison for art majors, health in prison for health science majors, politics (of prison) for political science majors, film (about prison) for film studies majors, law (and prison) for pre-law majors, and so on—we read works about prison, including some by people who currently were or had been imprisoned.[11] It became apparent that first-person perspectives, including one offered by Barbara Demming in her classic *Prisons That Could Not Hold*, cut through long-conditioned law-and-order ideology, and this began to give way in class discussions to empathy and to the basic sociological question: How do so many people end up in the hellholes that are prisons?

As my students and I realized how little we knew about the prison industrial complex in our midst, especially in the near vicinity in central New York, we made a plan to visit two prisons—in the fashion of Charles Dickens and Alexis de Tocqueville.[12] While the gesture may have been overly dramatic and somewhat problematic insofar as "touring" a prison risks rendering it a spectacle and objectifying the prisoners held there (as we see in such contemporary television voyeurism as MSNBC's *Lock Up*), my students and I came away from our half-day tours of the minimum security Onondaga County Department of Corrections and the maximum security Auburn Correctional Facility (which Tocqueville visited) with a much greater understanding of what and who we are talking about when we talk about prisons.

It is the active suppression of empathy, after all, that clears the way for retributive forms of justice to thrive, and empathy is hard won at a distance or through third-person analysis and argument. In order to bring more people into redemptive alignment with the lives and struggles of the millions locked up, they need to hear directly from those, like Steve, who can give a virtual and critical firsthand account of the prison industrial complex. I realize that for those deeply invested in retributive justice, the horrific conditions of confinement may not be in the least disturbing. On the contrary, they may be deeply satisfying. It is also likely that some people will take pleasure in witnessing close-up the suffering and/or destruction of the scapegoat, but these responses can, I've found, be significantly mitigated by the enlightened voices of prisoner-writers.

After editing Steve's first set of essays, I suggested that we add to the collection and produce a memoir in essays. After six years' effort, we published *Dead to Deliverance: A Death Row Memoir* with Split Oak Press. Early on, one of the few agents willing to read sample essays told me that he might reconsider his rejection were I or someone else to make Steve's work read more like Mumia Abu-Jamal's. A trained and experienced journalist, Abu-Jamal's lively, multi-layered prose might appeal more immediately to a broad book-buying audience—the one the agent must attract—but Steve is not, in fact, Mumia Abu-Jamal. I could not decide whether to be offended by this agent's candor—in effect, "we want all our black death-row inmates to be Mumia"—or appreciative, since the vast majority responded with form letters. We had a couple hopeful conversations with well-known progressive political presses, but resources were/are limited, manuscripts abundant, and I can't help reminding myself, too, that the Letter from Death Row is not one many people eagerly await or open with excitement. As the world changes and new, urgent issues vie daily for our time, the black hole of capital punishment remains unchanged and largely ignored.

Steve Champion's writing—in turns poetic, self-reflective, and critical—exists on the event horizon of this societal abyss. It should not escape—it is not supposed to escape—and yet it does. It is an open question whether it can reach an audience that includes sufficient numbers of people who are not already persuaded that our criminal justice system is fundamentally flawed and that capital punishment is a crime against humanity. As more and more people join the fight against the prison industrial complex, we should expect even more teachers and students, as well as readers at large, to take an interest in the expanding discourse of this social movement, and there is hope in that. Steve's essential message, that retributive criminal justice is a terrible substitute for social justice, is clear, powerful, and enduring. The responsibility remains for all of us to reflect redemptive light in as many directions as possible, and with whatever intensity and duration each of us can muster. We should not expect death row prisoners to redeem themselves without, in concert, endeavoring to redeem ourselves.

Notes

1. Mary E. Clark, "Skinner vs. the Prophets: Human Nature & Our Concepts of Justice," *Contemporary Justice Review* 8.2 (2005): 167.

2. See, for example, Rachel Libert, dir., *Beyond Conviction*, MSNBC, December 3, 2006; Gary Weiss and Rebecca Webber, "Intelligence Report: A New Kind of Criminal Justice," *Parade*, October 25, 2009, 6.

3. See my essay "Between Ivy and Razor Wire: A Case of Correctional Correspondence," *Reflections: A Journal of Writing, Service Learning and Community Literacy* 4.1 (2004): 62–75.

4. In 1980, there were approximately thirty thousand alcohol-related driving fatalities (National Highway Traffic Safety Administration FARS data, 2008), while the number of homicides, the vast majority of which were not gang-related, was approximately twenty-three thousand (10.2 per 100,000 population with a population of 226,545,805). See *Bureau of Justice Statistics*, http://www.ojp.usdoj.gov/bjs/homicide/hmrt.htm.

5. According to the U.S. Congressional Research Services Annotated Constitution: 1) "A prison inmate retains only those First Amendment rights that are not inconsistent with his status as a prisoner or with the legitimate penological objectives of the corrections system. The identifiable governmental interests at stake in administration of prisons are the preservation of internal order and discipline, the maintenance of institutional security against escape or unauthorized entry, and the rehabilitation of the prisoners"; and 2) "the Court invalidated mail censorship regulations that permitted authorities to hold back or to censor mail to and from prisoners whenever they thought that the letters 'unduly complain,' 'express inflammatory . . . views or beliefs,' or were 'defamatory' or 'otherwise inappropriate.' The Court based this ruling not on the rights of the prisoner, but on the outsider's right to communicate with the prisoner by sending or receiving mail. The Court held that regulation of mail must further an important interest unrelated to the suppression of expression; regulation must be shown to further the substantial interest of security, order, and rehabilitation, and it must not be utilized simply to censor opinions or other expressions. Further, a restriction must be no greater than is necessary or essential to the protection of the particular government inter-

est involved." *CRS Annotated Constitution. Cornell University Law School: Legal Information Institute*, http://www.law.cornell.edu//.html.

6. See, for instance, Phyllis Kornfield, *Cellblock Visions: Prison Art in America* (Princeton: Princeton Univ. Press, 1997).

7. Steve Champion, *Dead to Deliverance: A Death Row Memoir* (Vestal, NY: Split Oak Press, 2010), 123.

8. Steve received honorary mention in the short fiction category in the 1995 PEN Prison Writing Contest and in 2004 won first place in nonfiction for his essay "His Spirit Lives On: George E. Marshal." Also see Steve Champion, "The Geography of Death Row: Essays from Inside San Quentin," *ProudFlesh: New African Journal of Culture* 4 (2006), http://www.proudfleshjournal.com//.html; "First Day Inside: A Death Row Record," *Maxim*, May 2005: 136–37; Anthony Ross, Steve Champion, and Stanley Tookie Williams, *The Sacred Eye of the Falcon: Lessons in Life from Death Row* (Syracuse, NY: Kerr Publishing, 2007); Anthony Ross and Steve Champion, "The Paradigm of Abuse: San Quentin's Adjustment Center Revisited," *San Francisco Bay View*, May 2007: Web. 24 Oct. 2009. Titles of Steve's coauthored prison pamphlets are "Walking It Like You Talk It" (2005), "The Ninth Ground" (2004), and "Everything of Value You Must Carry with Your Hands" (2007).

9. Ross et al., *Sacred Eye*, i.

10. Ibid., 16.

11. Our reading list included *Criminal Injustice: Confronting the Prison Crisis*, ed. Elihu Rosenblatt (Boston: South End, 1999) and *The Real War on Crime: Report of the National Criminal Justice Commission*, ed. Steven R. Donziger (New York: Harper Perennial, 1996).

12. See Charles Dickens, *American Notes for General Circulation*. 1842. (London: Echo Library, 2006); Alexis de Tocqueville, *Democracy in America*. 1835, 1840. (New York: Penguin Classics, 2003).

Leaving Death Row A Screenplay

ELIZABETH ANN STEIN

PRISON HALLWAY

The handcuffed hands of TOMMY, 32, a convicted murderer whose poor, rural manner belies an extensive self-education acquired during ten years on Texas's Death Row. He moves with a modicum of dignity preserved against the odds.

CACAPHONY of twenty other visits ping-pongs off the walls. Tommy stops at a door; CLANGING as his GUARD unlocks it.

> GUARD
> Go on, Casanova.

DEATH ROW VISITORS' ROOM

A wall of concrete, steel mesh, and bullet-proof Plexiglas separates VELA, an idealistic, twenty-six-year-old Bulgarian student activist, and the PREACHER from the four-by-four cage in which Tommy stands, hands thrust through a slot in the door. The Guard locks the door, then unlocks Tommy's cuffs and clips them to his belt, hovering nearby. Tommy gives Vela a disarming smile. Vela, wearing street clothes, is overcome by emotion, springs out of her chair, places her hand on the Plexiglas and pledges her undying love—in Bulgarian.

> VELA
> Dokato ima zvezdi po nebesata i ptitsite letiat po nebosvoda, az se zaklevam moyata lubov kum teb da ne umre, moi budesht suprug.

Tommy, taken aback by what sounds like the gibberish of the religiously fevered, glances at Preacher, who signals reassurance. Calmed and back in control, Tommy places his hand on the other side of the Plexiglas from Vela's.

> TOMMY
> Likewise, I'm sure.

2. Stills from *Leaving Death Row*, filmed at the visiting area of the Houston Police Department's Southeast Jail. Vela (Julitta Pourciau) meets with Tommy (Anthony Hernandez) as the Guard (Richard Sabbara) and Preacher (Steven Pollard) look on. Photos courtesy Gary Chason.

The Guard reacts with disdain. Throughout, Tommy and his visitors maintain awareness of the Guard's presence.

Tommy is back to his charming self. He and Preacher exchange a knowing glance as Vela continues in Bulgarian, carried away with excitement.

> VELA
> Chuvstvam se kato printsesa, koyato vizda svoya prints za purvi put . . .

Vela, realizing she is going on in her native tongue, stops suddenly.

> VELA
> I am sorry. Finally, I see you, Tommy.

She considers him.

> VELA
> You are very . . . uh . . . pretty.

Tommy and Preacher laugh. Vela realizes she misspoke and joins good-naturedly. Tommy sits as they talk. Vela follows suit.

> TOMMY
> I don't represent that remark, but I'll take what I can get. I know how to do that.

Vela, melting to Tommy's charismatic presence, starts to say something urgent.

> VELA
>
> Can we make the wedding now? I must—

She catches herself, glances at the Guard, then switches to a different topic.

> VELA
>
> My trip was very well.

> TOMMY
>
> I hope you didn't get too tired, darling.

> VELA
>
> No tired. The ear-stoppers helped.

> TOMMY
>
> Uh . . . ear plugs?

> VELA
>
> Yes. Ear plugs. The VCR was kaput.
> (Horrified)
> So they played music!

> TOMMY
>
> (Puzzled)
> That doesn't sound so bad.

> VELA
>
> The national anthem of Bulgaria? From Sofia to Amsterdam?!

> TOMMY
>
> Well, bless your heart.

During the last exchange, the Guard moves on. Tommy directs his attention to Preacher. All three switch to a conspiratorial whisper.

> TOMMY
>
> You ready?

> PREACHER
>
> I am.

He glances at Vela, concerned at how naïve she seems.

> PREACHER
> Are you certain this is the right thing? For both of you?

> VELA
> I am. Certainly.

Preacher is still skeptical, worried.

> TOMMY
> (Increasingly agitated)
> Yes, it's right.
> (Beat)
> Let's do it.
> (Angry but sotto voce)
> I ain't going to Peckerwood Hill.
> (Louder)
> They won't put me in Peckerwood Hill.

The three look up in alarm. Tommy's mild outburst has reached the Guard who saunters back.

> GUARD
> (Looking suspicious)
> Who you calling "Preacher"?

> TOMMY
> No Preacher. This here is Prejean (PRE-zhun). Percy Prejean. My cousin. My fiancé's ride. That's all.

Guard eyes the group warily, lingers on.

> PREACHER
> So, we'll continue to pursue a stay of execution. You mustn't abandon hope.

> TOMMY
> (Trying unsuccessfully to hide hopelessness)
> Yeah, right.

Guard, bored again, saunters off.

VELA
Please, let us continue.
(Beat. To Tommy)
What is this hill of . . . wooden pecker?

Tommy and Preacher do a take at each other, suppressing laughter.
Tommy looks guiltily at Preacher, who registers surprise.

TOMMY
Nothing, honey.

PREACHER
You haven't told her about Peckerwood Hill? About the
disposition of your earthly remains?

VELA
(Upset)
His . . . what? If I will be the wife and you the husband,
we must tell all things. What does happening? What
remains? We appeal, no?

TOMMY
(Soothingly)
That's right, sweet thing. There's nothing I won't
share with you. Preacher's just talking about an
administrative detail.
(To Preacher, impatiently)
Let's get to the main event.

Vela is unconvinced, Preacher quietly intense.

TOMMY
Preacher, we'd be obliged . . . please?

Off Preacher's silent intensity, Tommy pauses. Preacher reaches a
decision.

PREACHER
(Quietly)
Not until you tell her.

VELA
Tell me what?

                    TOMMY
                    I don't know what he's talking . . .
                    PREACHER
                    (Interrupting Tommy after "he's")
                    You must tell her.

Vela and Tommy stare at Preacher. Sensing a spectator moment, the
Guard saunters back, forcing the gang of three to act like all is OK.

                    TOMMY
                    I'd love to see those pictures of my future in-laws —
                    Vela (mispronouncing it as VEE-lah).

                    VELA
                    Vela (VEH-lah). My name is said like Vela.

                    TOMMY
                    (Upset at bungling a key detail of the seduction)
                    Right. Vela, Vela, like Velveeta.

Guard snickers and, superiority restored, saunters off. The gang returns
to whispers.

                    PREACHER
                    I mean it. I won't do the ceremony here, or by proxy, if
                    you don't disclose to Vela the reason for your decision
                    to enter this holy state.

                    VELA
                    (Panicking)
                    But I have come this long miles . . . broke my bank, to
                    make this marriage. And you say we cannot?

There is a long silence in which Preacher stares at Tommy, Vela implores
him, and Tommy squirms, finally breaking down. He maintains low
tones, to keep guard away.

                    TOMMY
                    Peckerwood Hill.

                    VELA
                    I have heard of woodpeckers. What is the significance?

TOMMY

Ain't no bird. It's a place. When a convict, a convict
with no family, passes on, that's where he goes. You
don't believe me, go see for yourself. There's rows and
rows and rows of concrete crosses. Prisoners tend it.
Dig the graves, make the markers. The prison kills you
legally—throws you out the back door. Or lets you die
by not giving you medicine for . . . AIDS or some other
disease you catch in here. You go to Peckerwood Hill
because nobody claims your body. Nobody claims your
body.

Long pause.

TOMMY

I'm sorry, Vela. I lied. My letters to you—and I have to
confess, I wrote to ten other women—they weren't for
love.
(Lengthy beat)
I just want somebody to claim my body.

Tommy knows the game is up. Defeated, gets up to call guard. Till now,
Vela has been staring at him with an unreadable look.

VELA

(With quiet dignity)
I will not claim your body.

Tommy reacts with a gesture of acceptance, continues to look for the
guard. Another long pause. Vela stands as if to leave, the latest in a world-
girdling line of romantics who met a con artist and fell in love anyway.

VELA

We fight execution. I will not let you die.

Tommy sees her in a new light; a long-dampened belief in the possibility
of altruism—even love—is rekindled.

VELA

You ready?

PREACHER

I am.

> PREACHER
> Are you certain this is the right thing. For both of you?

After a long beat, Tommy indicates the positive.

> PREACHER
> Dearly beloved . . .

FADE OUT

My journey to death row started in 2006 on a bright and cold February morning at the training field house of the Eastham Unit of the Texas Department of Criminal Justice (TDCJ). Thirty of us were five weeks into the basic correctional officer class that every new TDCJ hire attends to prepare for assignment to a working unit. Bad drug tests and attitude problems had reduced our class from forty or so. Once we graduated and hit the prison floor, another 30 percent of us would depart within the first six months for a variety of reasons, including the inability to cope with convicted felons for six or more days out of every nine, for smuggling tobacco, drugs, or other contraband into the unit, and for falling into an "inappropriate" relationship with an inmate.

Working at TDCJ, I met some of the finest, most professional men and women I had ever encountered, but they were generally outnumbered by officers who either didn't give a damn or were outright crooked. The inmates, with twenty-four hours a day to study their keepers, had little trouble separating the "marks" whom they could manipulate and exploit from the officers who did the best job they could while maintaining a sense of basic humanity at their core. In an environment where the strong prey upon the weak, and kindness is often taken for weakness, I was soon to discover that one of the biggest difficulties facing honest officers was separating the good guys from the bad guys on both sides of the bars.

We were a mixed bunch: young women with children who were looking for a job that paid well by local standards and included benefits, and young men just out of a local high school with no other job prospects; there were others, mostly men with prior TDCJ service, who were returning because their original jobs hadn't panned out; a smattering of middle-aged men and women who needed a job where the only requirements were a high school diploma, a clean criminal record, and the ability to pass a simplistic exam; and ex-soldiers back from Iraq and Afghanistan whose skills centered mainly around serving as riflemen in a combat zone. We were in many ways like new inductees into the French Foreign Legion, with no past worth recounting and an uncertain future.

Our starting salary was $19,000 a year, a fact that constituted real sticker shock for a former university press director who had retired from a position that paid six times that amount a few months previously. My thirty-year career in scholarly book publishing had been ended abruptly (or so I thought at the time) by an addiction to drugs and alcohol that had begun in an Army helicopter combat assault troop in Viet Nam in 1969 and spanned most of my adult life. I was six weeks out of rehab when I started working at the TDCJ, clean but not really sober, and filled with a mixture of resentment at my loss of station, relief that my long-suffering wife had once again taken me back, and curiosity about what strange and dramatic things my new career might offer.

The last book I published before my professional demise was with veteran CNN war correspondent Walter Rogers. *Sleeping with Custer and the 7th Cavalry: An Embedded Reporter in Iraq* is a chronicle of Walt's dangerous journey with the armored Army reconnaissance unit that spearheaded the initial assault from the Kuwaiti border into Baghdad. Walt and I had become fast friends during many satellite phone calls and e-mails while he was in the war zone, and when we finally met face-to-face at his family cabin on an island on a small New England lake, it was like two old comrades coming together. Over steaks and beer, Walt correctly identified me as a "war junkie," and I was both proud and troubled by his assessment. I had started the first painful steps in identifying those things in my past that had addicted me to a life of personal and professional risk-taking long past the point where most of my peers had settled into a reasonably calm middle age.

I realized at the TDCJ academy that I was still seeking the trouble and chaos I had so often compulsively welcomed into my life. Fearing that I would lapse back into substance abuse, I determined to stay mindful about my response to the new and stressful environment. I wasn't overly concerned about my safety. I was afraid that I might like it too much.

Now I was huddled against the biting cold of a wind blowing south from the North Texas plains, alongside my new colleagues who didn't give a damn about how many brilliant books I'd published or how I once hosted five-martini power lunches in Manhattan and Los Angeles with great luminaries of Civil War history and post–Cold War film studies. I was still dreaming most nights about the small brown prescription bottles of painkillers I always carried in the pockets of my Brooks Brothers blazer, and the well-aged single-malt scotch that had long been my drink of choice. Later, after I had spent hours listening to the stories of men who had passed much of their adult lives incarcerated because of the same chemical dependencies, it became easier to trade in my bitterness for gratitude.

Eastham is a classic Texas prison farm on the western edge of the Piney Woods, surrounded by thousands of acres of rich soil that has been deposited for centuries by the Trinity River, which runs just to the south of the unit and separates it from the Ferguson Unit. Established in 1917 and named after the original landowners, Eastham is situated on more than twelve thousand acres, a dozen miles west of the small town of Trinity, and surrounded on all sides by a tranquil landscape of small farms, winding country roads, and forests of pine and oak.

Field crew inmates wearing prison whites and boots leave the prison five days a week to harvest everything from jalapeño peppers to watermelon and potatoes. Accompanied by officers on horseback wearing straw cowboy hats and carrying semiautomatic rifles and Smith & Wesson revolvers, the field crews leave early in the morning and return late in the afternoon to be stripped naked and searched before showering down and heading back to their cells in fresh whites. Except for the modern weapons and radios, the landscape of daily life hasn't changed much since the 1920s, when Clyde Barrow's brother broke him out from a field crew on Eastham, or the 1960s, when photographer Danny Lyon made the iconic images that appear in his heartbreaking book, *Conversations with the Dead*.

Eastham, known as "the Ham" by veteran correctional officers and seasoned convicts, is the northernmost anchor of the TDCJ Region 1 prison group, which is headquartered in Huntsville. There are thirteen Region 1 prisons located within a thirty-mile circle around downtown Huntsville, including Eastham, Ellis, Ferguson, Huntsville, Estelle, Byrd, Holliday, Wynne, Goree, Lewis, Duncan, Goodman, and Polunsky, where the TDCJ Death Row is located. These thirteen units house over twenty-four thousand inmates incarcerated for crimes ranging from capital murder and rape to drug offenses and home burglary. They are all, in varying degrees, dangerous and sometimes deadly places for inmates to live and correctional officers to work.

On this late winter morning my fellow trainees and I were standing in front of the Eastham field house, located on the entry road to the unit. We were waiting for a bus to take us to the Walls Unit in Huntsville, about a half hour to the south, for our second tour inside a working prison.

Our first visit had been to the Eastham Unit just down the entry road, and it had been a revelation. The Ham is one of the monsters in the TDCJ system, a maximum-security unit that houses many inmates who will live out their days inside its walls and who have little to lose if they are convicted for assaulting correctional officers or each other. The Administrative Segregation (Ad Seg) section of Eastham—where inmates judged too dangerous, or sex offenders judged too much at risk to live in the general prison population, are locked down twenty-three hours a day in small, one-man cells—has a population of over five-hundred souls.

As we filed past the main guard picket at the front entrance to Eastham, we wore new grey uniforms and spit-shined boots that marked us as "fish," a term applied to both officers who were still in training and inmates new to the TDCJ prison system. The uniforms, made in the millinery prison shops, were an ill-fitting polyester blend that lacked the heavy starch feel and faded appearance that came only after many dozens of washings in a prison laundry.

Catcalls and laughter followed us down the main hallway of the prison when we made our appearance and continued as we spent the day shadowing veteran officers as they worked the cell runs, rec yards, and mess hall, and pulled inmates one at a time out of the Ad Seg cells for showers and solitary recreation. The younger female trainees bore the brunt of this verbal abuse, hearing graphic descriptions, shouted from all sides, of what inmates who had not touched a woman for twenty years wanted to do with them. Our visit was intended, among other things, to be an introduction to the reality of prison life, and it served its purpose. Several candidates resigned from the academy the following week, saving the state of Texas the further time and expense of having them quit on their first day on the job.

Although the Huntsville Unit does not house maximum-security inmates and is not considered a particularly dangerous unit to work, we were nervous as we waited for our bus to the Walls; our tour would include a visit to the Death House. I had seen an execution chamber before, at Angola State Prison in Louisiana, while attending a criminology conference in New Orleans, but my visit was during a hiatus in executions, and the cell where the condemned man spends his last hours and the execution gurney itself were dusty and bare. Sister Helen Prejean's book *Dead Man Walking* and the subsequent movie were centered at the Angola Death House. My memories of the death chamber there were somehow removed from reality. In Texas in 2006, executions were taking place at the rate of two or more a month, and I anticipated a scene that would be entirely different.

Our bus, normally used to transport inmates, arrived about 7:30 A.M., and as we boarded, the odor of the portable toilet rose up to meet us. It was my first introduction to the raw, ugly odors that one encounters in prison:

intestinal gas, stale sweat, greasy hair, rotten teeth, and, on a bad day, the acrid coppery odor of blood coagulating on the concrete floor after a stabbing or particularly brutal fight. Childhood allergies had long left me with the habit of breathing through my mouth rather than my nose, and that behavior would serve me well in an environment where strip-searching two hundred naked, sweat-dripping inmates fresh off the recreation yard at the peak of a Texas summer and supervising convicts clearing a hopelessly clogged toilet were daily occurrences. I later discovered that the stink came home with us after each shift, embedded in our sweaty uniforms. I always stripped off my grays in the garage of my home before entering a scalding hot shower.

The Walls Unit derives its name from the massive red brick walls that date from the construction of the prison in 1849. The unit sits within two blocks of Sam Houston University, which houses the Correctional Management Institute of Texas and the George J. Beto Criminal Justice Center, named for a former penology professor and director of the TDCJ who made improvements in the Texas prison system between 1962 and 1972. Huntsville itself is a TDCJ company town, and at lunchtime dozens of officers may be seen dining at the country cafés and pizza joints near the county courthouse in the town square. The Walls Unit is also a prerelease facility where inmates from prisons around East Texas are transferred a few weeks prior to their release. At the Greyhound bus station, four blocks east of the courthouse, newly released or paroled ex-cons gather in the late afternoon waiting to catch a ride home, all carrying orange mesh bags holding personal property and many wearing castoff clothes donated to the prison by local charities or abandoned in the unit property room.

We exited the bus in the parking lot adjacent to the visitor's center facing the main entrance to the Walls and formed up in three rows. Sergeant Garcia, our training officer and an expert in hand-to-hand defensive tactics, gave us last-minute instructions about what to do, and what not to do, once we were inside the unit. We marched across the street and filed through the front door of the prison. Once inside we turned in our IDs at the visitor's control picket, just as family members are obliged to do when entering the prison for visitation, and were buzzed through the crash gate into the teeming body of the Walls.

To the uninitiated, the interior spaces of a prison are chaotic and confusing. There is a cacophony of sound: inmates yelling back and forth, cryptic sounds of officers' radios, multiple television stations, inmates on the yard playing cut-throat basketball, handball, and soccer, and men with huge shoulders and tattooed backs clanging weights. Crash gates slide open and shut with a heavy metallic whine. I was soon to learn that a veteran correctional officer, like a soldier in combat, begins to tune out all of this extraneous noise and listen on a deeper level for the important things: the sound of a fight down a cell run or in a fifty-man dormitory tank, or the call for all available officers to respond to an altercation or a suicide attempt.

The internal architecture of a prison appears, at first sight, to be a concrete maze. There are heavy steel crash gates that separate cell runs from mess halls, and kitchens from laundries. A main control picket, enclosed by thick walls and heavy glass, holds the keys that are issued to officers for security doors in their sector and the cans of pepper spray each officer carries. (The pepper spray canisters are weighed at the beginning of each shift as they are handed out and again at the end of the shift, when they are passed back into the control picket, to ensure that no "accidental" discharges have taken place.)

Older prisons, and that term describes most in the TDCJ system, are permeated by a deep grime that has built up over decades: the wide hallways are mopped daily and buffed occasionally, and many inmates keep their cells as clean as possible with the materials they have at hand, but the corners and stairways and communal shower rooms that are cleaned by inmate trustees are dark and glazed with dirt. Staph infections among inmates are common and render up putrid stinking wounds if not treated promptly. Most TDCJ units are not air-conditioned, and in the middle of a Texas summer they bake in a sodden heat, with inside temperatures exceeding one hundred degrees for weeks at a time. Inmates may purchase small, transparent, personal fans from the commissary but they do little except recirculate the hot air. Everyone suffers in the heat.

In maximum-security prisons like Eastham, inmates who are imputed by tattoos or other information to be affiliated with a Security Threat Group (STG) are also housed in Administrative Segregation. There are over a dozen of these groups officially recognized as STGs by the TDCJ: the Mexican Mafia, Texas Syndicate, Tango Blast, Latin Kings, and MS-13, along with other Latino gangs, and the Aryan Brotherhood, Skinheads, Peckerwoods, and other white supremacy groups. While Crips and Bloods are generally considered to be STGs they, unlike Hispanic gangs, are usually broken up into neighborhood "sets" both on the street and inside prison, and they do not join together to create problems in a unit. You can have a problem with the West Side Gangster Crips and be just fine with the 29th Street Bloods on the inside, but if you have an issue with a Latin King he'll be backed up by every other member of his gang. In Texas prisons, fights between black inmates are generally a personal one-on-one affair; warfare between the Barrio Azteca and the Hermano Pistolero Latino, on the other hand, is organized, disciplined, and often deadly.

Long-term occupants in Ad Seg include inmates convicted of child sexual molestation and child murder. On the Luther Unit in Navasota, I encountered a thirty-five-year-old white convict named Mr. Mays. He was invariably polite and undemanding, and always thanked me for giving him an extra carton of milk or serving of pancakes with peanut butter when I fed him breakfast at 3:30 A.M. Mr. Mays fell out of Dallas on two counts of aggravated child sexual assault in 2001, and his earliest parole date was 2045. (I wasn't supposed to know his crime or his sentence, but that information was easy to come by on the TDCJ website offender search tool.) Given his charges and his appearance, it was unlikely that he would ever see the free world again.

On the unit where Mr. Mays had previously been incarcerated, other inmates had discovered the nature of the charges that had bought him so much time. One day some of them caught him on the rec yard and carved the words "BABY RAPER" across his forehead from his hairline to his eyebrows with a steel shank. They rubbed black prison-made tattoo ink into the wound and left him bleeding and maimed, justifiably confident that fear for his life would keep him from identifying them.

Mr. Mays had several plastic surgeries at the TDCJ hospital in Galveston, but they did little to improve his appearance. He always wore the long-billed baseball cap most often seen on kitchen trustees, but when I pulled him out of his cell for a shower he had to leave the cap behind, and the black letters ripped across his forehead seemed to leap out from his pale white forehead. I showered Mr. Mays dozens of times while working at Luther, but it was always shocking to see the grotesque, indelible signature of his crime as I cuffed him up.

In the spring and summer of 2006 I spent many nights working alone in the sweat box that was the Luther Unit Ad Seg. The temperature at midnight remained above the century mark, and the inmates sprawled naked on the concrete floors of their tiny cells in a vain attempt to escape the heat. As I did the half-hour cell checks I dragged along behind me a large plastic ice cooler meant to hold the lunches and sodas of officers, throwing leftover ice on the nude bodies and talking to anyone who had the need and energy. Most people from the free world would find conditions in the Luther Seg to be, quite literally, hell on earth.

Inmates may be kept in Seg for weeks or months or years, but the citizens of death row are routinely held in isolation for over a decade as mandated and court-granted appeals grind on. The death row section on the TDCJ website notes that the average time a condemned prisoner spends on death row between conviction and execution is 10.26 years. The shortest stay was that of Joe Gonzales, who was put to death after 248 days in 1996, while the longest was endured by Excell White, who waited 8,854 days, or 24 years, to ride the needle in 1999. Condemned inmates are frequently described as "changed men" by family, friends, and prison officials by the time they are escorted to the execution chamber, and with good reason.

In a March 2009 article in the New Yorker entitled "Hellhole," surgeon and author Atul Gawande explores the persistent and corrosive mental damage done to prison inmates serving extended terms in solitary confinement. Gawande compares the resulting depression, despair, and irrational anger to what is known about the long-term effects of social and physical isolation suffered by prisoners of war, like Senator John McCain in North Viet Nam, or noncombatants like Associated Press correspondent Terry Anderson who spent seven years as a hostage of Hezbollah in Lebanon. In comparing the experiences of high-profile captives with those of prisoners in the isolation cells of federal and state prisons in this country, Gawande asserts that "whether in Walpole (maximum-security prison) or Beirut or Hanoi, all human beings experience isolation as torture." He further draws a parallel between the conditions of these prisoners and those "enemy combatants" held at Guantánamo Bay:

> Our willingness to discard these standards for American prisoners made it easy to discard the Geneva Conventions prohibiting similar treatment of foreign prisoners of war. . . . In much the same way that a previous generation of Americans countenanced legalized segregation, ours has countenanced legalized torture.

I was not yet aware of the horrors of Administrative Segregation or the daily routine of death row as I followed my cohort of trainee officers up a stairway to the second floor of the Walls for a general briefing by several veteran TDCJ detention officers.

Following the briefing we were split into smaller groups, and our tour through the steel-and-concrete maze began. My group explored cell runs and large holding areas where inmates with worn, gray, wool blankets pulled over their heads and shoulders lounged. In the inner courtyard of the unit, trustees worked in the flower beds and leisurely swept the concrete walkways. Their sideways glances and smiles marked us for what we were: another group of COs in training. We saw the old educational-complex building where an eleven-day siege that started in the third-story library in 1974 left two female hostages and two prisoners dead. In the dappled morning sunlight it all looked deceptively calm and peaceful.

After several hours of sightseeing we gathered in the ODR, the Officers' Dining Room, for lunch. It was bright and clean, and kitchen trustees brought our trays to the table. The food didn't look bad at first glance: misshapen TDCJ hotdogs processed on the Ellis Unit hog farm, beans, onions, winter greens, and iced tea. It didn't taste exactly like free-world chow, but it was edible. The ODR inmate cooks on some units are famous for turning basic TDCJ food into something a bit more toothsome for the officers, and both inmates and officers carry Louisiana pepper sauce to brighten up underseasoned meals.

On Juneteenth, celebrated as Black Independence Day in Texas, most units serve fatty ribs and barbecue brisket, while there are enchiladas for Cinco de Mayo, and turkey with dressing for Christmas and the Fourth of July. The mess hall at the Walls is also where the condemned man's last meal is prepared, with requests honored as long as they can be created from food at the unit. No lobster or mangos, no T-bone steak or fresh salmon. Comfort food like fried chicken is a favorite for last meals, along with tacos and chocolate cake. Sometimes those about to die eat it all and sometimes it is left untouched.

The final event of the day was the one we had all been waiting for: a walk through the Walls Death House. An officer who worked on the volunteer five-person "tie down" team, which escorts the condemned from a holding cell to the execution chamber and secures him or her on the gurney with leather straps, spoke to us about procedure and protocol: how the prisoner is driven in a prison van from death row to the Polunski Unit at Livingston, about forty minutes south of Huntsville, on the morning of the execution; how he or she is free to speak with family members on a telephone for most of the afternoon. The prison chaplain, who remains just outside the holding cell as a spiritual comfort, walks behind the condemned person across the hallway to the execution chamber and stands at the foot of the gurney.

My group left the meeting room and headed across the inner courtyard of the Walls. The Death House is a low compact building at the southeast corner of the prison, under a guard picket perched thirty feet above the ground. I remember seeing a young black female officer on the wall above us carrying an AR-15 assault rifle at port arms and wearing a padded TDCJ jacket. She seemed to be frowning slightly, as if we were invading her turf.

I had encountered death before—violent death as a young man in the jungles of Viet Nam and, years later, when my infant son died in my wife's arms three days after his birth. My father and mother were both gone, as were good friends who had succumbed to the diseases of middle and old age. For all of that, I had never been confronted with institutional death, where the penalty was meted out by a trained team of professionals on the payroll of the state.

My recollections of the Texas Death House have been distorted by time and emotion. I record them here as they remain in my memory.

We entered through a door on the south side of the building and walked into a short narrow hallway with a low ceiling. The small talk that had characterized the morning tour had ceased and we listened in silence as our guide walked ahead of us. We passed several small rooms on the left side of the hallway. In the second one I saw, laid out on a table against the wall, a neatly folded set of clean prison whites, and next to them a new pair of plastic shower slides. On top of the white uniform was a small towel and four small bars of bluish prison-made soap. An execution was scheduled for the next evening, and preparations were in place.

Dead man's clothes, dead man's soap.

At the end of the hallway on the left side was a room that held eight small cells and tables. Several of the cells were set up in the normal fashion, with mats, sheets, and blankets on the rack and a toilet in one corner. One cell contained a shower, and another was a violent cell, devoid of any furnishings, where the condemned would be placed if the stress of the final hours became too great. On one of the tables was a telephone.

Directly across the hallway from these holding cells was the execution chamber. It is a small room with green walls and a clean white floor, and a digital clock hanging on the wall to record the time of death. The centerpiece of the chamber is a hospital gurney bolted to the floor, with four sets of leather straps to secure the prisoner. The gurney was covered with a white sheet. I touched it and found a slightly rough finish.

On one wall are the separate rooms from which members of the victim's family and the prisoner's family witness the execution. On the opposite wall is a rectangular hole from which the intravenous lines carry three chemicals into the death chamber: a lethal dosage of the barbiturate sodium thio-pental, which is supposed to bring about near-instant sedation; the muscle relaxant pancuronium bromide, which collapses the prisoner's lungs and diaphragm; and finally potassium chloride, which stops the heart.

The chemicals begin to flow at a prearranged signal from the warden, who stands at the head of the gurney. The TDCJ website notes that the condemned is normally pronounced dead approximately seven minutes later. Several telephones are mounted on the wall, one a direct line to notify the warden if a last minute stay of execution has been granted.

On the evening following our visit, at approximately 6:00 P.M., Robert Neville Jr. would be escorted the few steps from his holding cell into the execution chamber to die. The TDCJ death row webpage notes that in life Neville was, at six feet tall and 140 pounds, a lanky blue-eyed redhead born in 1974 in Tarrant County, Texas. He worked as a laborer and had left school in the 11th grade. Eight months after being paroled in June 1997, after serving time for burglary of a motor vehicle, Neville and codefendant Michael Wayne Hall shot Amy Robinson, a nineteen-year-old white female, whom they knew from work, seven times with a .22 caliber pistol. Neville and Hall attempted to flee to Mexico but were apprehended at the border.

Neville's last words display a small measure of repentance for the grief he has caused:

Yes. Ms. Carolyn Barker and Tina, I would like to apologize to you all. To Amy's sister, and everybody else here. I love you all. I hope you can find it in yourselves to forgive me and I hope all of this here will kinda settle your pain and I hope the Lord will give you comfort and peace. And I just want you to know that I am very sorry for what I done. And if I see Amy on the other side, I will tell her how much you love and miss her and we will have a lot to talk about. Mom, Dad, and Charlotte—I am sorry for putting you through all this pain and stuff. (TDCJ death row webpage)

Neville's words mark a basic conflict in my own nature. If he had murdered my wife or sister or mother, would I want to hear his hope of meeting his victim in another life? Would I, like the angry God of the Old Testament, demand an eye for an eye, a life for a life? Or would I be content knowing that he would be locked away for the rest of his natural life?

Neville's codefendant remains on death row.

After a short question-and-answer session, we filed out of the Death House and returned to the administrative section of the Walls Unit across the inner courtyard, now cast in the shadows of the late winter afternoon.

For years I have remembered the cool, clean room with the gurney and the green walls and the white-faced clock on the wall.

Most of my colleagues professed to find our visit spooky but satisfying. A few offered up their preference for the Huntsville Unit after completing training, with the hope that they would eventually be allowed to volunteer for the execution team and participate in bringing final justice to the worst enemies of our state. We went single-file downstairs through the electronically controlled crash gate, picked up our ID badges, and walked out the front door of the Walls into the growing darkness, again forming up in ranks before boarding the bus for the ride back to Eastham.

Texas remains the state where the most executions are carried out because the death penalty is supported by the majority of its citizens. And our politicians, like politicians everywhere, are loath to support any reform that might endanger their reelection to local and state office. To my knowledge, none of our state senators or representatives has ever been voted out of office for taking an aggressive public stand against crime, and in these parts that means vocal and enthusiastic support for state-sanctioned execution. The majority view is that it is far better to risk depriving an innocent person of his or her life than to risk the possibility that a guilty man might escape a just punishment. This politically expedient fact is not lost on Governor Rick Perry, and it was certainly obvious to his predecessor, George W. Bush.

I never worked on death row, but in the years following my visit to the Death House, I met and spoke at length with over a dozen men convicted of murder, some serving time in TDCJ and some awaiting transport to prison in the Brazos County Sheriff's Office Detention Center. They had, for various reasons, been judged not worthy of receiving the death penalty and were instead exiled from society for part or all of their lives.

One was a meth-ravaged eighteen-year-old blond kid who fatally shot his sister's boyfriend five times; another, a standout basketball player at a local high school before graduating and discovering crack cocaine, had nearly decapitated, with a knife, the woman who was his dealer; a third, a middle-aged Houston attorney who murdered his law partner and his wife with a pistol after he found them in a naked embrace in his office, and subsequently shot away most of his lower jaw in a failed suicide attempt, would likely spend the rest of his life in a locked infirmary cell on the Luther Unit, too maimed to join the general prison population.

With few exceptions these killers came from a background of poverty, ignorance, and violence. They had fathers and sometimes mothers who were absent, either doing time, chasing dope, or running the streets. They were sometimes the youngest generation of extended criminal families, with hardcore offenders for brothers, uncles, cousins. Many were victims of severe physical, psychological, or sexual abuse as children, and some would immediately be identified in the free world as suffering from some diagnosable form of mental illness or mild retardation.

In my experience, none of them disputed the fact that they had taken the life of another human being, although many disputed the motives and circumstances of the crimes. Some were intelligent and entertaining to talk with, and some were just thugs who proudly wore the scars and prison tattoos of street gangs and a lifetime of incarceration. The one who haunts me the most is John Thuesen, a young Marine Corps veteran of the war in Iraq with startling blue eyes and close-cropped blond hair, who was attending a local community college on the GI Bill when he shot his former girlfriend and her brother to death after she broke up with him. He then called 911, and when the police arrived they found him kneeling over the dead woman attempting to give her CPR. John now lives on death row. In the eighteen months between his arrest and conviction, we spoke every night I was on duty at the jail, about PTSD and his experiences in Iraq, and his family and many other things. John never talked about his dead girlfriend and I never asked him.

Through five years of employment with various organizations in the Texas criminal justice system, I have confronted a few individuals whose crimes were so heinous that I would have been gratified, momentarily, to kill them with my own hands. My personal feelings about capital punishment have been tested. There are some criminals who must be locked away from society in perpetuity because they have proven themselves to have no respect for human life and welfare. Judicial execution, however, has no value as a deterrent. It represents a desire for revenge, and that is an emotion that we cannot afford to embrace.

We can see from the present course we are following that violence only begets more violence and killing only leads to more killing. It is possible to have justice without revenge and hate. The death penalty is not the answer.

—Loretta Filipov, whose husband, Alexander Filipov, was killed on September 11, 2001

Billy Budd and Capital Punishment
A Tale of Four Centuries

H. BRUCE FRANKLIN

At present there are only two classes of the community who yet favor
capital punishment and these are clergymen and prosecuting attorneys.
— New York State Assemblyman Galen Hitt, 1890

No work of literature probes more deeply into the guts of capital punishment than Herman Melville's *Billy Budd, Sailor.* Set in the last decade
of the eighteenth century, finished just before the author's death in the
last decade of the nineteenth century, this novella has continued to provoke fierce controversies about its meanings ever since it was discovered in
manuscript shortly after the First World War. Yet strangely enough, amid all
the competing interpretations of Captain Vere's decision to sentence Billy
Budd to death by public hanging, no previous writer seems to have noticed
that the issues of capital punishment itself, as well as its history, are central to the story.[1]

Why not? The answer to this question reveals strange features of the cultural history of capital punishment and highlights the profound relevance
of the story to twenty-first-century America.

Look at the first issue of *Cardozo Studies in Law and Literature*, published in
1989 and devoted entirely to *Billy Budd* because — in the words of law professor Richard H. Weisberg — this is "the text that has come to 'mean' Law
and Literature."[2] Yet even the ten essays that comprise this journal ignore
the fundamental issues raised by capital punishment. About the only exception comes from Weisberg's antagonist, Judge Richard A. Posner of the
U.S. Court of Appeals for the Seventh Circuit, who reviles those who "condemn Vere's conduct" as mere "liberals" who are "uncomfortable with authority, including military authority, and hate capital punishment." ("Most
literary critics are liberals," adds Posner, who styles himself a "new critic"
and who was later a prominent candidate for the U.S. Supreme Court.) According to Judge Posner, "we must not read modern compunctions about
capital punishment into a story written a century ago."[3]

Posner here expresses the historical myopia of late twentieth- and early
twenty-first-century American culture that sees itself as more enlightened and progressive than the late nineteenth century about capital pun-

ishment. Quite to the contrary, most late nineteenth-century Americans would likely be appalled and amazed by the state of capital punishment in contemporary America, which added sixty new federal crimes punishable by death (in the Crime Bill of 1994) and where two thirds of the citizens consistently support not only the death penalty but also clamor for executions to be broadcast on television.[4]

During the very years that Herman Melville was composing Billy Budd— 1886 to 1891—national and even international attention was focused on the century-long battle to abolish capital punishment in America, then reaching a strange climax in New York, the very state where he was living. Why had we overlooked something so obvious? Is it because we were ignorant of the history of capital punishment in the nineteenth century, including its profound influence on American culture?[5] Or had we become desensitized to the implications of the issue that were so manifest to nineteenth-century Americans? In any case, when we do contextualize Billy Budd within the American history of capital punishment and its bizarre outcome in New York during the years 1886 to 1891, the story transforms before our eyes.

If Billy Budd had been published in 1891, when Melville wrote "End of Book" on the last leaf of the manuscript, few readers at the time could have failed to understand that the debate then raging about capital punishment was central to the story, and to these readers the story's position in that debate would have appeared unequivocal and unambiguous. Indeed Billy Budd flows from—and within—that American movement against capital punishment. It dramatizes each of the crucial arguments and concepts of that movement. And it brings into vivid focus and contemporary relevance the key issues of the nineteenth-century debate: Which offenses, if any, should carry the death penalty? Does capital punishment serve as a deterrent to killing or as an exemplary model for killing? What are the effects of public executions? Is hanging a method of execution appropriate to a civilized society? Is an impulsive act of killing by an individual more—or less— reprehensible than the apparently calmly reasoned act of judicial killing? Is capital punishment essentially a manifestation of the power of the state? A ritual sacrifice? An instrument of class oppression? A key component of the culture of militarism? Participants on all sides of the debate seemed to agree on only one thing: that the most appalling period in the history of capital punishment within modern civilization was the reign of George III in England.

When the officers whom Captain Vere has handpicked for his drumhead court appear reluctant to convict Billy and sentence him to death, Vere forcefully reminds these subordinates that they owe their "allegiance" not to "Nature," their "hearts," or their "private conscience," but entirely to "the King" and his "imperial [conscience] formulated in the code under which alone we officially proceed." [6] The time is 1797, the king is George III, and the code to which Vere refers was known in the nineteenth century as the "Bloody Code."

During the reigns of the Tudors and Stuarts, fifty crimes had carried the death penalty, and more were slowly added. The most spectacular increase then came during the reign of George III, when sixty offenses were appended to the death penalty statutes.[7] By the last third of the nineteenth century, George III's Bloody Code had been universally repudiated and condemned, both in England and America.[8] As the battle against capital punishment raged while Melville was composing Billy Budd, partisans on both sides agreed that eliminating most of the code's capital offenses constituted one of the century's notable achievements in human progress. Not surprisingly, opponents of the death penalty cited the Georgian code as barbaric and anachronistic, even for the eighteenth century. For example, a widely reprinted 1889 article referred to "Georgian justice" as "a scandal to the rest of the civilized world," and agreed with Mirabeau's verdict at the time that "the English nation is the most merciless of any that I have heard or read of."[9] Even advocates of capital punishment celebrated the progress away from the Bloody Code, pointing out that by the early 1880s capital offenses in England had been reduced to "three classes" of deliberate murder, none of which included "crimes committed under circumstances of great excitement, sudden passion, or provocation."[10] Articles favoring capital punishment published during the late 1880s argued that the death penalty should certainly "be restricted to murder committed with malice prepense, by a sane person, in resisting arrest, or in the commission of another felony."[11] Billy Budd, remember, is charged not with murder but with striking "his superior in grade"; "apart from its effect the blow itself is," as Captain Vere states, "a capital crime" under the Articles of War of the Georgian code (272). Nobody on the ship believes the sailor acted with premeditation or malicious—much less murderous—intent, but Vere instructs the court that they must disregard all questions of intent (274).

In the midst of America's revolution against George III's imperial regime, there were some attempts to abolish capital punishment for all crimes except murder and treason. For example, Thomas Jefferson and four other Virginia legislators drafted such a law in early 1777, but it was not considered until 1785, when it was defeated by a one-vote margin in the state's House of Delegates.[12]

The most influential legal act came in 1794, three years before the action of Billy Budd, when the state of Pennsylvania became the first to codify into law the innovative concept of "degrees" of murder. Capital punishment was restricted to murder in the "first degree," defined as "wilful, deliberate and premeditated killing."[13] Two years later, New York reduced the number of capital crimes from thirteen to two—murder and treason—while also abolishing whipping as a punishment for any crime.[14] In the ensuing decades, state after state in the North and West followed the lead of Pennsylvania and New York in reducing capital offenses, and the movement for complete abolition of the death penalty steadily gained momentum into the 1850s. Maine in 1837 and New Hampshire in 1849 passed moratoria on all executions; Massachusetts limited the death penalty to first-degree murder in 1852; and one house of the state legislature voted to abolish the death penalty in Ohio (1850), Iowa (1851), and Connecticut (1853). Capital punishment was abolished altogether in Michigan (1846), Rhode Island (1852), and Wisconsin (1853).[15]

Among the champions of the surging campaign for abolition were many of the republic's cultural leaders, such as Henry Wadsworth Longfellow, John Greenleaf Whittier, John Quincy Adams, Lydia Maria Child, Theodore Parker, Margaret Fuller, and Henry Ward Beecher. The two great newspapers of New York City were for decades edited by prominent opponents of capital punishment, William Cullen Bryant of the New York Evening Post (1829–1878) and Horace Greeley of the New York Tribune (1841–1872).[16]

In the slave South, however, George III's Bloody Code had its distinctively American counterpart in the myriad of offenses defined as capital if committed by slaves. Capital punishment as an instrument of class oppression has never been demonstrated more blatantly, an argument made frequently in the anti–death-penalty literature. For example, in 1844 Universalist minister Charles Spear of Massachusetts cited the laws of the South as examples of the class content of capital punishment and reasons for its total abolition. Georgia had a mandatory death sentence for the following crimes: "Rape on a free white female, if a slave. Assaulting free white female with intent to murder, if a slave. Burglary or arson of any description contained in penal code of state, if a slave. Murder of a slave or free person of color, if a slave."[17] On the other hand, a white man in Georgia convicted of raping a slave woman or free woman of color faced a fine and/or imprisonment, at the discretion of the court.[18] In Alabama, Spear noted, it was not a capital crime to kill a black, but there was a mandatory death penalty for these offenses: "Murder, or attempt to kill any white person. Rape, or attempt to commit, if a slave, free negro or mulatto. Insurrection or rebellion against the white inhabitants. Burglary. Arson. Accessary [sic] to any of the above crimes." Missouri provided that any "negro, mulatto, or free colored person" committing rape would be executed by means of castration. Virginia had seventy-one crimes that were capital offenses for slaves. These included burglary, forgery, stealing a horse or harboring a horse thief, "wilfully setting fire to any stack or cock of wheat," theft of money or goods "of the value of four dollars," and, of course, raping or attempting to rape a white woman.[19] In 1848, Virginia passed a new statute requiring the death penalty for blacks for any offense that was punishable by three or more years imprisonment if committed by whites.[20]

The political content of capital punishment was also manifest in the legal codes that supported the institution of slavery. Pre–Civil War North Carolina had a mandatory sentence of death for any person guilty of concealing a slave with intent to free him[21] or for "circulating seditious publications among slaves, second offence."[22] Georgia imposed a mandatory death penalty for "circulating insurrectionary papers, either by a white, a negro, mustizzo, or free person."[23] Missouri law required mandatory execution for "exciting insurrection among slaves, free blacks, or mulattoes." Louisiana had a mandatory death penalty for anyone guilty of "writings of a seditious nature."[24]

From the mid-1850s through the Civil War, the movement to abolish the death penalty was overwhelmed by the movement against slavery.[25] When revived in the late 1860s, the anti–capital-punishment movement often seemed to its adherents to be part of inexorable global progress. By 1889 they could cite the abolition of the death penalty, by law or in practice, in Holland, Finland, Belgium, Prussia, Portugal, Tuscany, and Rumania.[26] To maximize shock value, they often focused on what many regarded as the most barbaric aspects of capital punishment as practiced: public execution and hanging.

Public execution and hanging, which are integral to Captain Vere's arguments for the necessity of killing Billy Budd, played a complex role in the debates of the last third of the nineteenth century. As abolitionists emphasized the grotesque and sordid spectacles of public hangings, they often played into the hands of retentionists, who saw that their best strategy for preserving the death penalty lay in cleansing it of the features almost universally condemned as loathsome remnants of a savage past.[27]

Between 1833 and 1849 fifteen states abolished public executions,[28] and the movement to banish the practice altogether was unstoppable in the postwar decades. From the late 1860s through the end of the century, hanging became the focal point of abolitionist and reformist arguments, and New York became the pivotal battleground. In his 1889 Putnam's article "The Gallows in America," Edmund Clarence Stedman (who was to become Melville's most enthusiastic patron during the period of Billy Budd's composition) dwells on the horrors of hanging to convince readers, especially in New York, to abolish the death penalty entirely. "Let the Empire State" join Michigan in ending capital punishment, Stedman declares, "and within ten years thereafter the gallows will be banished from every State in the Union."[29] Although he acknowledges that through "new scientific knowledge" some "painless mode of killing may be discovered—as by an electric shock," the movement against the death penalty is growing "so rapidly that there is small likelihood of its modification by new forms."[30] Stedman did not foresee how one of the most bizarre chapters in nineteenth-century American technological and cultural history—the "Battle of the Currents"—would help preserve capital punishment in New York and much of the nation all the way into the twenty-first century.

In the early 1880s Thomas Alva Edison and his Edison Corporation dominated the emerging electrification of urban America, especially in the New York City area. Edison, however, was obsessively committed to direct current (DC), which could not be economically transmitted more than a mile or two. In 1886 George Westinghouse's newly incorporated Westinghouse Electrical and Manufacturing Company placed into operation the first alternating current (AC) generating station, and demonstrated that AC could be transmitted over great distances. Meanwhile, Civil War–hero General Newton Curtis, elected to the New York Assembly in 1884, had launched a major campaign to abolish the death penalty in New York.[31] In 1885 Governor David Hill, anxious to preserve capital punishment while recognizing the prevalent revulsion against hanging as a "remnant of the dark ages," asked the legislature to create a commission to explore ways of carrying out the death penalty "in a less barbarous manner."[32]

In early 1887 Westinghouse moved into direct competition with Edison in New York City, touching off the Battle of the Currents.[33] Edison's strategy was to convince the public that AC was too dangerous for domestic use. So in 1887 he began a gruesome publicity campaign, inviting reporters, particularly from the New York newspapers, to witness theatrically staged electrocutions of cats, dogs, calves, and horses. Edison even managed to get the members of the New York State Commission to Investigate and Report the Most Humane and Practical Method of Carrying into Effect the Sentence of Death to attend his AC electrocution of neighborhood dogs.[34] Edison's main operative was one Harold P. Brown, who pretended to be acting independently, even after the New York Sun printed a series of forty-five letters between Brown and Edison, as well as between Brown and the companies covertly acting for Edison.[35] In 1888, Brown staged at Columbia College's School of Mines an especially cruel execution of what the New York Herald called "a large mongrel Newfoundland"; the show produced sensational accounts in the New York dailies and even a ballad.[36] Meanwhile, Brown was secretly conspiring with New York State prison authorities to purchase three Westinghouse AC generators and set them up in prisons to be wired to a proposed "electric chair."[37] The object was to arrange for human executions to be conducted by electrocution with AC, thus terrorizing the population about the lethal menace posed by Westinghouse's technology. From now on, according to Edison and his cohort, condemned felons would not be hanged but "Westinghoused."[38] Brown concluded a self-serving 1889 article in the North American Review with these words: "Strenuous efforts have been made to befog the public mind in order to prevent the use of the alternating current for the death-penalty, lest the public should learn its deadly nature and demand that the Legislature banish it from streets and buildings, thus ending the terrible, needless slaughter of unoffending men."[39]

New York City's newspapers charged into the Battle of the Currents. The New York Evening Post, no longer edited by that ardent foe of capital punishment, William Cullen Bryant, favored electrocution. The New York Tribune and New York Times were both zealous allies of Edison and defenders of capital punishment.[40] The Times in 1887 editorialized in favor of replacing hanging—which it characterized as sheer "barbarity"—with electrocution, which it envisioned as so quick and deadly as to be a form of "euthanasia"; it urged "the State of New York to be the first community to substitute a civilized for a barbarous method of inflicting capital punishment, and to set an example which is sure of being followed throughout the world."[41] When the New York State Commission in January 1888 reported, to no one's surprise, in favor of electrocution, the Tribune and Times presented the recommendation as major and welcome news. Besides their news coverage, both papers had days of lengthy editorials extolling electrocution. The Tribune declared that electrocution would be "a step toward humanity and decency."[42] In another editorial the same day, the Tribune evoked the almost universal repugnance against hanging: "The American people are practically unanimous in desiring that the present cruel and clumsy method of execution shall be relegated among the other barbarisms of punishment."[43] Both newspapers also approved of the recommendation that all executions be held within the walls of a prison, with the number of witnesses—all to be selected by prison authorities—limited to twelve. The only caveats, expressed by both papers, had to do with the commission's recommendations that the executed person's body should "in no case be delivered to any relative or other person whatsoever" and that any newspaper publishing an account of an execution other than "the statement of the fact that such convict was on the day in question duly executed according to law at the prison" would be "guilty of a misdemeanor."[44] The *Times* commended the intent of these prohibitions, which was to keep the executed criminal from becoming "a hero" of the masses and prevent "such a display of sympathy with crime as was furnished by the funeral of the Anarchists in Chicago." The editorialist argued, however, that to "make a mystery" of an execution such as that of "the Chicago Anarchists" would be "proceeding too much in the line of a despotic Government to be acceptable here."[45]

During the next two and a half years New York was embroiled in legal suits and political maneuvering that brought national and worldwide attention to its struggles with the issue of capital punishment. Lawyers for William Kemmler, the intended victim of the first electrocution, went to court to prevent this "cruel and unusual punishment." Edison merged his company into General Electric, partly to fight the legal suits filed by Westinghouse to keep its equipment from being used to electrocute Kemmler. General Curtis submitted his second assembly bill to outlaw capital punishment. The *Tribune* and the *Times* now began to impugn General Curtis's motives, implying that he was acting merely as a bribed agent of Westinghouse (charges refuted by his efforts years later as a member of Congress to abolish the death penalty for the whole nation). The personal attacks on Curtis got fiercer when his bill to abolish capital punishment was passed by the New York Assembly on May 1, 1890, by a vote of seventy-four to twenty-nine.[46]

The bill was not, however, approved by the state senate. All the recommendations of the state commission—including criminal penalties for publishing descriptions of executions—now became the unchallenged law of New York. So on August 6, 1890, William Kemmler became the first victim of the modern, civilized form of execution by electricity.

The spectacle was hardly the "euthanasia" earlier promised by the *Times*. Indeed the front page of the *Times*, the following day, violated the very law that had mandated Kemmler's electrocution by publishing a description of "the most revolting circumstances" that "placed to the discredit of the State of New York an execution that was a disgrace to civilization." The witnesses, "men eminent in science and in medicine," were so physically "nauseated" by the gory spectacle that "they almost unanimously say that this single experiment warrants the prompt repeal of the law." The article ended by noting that the witnesses all acted "as though they felt that they had taken part in a scene that would be told to the world as a public shame, as a legal crime."[47]

One of the attending physicians selected to conduct the autopsy on Kemmler published in October 1890 an impassioned appeal to abolish the death penalty, opening with an evocation of the "world-wide interest" in the execution: "When the harrowing details of the death chamber were tingled along the telegraph wires of the country, and their impulses were throbbed through the cable, the entire civilized world viewed the scene with astonished horror."[48] In an influential volume linking capital punishment to war, published in January 1891, Andrew Palm noted that the Kemmler execution was "denounced as horrible, brutal, atrocious, a disgrace to humanity, etc. English editors were just as much shocked as their brethren on this side of the Atlantic, one London daily declaring that Kemmler's execution sent a thrill of horror around the globe."[49]

It was in this context that Melville composed *Billy Budd*, which he began in 1886 and concluded in April 1891, eight months after Kemmler's execution. Although Melville's contemporaries, who almost universally abhorred hanging, might have shuddered at Captain Vere's instantaneous decision that Billy "must hang" (232), the story is carefully crafted to keep the *means* of execution from being a significant issue.

When he is hanged, Billy evinces none of the hideous agonies familiar to the crowds at public hangings and described with sickening detail in countless nineteenth-century essays and books. There is not even the almost invariable muscular spasm or involuntary ejaculation. Chapter 26, obtrusively inserted between Billy's transcendent death and the sailors' reaction, is devoted to a discussion of this perfect lack of motion. The purser suggests that this "singularity" must be attributed to Billy's "will power." In the surgeon's response we can hear a parody of the debate transpiring in Melville's New York about the most humane and scientific way to kill a person: "In a hanging scientifically conducted—and under special orders

I myself directed how Budd's was to be effected—any movement follow-ing the complete suspension and originating in the body suspended, such movement indicates mechanical spasm in the muscular system. Then the absence of that is no more attributable to will power, as you call it, than to horsepower" (321–22). Admitting to the purser that this "muscular spasm" is almost "invariable," the surgeon acknowledges that "I do not, with my present knowledge, pretend to account" for its absence: "Even should we assume the hypothesis that at the first touch of the halyards the action of Budd's heart, intensified by extraordinary emotion at its climax, abruptly stopped—much like a watch when in carelessly winding it up you strain at the finish, thus snapping the chain—even under that hypothesis how account for the phenomenon that followed?" (323).

The purser then asks, "Was the man's death effected by the halter, or was it a species of euthanasia?" "Euthanasia," replies the surgeon, has dubious "authenticity as a scientific term" (324). Though it may outwardly resemble the "euthanasia" the New York Times had erroneously predicted for electro-cution, Billy's death by hanging clearly transcends not only the surgeon's scientific understanding but also the debate about the modalities of capi-tal punishment swirling around the composition of the story. More pro-foundly relevant to Billy Budd are the terms of the debate about the funda-mental issue of capital punishment itself. Indeed, the essence of the issue structures the story.

We witness two killings aboard HMS Bellipotent. One comes from the im-pulsive, involuntary fatal blow Billy Budd strikes to the forehead of Clag-gart. The blow is partly in response to Captain Vere's exhortation to the stammering Billy, "Defend yourself!" Vere recognizes that Claggart has been "struck dead by an angel of God," and he and his drumhead court all acknowledge that Billy acted without malice, forethought, or any murder-ous intent. The other killing is carried out under cover of law, after reasoned argumentation, and by the state acting through the agency of Captain Vere and his officers.

Which of these two acts constitutes murder? Budd is not even accused of murder. But what about Vere's act? Could it fall under the 1794 Pennsyl-vania definition of murder in the "first degree," that is, "wilful, deliberate and premeditated killing"?

And this is precisely how the argument against capital punishment was framed during the years Melville was writing. The fact that hangings were conducted by the state under cover of law did not, to opponents of the death penalty, absolve them from being murders. Indeed the terms widely used for these killings were "legal murders," "legal killing," and "murder by law."[50] The following commentaries, published in 1890, could apply directly to the two killings on the *Bellipotent*:

> [W]hen a criminal is judged, all the extenuating circumstances shall be taken into consideration. Were this rule observed, the victim of the law would seldom appear in so bad a light as the government that passed the sentence. Let me illustrate the thought: a man commits a murder: the government in turn sentences the man to death. Here we have two parties who have presumed to take a human life. . . . [T]he question now arises, upon the shoulders of which party rests the greatest guilt? A most solemn thought. There are many extenuating circumstances in the first instance, but what can be said in justification of the government?[51]

> [C]apital punishment administered in any form is essentially a relic of a barbarous age. . . . [T]he State always acts with coolness and deliberation, while ninety per cent. of her children slay their fellowmen in the frenzy of passion.[52]

Although Captain Vere has already decided, before he convenes his drumhead court, that Billy "must hang," the three officers he handpicks are quite reluctant to convict and sentence the handsome sailor. In the trial, during which Vere acts as sole witness, prosecutor, and, ultimately, commander of the jury, he finds it necessary to overwhelm his three subordinates with a deluge of arguments. One is precisely that they must "let not warm hearts betray heads that should be cool" (270).[53]

Vere makes his first argument while still in his role of witness (though later he tells the officers, "Hitherto I have been but the witness, little more" [265]): "Quite aside from any conceivable motive actuating the master-at-arms, and irrespective of the provocation to the blow, a martial court must needs in the present case confine its attention to the blow's consequence, which consequence justly is to be deemed not otherwise than as the striker's deed" (256). By arguing, especially in such legalistic phraseology, that his court is *not* to consider extenuating circumstances or motive, Vere is underlining for readers in 1891 the fundamental injustice of the proceedings. The three officers, in fact, are disturbed by this manifestation of "a prejudgment on the speaker's part" (258). Later Vere reiterates, "Budd's intent or non-intent is nothing to the purpose" (274).

As discussed earlier, Vere's extended argument that the officers owe their allegiance not to "Nature," their "hearts," or their "private conscience," but entirely to King George III and his "code under which alone we officially proceed" would to any late nineteenth-century audience be an emphatic reminder of the barbaric Bloody Code for which Vere is acting as agent. Vere insists, in fact, that he and his officers must act *merely* as agents and instruments of that law: "For the law and the rigor of it, we are not responsible. Our vowed responsibility is in this: That however pitilessly that law may operate in any instances, we nevertheless adhere to it and administer it" (270). Each of Vere's arguments defends one or more of the most egregious features of the Georgian code. To late nineteenth-century readers, this would serve as a conspicuous reminder of the horrors of Georgian justice from which nine decades of reform had liberated both the United States and Britain.

Immediately after insisting that his officers may not consider "Budd's intent or non-intent," Vere claims that they are taking too much time (a blatantly specious argument, especially in light of the time later spent in the execution and burial rituals): "Strangely we prolong proceedings that should be summary—the enemy may be sighted and an engagement result. We must do; and one of two things must we do—condemn or let go" (275). In response, the sailing master, the one trial officer who had not previously spoken, asks "falteringly," "can we not convict and yet mitigate the penalty?" (275).

Insisting that this would not be "lawful," Vere highlights for readers one of the most universally condemned aspects of the code under which he operates: *mandatory* death penalties. Opponents of capital punishment of course focused on the inflexible brutality and cruelty thus codified into law and passing for justice. Joining them, however, were some of the most ardent defenders of capital punishment, including many judges and district attorneys, who were continually encountering juries that—like the sailing master—would rather acquit than consign a criminal to death. In the period from 1860 to 1895, eighteen states shifted from mandatory to discretionary capital punishment, with legislators usually citing the reluctance of juries to participate in capital punishment.[54]

At this point in the trial, Vere abruptly shifts from all his previous arguments—which were based on the premise that he and his drumhead court *must*, under law, sentence Billy to death—to the argument that finally convinces his officers: they *should* hang Billy in a public execution. "His closing appeal," the narrator informs us, is not to their reason but "to their *instinct* as sea officers" (280; italics mine), and this is what makes it so convincing—at least to them.

This appeal is based solely on the doctrine of deterrence, the main argument preserving capital punishment throughout the nineteenth century and ever since. By the late 1880s, however, vast amounts of statistical and other evidence had demonstrated that there is little if any reasonable basis for the belief that capital punishment deters any of the crimes for which it is imposed. Nevertheless, the defenders of capital punishment, like Vere, tended more and more to abandon the argument that it was just, fair, appropriate, or ordained by God, and more and more to rely on belief in its value as a deterrent to crime. They appealed not so much to evidence as to the fear of violent crime widespread among the privileged and affluent classes, a fear which they of course encouraged.[55]

Like the typical nineteenth-century defender of capital punishment, Vere appeals to the fear of the fellow members of his privileged class on the *Bellipotent*, in other words to "their instinct as sea officers." There is, however, one fundamental difference between the deterrence argument familiar to nineteenth-century readers and Vere's decisive argument. The customary argument was (and is) that capital punishment deters the particular crime by making an example of the criminal. Vere's argument—far more cynical—is that hanging Billy Budd before the crew will intimidate them and reinforce the "arbitrary discipline" exerted over them by the officers, while *not* hanging him would encourage mutiny. Mutiny is the crime of which Claggart had falsely accused Billy and of which Vere and his officers know Billy is innocent. But, argues Vere, "the people," because they "have not that kind of intelligent responsiveness that might qualify them to comprehend and discriminate," will believe that Billy has committed "a flagrant act of mutiny" and will therefore emulate him if he is not appropriately punished for it. For readers in 1891, Vere's argument, so persuasive to his subordinate officers, would seem so obviously specious and illogical as to appear virtually a parody of the usual defense of capital punishment for the sake of deterrence:

Gentlemen, were that clearly lawful for us under the circumstances, consider the consequences of such clemency. The people [the ship's company] have native sense; most of them are familiar with our naval usage and tradition; and how would they take it? Even could you explain to them—which our official position forbids—they, long molded by arbitrary discipline, have not that kind of intelligent responsiveness that might qualify them to comprehend and discriminate. No, to the people the foretopman's deed, however it be worded in the announcement, will be plain homicide committed in a flagrant act of mutiny. What penalty for that should follow, they know. But it does not follow. *Why?* they will ruminate. You know what sailors are. Will they revert to the recent outbreak at the Nore? Ay. They know the well-founded alarm — the panic it struck throughout England. Your clement sentence they would account pusillanimous. They would think that we flinch, that we are afraid of them — afraid of practicing a lawful rigor singularly demanded at this juncture, lest it should provoke new troubles. What shame to us such a conjecture on their part, and how deadly to discipline. (276–78)

In other words, because "we" are afraid of "the people," "we" have to hang Budd because otherwise "they" would think "we" are afraid of "them"!

One influential article published in January 1890, entitled "The Crime of Capital Punishment," directly attacks Vere's final and most effective argument — "legal killing . . . is done merely as a warning to evil-doers and for the safety of society" — as "an afterthought, an explanation which the growing humane sentiment of *the people* is forcing from the barbarians who defend and practise murder by law."[56]

The same article goes on to focus on the role of the clergy in the actual administration of capital punishment:

At every scaffold there is a strange and significant union of Church and State. The State is there in the person of the hangman. The Church is there in the person of the priest or minister. It is the old familiar scene of the State doing deeds of violence and blood in the name of law and order, and with the sanction and concurrence of religion.[57]

Melville seems to be extrapolating from this passage, or many similar ones of the period, in his commentary on the chaplain's inability to lift "a finger to avert the doom of such a martyr to martial discipline" and on his overall role, which links the execution to the essential purpose of the *Bellipotent*:

Bluntly put, a chaplain is the minister of the Prince of Peace serving in the host of the God of War — Mars. As such, he is as incongruous as a musket would be on the altar at Christmas. Why, then, is he there? Because he indirectly subserves the purpose attested by the cannon; because too he lends the sanction of the religion of the meek to that which practically is the abrogation of everything but brute Force. (312)

The response of the crew to Billy's execution is a direct refutation of Vere's deterrence argument, in which he suggested to his officers that the threat of imminent mutiny was smoldering on the ship. Although the story is labeled an "Inside Narrative," it reveals not the faintest hint of any such possibility prior to Billy's death. Discipline is breached only after Billy's hanging and in response to it, in the midst of the rituals of the public execution and subsequent burial (326, 330, 331).

The true significance of the killing of Billy Budd comes out in these scenes. Like many of the arguments raised against the death penalty between the 1790s and the 1890s, Billy Budd strips away the illusions of justice and deterrence to reveal the essence of capital punishment: human sacrifice, a ritual of power in which the state and the ruling class demonstrate, sanctify, and celebrate their ultimate power—the power of life and death—over the classes they rule.

By the last third of the nineteenth century, public execution had been thoroughly discredited and legally abandoned in England as well as in most of the United States. Nevertheless, crowds continued to find ways to view hangings that were officially closed to the public. When, for example, a "private" execution took place at the Tombs in New York City, "the neighboring buildings are black with people, seeking to look down over the prison walls and witness the death agonies of the poor wretch."[58] Such scenes were a main target of the stipulation in the New York electrocution law that executions must take place inside the walls of a prison. One principal argument against public executions had been their effects on the "mobs" that came to watch. This reasoning is ironically echoed in the strange "murmur" that runs through the sailors forced to witness their shipmate's execution: "it seemed to indicate some capricious revulsion of thought or feeling such as mobs ashore are liable to, in the present instance possibly implying a sullen revocation on the men's part of their involuntary echoing of Billy's benediction" (326).

Another argument against public execution was that, contrary to its alleged deterrent effect, it tended to transform the criminal into both a victim and a "hero."[59] The sailors, pointedly refuting Vere's prediction about them, "instinctively felt that Billy was a sort of man as incapable of mutiny as of wilful murder." To them he becomes more than a hero. The very spar from which he was hanged is metamorphosed into the object of their veneration: "To them a chip of it was as a piece of the Cross" (345–46).[60]

Billy Budd is not, of course, a mere treatise against capital punishment. Melville is using contemporaneous awareness about the issue to explore the larger ethical, philosophic, and political questions it so dramatically focuses. Undoubtedly New York Assemblyman Galen Hitt was overstating the case when he claimed in early 1890, "at present there are only two classes of the community who yet favor capital punishment and these are clergymen and prosecuting attorneys."[61] Nevertheless, Melville could safely assume that almost all potential readers in 1891 would regard public execution and hanging as relics of a barbarous past, would be sensitized to the larger issues surrounding capital punishment, and would already either oppose the death penalty outright or consider it warranted only for first-degree murder and treason. Even the most ardent proponents of the death penalty in late nineteenth-century America would be embarrassed by positions such as these: "Vere justifiably condemns Billy to death" (Peter Shaw); Billy Budd is a "murderer and a cause of his own death" and Melville "is to be identified" with Captain Vere (Milton Stern); "the virtuous man, Captain Vere," must "punish the violence of absolute innocence"—that is, must kill Billy Budd—since "absolute, natural innocence" is "at war with the peace of the world and the true welfare of mankind" (Hannah Arendt).[62] Readers in 1891 would be far more likely to wonder, like the surgeon (235) and the narrator (236–37), whether Vere is insane.

There remains a question that by now must have occurred to most readers of this essay: Do not military circumstances, especially during war, demand the kind of martial law under which Vere proceeds (or claims to proceed[63])? Perhaps the most passionate and detailed refutation of this position was presented in chapter after chapter of a book published in 1850, bearing the ambiguously ominous title *White-Jacket or The World in a Man-of-War*, and written by a man who had himself served as a common seaman on a man-of-war—Herman Melville. Ascribing British naval law to a "barbarous feudal aristocracy" that had regained power in the Restoration and its sequel, Melville argued that in the Interregnum, "a period deemed so glorious to the British Navy, these Articles of War were unknown." Therefore, he reasoned, "such tyrannical ordinances are not indispensable—even during war—to the highest possible efficiency of a military marine." He pointed out that Admiral Nelson (lionized in *Billy Budd*) opposed corporal punishment and routinely reassigned "wholly ungovernable" seamen to an admiral who "held in abhorrence all corporal punishment," thereby winning the loyalty of these men. "The mutinous effects of government abuses in the Navy," according to Melville, "developed themselves at the great mutiny of the Nore." He summed up his view in these words:

Certainly the necessities of navies warrant a code for its government more stringent than the law that governs the land; but that code should conform to the spirit of the political institutions of the country that ordains it. It should not convert into slaves some of the citizens of a nation of freemen.

He then denounced the American Articles of War as "an importation from abroad, even from Britain, whose laws we Americans hurled off as tyrannical, and yet retained the most tyrannical of all." [64] Melville frequently consulted White-Jacket while composing Billy Budd on a writing box to which he had glued the motto: "Keep true to the dreams of thy youth." [65]

On another level, the relations between martial law and civil society had more disturbing implications for Melville in 1891 than in 1850. As he was writing Billy Budd, the rising tide of imperialism, with its corollary of militarism, was threatening the basic republican and democratic values expressed so passionately in White-Jacket. In 1850 he could plead for extension of the highest laws of the land to its ships at sea. But by 1891, as the nation was about to build its first large-scale standing navy to prepare for its imperial manifest destiny, Melville envisioned the governance of the warship becoming dominant over the laws of the land. [66] Like many of his contemporaries, he saw that the essence of capital punishment is the state's power over life and death, a power boundlessly expanded in war. He dramatized the deadly meaning of capital punishment for the eighteenth, nineteenth, twentieth, and twenty-first centuries in the kidnapping of Billy Budd from the peaceful merchant ship Rights of Man and his execution on the aptly named man-of-war Bellipotent. So Billy Budd's messages about capital punishment seem to become ever more timely in our epoch of permanent warfare.

Notes

1. The contesting interpretations of Billy Budd are analyzed by Geraldine Murphy in "The Politics of Reading Billy Budd," American Literary History 1 (Summer 1989): 361–82.

2. Richard H. Weisberg, "Editor's Preface," Cardozo Studies in Law and Literature 1 (Spring 1989). Weisberg has done a thoughtful analysis of legal issues in the story in "How Judges Speak: Some Lessons on Adjudication in Billy Budd, Sailor with an Ap

plication to Justice Rehnquist," *New York University Law Review* 57 (April 1982): 1–69 and *The Failure of the Word: The Protagonist as Lawyer in Modern Fiction* (New Haven: Yale Univ. Press, 1984), 131–59. See also Susan Weiner, *Law in Art: Melville's Major Fiction and Nineteenth-Century American Law* (New York: Peter Lang, 1992), 139–66.

3. Richard A. Posner, "Comment on Richard Weisberg's Interpretation of *Billy Budd*," *Cardozo Studies in Law and Literature* 1 (Spring 1989): 71–79. A rewritten version of this essay appears in Posner's *Law and Literature*, 3rd ed. (Cambridge: Harvard Univ. Press, 2009). Posner's reading of *Billy Budd* is demolished by Judge Juan Ramirez Jr. and Amy D. Ronner in "Voiceless Billy Budd: Melville's Tribute to the Sixth Amendment," *California Western Law Review* 41 (Fall 2004): 103–45.

4. Frank Newport, "In U.S., Two-Thirds Continue to Support Death Penalty; Little Change in Recent Years Despite International Opposition," http://www .gallup.com/poll/123638/in-u.s.-two-thirds-continue-support-death-penalty.aspx, and *"Two-thirds of Americans Support TV Executions,"* http://www.msnbc.msn.com/ id/4353934/ns/us_news-crime_and_courts.

5. In his groundbreaking article "The Movement to Abolish Capital Punishment in America, 1787–1861," *American Historical Review* 63 (October 1957), 23–46, David Brion Davis was shocked to discover that this movement is "seldom mentioned in the standard social and intellectual histories of the period" (23). This article did most of the spadework for more recent studies and offers a comprehensive exploration of the philosophic background for nineteenth-century American arguments opposing and defending capital punishment. Paul Christian Jones, *Against the Gallows: Antebellum American Writers and the Movement to Abolish Capital Punishment* (Iowa City: Univ. of Iowa Press, 2011), demonstrates that the movement against the death penalty in antebellum America was far more pervasive and culturally influential than previous scholars had imagined.

6. Herman Melville, *Billy Budd, Sailor (An Inside Narrative)*, ed. Harrison Hayford and Merton Sealts Jr. (Chicago: Univ. of Chicago Press, 1962), 267–72. Subsequent references to this text will be by parenthetical number.

7. David D. Cooper, *The Lesson of the Scaffold: The Public Execution Controversy in Victorian England* (Athens, Ohio: Ohio Univ. Press, 1974), 27. Cooper devotes a chapter to "The Bloody Code" of George III. See also Hugo Adam Bedau, *The Death Penalty in America*, 3rd ed. (New York: Oxford Univ. Press, 1982), 6. Curiously, the number of death penalty offenses added under George III is the same as the number added under President Bill Clinton by the Crime Bill of 1994.

8. See Cooper's volume for the history of the movement against capital punishment, public execution, and hanging in England.

9. B. Paul Neuman, "The Case against Capital Punishment," *Eclectic Magazine* 113

(October 1889), 518–25. (American reprint from British Fortnightly Review 52 [September 1889]: 322–33.)

10. Samuel Hand, "The Death Penalty," North American Review 133 (December 1881), 541–50; reprinted in Selected Articles on Capital Punishment, compiled by Lamar T. Beman (New York: H. W. Wilson Company, 1925), 178.

11. J. M. Buckley, "Capital Punishment," Forum 3 (June 1887), 381–91; as reprinted in Beman, 94. See also W. C. Maude, "Shall We Abolish the Death Penalty for Murder?" Month 65 (February 1889): 168–79.

12. Voices Against Death: American Opposition to Capital Punishment, 1787–1975, ed. Philip English Mackey (New York: Burt Franklin & Co., 1976), xiv.

13. Bedau, Death Penalty, 4; Sarah T. Dike, Capital Punishment in the United States (Hackensack, NJ: National Council on Crime and Delinquency, 1982), 7–8; Mackey, Voices, xvi.

14. Philip English Mackey, Hanging in the Balance: The Anti–Capital Punishment Movement in New York State, 1776–1861 (New York: Garland Publishing, 1982), 69; Mackey, Voices, xvi–xvii.

15. Mackey, Voices, xxvi–xxvii.

16. In 1850, Melville had purchased Greeley's Hints toward Reforms, in Lectures, Addresses, and Other Writings (New York, 1850) according to Merton Sealts Jr., Melville's Reading: A Check-List of Books Owned and Borrowed, offprinted from Harvard Library Bulletin (Cambridge, MA: Harvard Univ. Press, 1950), 130. This volume included Greeley's attack on the death penalty, "Death by Human Law" (301–10).

17. Charles Spear, Essays on the Punishment of Death, 10th ed. (London: self-published, 1845), 224. Originally published in 1844, this volume exerted a major influence on the movement against capital punishment in England as well as in America.

18. William J. Bowers, with Glenn L. Pierce and John F. McDevitt, Legal Homicide: Death as Punishment in America, 1864–1982 (Boston: Northeastern Univ. Press, 1984), 140.

19. Spear, Essays, 224–31.

20. Bowers, Legal Homicide, 140.

21. Bedau, Death Penalty, 8.

22. Spear, Essays, 223.

23. Ibid., 224.

24. Ibid., 225–26.

25. Louis P. Masur, Rites of Execution: Capital Punishment and the Transformation of American Culture, 1776–1865 (New York: Oxford Univ. Press, 1989), 160; Mackey, Voices, xxvii; Davis, "Movement," 45–46.

26. Neuman, "Case," 524.

27. In pre-1850 England, even those who were in favor of public executions admitted that they were "depraving," "ugly," "disgusting," "evil," and "brutalizing" (Cooper, 50).

28. Mackey, *Voices*, xx.

29. Edmund Clarence Stedman, "The Gallows in America," *Putnam's Magazine* 13 (February 1889), 225–35. Stedman met Melville in 1888. On October 20, 1888, Melville returned books lent to him by Stedman with a letter in which he wrote, "And your own book in many of its views has proved either corroborative or suggestive to me." In 1890 Stedman arranged a dinner for Melville at the Author's Club, one of the few recognitions of the author in his later years. Stedman's son Arthur became a good friend of Melville in the last two years of the writer's life and after Melville's death worked with Elizabeth Melville in reissuing four of his books. See Jay Leyda, *The Melville Log* (New York: Harcourt, Brace, 1951), I, xxxiii; II, 804–6.

30. Stedman, "Gallows," 230.

31. See entry for Newton Martin Curtis, *Dictionary of American Biography* (New York: Scribner, 1943).

32. Lawrence Meir Friedman, *Crime and Punishment in American History* (New York: Basic Books, 1993), 171.

33. For the Battle of the Currents, see Matthew Josephson, *Edison: A Biography* (New York: McGraw Hill, 1959), 344–50; somewhat different perspectives are offered in Robert Silverberg, *Light for the World: Edison and the Power Industry* (Princeton, NJ: D. Van Nostrand, 1967), 238–43; Ronald W. Clark, *Edison: The Man Who Made the Future* (New York: G. P. Putnam's Sons, 1977), 157–60; and Margaret Cheney, *Tesla: Man Out of Time* (Englewood Cliffs, NJ: Prentice-Hall, 1981), 41–49. A more detailed account is Thomas P. Hughes, "Harold P. Brown and the Executioner's Current: An Incident in the AC-DC Controversy," *Business History Review* 32 (Spring 1958): 143–65. For some of the Battle's cultural ramifications, including its role in Twain's *A Connecticut Yankee in King Arthur's Court*, see H. Bruce Franklin, *War Stars: The Superweapon and the American Imagination* (Amherst, MA: Univ. of Massachusetts Press, 2008): 54–77.

34. "Lightning for Murder," *New York Tribune*, January 17, 1888. The dogs and cats were pets gathered from the West Orange, New Jersey, neighborhood of Edison's laboratory by schoolboys who were paid twenty-five cents for each animal, leading to the decimation of the local animal population (Josephson, 347).

35. *New York Sun*, August 25, 1889.

36. Hughes, "Harold," 148–49.

37. For Brown's machinations and the covert operations of Edison's front organizations, see Hughes, "Harold," 156–58.

38. Josephson, *Edison*, 348; Cheney, *Tesla*, 45.

39. Harold P. Brown, "The New Instrument of Execution," *North American Review* (November 1889): 586–93. In the same issue, the editors ran "Dangers of Electric Lighting," an anti-AC article by Edison himself; in September, the *North American Review* had published another article favoring electrocution, "Capital Punishment by Electricity," by Elbridge T. Gerry, the chairman of the New York Commission who was secretly working with Brown.

40. After the death of editor Horace Greeley, the *New York Tribune* soon ceased being one of the foremost voices in favor of abolishing capital punishment.

41. "Capital Punishment," *New York Times*, December 17, 1887.

42. "Electricity or the Rope," *New York Tribune*, January 22, 1888.

43. "A New Agent of Death," *New York Tribune*, January 22, 1888.

44. "Death by Electricity" and "The Abolition of Hanging," *New York Times*, January 17, 1888; "Lightning for Murder," *New York Tribune*, January 17, 1888.

45. "The Abolition of Hanging"; the reference is to the workers' leaders hanged in 1887 for the 1886 Haymarket bombing. For a discussion of relations between the Haymarket hangings and *Billy Budd*, see Robert K. Wallace, "Billy Budd and the Haymarket Hangings," *American Literature* 47 (1975): 108–13.

46. "Gen. Curtis of St. Lawrence . . . ," *New York Times*, March 29, 1890; "Forty-eight Hours after the News . . . ," *New York Times*, May 2, 1890; "Is It the Dynamo Again? Rushing through the Bill to Abolish Capital Punishment," *New York Tribune*, May 2, 1890; "The Death Penalty," *New York Tribune*, May 3, 1890; "Capital Punishment," *New York Tribune*, May 6, 1890.

47. "Far Worse than Hanging; Kemmler's Death Proves an Awful Spectacle," *New York Times*, August 7, 1890.

48. Dr. George F. Shrady, "The Death Penalty," *Arena* 2 (October 1890), 513–23.

49. Andrew J. Palm, *The Death Penalty: A Consideration of the Objections to Capital Punishment, with a Chapter on War* (New York: G. P. Putnam's Sons, 1891), 100.

50. Davis, "Movement," 33. For an example published while Melville was writing *Billy Budd*, see Hugh O. Pentecost, "The Crime of Capital Punishment," *Arena* 1 (January 1890), 175–83.

51. Benjamin O. Flower, "Shall We Continue to Kill Our Fellowmen?" *Arena* 1 (January 1890), 243–45.

52. Benjamin O. Flower, "Thoughts on the Death Penalty," *Arena* 2 (October 1890), 636–38.

53. Note the echo of the narrator's comment about those possessed by "depravity according to nature": "Toward the accomplishment of an aim which in wantonness of atrocity would seem to partake of the insane, he will direct a cool judgment sagacious and sound" (133–34).

54. Mackey, *Voices*, xxx.

55. An 1889 article published in England and the United States gave statistics showing that the homicide rate had dropped in each state as well as each European country that had abolished capital punishment (Neuman, 524).

56. Pentecost, "Crime," 175–76, italics mine.

57. Pentecost, "Crime," 178.

58. James D. McCabe Jr., *Lights and Shadows of New York Life* (1872), as quoted in Friedman, 170.

59. "The Abolition of Hanging," *New York Times*, January 17, 1888.

60. Compare Stedman, "Gallows," 227: "Great and good men have been hanged, and it was said of one, that he 'made the gallows glorious, like the Cross'" (the internal quotation is from Emerson's eulogy of John Brown).

61. "Is It the Dynamo Again? Rushing through the Bill to Abolish Capital Punishment," *New York Tribune*, May 2, 1890.

62. Peter Shaw, *Recovering American Literature* (Chicago: Ivan R. Dee, 1994), 76; Milton Stern, *The Fine Hammered Steel of Herman Melville* (Urbana: Univ. of Illinois Press, 1957), 26–27; Hannah Arendt, *On Revolution* (New York: Viking, 1965), 79.

63. Vere is actually not following but violating the very code under which he claims to be operating. This violation was first pointed out by C. B. Ives, "*Billy Budd* and the Articles of War," *American Literature* 34 (1962): 31–39; it has been explored further by other critics, including Stanton Garner, "Fraud as Fact in Herman Melville's *Billy Budd*," *San Jose Review*, 4 (May 1978), 82–105, and, most thoroughly, Weisberg, *Failure*, 144–59. Vere's modern defenders (such as Posner, right on through the 2009 edition of his *Law and Literature*) take the position that Melville was simply unfamiliar with British naval law, an argument refuted by the detailed exploration of this law, based on thorough research, in *White-Jacket*; see Howard P. Vincent, *The Tailoring of Melville's White-Jacket* (Evanston, IL: Northwestern Univ. Press, 1970), 103–6.

64. The quotations are from *White-Jacket or The World in a Man-of-War*, eds. Harrison Hayford, Hershel Parker, and G. Thomas Tanselle (Evanston, IL: Northwestern Univ. Press, 1970), chapters 35, 36, 71.

65. Merlin Bowen, *The Long Encounter* (Chicago: Univ. of Chicago Press, 1960), 217.

66. For an analysis of *Billy Budd* in the context of the end-of-the-century movement toward imperialism, see H. Bruce Franklin, "From Empire to Empire: *Billy Budd, Sailor*," in *Herman Melville: Reassessments*, ed. Robert Lee (London: Vision Press, 1984; New York: Barnes and Noble, 1984): 199–216.

December 26, 1862 Chaska

Mankato, Minnesota

After the *massacre*, three hundred Sioux were tried
and condemned, but Lincoln made that thirty-eight.
They'd raped or murdered—one, Chaskadon, knifed
a pregnant woman, carved the baby out—
but Chaska got jail time; a woman testified
he'd saved her life.
     The gallows was a crowded
square built to hang, at once, *ten men each side.*
Singing in *doleful harmony,* hooded, bound,
they tried to take one another by the hand.
Sarah Wakefield, the woman Chaska saved,
read this in the papers, and saw that he'd been hanged.
Officials apologized for their mistake:
Chaskadon, not Chaska, was to have died.

  I am not ashamed to acknowledge that I cried.

August 23, 1927 Nicola Sacco

Charlestown, Massachusetts

Vanzetti said to quit the hunger strike,
but Sacco stalled: why fatten up before
you're killed? When he ate, he ate for strength to write
Be strong, dear Dante. Comfort your mother. Or
Ines, in every angle, this sad walled cell
and everywhere my gaze rests, I love you
much, then so much. On the twenty-third, the tall
doors of the Athenaeum's Reading Room
saw someone slip small fliers into all
the magazines: *their voices are gone, but will*
be remembered in gratitude and tears. Exalted
shall be these *working men and dreamers,* killed
by *Judges, Scholars, Governors* whose names
have gone down into everlasting shame.

May 3, 1946 Willie Francis
Saint Martinsville, Louisiana

They brought Louisiana's only chair
in a pick-up from Angola into Saint
Martinsville Parish, to the Court House, where
a fifteen-year-old colored boy had lain
on straw for months. Jailhouse on the second floor:
Death kindly took the elevator. Wires
were tossed from dynamo to window. Four
men setting up the chair passed flasks, dead tired
and innocent of amps. They called the priest,
and pulled the switch, and thought he'd die. He shook
and lurched and gasped—*You're not supposed to breathe!*
They shut it down, freed him from straps and hood.
Then Willie Francis stood up without help
and—miracle, miracle—walked back to his cell.

October 9, 2002 Aileen Wuornos
Starke, Florida

That makeup on Charlize Theron, and how
the murders piled up; the first in self-
defense, then all the rest. In theatres, crowds
of people streamed out: silent, shocked. Her death
warrant's online: Adobe Acrobat.
And Netflix has two documentaries
with interviews and trials, old photographs.
She says she's getting *all the tears out of me*
and stuff so I won't cry and jazz. To tough
it out as tough as I can. This used to be
called "dying game." In the end, that wasn't enough:
You sabotaged my ass, society!
Inhumane fucking living bastards and bitches
who used me for money, for books, and movies and shit.

Antigallows Activism in Antebellum American Literature

JOHN CYRIL BARTON

During the colonial period and in the early years of the Republic, "Hanging Day" and its practices—the execution sermon, the condemned's last words or dying confession, the public spectacle of the execution, and official narratives or popular broadsides documenting the event—were designed to promote religious order and good citizenship. However, the role and place of the death penalty changed dramatically in the decades following the Revolutionary War. In the late eighteenth and early nineteenth centuries, the Enlightenment ideal of a less severe, more proportional government and belief in the benevolence of human beings, coupled with a republican disdain for the so-called "right" of a state to take citizens' lives, led prominent thinkers from Benjamin Franklin, Thomas Jefferson, and James Madison to John Quincy Adams, Lydia Maria Child, Wendell Phillips, and Margaret Fuller to challenge the scope and legitimacy of capital punishment.

The reformation of penal codes and capital statutes had long been a concern in Pennsylvania (in 1794 the state abolished the death penalty for all offenses except first-degree murder), but the reform movement became a topic of national interest in the nineteenth century. In the 1820s, influential lawyer and politician Edward Livingston presented landmark arguments for the abolition of capital punishment before the Louisiana state legislature, and the spirit of reform peaked in the 1830s, 40s, and early 50s when social organizations such as the New York and Massachusetts Societies for the Abolition of Capital Punishment were formed. Many Northern and some Southern states began revising capital statutes and moving executions from the public square to the enclosed, "private" space of the prison yard. New York, Massachusetts, and New Hampshire came close to abolishing capital punishment, and bills calling for abolition passed or nearly passed in one of the legislative houses in New Jersey, Vermont, Ohio, and Connecticut. In 1837, Maine passed a bill that sentenced those convicted of capital crimes to solitary confinement and made executions require an executive warrant issued by the governor one year after the pronouncement of a death sentence. The "Maine Law" helped prevent any death sentence in the state from being carried out for twenty-seven years.

By 1853, three states—Michigan in 1847, Rhode Island in 1851, and Wisconsin in 1853—had abolished the death penalty. Largely due to the impending Civil War, however, and the inevitable violence associated with the effort to abolish slavery, a movement with which the reformation of capital punishment was intimately connected,[1] death penalty abolitionism lost its momentum, not fully to return to the public spotlight until the turn of the twentieth century.[2]

The antigallows movement in antebellum America spurred legislative reports, political writings, and imaginative journalism as well as poetry and fiction. Abolitionists drew on religious and political arguments to claim that capital punishment violated human and civil rights, and they challenged arguments about deterrence. Robert Rantoul Jr., a Massachusetts politician, and John L. O'Sullivan, a prominent New York Democrat and editor of the *The United States Magazine and Democratic Review*, made innovative arguments about the inappropriateness of capital punishment in a republic. Famous literary figures contributed to the debate by publishing in O'Sullivan's journal, including Nathaniel Hawthorne, John Greenleaf Whittier, and Walt Whitman. Others such as Henry Wadsworth Longfellow and Herman Melville criticized the death penalty in their work, and some popular writers—notably William Gilmore Simms, George Lippard, Sylvester Judd, and E. D. E. N. Southworth—questioned in their novels the purpose of the gallows. The campaign to abolish capital punishment was an important part of the context that helped bring about the American Renaissance and in some ways reveals as much about the democratic assumptions informing the invigoration of American literature at midcentury as did the campaign to abolish slavery.

"Dramatick Effect": *Logan* and Livingston

The final chapter of David Brion Davis's classic study *Homicide in American Fiction* (1957) provides a starting point for inquiry into antebellum literature and the death penalty. As its title suggests, *Homicide in American Fiction* attends primarily to questions about murder, but in its final chapter Davis turns to capital punishment, claiming that "American fiction in the second quarter of the nineteenth century reveals a curious synthesis of . . . two positions": "reformers who emphasized the effect of environment on moral behavior, arguing that criminals should be cured instead of being punished, and traditionalists who finally abandoned the rationalistic theory of deterrence and fell back upon a doctrine of intrinsic and absolute justice."[3] More than a "curious synthesis," U.S. fiction helped to shape cultural debates over capital punishment. A case in point is John Neal's *Logan: A Family* (1822), a popular, two-volume work that dramatizes, with extended discussion, a public execution.

Early in Volume II of *Logan*, Neal's protagonist, Harold, witnesses the hanging of several men convicted of piracy. The executions take place on board a commercial ship as Harold travels to England. The narrator vividly portrays the hangings, describing how the condemned were "successively drawn up . . . and then let down part way, with a sudden jerk, which caused the dislocation of their necks, like the report of a pistol."[4] At the sight and sound of these acts, Harold's "blood curdled" and his "heart turned sick, cold, cold as ice" (L, 8). When the last of the men is hanged (one has been pardoned at the last moment), Harold tells a stranger near him that he feels as if he "were a witness against these men" (L, 9). In response, the stranger asks, "And what think you of the reprieve?" to which Harold replies: "I like that. I love mercy. I could kneel down and thank them for sparing one life. And the very sailors—see how they are affected by it! The populace too, in the boats—they are crying" (L, 9). The sentiment of Harold's answer prompts a firm rejoinder from the stranger: "No. You are deceived. . . . That reprieve was injudicious. Punishment should be *certain*. *Certainty* does more than quantity, in penal codes, to counterbalance temptation. Were there but one man in a million pardoned, every criminal would hope that himself would be that man. Each expects the prize in a lottery. No! these people are not weeping. . . . They love sensation—they love spectacles" (L, 9).

As Harold persists in his objections, the dialogue takes shape as an object lesson in Enlightenment attitudes toward hanging and the deleterious psychological effects of public executions. Harold represents the young romantic subject (Byron's Childe Harold serves as a model) while the older stranger plays the role of a wise, skeptical philosopher. When Harold insists that the sympathy of the spectators reflects society's innate love of humanity and abhorrence of a justice system that inflicts death for crime, the stranger again corrects him: "The populace will assemble to execute a felon to day, with their own hands, and to morrow beset the throne of justice for his pardon. I have seen this, again and again. I have seen ten thousand people in tears because a handsome boy was to be executed; and I have seen the officer who brought his pardon, hooted and pelted from the ground, by a part of the same mob. Men sometimes sit down to cry—and it is dangerous to disappoint them. They have made up their minds to be sentimental, and woe to him who interferes or interrupts them" (L, 9). The stranger remarks further on the harmful effects: "There are several things to condemn in this affair," he explains. "In the first place, all the pirates are represented as penitent, and *assured* of heaven. In the next place, he who is pardoned is kept in ignorance of it, till the last moment" (L, 10).

The dramatic effect of the pardon prompts Harold to interrupt the stranger to comment that "not the criminal only, but the populace [will] remember it, with greater seriousness," since the pardoned convict "has suffered all but death: —the ignominy, the anticipation, the horrour, and the pain of such a death is nothing, absolutely nothing" (L, 11). In fact, Harold adds, the act of hanging itself was relatively uneventful and even merciful compared to the dreadful anticipation of each execution: "I felt relieved when their necks were snapped. I expected something a thousand times more horrible—but how instantly they were motionless! Oh, there is no death so easy!" (L, 11). Harold's sentiment illustrates the stranger's argument against both the mode of capital punishment and the practice of issuing last-minute pardons: "Right, young man," the stranger replies,

> Hence the glaring impolicy of such executions; hence too the frequency of suicide by hanging. Poor wretches! they see that the pain is momentary; all feel as you did, at the sight of the first execution. They expect to fall down, when the signal is given, and yet they find that the reality is nothing to the terrours of their own imaginations. But let me proceed. By delaying the reprieve until the last moment, for a presumptuous and idle piece of dramatick effect—*they teach every man, at the gallows, to expect, even to the last moment, the very last, a reprieve.* (L, 11)

The exchange between Harold and the stranger highlights concerns that would preoccupy the antigallows movement in the decades preceding the Civil War: (1) the deleterious effects of public executions and staged reprieves; (2) the complicity of witnesses; (3) the Enlightenment principle of *certainty* in punishment over severity (or "quantity," as the stranger says) as a useful deterrent; (4) the base desires of violence and spectacle to which public executions cater; and (5) the false pretense of forgiveness and salvation that the ritual of legal violence instills in the criminal mind. As the dialogue in *Logan* continues, Harold's response to the stranger's argument brings out this fifth and final point: "Gracious God," he exclaims, "hence, every man goes out of the world unprepared, in reality!" to which the stranger replies: "Yes—and hence too, the hardihood and carelessness, with which the most detestable ruffians go out of it; depriving the scene of all its terrors, making it a brutal farce, a trial of insensibility" (L, 11).

Logan was published in 1822, the same year Edward Livingston presented the first of his arguments against capital punishment before the Louisiana legislature. A former congressman and mayor of New York, forced to Louisiana by financial scandal, Livingston was elected a member of the state assembly in 1820. In 1821, he drafted a revision of the state's criminal statutes. A year later he delivered his eloquent *Report on the Plan of a Penal Code*, a lengthy section of which called for the abolition of the death penalty.

Like the stranger in *Logan*, Livingston found capital punishment to be barbarous and ineffective. Livingston, however, attended to the criminal passions (notably ambition and avarice) aroused in the spectators of executions. When the "inflection of death" becomes frequent, "it loses its effect," Livingston claimed; "the people become too much familiarized with it to consider it as an example; it is changed into a spectacle, which must frequently be repeated to satisfy the ferocious taste it has formed."[5] At the same time, when executions are infrequent and "kept for great occasions, and the people are seldom treated with the gratification of seeing one of their fellow-creatures expire by the sentence of the law; a most singular effect is produced; the sufferer, whatever be his crime, becomes a hero or a saint; he is the object of public attention, curiosity, admiration, and pity" (EL, 44). In either case, Livingston echoed arguments in Neal's novel, especially the claim that the condemned becomes an object of sympathy in the eyes of the populace.[6] "Thus the end of the law is defeated," Livingston concluded; "the force of the example is totally lost, and the place of execution is converted into a scene of triumph for the sufferer, whose crime is wholly forgotten, while his courage, resignation, or piety, mark him as the martyr, not the guilty victim, of the laws" (EL, 45).

Livingston and Neal, one from law and the other from literature, speak against the death penalty near the beginning of a reform movement that would play a prominent role in the cultural politics of the antebellum period. As a Pennsylvania paper declared in 1844: "The subject of capital punishment is claiming much and increasing attention, not only in our own State, but in many other parts of the country."[7] In his 1866 autobiography, Neal positions his writing as part of this movement and reflects, "I believe that the changes which have followed year after year, both abroad and at home, in the mode of execution, originated with my 'Logan.'"[8] Neal also identifies the source for his gallows scene:

> When I wrote "Logan," after having seen two pirates, and two young men strangled by law, in the midst of a noisy, riotous crowd in Baltimore, at noon-day, with the blue heavens, the green earth, and the golden sunshine testifying against their dread "taking off," I urged our lawgivers, if they would still insist upon strangling men, women, and children, to do it within the walls of a prison, at midnight, and with the tolling of a large, ponderous bell, or the sound of cannon, like minute-guns at sea; that murderers, and ravishers, and house breakers, and thieves, and highwayman, might be startled from their sleep, and set a-thinking; or be disturbed in their midnight revels, or their unaccomplished depredations, as by a voice from the other world, filling them with dismay, or with a mysterious unutterable horror, according to their guilt, in their dread loneliness and desolation.[9]

Neal calls for more effective means of administering capital punishment, also hinted at by the stranger in *Logan*: "Another defect is this;" the stranger tells Harold, "men are executed in daylight, and the mob go home, about their usual occupations. . . . But let executions be conducted at night, by torch light, with tolling bells, at midnight, and what would be their sensations then!" (L, 13). This change, of course, was never implemented, but Neal did credit *Logan* with prompting a reform development: the movement of executions from the public square to the enclosed space of the prison yard. Indeed, Neal's argument for prohibiting public executions in *Logan* preceded the first actual state law of that kind by eight years.[10]

A War of the Nation against a Citizen: Origins of U.S. Abolitionism

The origins of the movement to abolish capital punishment in antebellum America can be found in Cesare di Beccaria's *On Crimes and Punishments*, a short treatise on the reformation of criminal law first published in 1764. Upon publication in Italy and its translation throughout Europe, Beccaria's book attracted attention and sparked debate. Interest in Beccaria's ideas were every bit as keen in England and colonial America. The first English edition of *On Crimes and Punishments* was published in London in 1767 and advertised in New York in 1773. The first American editions of Beccaria's treatise were published in Charleston in 1777 and in Philadelphia in 1778.[11]

Drawing upon Montesquieu's *The Spirit of Laws* (1748), Beccaria argued for less severe, more proportionate punishments in criminal law and reasoned that the death penalty was neither necessary nor useful. Capital punishment was not necessary, he claimed, because in times of peace life imprisonment would protect society from dangerous members.[12] It was not useful because the harshness of the penalty did not leave a lasting impression upon those whom it intended to deter. In Beccaria's words, "It is not the severity of punishment that has the greatest impact on the human mind, but rather its duration, for our sensibility is more easily and surely stimulated by tiny repeated impressions than by a strong but temporary movement."[13] For Beccaria, life imprisonment deterred crime because the punishment would be "spread out over a lifetime" whereas "capital punishment exercises all its powers in an instant."[14] If, as Montesquieu stated in *The Spirit of Laws* and Beccaria reiterated in *On Crimes and Punishments*, any punishment that was unnecessary was "tyrannical," then the death penalty epitomized tyranny.[15]

Beccaria's attack on the death penalty challenged the social contract theories of Montesquieu and Rousseau. Like Rousseau, he subscribed to a theory of government in which citizens renounced part of their individual liberty to form a social compact. According to Beccaria, members of a social contract never gave the state the right to take their lives. To do so would be to contradict the underlying principle of the contract itself. "By what alleged right can men slaughter their fellows?" Beccaria asked. "Certainly not by the authority from which sovereignty and law derive. That authority is nothing but the sum of tiny portions of the individual liberty of each person; it represents the general will, which is the aggregate of private wills. Who on earth has ever willed that other men should have the liberty to kill him? How could this minimal sacrifice of the liberty of each individual ever include the sacrifice of the greatest good of all, life itself?" As his emphasis upon liberty suggests, Beccaria's argument hinged upon the individual liberties the social contract was created to protect. Foremost among these was the right to life, "the greatest good of all." From this line of reasoning, Beccaria concluded: "The death penalty, then, is not a *right* . . . but rather a war of the nation against a citizen, a campaign waged on the ground that the nation has judged the destruction of his being to be useful or necessary."[16]

This description of capital punishment as a civil war between a nation and its citizens must have caught the attention of Beccaria's many liberal-minded American readers. As Louis Masur notes, "No less a figure than Thomas Jefferson credited Beccaria with awakening the world to the unnecessary severity of capital punishment."[17] Also influenced by Beccaria was Benjamin Rush, the foremost physician in America during the late eighteenth century and, like Jefferson, a signer of the Declaration of Independence. Rush emerged as the first great spokesperson for the anti-gallows movement in the newly formed United States. He expressed his views in an essay delivered on March 9, 1787, at the home of Benjamin Franklin, and later published as *An Enquiry into the Effects of Public Punishments upon Criminals and upon Society*. In 1792, a year after the Bill of Rights was ratified, Rush published *Considerations on the Injustice and Impolicy of Punishing Murder by Death*, his definitive statement on abolition. His attack was centered on moral and religious objections, a dominant line of reasoning in the abolition movement from the late eighteenth to the mid-nineteenth century.

Rush also drew a persuasive contrast between monarchical and republican forms of government:

> Kings consider their subjects as their property; no wonder, therefore, they shed their blood with as little emotion as men shed the blood of their sheep or cattle. But the principles of republican governments speak a very different language. They teach us the absurdity of the divine origin of kingly power. They approximate the extreme ranks of men to each other. They restore man to his God—to society—and to himself. They appreciate human life, and increase public and private obligations to preserve it. They consider human sacrifices as no less offensive to the sovereignty of the people, than they are to the majesty of heaven. They view the attributes of government, like the attributes of the deity, as infinitely more honoured by destroying evil by means of merciful than by exterminating punishments. The united states have adopted these peaceful and benevolent forms of government. It becomes them therefore to adopt their mild and benevolent principles.[18]

For Rush, the death penalty in a republic was "like a human sacrifice in religion";[19] in developing this analogy, he conflated legal and extralegal forms of capital punishment, suggesting an undeniable similarity between them—a similarity the state tries to hide with elaborate rituals and formal procedures. In this respect, Rush's attack on capital punishment (along with that of Beccaria) laid the foundation for what we can call the republican argument against the death penalty.[20]

Antebellum reformers built on this argument, including Livingston and Robert Rantoul Jr., a prominent lawyer and leading Democrat in Massachusetts. From 1835 to 1838, Rantoul delivered annual reports in favor of abolition. The most famous was his 1836 *Report on the Abolition of Capital Punishment*. Claims of capital punishment as barbaric and a remnant of despotic regimes were common enough in the nineteenth century, but, as Hugo Adam Bedau suggests, Rantoul was perhaps the only abolitionist prior to the mid-twentieth century to argue against capital punishment on the grounds that it was inconsistent with the Bill of Rights.[21] In his *Report*, Rantoul summoned the Eighth Amendment prohibition of cruel and unusual punishment: "The whipping-post and the pillory survived, for a period, the constitutional prohibition of cruel and unusual punishments. They have disappeared, and the gallows, which is more unusual than either of those barbarities had been, and infinitely more cruel and revolting, must soon follow in their train" (451). If Rantoul was the leading opponent of the gallows in the 1830s, John O'Sullivan was the foremost advocate for abolition in the 1840s, and public debate unfolded in the pages of O'Sullivan's influential journal, *The United States Magazine and Democratic Review*.

O'Sullivan, Abolitionism, and Literary Contributions

Like Rantoul, O'Sullivan was trained as a lawyer and committed to the Democratic Party, but he came to politics as a young newspaper and periodical editor. In 1840, O'Sullivan won a seat in the New York State Assembly with a campaign largely based on reformation of capital punishment. In 1841, he was appointed chair of a committee to consider the expediency of abolishing the death penalty. That committee presented an abolition bill that, after considerable delay in the House and negative publicity by opponents, was defeated by a slim margin. O'Sullivan was convinced that the measure would pass the following year, but it failed by the same margin. First printed for the state assembly on April 14, 1841, O'Sullivan's *Report in Favor of the Abolition of the Punishment of Death by Law* offered a compendium of "leading arguments and evidences, derived from revelation, reason, and experience."[22] The *Report* was reprinted as a book later that year. By October, "being called for by public demand" (*Report*, 4), a second edition of O'Sullivan's book was published, and for the next twenty years it served as the standard reference in capital punishment debates.[23]

The strength of O'Sullivan's *Report* lies in its popular reformulation of arguments developed by Beccaria, Rush, Livingston, and Rantoul. Part statistical analysis with utilitarian and republican arguments, and part moral anecdote and exegesis of Biblical authority, the *Report* appealed to sympathy, reason, and historical example. O'Sullivan also emphasized the question of deterrence and the adverse psychological impact of executions. The punishment of death for murder, Livingston had argued, not only "fails in any repressive effect, but . . . promotes the crime" (EL, 201). Livingston cited an incident reported in a Pennsylvania newspaper in which a man committed murder on the way back from a public execution. For Livingston, this example illustrated the proclivity of the human mind "to imitate that which has been strongly impressed on the senses" (EL, 201–202). Reformulating and quoting Livingston at length (he even cites the example from the Pennsylvania paper), O'Sullivan detailed the death penalty's failure as a deterrent, singling it out in his book as the "strongest objection against the punishment of death" (Report, 84). He offered this pithy statement, italicized and repeated: "*the executioner is the indirect cause of more murders and more deaths than he ever punishes or avenges*" (Report, 85, 98). By highlighting the executioner, O'Sullivan called attention to human agency and placed responsibility for murder on the hangman but, more importantly, on anyone who supported the gallows in the face of surging reform.

At the center of this reform movement was *The United States Magazine and Democratic Review*, founded and edited by O'Sullivan. In the 1840s, the *Democratic Review* published dozens of articles advocating the abolition of the death penalty. O'Sullivan wrote some of these articles himself, such as "Capital Punishment" (April 1843), "The Anti-Gallows Movement" (April 1844), and "The Gallows and the Gospel: An Appeal to Clergymen Opposing Themselves to the Abolition of the One, in the Name of the Other," the lead article in the March 1843 issue. Framed as an appeal, "The Gallows and the Gospel" attacked the position of clergymen who defended the death penalty: "Some of you appear to have felt especially called upon to cast yourselves in the path of this advancing movement of opinion; to have taken the institution in question under your particular professional patronage and protection, and marshalling yourselves in organized array, as it were, around the foot of the Scaffold, have seemed ambitious to assume the function of the very Body-Guard of the Hangman."[24] O'Sullivan envisioned capital punishment debates as a virtual war: on one side, reformers firing salvos at the gallows; on the other, retentionist clergymen "marshalling" themselves around the scaffold to serve as the hangman's "Body-Guard."

Although addressed to clergy, O'Sullivan's audience was "the large number of the undecided and indifferent, who may never have had a combined opportunity and disposition" to approach the death penalty through "Biblical criticism" and applied Christian ethics ("Gallows," 228). He sought to provide that opportunity by presenting "an outline of the Scriptural Argument by which we refute the common objections opposed to us from the Bible, and on which we claim the right to invoke their favor and cooperation with these efforts" ("Gallows," 228). Contrary to popular opinion, he argued that "the Bible contains no injunction nor sanction of the practice of capital punishment; but . . . the very reverse is most unequivocally impressed upon its pages, in their outset as in their close" (Report, 29). He read Genesis 9:6 ("Whoso sheddeth the blood of man, by man his blood shall be shed") as prophecy rather than injunction. That is, the verse serves as a prediction or a denunciatory warning of a possible future event, much like the proverb derived from Matthew 26:52, "He who lives by the sword dies by the sword," or the one from Revelations 13:10, "He that leadeth into captivity shall go into captivity." It does not, for O'Sullivan, function as a universal commandment such as "Thou shall not kill" (Exodus 20:13).

Unsurprisingly, the sixth commandment played a crucial role in O'Sullivan's thinking. That commandment stands "naked and sacred" in its "simplicity" and is "absolute, unequivocal, universal" (Report, 22). It cannot be transformed into "Thou shall not commit murder—but mayest kill him who has committed murder." To be sure, it contains "no proviso—no exception—no qualification" (Report, 22). O'Sullivan also found evidence against capital punishment in the story of Cain and Abel, which he identified in "The Gallows and the Gospel" as the "lesson set by the example of God himself in the case of the first murder" (233). In the Report, O'Sullivan pushed this reading further: "Yet was death the sentence of Cain? On the contrary, his doom is written that he should be 'a fugitive and a vagabond in the earth,' the earth ceasing to yield her strength to his tillage and a mark being set on him, 'lest any finding him should kill him'" (28). What is more, God reiterated the proscription on taking Cain's life with these words: "Whoso slayeth Cain, vengeance shall be taken on him seven-fold" (28).

In his spirited assault upon traditional Biblical interpretations, O'Sullivan certainly had in mind Reverend George Barrell Cheever, a Presbyterian minister and defender of the gallows who authored Punishment by Death: Its Authority and Expediency (1842). In his famous defense of capital punishment, Cheever championed the gallows, building his argument on an appeal to divine authority in Genesis 9:6. Further, a month before "The Gallows and the Gospel" was published, O'Sullivan had debated Cheever in New York City on the question, "Ought Capital Punishment To Be Abolished?"[25] The debates, held at the Broadway Tabernacle on January 27, February 3, and February 17, were well attended and generated press for some time to come.

A literary rendition of the O'Sullivan-Cheever debates emerges from the pen of Nathaniel Hawthorne, a friend of O'Sullivan and a contributor of over twenty works to the *Democratic Review*, including "Egotism, or the Bosom Serpent," published alongside "The Gallows and the Gospel." The debate occurs in a pivotal moment in "Earth's Holocaust," Hawthorne's 1844 tale which recounts the narrator's journey to the American Midwest to witness the immolation of the world's "worn-out trumpery," its "condemned rubbish."[26] Midway through the tale, following the destruction of signs of rank and social prestige, liquors and tea, articles of high fashions and instruments of war, the body of reformers responsible for the great bonfire—this "Earth's Holocaust"—turns its attention to instruments of capital punishment: "old implements of cruelty—those horrible monsters of mechanism—those inventions which it seemed to demand something worse than man's natural heart to contrive, and which had lurked in the dusky nooks of ancient prisons, the subject of terror-stricken legends" ("Earth's," 392).

Halters, headsmen's axes, and the guillotine are among the instruments of death thrown into the fire, but the imminent destruction of the gallows generates the most interest from the crowd, even sparking a debate between two men likely drawn from Cheever and O'Sullivan respectively: "Stay, my brethren!," cries a defender of capital punishment as the gallows is about to be thrust into the fire. "You are misled by a false philanthropy!— you know not what you do. The gallows is a heaven-oriented instrument! Bear it back, then, reverently, and set it up in its old place; else the world will fall to speedy ruin and desolation!" ("Earth's," 393) In response, "a leader in the reform" commands his brethren: "Onward, onward! . . . Into the flames with the accursed instrument of man's bloody policy! How can human law inculcate benevolence and love, while it persists in setting up the gallows as its chief symbol! One heave more, good friends, and the world will be redeemed from its greatest error!" ("Earth's," 393). The gallows is finally pushed into the fire, and this act appears to be a good thing, as Hawthorne's narrator had moments earlier applauded the destruction of halters, axes, and the guillotine, commenting that their immolation "was sufficient to convince mankind of the long and deadly error of human law" ("Earth's," 392). Yet one cannot say for certain that this radical reform will benefit society, since the tale moves into parody as marriage certificates, written constitutions of all kinds, works of literature, and even the Bible become fuel to feed the fire.

While it might be a stretch to call "Earth's Holocaust" abolitionist in orientation, one can say that about Hawthorne's "The New Adam and Eve," a story first published in the February 1843 *Democratic Review*, just one month before O'Sullivan's "The Gallows and the Gospel." In this story, Hawthorne imagines the return of the world's primogenitors after the "Day of Doom has burst upon the globe, and swept away the whole race of men."[27] Eventually, the "New" Adam and Eve enter a prison and wander through its bleak corridors and narrow cells. The novelty of Adam and Eve's experience provides Hawthorne's narrator with the opportunity to comment on the sad state of crime and punishment with which the recently deceased world was plagued, but nothing within the prison provokes strong reaction from Adam and Eve or the narrator. All that changes when, "passing from the interior of the prison into the space within its outward wall, Adam pauses beneath a structure of the simplest contrivance, yet altogether unaccountable to him" ("Adam," 255). This structure, we are told, "consists merely of two upright posts, supporting a transverse beam, from which dangles a cord" ("Adam," 255). The menacing object that Adam finds "altogether unaccountable" is the gallows, and its foreboding presence elicits a shudder "with a nameless horror" from Adam. He asks Eve what "this thing" could be. "'I know not,' answers Eve, 'but, Adam, my heart is sick! There seems to be no more sky,—no more sunshine!'" ("Adam," 255) Without knowledge of the world to which the gallows belongs, neither Adam nor Eve can place "this thing" within an interpretive frame, but intuition sends horror through Adam and affects Eve with heartache and despair.

The narrator reflects on the couple's reaction:

> Well might Adam shudder and poor Eve be sick at heart; for this mysterious object was the type of mankind's whole system, in regard to the great difficulties which God had given to be solved—a system of fear and vengeance, never successful, yet followed to the last. Here, on the morning when the final summons came, a criminal—one criminal, where none were guiltless—had died upon the gallows. ("Adam," 255)

This authorial intrusion endorses Adam and Eve's moral response and raises questions about "a system of fear and vengeance, never successful, yet followed to the last." This description calls attention to the negative aims of the death penalty (i.e., "fear" and "vengeance"), which are given dramatic expression through the example of that "final summons" when "a criminal—one criminal, where none were guiltless—had died upon the gallows." By shifting midsentence from the indefinite, "a criminal," to the definite, "one criminal," the narrator suggests the finality of all executions and the singularity of this one, and the emphasis on the universal guilt of humanity undercuts the moral superiority that typically justifies the death penalty.

Other prominent literary figures also wrote antigallows work for the *Democratic Review*. Four months before "The New Adam and Eve," John Greenleaf Whittier published "Lines, Written on Reading Several Pamphlets Published by Clergymen Against the Abolition of the Gallows" in the October 1842 issue. With an appeal to sympathy and compassion, and by situating the gallows at the end of a history of cruelty inflicted by men in the name of God, Whittier indicted capital punishment and asked those of "milder faith": "Will ye become the Druids of our time? / Set up your scaffold-alters in our land, / And, consecrators of Law's darkest crime, / Urge to its loathsome work the Hangman's hand?"[28] By linking the death penalty to a barbaric past, Whittier strove to show that capital punishment was incompatible with democratic principles and civil liberties.

Whittier extended this argument in a second antigallows poem, "The Human Sacrifice," published in the May 1843 *Democratic Review*. The poem was written expressly for the abolitionist cause and specifically, as Whittier states in its introductory note, in response to a clergyman's "warm eulogy upon the gallows" published in a number of leading papers. Sentimental and symbolic, "Human Sacrifice" explores the thoughts of two individuals: a sympathetic condemned man, confined to his cell and waiting death in an hour's time, and the minister who presides over the execution, "Blessing with solemn text and word / The gallows-drop and strangling cord." The minister's blessing sanctions what Whittier on two occasions calls "the crime of Law."[29] This blessing recalls readers to the human sacrifice in the poem's title, a conception of capital punishment articulated fifty years earlier in Rush's claim that "[a]n execution in a republic is like a human sacrifice in religion."[30]

While Whittier's antigallows poems may have been occasioned by remarks from clergymen, their publication in the *Democratic Review* served another end as well. To the disappointment of O'Sullivan and other abolitionists, William Wordsworth had recently published a series of sonnets in support of the death penalty. In the March 1842 *Democratic Review*, O'Sullivan laid the groundwork for a counterattack in an essay titled "Wordsworth's

Sonnets on the Punishment of Death."[31] He expresses regret that the "great English master" has written in support of "one of the most hideous and horrible barbarisms yet lingering to disgrace the statute-books of modern civilization."[32] O'Sullivan acknowledges that, because of "the strongly conservative cast of his mind and political opinions," one could not expect Wordsworth to come out in favor of abolition. "Yet," he continues, "to behold him take to the sacred lyre, and attune its chords to the harsh creaking of the scaffold and the clanking of the victim's chains, seems almost a profanation and a sacrilege—as though a harp of heaven were transported from its proper sphere and its congenial themes, to be struck by some impious hand to the foul and hideous harmonies of hell."[33] O'Sullivan cites in full Wordsworth's fourteen "Sonnets on the Punishment of Death" and offers a stanza-by-stanza analysis. He also cites in full an antigallows poem by Lydia Huntley Sigourney. By quoting Sigourney's "The Execution" and publishing Whittier's poems, O'Sullivan attempted to displace Wordsworth's "Sonnets" with imagery and poetic language that argue for abolition.

In November 1845, Walt Whitman joined the conversation in the *Democratic Review* with "A Dialogue," an imaginative essay that stages a conversation between a condemned murderer and society on the eve of an execution. Again, the high stakes and sharply delineated contours of capital punishment dramatize the confrontation between the citizen-subject and sovereign authority. Like Hawthorne's "The New Adam and Eve," Whitman's "A Dialogue" is framed as a parable. It begins by posing the following question: "What would be thought of a man who, having an ill humor in his blood, should strive to cure himself by only cutting off the festers, the outward signs of it, as they appeared upon the surface?"[34] Whitman foregrounds questions about social complicity and responsibility for criminal acts; the "man" represents society as a whole, whereas the "festers" signify criminals who are "outward signs" of a diseased social body. As Whitman explains, "Put criminals for festers and society for the diseased man, and you may get the spirit of that part of our laws which expects to abolish wrong-doing by sheer terror—by cutting off the wicked, and taking no heed of the causes of the wickedness." Following this preamble, Whitman proceeds with the dialogue, an exchange between "the imposing majesty of the people speaking on the one side, a pallid, shivering convict on the other" ("Dialogue," 360).

The convict initiates the discussion by admitting to have committed a "wrong . . . in an evil hour" when "a kind of frenzy came over me, and I struck my neighbor a heavy blow, which killed him" ("Dialogue," 360). Summarizing the convict's crime in this manner emphasizes murder as an act typically perpetrated in a heat of passion and committed by a person much different in mind and disposition than the one now awaiting execution. To the convict's admission of guilt, society flatly responds: "you must be killed in return" ("Dialogue," 361). When the convict asks, "Is there no plan by which I can benefit my fellow-creatures, even at the risk of my own life?" society again replies tersely in the negative: "None . . . you must be strangled—choked to death. If your passions are so ungovernable that people are in danger from them, we shall hang you." The condemned asks, "Why?" suggesting that incarceration in a strong prison would protect society and that he would gladly work while in prison to defray the expense of housing him. Once again, society gives its blunt response of "No," adding that "we shall strangle you; your crime deserves it," to which the "murderer" (as Whitman now refers to him) asks: "Have you, then, committed no crimes?"

Putting society on the defensive enables Whitman's murderer to implicate "the people" in the production of crime. The dialogue shifts to a discussion of crimes that, in society's words, have not "come within the clutches of any statute," but lead daily to the ruination and even death of many ("Dialogue," 361). This inadvertent admission of guilt permits the convict to comment on social responsibility and to expose a double standard in a theory of justice which holds that an individual, when sinned against, should forgive, while society ought to withhold forgiveness and exact payment in kind. When the convict asks why should not the people, like the individual, be guided by the principle of forgiveness, society responds, "The case is different. . . . We are a community—you are but a single individual. You should forgive your enemies." The condemned poses a rhetorical question and answers by way of analogy:

"And are you not ashamed," asks the culprit, "to forget that as a community which you expect me to remember as a man? When the town clock goes wrong, shall each little private watch be abased for failing to keep the true time? What are communities but congregated individuals? And if you, in the potential force of your high position, deliberatively set examples of retribution, how dare you look to me for self-denial, forgiveness, and the meekest and most difficult virtues?" ("Dialogue," 361)

The convict's comparison of the "town clock" to "each little private watch" suggests that the internal watches of each citizen are set according to the town clock. If society sets the example of retribution, how can the people expect an individual, when provoked or enraged, to act according to a different and higher standard? The convict reinforces his point by saying that he killed simply because his "blood was up," even though he knew the penalty for such a crime would be death. The convict deploys a series of questions that society cannot answer satisfactorily. Readers are left with a clear sense of the moral horrors and contradictions of a justice system that condemns lethal violence by using such violence and hypocritically demands forgiveness from private citizens for acts it deems unforgivable.

Near the end of "A Dialogue," the conversation turns to the death penalty's spectacle of violence. The convict and society agree that such a spectacle is "degrading and anti-humanizing," and society congratulates itself on the passage of recent laws making executions in many states private. The convict, however, points out that executions are still public in many states and, more importantly, that so-called "private" executions are by no means private when "everybody reads newspapers, and every newspaper seeks for graphic accounts of these executions" so that "such things can never be private" ("Dialogue," 362). The convict accuses newspapers and print media of carrying out, as it were, *literary executions*. Thus, he disabuses society of the notion that executions have become private and less visible.

> The whole spectacle of these . . . executions is more faithfully seen, and more deliberately dwelt upon, through the printed narratives, than if people beheld it with their bodily eyes, and then no more. Print preserves it. It passes from hand to hand, and even boys and girls are imbued with its spirit and horrid essence. Your legislators have forbidden public executions; they must go farther. They must forbid the relation of them by tongue, letter, or picture; for your physical sight is not the only avenue through which the subtle virus will reach you. Nor is the effect lessened because it is more covert and more widely diffused. Rather, indeed, the reverse. ("Dialogue," 362–63)

By advocating restrictions upon the press, Whitman's convict pushes the argument further than Whitman himself would take it.[35] After all, in publishing "A Dialogue," Whitman participates in the very discursive activity against which the convict speaks. And Whitman, the journalist, published other such pieces, including a bitterly sarcastic "Hurrah for Hanging!" in an issue of the Brooklyn *Daily Eagle* (1846). That article, Whitman explains, was occasioned by "the butcher[ing] of five human beings last week in

Cayuga co., in this state."[36] He concluded the *Daily Eagle* report by ironically urging readers to "let the law keep up with the murderer, and see who will get the victory at last."[37] Whitman also promoted the discussion of reports on capital punishment in the meetings of the Brooklyn Association for the Abolition of the Death Penalty, an organization Whitman cofounded in 1846.

Still, the point Whitman's convict makes is an important one: the so-called privatization of lawful hangings in no way diminishes the psychological impact they may have. Indeed, the proliferation of printed narratives of executions occurred in large part because the spectacle of lawful violence had moved behind prison walls. For this reason, and due to unprecedented debates about capital punishment in the decades preceding the Civil War, one could follow the convict and say that executions in the 1840s and early 50s had never before been so public.

Classic American Literature and Capital Punishment

Today these debates are largely forgotten by critics of American literature. Yet this controversy helped to generate the "American Renaissance" in the early 1850s. Whitman was a crucial figure in the death penalty abolitionist movement, and if, as David S. Reynolds has suggested, Whitman's "Hurrah for Hanging!" was likely influenced by "Hurrah for the Gallows!"[38] a sardonic chapter lampooning capital punishment in George Lippard's best-selling *The Quaker City* (1845), then debates about capital punishment themselves lie "beneath the American Renaissance" and constitute some of the roots that led to the midcentury flourishing of American literature.

These debates left an indelible imprint on many works by classic American writers. Henry David Thoreau made his own argument against hanging in "A Plea for John Brown" (1859), advocating a theory of individual rights and the state similar to Rantoul's. Delivered on several occasions in the weeks following the raid upon Harpers Ferry, Thoreau's speech turned the imminent execution of John Brown into a call for continued and even violent disobedience to laws supporting slavery. He deified Brown, transforming him into a martyr: "Some eighteen hundred years ago Christ was crucified; this morning, perchance, Captain Brown was hung. These are two ends of a chain which is not without its links."[39]

There is also the famous opening of Nathaniel Hawthorne's *The Scarlet Letter* (1850), which stages the scene of capital punishment even though an execution itself does not occur. The novel begins with the image of "The Prison Door," out of which Hester Prynne emerges like a "condemned criminal" coming "forth to his doom."[40] A crowd gathers to witness the punishment of Hester "on whom the sentence of a legal tribunal had but confirmed the verdict of public sentiment" (*Scarlet* 37). Just before the punishment commences, some spectators push forward as if to be "nearest to the scaffold at an execution" (*Scarlet* 38). Even the dialogue among spectators concerns the place and purpose of capital punishment: "This woman has brought shame upon us all and ought to die," a matronly woman declares. "Is there not law for it? Truly there is, both in the Scripture and the statute-book." In response, a man from the crowd asks, "Is there no virtue in woman, save what springs from a wholesome fear of the gallows?" (*Scarlet* 39). Hester is not executed, and neither she nor the crowd expects such a punishment to occur, but her presence on the scaffold rehearses the ritual of capital punishment.

Popular antebellum novels and romances responded to the gallows, such as Lippard's *The Quaker City* (1845), Sylvester Judd's *Margaret* (1845; rev. 1851), John Ludlum McCollum's *The Glenns* (1851), Talvj's *The Exiles* (1853), Elizabeth Oakes Prince Smith's *The Newsboy* (1854), and Lee Day Kellogg's *Merrimack* (1854). William Mayo Starbuck and Julia A. Mathews wrote short stories ("The Captain's Story" and "The Red Cloak; or Murder at the Roadside Inn," respectively) that directly criticized capital punishment. Lydia Maria Child wrote two antigallows stories, "Elizabeth Wilson" (1846) and "The Juryman" (1857), and argued against the death penalty in more than one of her widely read *Letters from New York*. William Gilmore Simms and E. D. E. N. Southworth both wrote several novels that supported the antigallows campaign.[41] One of the period's most dramatic enactments of a death sentence occurs in Herman Melville's *White-Jacket* (1850). Melville links flogging and the death penalty to a barbarous past antithetical to the principles of American democracy.

In an overview essay on capital punishment in U.S. literature, Nancy Morrow discounts the impact that the death penalty had on nineteenth-century American writers: "Although the debate about capital punishment was quite ardent, it served relatively infrequently as the source of inspiration for imaginative literature before the 1920s, especially in comparison with its widespread use in novels, plays, and films since then."[42] On the contrary, works by classic American writers registered the concerns of the antigallows movement. That campaign influenced a number of then-popular but now-forgotten fiction writers traditionally positioned "beneath" the American Renaissance. Considerable energy has been devoted—and rightly so—to revising our understanding of the American

Renaissance (and what lies beneath) in terms of the movement to abolish slavery. I have tried to lay the groundwork for understanding the American Renaissance in terms of that "other" antebellum abolition movement, a movement still unfulfilled in a country that once led a campaign to prevent the state from exercising the power to curtail the most important civil liberty of all—life.[43]

Notes

1. Louis Masur writes, "In the minds of abolitionists such as William Lloyd Garrison and Wendell Phillips, one campaign, against slavery or the gallows, was inseparable from the other. Both slavery and capital punishment, they argued, represented systems of brutality that coerced individuals, and both institutions merited attack" (157). Other opponents of slavery, such as Theodore Parkman and Lydia Marie Child, also spoke out against the death penalty. Frederick Douglass and Susan B. Anthony organized an anti-death penalty meeting in Rochester, New York, in 1858. However, alliances between these movements were not always clear-cut. John L. O'Sullivan, the leading spokesperson against the death penalty in the 1840s, supported the Confederacy, and George Barrell Cheever, foremost defender of the gallows in the 1840s, became a leader in the anti-slavery cause.

2. My overview draws from Stuart Banner, *The Death Penalty: An American History* (Cambridge: Harvard Univ. Press, 2002); Louis P. Masur, *Rites of Execution: Capital Punishment and the Transformation of American Culture* (New York: Oxford Univ. Press, 1989); Karen Halttunen, *Murder Most Foul: The Killer and the American Gothic Imagination* (Cambridge: Harvard Univ. Press, 1998); Philip English Mackey, ed., *Voices Against Death: American Opposition to Capital Punishment, 1787–1977* (New York: Burt Franklin, 1977); David Brion Davis, "The Movement to Abolish Capital Punishment in America, 1787–1861," *American Historical Review* 63.1 (1957): 23–46; and Davis, *Homicide in American Fiction* (Ithaca: Cornell Univ. Press, 1957).

3. Davis, *Homicide*, 299.

4. John Neal, *Logan: A Family History*. 2 Vols. (Philadelphia: H.C. Carey and I. Lea, 1822), 8. Subsequent references to this text will be cited parenthetically as L.

5. Edward Livingston, *The Complete Works of Edward Livingston on Criminal Jurisprudence*, vol. 1. Reprint Series in Criminology, Law Enforcement, and Social Problems (Montclair, NJ: Patterson Smith, 1968), 43. Subsequent references to this text will be cited parenthetically as EL.

6. For Livingston's impact in France, see Sonja Hamilton, *La Plume et le Couperet: Enjeux Politiques et Littéraires de la Peine de Mort Autour de 1830*. Ph.D. dissertation, Johns Hopkins Univ. Press, 2003, 71–73.

7. Quoted in Masur, *Rites*, 117.

8. John Neal, *Wandering Recollections of a Somewhat Busy Life: An Autobiography* (Boston: Roberts Brothers, 1869), 390.

9. Ibid., 390.

10. See Mackey's introduction to *Hanging*. For the movement toward private executions, see Banner, chapter 6.

11. Masur, *Rites*, 52. See Paul Spurlin, "Beccaria's Essay on Crimes and Punishments in Eighteenth-Century America," *Studies on Voltaire and the Eighteenth Century* 27 (1963): 1489–1504.

12. Beccaria found the death penalty justifiable only in times of war when the imprisonment of a political figure jeopardized the security of the state or when the execution of a condemned citizen was "the one and only deterrent to dissuade others from committing crimes." Cesare di Beccaria, *On Crimes and Punishments*, ed. David Young (Indiana: Hackett Publishing Company, 1986), 48.

13. Beccaria, *On Crimes*, 49.

14. Ibid., 50.

15. Montesquieu takes up the question of sovereign authority in relation to civil and criminal laws in Vol. 1, Book VI of *The Spirit of Laws*. In Book XIX, he writes, "All punishment which is not derived from necessity is tyrannical." Baron de Montesquieu, *The Spirit of Laws* (New York: Prometheus Books, 2002), 299.

16. Beccaria, *On Crimes*, 48.

17. Masur, *Rites*, 53.

18. Benjamin Rush, *Considerations on the Injustice and Impolicy of Punishing Murder by Death* (Philadelphia: Carey, 1792), 18–19.

19. Ibid., 16.

20. My use of the term republican argument is indebted to Masur (66).

21. Hugo Adam Bedau, preface in *Voices Against Death: American Opposition to Capital Punishment, 1787–1977*, ed. Philip English Mackey (New York: Burt Franklin, 1977), v.

22. John O'Sullivan, *Report in Favor of the Abolition of the Punishment of Death by Law* (New York: Arno Press, 1974), 5. Subsequent references to this text will be cited parenthetically as *Report*.

23. Robert D. Sampson, *John L. O'Sullivan and His Times* (Kent, OH: Kent State Univ. Press, 2003), 101.

24. John O'Sullivan, "The Gallows and the Gospel," *United States Magazine and Democratic Review* 12 (March 1843), 227. Subsequent references to this text will be cited parenthetically as "Gallows."

25. For the O'Sullivan-Cheever debates, see Philip English Mackey, *Hanging in the Balance: The Anti–Capital Punishment Movement in New York State, 1776–1861* (New York: Garland, 1982); Masur, *Rites*; Sampson, *O'Sullivan*.

26. Nathaniel Hawthorne, "Earth's Holocaust," in *The Centenary Edition of the Works of Nathaniel Hawthorne*, eds. William Charvat, Roy Harvey Pearce, and Claude M. Simpson. Vol. 10, *Mosses from an Old Manse*, eds. J. Donald Crowley and Fredson Bowers (Columbus: Ohio State Univ. Press, 1974), 381. Subsequent references to this text will be cited parenthetically as "Earth's."

27. Hawthorne, *Mosses*, 247. Subsequent references to this text will be cited parenthetically as "Adam."

28. John Greenleaf Whittier, "Lines, Written on Reading Several Pamphlets Published by Clergymen against the Abolition of the Gallows," *United States Magazine and Democratic Review* 11 (October 1842), 375.

29. John Greenleaf Whittier, *Complete Poetical Works of John Greanleaf Whittier* (Boston: Houghton, Mifflin and Co., 1881), 476, 477.

30. Rush, *Considerations*, 19.

31. "Wordsworth's Sonnets on the Punishment of Death," *United States Magazine and Democratic Review* 10 (March 1842), 272. This article was published without an attribution, but it is reasonable to assume that O'Sullivan wrote the response.

32. "Wordsworth's Sonnets," 272.

33. Ibid., 273.

34. Walt Whitman, "A Dialogue," *United States Magazine and Democratic Review* 17 (November 1845), 360. Subsequent references to this text will be cited parenthetically as "Dialogue."

35. For a short time, New York did make it illegal for the press to provide details of an execution. See Michael Madow, "Forbidden Spectacle: Executions, the Public and the Press in Nineteenth-Century New York," *Buffalo Law Review* 43 (Fall 1995): 467; and Lieberman in this collection.

36. Walt Whitman, *The Uncollected Poetry and Prose of Walt Whitman*, vol. 1, ed. Emory Holloway (New York: Peter Smith, 1932), 108.

37. Ibid., 109.

38. George Lippard, *The Quaker City; or the Monks of Monk Hall*, ed. David S. Reynolds (Amherst: Univ. of Massachusetts Press, 1995), xxxi.

39. Henry David Thoreau, "A Plea for John Brown," *Political Writings*, ed. Nancy L. Rosenblum (Cambridge: Cambridge Univ. Press, 1996), 156.

40. Nathaniel Hawthorne, *The Scarlet Letter and Other Writings*, ed. Leland S. Person (New York: W.W. Norton, 2005), 36. Subsequent references to this text will be cited parenthetically as *Scarlet*.

41. For Southworth, see Paul Christian Jones, "'I put my fingers around my throat and squeezed it, to know how it feels': Antigallows Sentimentalism and E. D. E. N. Southworth's *The Hidden Hand*," *Legacy* 25.1 (2008): 41–61. For Simms,

see John Cyril Barton, "William Gilmore Simms and the Literary Aesthetic of Crime and Punishment," *Law and Literature* 22:2 (2010): 222–43.

42. Nancy Morrow, "Capital Punishment" in *American Literature through History*, Vol. I, eds. Tom Quirk and Gary Scharnhorst (New York: Scribners, 2006), 202.

43. Alexis de Tocqueville comments in *Democracy in America* (1840): "There is no country where criminal justice is administered with more kindness than in the United States. Whereas the English seem to want to preserve carefully the bloody traces of the Middle Ages in their penal legislation, the Americans have almost made the death penalty disappear from their codes." Alexis de Tocqueville, *Democracy in America*, trans. Harvey C. Mansfield and Delba Winthrop, vol. 2 (Chicago: Univ. of Chicago Press, 2000), 538.

Electric Sensations and Executions in Gertrude Atherton's *Patience Sparhawk and Her Times*

JENNIFER LEIGH LIEBERMAN

> *An execution under the law ought to be the more terrible for the solemnity and impressiveness with which it is performed. It ought to be certain, swift, and painless. At its best hanging does not fulfill these requirements, while when it is bungled it becomes a spectacle which revolts civilized spectators or readers and inspires them with indignation rather at the law and its ministers than at the law-breaker who is answering for his offenses. There should be no doubt of the acceptance by the Legislature of the report of the [Gerry] commission. It will be creditable to the State of New York to be the first community to substitute a civilized for a barbarous method of inflicting capital punishment, and to set an example which is sure of being followed throughout the world.*
> — *"Capital Punishment,"* New York Times, *December 17, 1887*

This *New York Times* article illustrates how certain technological fantasies about the electric chair were promulgated in late nineteenth-century American newspapers. Such coverage often contended that electricity would provide a more "civilized," "sensible" form of capital punishment by replacing the public spectacle of hanging. As Dwight Conquergood argues, "Much of the debate surrounding the death penalty since the 1890 invention of the electric chair has focused on the performance technology of executions."[1] While proponents lauded the electric chair as a "humane" mode of killing, the actual practice continued to dehumanize the prisoner. The Gerry Commission, which proposed that New York adopt an electrical method of execution, presumed that a technologically advanced method of capital punishment would preempt the "problem" of "revolt[ing] civilized spectators or readers." By explicitly citing readers' responses in their promotion of electric execution, the commission report demonstrates that the motivation to find a humane method of execution was inextricably connected to the perceived need to preempt public sentiment. As with lethal injection, the turn to the electric chair was less about humanitarian regard for the men and women executed than a political need to manage public response to state killing. The possibility that the public would sympathize with the condemned was further delimited by the Electric Execution Act

(1888), which instituted a press gag clause intended to control journalistic reports.

Yet even before the gag statute was repealed in 1892, late nineteenth-century reports of electric execution did not have the effect that the New York state legislature feared.[2] Fictional and journalistic accounts of electrocution frequently minimized sympathy for the condemned by stressing the "unreal" quality of the death and focusing more on the awesome power of the electric apparatus than on the person being executed. In contrast, Gertrude Atherton's popular novel *Patience Sparhawk and Her Times* (1897) critiques cultural fantasies about electric execution while addressing the crucial issue of public sentiment. Unlike novels that came before it, which incorporate accidental or nonstate electrocutions—notably Mark Twain's *A Connecticut Yankee in King Arthur's Court* (1889)—*Patience Sparhawk* deals with legal electrocution. Atherton illuminates a fundamental problem with the rationalized, technological progress that the electric chair was intended to epitomize: the public's knowledge of the chair was mediated primarily through sensationalistic representations. *Patience Sparhawk* implicates methods of representing the death penalty with the practice itself and depicts modern Americans as more interested in the sensational story than in justice.

By drawing attention to the performance of electrocution and raising questions about how states use technology to legitimize capital punishment, the novel recognizes a disturbing trend that Hugo Bedau and Austin Sarat identify in capital punishment discourses today: the electric chair failed to make executions more rational or humane because the popular emphasis on the promise of a technologically perfected execution method turned public attention from *whether* modern American states should continue to practice capital punishment to *how* these states would practice it most efficiently.[3] *Patience Sparhawk and Her Times* uses the form and length of the novel to emphasize how this fantasy of instant death often obscures the fact that the wait between sentencing and execution is a form of torture itself.

Electric Execution with the Touch of a Button

In 1886, the state of New York appointed a commission "to investigate and report at an early date the most humane and practical method known to modern science of carrying into effect the sentence of death in capital cases."[4] The Gerry Commission turned in its report on January 17, 1888, recommending electricity as the most effective alternative to hanging. Five months later, New York passed Chapter 489 of the Laws of New York—the Electric Execution Act—which was predicated on two claims: (1) that the barbarity of capital punishment could be eliminated by adopting a new scientific method, and (2) that public sentiment against capital punishment, fueled by affective representations of hangings, could be mitigated by a "practically" humane alternative. This law did not define the legal parameters by which state prisons could acquire apparatuses for electrocutions or describe how these devices might work. Even before an electrocution apparatus had been invented, the law included a press gag clause and a rigid description of how electric executions could be described to the public: "No account of the details of any such execution, beyond the statement of the fact that such a convict was on the day in question duly executed according to the law at the prison, shall be published in any newspaper. Any person who shall violate or omit to comply with any provision of this section shall be guilty of a misdemeanor."[5] In addition to inventing a new method of execution, the Electric Execution Act sought to impede public sentiment against capital punishment through technological modification and privatization.

Fear of public sympathy for executed individuals has been a long-standing concern in American political history. Kristin Boudreau argues that American nationhood is predicated on public sentiments, or emotional connections, ranging from the feeling that a certain law is morally sensible to the abstract affinity for "fellow citizens" across the country.[6] Yet she notes that these emotional bonds could be strengthened or challenged by personal sympathies, such as pity for a repentant convict who becomes the victim of a brutal hanging. To resolve this problem, inventions that promised to routinize hanging, such as the "upright jerker," gained widespread use in the mid-nineteenth century.[7] Even with these so-called improvements, hangings were inconsistent and frequently disturbing. As a result, between 1830 and 1860, every Northern state moved hangings from a public space into the prison yard.[8] The invention of the electric chair further ensured that executions could be more private and rigorously controlled.

In addition to inventing a layer of bureaucracy that distanced citizens from the process of capital punishment, the Electric Execution Act encouraged activists who opposed hanging to reconceptualize capital punishment as a technological process rather than an atavistic ritual. The abstract promise of instant death made execution palatable, even fascinating, to many Americans—and the role that Thomas Edison and George Westinghouse's "Battle of the Currents" played in the chair's implementation added intrigue to the already provocative idea of state-sanctioned electric death.[9]

Edison notoriously opposed the death penalty in any form before Alfred Southwick, a member of the Gerry Commission, convinced him that his endorsement of electric execution might be profitable. Edison realized that using a Westinghouse AC (alternating current) generator in an electric execution chamber might discourage the public from adopting AC power, although it could travel more efficiently across longer distances than his DC (direct current) power distribution system. Westinghouse fought back, hiring lawyers to challenge the constitutionality of electric execution and even refusing to sell New York (and later Ohio) prisons AC generators. In the end, the electric chair was powered by a Westinghouse generator, but this did not have the effect Edison hoped for or Westinghouse feared. Instead of inciting fear of the power of AC current, newspaper coverage of the Battle of the Currents inspired curiosity. Debates over which inventor-celebrity would "win" the battle overshadowed discussion about the actual fates of people condemned to execution.

Perhaps most importantly, Edison's desire to thwart the rise of AC power helped construct the most potent technological fantasy about electric execution. When asked to describe how the process of electrocution would work, Edison explained, "'When the time comes, touch a button, close the circuit, and'—Edison snapped his fingers—'it is over.'"[10] Although Edison specified that the current should "come from an alternating machine," public interest in the chair gradually crystallized into the frightening but provocative image of technological supremacy that Edison casually referenced: the incongruously small, death-dealing electric button. The fatal button appeared across journalistic and fictional representations, and the type of electric current that powered the chair was gradually forgotten.

Edison's mention of the electric button demonstrates the extent to which electrocution was conceptualized as a technological alternative to hanging before the first electric chair was designed. After the Electric Execution Act passed, many questioned whether this new method would ameliorate public sentiment against capital punishment, but few questioned that such a device would demonstrate the awesome power of modern technology and the state acting in concert. Even critics of the death penalty imagined the electrocution apparatus to be potent and gracefully compact, as in William Dean Howells's 1888 letter to the editor of *Harper's Weekly*: "I understand that the death-spark can be applied . . . without even arousing the victim. . . . I have fancied the executions throughout the State taking place from the Governor's office, where his private secretary, or the Governor himself, might . . . dismiss a murderer to the presence of his Maker with the lightest pressure of the finger."[11] The presumed ease of electrocution signified by the electric button becomes part of the problem, Howells argues, because killing should never be easy.

Mark Twain's *Connecticut Yankee in King Arthur's Court* (1889) similarly criticizes electrocution while maintaining the technological fantasy of instant death. Also published before the electric chair was implemented but after the Electric Execution Act was passed into law, *Connecticut Yankee* imagines the technology of electrocution in a lengthy dialogue that ends with Hank Morgan, the protagonist, detailing the most cost-effective mechanism to his thoroughly modernized sixth-century apprentice, Clarence:

> You don't want any ground-connection except the one through the negative brush.
>
> The other end of every wire must be brought back into the cave and fastened independently, and without any ground-connection. . . . [O]bserve the economy of it. . . . [Y]ou are using no power, you are spending no money, for there is only one ground-connection till those horses come against the wire.[12]

This passage details the hardware of a simple and efficient electrocution apparatus. While Morgan portrays the apparatus as a circuit that will ground itself through bodies with no need for external intervention, he also describes the moment of electrocution, like Edison and Howells, in terms of a simple button: "I touched a button, and shook the bones of England loose from her spine."[13] The hyperbole of breaking the nation's spine with the mere push of a button emphasizes the raw power of electricity and the ease with which Morgan controls it, but the disparity between Twain's descriptions of the method and the moment of electrocution is suggestive. Although he describes the construction of the electrocution apparatus with rational, scientific language, his depiction of actual electrocutions is hyperbolic and excited, peppered with exclamation marks. The astounding body count of twelve thousand knights, though horrifying, denotes the awesome destructive power Twain imagined. In this way, *Connecticut Yankee* illustrates the popular tendency to displace technical understandings of electrocution with the larger fantasy of technological control, epitomized by the electric button that effortlessly extinguishes life.

Rockwell and the Mathematical Impossibility of Pain

Similar to Edison, Howells, and Twain, Alfonso David Rockwell's writings illustrate how fantasies about the instant operability of the electric button could displace the material process of electrocution. Rockwell was an electrical medical expert whose testimony in the U.S. Supreme Court case "In RE Kemmler" (136 U.S. 436) helped to determine that electrocution would not be considered cruel or unusual punishment. Rockwell witnessed the electrocution of scores of animals in order to advise the New York state government about the most effective techniques for implementing the new law. He had directed electricity through many bodies in his medical practice, and he thoroughly understood the mechanisms of the electric chair. Yet curiously, he described hangings that he never witnessed as more "real" than the electrocutions he attended and helped to orchestrate.

In his autobiography, *Rambling Recollections* (1920), Rockwell devotes an entire chapter to "Electro Execution," which begins with a brief description of how sympathy shaped his involvement in the chair's implementation: "It had long been conceded that the rope was a barbarous method of execution, but it is always difficult to substitute a new method for an old, and the long contest over this *merciful* change in the law of the State of New York proved no exception. If the law must kill, let it kill decently. Although no strong advocate for capital punishment I *revolted at the brutality of the* strangulation method." [14] Rockwell's emphasis on sympathy is characteristic of his medical ideology; his objective is the elimination of pain wherever possible—and to Rockwell, the gallows meant pain. Although he never witnessed an execution by hanging, he describes "the horrors of hanging" with some of the most vivid prose of his entire autobiography: "the first terrible fatal fall, the gradual choking, the blackening face, and protruding tongue, and above all the convulsive, agonizing and long-drawn-out struggle." [15] His description of the four successive electrocutions he witnessed at Sing Sing correctional facility are conspicuously less concrete: "as one after the other, these miserable victims . . . took their places in the death-chair . . . a species of dreamlike apathy seemed to steal over me. It all seemed so unreal and without human touch that I could fancy myself wafted to the middle ages." [16] Perhaps Rockwell's reference to the middle ages marks a perceived underlying barbarism to the process, or he simply found the scene fantastic, akin to the electrocutions in Twain's *Connecticut Yankee*. In either case, this sense of unreality, common in depictions of the electric chair, results in part from the physical displacement of the executioner from the execution chamber. As Austin Sarat argues, modern execution laws use "technology to veil the ugly reality of execution, separating cause and effect, and making it unclear who is actually ordering and doing the killing."[17]

Disparate representational treatment of hanging and electrocution also illuminates a trend in how Rockwell—and much of the American public—perceived these methods of capital punishment: death by hanging was tangible whereas death by electrocution was an unreal moment of technological sublimity. Lacking a suitable representational framework to comprehend death by an electric button, even an expert who helped modify the chair's hardware and witnessed electrocutions firsthand can only apprehend the experience as "unreal." Importantly, Rockwell does not use this sense of unreality to forgive his role in the death penalty. While he saw the electric chair as a moderate improvement over the brutality of hanging, he never saw it as a perfectible solution: "I experienced a feeling of shame and blood-guiltiness. As never before the awful meaning of the terms 'immutable' and 'irrevocable' was driven in. What if one of these men was not truly guilty?"[18]

Rockwell concludes with a description of the electric chair that mimics the rationalizing discourse that justified its invention, though he qualifies this with a trace of sympathy:

> Aside from the knowledge that a human life is being sacrificed, there is nothing revolting in the sight. With face covered and person securely bound, the victim awaits the final stroke, and the translation from life to death is quicker than thought, and with the mathematical impossibility of pain. . . . The certainty that no pain can be experienced under a lethal dose of electricity is evident from the fact that, while nerve force travels at the rate of but 100 feet a second, electricity travels at the rate of 160,000 miles a second. The brain, therefore, can have absolutely no time to experience a sensation, since the electrical current travels a million times faster than the nerve current.[19]

Although he describes "the mathematical impossibility of pain," Rockwell modifies this final passage with the provocative clause: "Aside from the knowledge that a human life is being sacrificed." In this manner, he signals that the rationalized discourse of instant death is insufficient to justify the practice; the scene can only be perceived as clean and scientific when the knowledge of death is set "aside."

The contrast between his dreamlike observation of the executions and his rationalization thereafter demonstrates that his sympathetic and scientific interpretations are complementary—both perspectives are necessary to comprehend the stakes of electric executions, but he experiences and describes them separately. Rockwell was not alone in this respect. An analogous split was perpetuated within most articles about the chair, which treated scientific expertise—including Rockwell's own testimonies—as separate from or antagonistic toward perspectives that sympathetically focused on the human component of the execution circuit. This fundamental division inflected electric chair narratives for years, adding to the device's ambiguous characterization by suggesting that any descriptive detail about the chair could be subjective and debatable.[20] Legal electrocution paradoxically became characterized as material and ethereal, alluring and terrifying.

The First Electric Chair Experiment

In the nineteenth and early twentieth centuries, debates about electricity's effects on the body inspired many to question the ethics of new technological practices. By the late 1890s electric execution often registered with the American reading public as "unreal" or—because of Edison and Westinghouse's corporate involvement—as propagandistic exaggeration. The increasing popularity of electrical medicine sparked arguments between doctors and electrical scientists about whether the pursuit of knowledge gave anyone the right to experiment with living human subjects, and this debate was intensified by the invention of the chair.[21] Newspapers staged a public conversation, using the first electric executions to question whether science (as an abstract, monolithic force) served the public or whether it used the public to serve its own interests. Although papers depicted electric executions as philosophical battlegrounds to question the role that ethics or empathy could play in modern science, even the most critical electric chair narratives tended to heighten the chair's iconic status, shifting readers' attention from the electrocuted body to a limited set of social issues.

The most famous of such public discussions surrounded the first use of the electric chair in the execution of William Kemmler. Since Kemmler plainly admitted to murder and there were no counterclaims suggesting his innocence, newspapers showed almost no compassion for the loss of his life. Instead, his story sparked debates about whose interests were served by the electric chair and by technological development in general. An example from *The National Police Gazette*, a sensational weekly journal, challenges the authority and ethics of the doctors and scientists who staged the electrocution.[22] According to the *Police Gazette*, Kemmler revealed the potential horror of this scientific method of execution with a simple request—"just don't let them experiment with me too much"—suggesting that, to Kemmler, becoming an object of scientific inquiry was the most frightening aspect of electrocution. The gory description which follows suggests that his execution was indeed a disturbing experiment:

The witnesses, all supposing the man was dead, crowded around the death chair. Somebody removed the electrode from Kemmler's head. Then something occurred that froze the blood in the spectator's veins, and, as one witness said, made him long that he should be struck blind, for he could not close his eyes or turn his head, and yet what he saw fairly made him dizzy with horror. . . . [T]he supposed lifeless chest began to move up and down in deep-strained breathing.

The report challenges the notion of instantaneousness, but it also transforms Kemmler's body into a sensational narrative by displacing him as a victim of state power and by using him as evidence against the authority of science. Kemmler's writhing, bleeding body attests not to a human's agony, but to the imperfect circuitry of the chair and the attending doctors' inability to diagnose his death. Such writing practices emphasize the spectator's suffering above the victim's, suggesting that the execution was problematic not because it "reminded [viewers] of the ferocity of the state's sovereign power over life itself," but because it was not palatable to a genteel audience.[23] Although descriptions of many bungled hangings often seemed more drawn out and painful than Kemmler's botched electrocution, his execution was considered a greater failure because it "suggested that the quest for a painless, and allegedly humane, technology of death was by no means complete."[24] Thus, while Kemmler's execution was horrifying, it did not eradicate the technological fantasy of the electric chair.

Less sensational reports than the *Police Gazette*'s discussed the desire to perfect electric execution more overtly.[25] On the morning after Kemmler's execution, the *New York Times* published a description of the event on its front page, supplemented on the second page by an article that hypothesizes, "Westinghouse Is Satisfied. He Thinks There Will Be No More Electrical Executions."[26] Like the *Police Gazette*, the *Times* article describes the admittedly bungled execution as a horrifying "experiment," but it argues that such experiments are an important step in the perfection of any process, including capital punishment. Indicating that abolishing the chair would serve Westinghouse's, and not society's, best interests, the *Times* suggests that the pain that the victim suffered would serve scientific progress. Although the forms of the *Police Gazette* and *Times* articles are different, both demonstrate how electrocution narratives often functioned liked sensationalist fiction, textualizing victims' bodies to question competing ideologies.[27] Through newspaper coverage, Kemmler's body can be perceived alternately as a scientific artifact that teaches experts more about electric medicine or as a casualty of the "battle" between Edison and Westinghouse.

Given this context, Atherton's novel *Patience Sparhawk and Her Times* takes on crucial significance as one of the few novels that directly addresses contemporary reading and writing practices as an important component in the social meanings of electric executions. Like the newspaper reports of Kemmler's execution, the novel raises questions about how to read the body of an accused criminal. Further, it links the violence of capital punishment to contemporary journalism and even assimilates its readers as voyeurs who perpetuate electric execution with their avid curiosity. The marked increase in sales of electrical medical devices following reports of Kemmler's electrocution suggests that electric chair narratives did not inspire outrage, fear, or sympathy, but instead sparked individuals' curiosity about the effects electricity would have on their own bodies.[28] Confronting this issue, Atherton suggests that late nineteenth-century Americans apprehend the electric chair as unreal because it has been overwritten by formulaic narratives from news stories. In contrast, Atherton shows that the form of the novel allows readers to apprehend the electric chair more critically than brief articles or narratives that focus solely on the chair's supposed instantaneity.

Atherton loosely based her criminal plot on a contemporary example she considered overly discussed: the 1893 trial and execution of Carlyle Harris. Though she made her protagonist female rather than male, she adapted the most recognizable elements of the case, including the type of murder (overdose of morphine), the courtroom rhetoric (the argument that an intelligent person would not administer an overdose of morphine because it would be "too obvious"), and the condemned's demeanor in the execution chamber (cooperative and reserved). Atherton's brief discussion of Carlyle Harris in her autobiography suggests that in her opinion there was nothing exceptional about his case to warrant this degree of popular interest.²⁹ Rather, she suggests that the public's voracious interest stemmed from the dramatic narrative structure of the trial and execution.

Patience Sparhawk and Her Times

Largely forgotten by literary critics, Patience Sparhawk and Her Times foresees important critiques that will be made by later electric chair fictions, such as Theodore Dreiser's novel American Tragedy (1925) and Sophie Treadwell's play Machinal (1928). Three decades after the publication of Patience Sparhawk, Dreiser and Treadwell created powerful characters who are driven to commit murder by systematic oppression. Their attempts to transcend restrictive social situations are met with the state's calculated, murderous response. Atherton, however, places an innocent character in the chair, raising different questions about truth, sympathy, and justice in modern America.

Patience Sparhawk was published by John Lane of the Bodley house, known for publishing controversial works, especially by and about "New Women." Although readers would expect John Lane's books to be less sensational and lowbrow than dime novels or criminal narratives, advertisements for Patience Sparhawk encouraged sensational expectations by describing the book as the "American maelstrom" and frequently quoting Atherton's claim that she "cannot write an article for a newspaper, much less a novel, without throwing the entire United States press into a ferment." ³⁰ Patience Sparhawk invites readers to expect a sensational or controversial conclusion, and Atherton uses these expectations to motivate her critique of the role that sensational journalism plays in the practice of capital punishment.

Patience Sparhawk is comprised of five books that detail Patience's life from an atavistic fifteen-year-old Californian, to the young wife of a boring wealthy member of the New York elite, and finally to an independent woman who leaves her husband (and his money) to become a journalist for the Day. In the final book of the novel, Patience is wrongly accused of killing her estranged husband, but condemned because the lower-class jury resents her snobbery and because she had a violent past; she had attacked her mother once at the age of fifteen. Although Patience is eventually saved, her rescue comes not through conventional appeals, but through the attempts of her love interest and lawyer, Garan Bourke, who does everything he can to save her, even encouraging a priest to elicit deceptively a confession from the woman whom he suspects of framing Patience.

The novel challenges the efficacy of the criminal justice system by stressing that Bourke must work around it to save Patience from wrongful execution, yet it does not promote radical systemic change. Although *Patience Sparhawk* features a powerful female protagonist with protofeminist autonomy and willfulness, it never considers that race or xenophobia were (and are) prominent factors in how the state implements capital punishment. It resolves the failure of the criminal justice system by resorting to romance, suggesting that a lack of active emotional agency is a larger cultural problem than the prejudices built into modern correctional institutions. Still, published four years after the press gag clause was repealed from the Electric Execution Act, and shortly after the English translation of Cesare Lombroso's popular *The Female Offender* (1895), *Patience Sparhawk* engages complex ideologies that sought to perceive bodies as texts.

The novel never mentions Lombroso directly, but several characters express concerns that Patience's innate constitution could be dangerous. At the age of fifteen, Patience's surrogate grandfather figure, Mr. Foord, tells her, "If you remain here you will grow up bitter and hard, and the result with your brain and temperament may be terrible."[31] Even Bourke tells Patience, "there's a force in you, and force doesn't go to waste, although it's more often than not misdirected."[32] In the first book of the novel, Patience lives up to these Lombrosian expectations. After her mother initiates an altercation, Patience "screamed harshly and springing at her mother clutched her about the throat. The lust to kill possessed her. . . . Instinctively she tripped her mother and went down on top of her." After this rage subsides, Patience "felt no repentance, no remorse." In fact, she even feels "elation" at becoming "the sensation of the hour."[33] However, by making Patience innocent, the novel suggests that biological determinism is an insufficient and even dangerous method of reading bodies. Atherton is less concerned with how her readers understand criminality than with whether they view Patience as many viewed Kemmler and Harris: unsympathetically, with voyeuristic interest in their deaths.

After problematizing Lombrosian methods for reading criminality onto bodies, *Patience Sparhawk* raises questions about other methods for textualizing human lives. The novel directly implicates writers in the process of capital punishment. Although her violent history contributes to her conviction, Patience's indictment is first inspired by the speculation of a sensational journalist from *The Eye*, a rival paper to her *Day*. Newspapers catalyze her wrongful conviction and eerily delimit Patience's behavior in the execution chamber, threatening to expedite her electrocution. By linking sensational journalism to the violence of capital punishment, Atherton lambastes journalists and readers for their voyeuristic interest in following a crime story to its most sensational conclusion—in this case the electrocution of an innocent woman.

Unlike Howells and Twain, who preserve in their writings the mythologized notion that electric death is instantaneous, Atherton suggests that nothing is instant about it. Her electric chair scene takes time. It sidesteps the aspect which held such fascination for the late nineteenth-century reader and writer—the moment the current kills—drawing attention to the fact that the chair's meanings are laboriously, consistently produced *around*, as well as within, the moment of electric shock through the circulation and production of stories. Like her contemporaries, Atherton was interested in the chair's hardware; she even traveled to Sing Sing to sit in the chair herself for research.[34] Yet in the novel she shifts attention away from the device to demonstrate that no matter how rational, mystified, or mishandled the apparatus, it is still almost exclusively apprehended through written representations.

This critical depiction of sensational journalism appears early in the novel, after Patience first finds herself rendered as "news." Excited to see her name in print, she feels "the same thrill she had experienced when the men looked askance at her after her assault upon her mother," but chastises herself for this suggestively charged "thrill": " 'What fools we mortals be!' she thought. 'If a woman is run over in the street she has a column, and if she goes to a hotel and commits suicide, she has two, and is a raving beauty.' "[35] Although she becomes a journalist shortly after this scene, her inner monologue draws an association between sensational journalism and violence by equating column lengths with the manner in which a woman dies.[36] She affiliates the feeling of seeing her name in print with the public's awareness of her private dispute with her mother. Not only did this altercation occur in the home, it was a revealing moment for Patience, who discovered an essential truth about herself by unleashing her atavistic instincts. The act of making such intensely private moments public, this passage implies, is always potentially violent.[37]

This antagonistic characterization of journalism gains intensity in the last book of the novel when Patience's awareness of herself as news trumps her fear of imminent death. She refuses brandy in the execution chamber because the "exaltation of heroism was beginning to possess her, and she would give no newspaper the chance to say that she owed her fortitude to alcohol."[38] Patience's comportment reveals her concern about how the journalists will depict her, and, since Carlyle Harris refused an alcoholic beverage before his execution, it is another novelistic reference to his case. This scene would have reminded readers of an actual electrocuted body, just as it solidified expectation that Patience's story will parallel Harris's, whose electrocution was followed by his loved ones' exclamations of his innocence.[39]

Atherton emphasizes the tragedy of Patience's metatextual perspective: "there was a sense of unreality in it all. She felt as if she was going to play some great final act; she could not realize that the climax meant her own annihilation."[40] Her sense of unreality does not make her imminent execution any less real within the novel, but it demonstrates the danger of apprehending the electric chair through melodramatic narrative frameworks. Although Patience is a willful and individually motivated character, in the execution chamber she can function only according to trite dramatic conventions. By interpreting the electrocution chamber as a setting in the journalists' sensational narratives and acting according to her perceived role in this setting, Patience casts off her agency and expedites the process of her own execution, thwarting the prison guard's attempts to stall in the hope that Bourke might find a way to save her. In this way, Atherton draws attention to the harmfulness of this performance. Since the reader knows that Patience is innocent, her adherence to the ritual of executing justice seems tragically absurd. In these final scenes, Patience's stubborn notion that refusing to fight back will force the journalists to describe her as heroic implies that the value systems which inform popular representational frameworks perpetuate, rather than objectively describe, capital punishment.

Atherton inscribes this critique onto the bodies of the journalists, as well. As they watched Patience enter the execution chamber and sit in the electric chair, they "regarded her with deep sympathy, and perhaps a bitter resentment at the impotence of their manhood. One looked as if he should faint. . . . Only one watched her with wolfish curiosity. He was the youngest of them all, and it was his first great story."[41] Only one of the journalists is inhumanly eager for the story, and even this young reporter's "wolfish[ness]" signifies "impotence" rather than vigor. This description engages the contemporary debate about whether journalists should remain detached or act on their sympathy and intervene in the news they report.[42] Ultimately, Atherton implies that by positioning themselves as "objective" observers, these journalists sacrifice their ability to effect change and even their own masculinity is challenged. Unlike these passive observers, Bourke is conspicuously *not* objective. As Patience's lawyer and lover, he is invested in her rescue. Rather than representing a feminized flaw, his emotional connection with Patience is the key component of his heroism and masculinity. Indeed, in the novel, the journalists' inability to foster such emotional connections is their moral undoing. Their writing fosters the sense of unreality about the electric chair that inhibits social action against it.

Atherton expands this critique by linking the culture of sensationalism that the journalists espouse with a broader lack of sympathy. The novel's electric chair sequence includes a description of women eagerly anticipating Patience's execution: "The women sat about on the slope opposite the prison, pushing the baby carriages absently back and forth, or gossiping with animation. Other women crowded up the bluff, settling themselves comfortably to await, with what patience they could muster, the elevation of the black flag."[43] These curious mothers represent a traditional domestic femininity, complicated by their cruel desire for Patience's electrocution. They do not lament or protest the execution of another woman; they revel in it.

As the scene shifts from the hilltop to the execution chamber, Atherton encourages readers to anticipate Patience's electrocution with similar excitement, collapsing their perspective with that of the women on the hill. By painting Patience as an areligious, outspoken heroine, she forces readers to wonder whether this character, who after all did try to kill her mother, should be rescued. The possibility of execution includes the classically tragic element of nearly missed love, and it offers a description of something that had not yet happened anywhere in the world: the electrocution of a woman.[44] One contemporary critic of the novel even said that Patience's rescue comes "somewhat to the regret of the sympathetic reader."[45] Another expressed detachment from Patience and Garan Bourke, while admitting that the novel "closes with an excellent report of a murder trial, in which there is an unmistakable touch of dramatic power."[46] This heightened interest in the criminal plot suggests that such readers' experiences coincided with those of the women on the hill; both voyeuristically await news of Patience's electrocution.

The drawn-out electric chair sequence amplifies readers' anticipation. Although Patience "walk[s] deliberately to the chair," the head-keeper interrupts the standard procedure to examine it "in detail" and to ask the electrician several questions about its operability.[47] His inspection of the device delays the narrative and intensifies the climax; it also draws attention to the frequency of mistakes associated with electric executions, reminding readers of the sensational possibility that the chair could malfunction. Atherton enhances this suspense by repeatedly describing sensations that seem to represent electrocution, and then clarifying that the current was not yet turned on: "Her mind was a sudden blaze of light—which light she thought with a stifled shriek."[48] With each metaphorically electrical detail, Atherton heightens the reader's curiosity for the "shocking" conclusion.

After building readers' excitement for Patience's electrocution, Atherton discharges the suspenseful energy in a suddenly romantic turn. On the last page of the novel, Bourke rescues Patience just as she braces for the electric shock:

> Suddenly her ears were pierced by a din which made her muscles leap against the straps. Was she in hell, and was this her greeting? She had felt a second's thankfulness that death had been painless.
>
> Then, out of the babel of sound, she distinguished words which made her sit erect and open her eyes, her pulses bound, her blood leap. . . . The cap had been removed, the men were unbuckling the straps. . . . Round her the newspaper men were pressing, shouting and cheering, trying to get at her hand to shake it.
>
> She smiled and held out her hand, but dared not speak to them. Pride still lived, and she was afraid she should cry.[49]

This final scene opens with Patience's muscles "leap[ing] against the straps," tantalizing readers with the promise of electrocution. By tricking her readers to imagine with Patience that the electrocution was over before the current was even switched on, Atherton pokes fun at the technological fantasy of instant and painless death. More importantly, by short-circuiting the electrocution narrative, she forces readers to confront their fantasies about electrocution and their urge to see the sensational narrative through to its end.

This conclusion does more than substitute romance for sensationalism. The journalists inhibit the novel's romantic conclusion, since Patience censors her emotional response to her rescue in their presence. To Atherton, every representation of electrocution is a fiction, an assemblage of fantasies about a "great story" and technological progress. By concluding with this hybrid of romance and sensation, she draws attention to the fact that readers are compelled by the mystery of electrocution, but also demonstrates that this attraction implies complicity in the outcome.

Conclusion

In recent years lethal injection has become the preferred "scientific" method of capital punishment, but the electric chair has yet to be entirely phased out. In 2007 Daryl Keith Holton became the first Tennessee inmate to be electrocuted in decades.[50] The fantasy of perfect disciplinary technology has been a distraction and a justification for over a century. Only a few years after the invention of the electric chair, Atherton recognized that American culture was becoming complacent with—and complicit in—the practice of capital punishment. Despite her piercing critique of sensationalism, however, Atherton likely would have preferred nineteenth-century voyeuristic curiosity to the blasé attitude many Americans have about capital punishment today. As we reconsider the cultural meanings of technological executions in the twenty-first century, *Patience Sparhawk* uses a biographical form that reminds us that executions are a human process, not a technological one. The finger that pushes the electric button and the body in the chair are connected by a larger human circuit, shaped by too many desires and prejudices, too many complicated actions and reactions, to be just, rational, instant, or scientific.

Notes

My gratitude to the Bakken Library and Museum for a 2008 Fellowship that enabled me to complete research for this essay.

1. Dwight Conquergood, "Lethal Theatre: Performance, Punishment, and the Death Penalty," *Theatre Journal* 54.3 (2002): 360.

2. Stuart Banner, *The Death Penalty: An American History* (Cambridge: Harvard Univ. Press, 2002): 163. For more on the repeal of the press gag clause see Craig Brandon, *The Electric Chair: An Unnatural American History* (London: McFarland & Co, 1999): 200–204; Richard Moran, *Executioner's Current: Thomas Edison, George Westinghouse, and the Invention of the Electric Chair* (New York: Alfred A. Knopf, 2002): 213.

3. See Hugo Adam Bedau, "An Abolitionist's Survey of the Death Penalty in America Today," in *Debating the Death Penalty: Should America Have Capital Punishment? The Experts on Both Sides Make Their Best Case*, eds. Hugo Adam Bedau and Paul G. Cassel (New York: Oxford Univ. Press, 2004): 20; and Austin Sarat, *When the State Kills: Capital Punishment and the American Condition* (Princeton: Princeton Univ. Press, 2001): 61–84.

4. Elbridge T. Gerry, Alfred P. Southwick, and Matthew Hale, "Report of the Commission to Investigate and Report the Most Humane and Practical Method of Carrying into Effect the Sentence of Death in Capital Cases" (Albany: Argus, 1888): 3.

5. "Electrical Execution Act," Chapter 489, *Laws of the State of New York* (July 1888).

6. Kristin Boudreau, *The Spectacle of Death: Populist Literary Responses to American Capital Cases* (New York: Prometheus Books, 2006): 21.

7. Banner, *Death Penalty*, 171–72.

8. Ibid., 146.

9. For more on Edison's role in the invention of the electric chair, see Elizabeth Barnes, "Communicable Violence and the Problem of Capital Punishment in New England, 1830–1890," *Modern Language Studies* 20.1 (2000): 24; H. Bruce Franklin, "Billy Budd and Capital Punishment: A Tale of Four Centuries," in this collection.

10. Mark Essig, *Edison and the Electric Chair: A Story of Light and Death* (New York: Walker, 2003): 133.

11. William Dean Howells, "Execution by Electricity," *Harper's Weekly*, January 14, 1888, 23b.

12. Mark Twain, *A Connecticut Yankee in King Arthur's Court*, ed. Shelly Fisher Fishkin (New York: Oxford Univ. Press, 1996): 542.

13. Ibid., 554.

14. Alfonso David Rockwell, *Rambling Recollections: An Autobiography* (New York: P.B. Hoeber, 1920): 221, emphasis added.

15. Ibid., 232.

16. Ibid., 231.

17. Sarat, *When the State Kills*, 64. See Roger Neustadter, "The Death Penalty in the Industrial Age," *Journal of American Culture* 12.3 (1989): 80.

18. Rockwell, *Rambling*, 231.

19. Ibid., 232.

20. According to Karen Roggenkamp, the American reading public expected news stories to be somewhat fictionalized. See *Narrating the News: New Journalism and Literary Genre in Late Nineteenth-Century American Newspapers and Fiction* (Kent, OH: Kent State Univ. Press, 2005): 56.

21. For example, see George Miller Beard, "Experiments with Living Human Beings," *Popular Science Monthly*, March 1879, 611–757.

22. "Electrocuted," *National Police Gazette*, August 23, 1890, 6.

23. Sarat, *When the State Kills*, 62.

24. Ibid., 62.

25. For descriptions of the electric chair that emphasize the scientific process, see "Kemmler's Death Chamber: How the Electric Current Is to Be Transmitted to His Body," *New York Times*, April 26, 1890, 2; and "Capital Punishment," *New York Times*, December 17, 1887, 4.

26. "Far Worse than Hanging," *New York Times*, August 7, 1890, 1; "Westinghouse Is Satisfied," *New York Times*, August 7, 1890, 2.

27. On reading bodies and execution, see Sarat, *When the State Kills*, 71–81. On sensationalism and bodies, see Jonathan Elmer, *Reading at the Social Limit: Affect, Mass Culture, and Edgar Allan Poe* (Stanford: Stanford Univ. Press, 1995): 102.

28. Carolyn Thomas de la Peña, *The Body Electric: How Strange Machines Built the Modern American* (New York: New York Univ. Press, 2003): 113.

29. Gertrude Atherton, *Adventures of a Novelist* (New York: Liveright, 1932): 151, 222.

30. "Patience Sparhawk and Her Times," *The Dial: A Semi-monthly Journal of Literary Criticism, Discussion and Information*, October 1, 1897, 170; and "Topics of the Times," *New York Times*, May 15, 1898, 18.

31. Gertrude Atherton, *Patience Sparhawk and Her Times* (New York: Macmillan, 1908): 49.

32. Ibid., 56.

33. Ibid., 43.

34. Emily Wortis Leider, *California's Daughter: Gertrude Atherton and Her Times* (Stanford: Stanford Univ. Press, 1993): 147.

35. Atherton, *Patience Sparhawk*, 290.

36. For more on Atherton's representations of journalism, see Jean Marie Lutes, *Front Page Girls: Women Journalists in American Culture and Fiction: 1880–1930*, (Ithaca: Cornell Univ. Press, 2006): 104.

37. Atherton, *Patience Sparhawk*, 43.

38. Ibid., 482.

39. "Carlyle W. Harris Is Dead," *New York Times*, May 9, 1893, 8.

40. Atherton, *Patience Sparhawk*, 481.

41. Ibid., 483.

42. Roggenkamp, *Narrating*, 98.

43. Atherton, *Patience Sparhawk*, 479.

44. The first woman to be executed in the electric chair was Martha M. Place at Sing Sing Prison on March 20, 1899.

45. "The Epic of the Advanced Woman," *The Chap-Book; Semi-Monthly: A Miscellany & Review of Belles Lettres*, April 15, 1897, 444.

46. "Literature," *The Critic: A Weekly Review of Literature and the Arts*, April 24, 1897, 283.

47. Atherton, *Patience Sparhawk*, 484.

48. Ibid., 486.

49. Ibid., 488.

50. Dan Barry, "Death in the Chair, Step by Remorseless Step," *New York Times*, September 16, 2007, 1.

CAST OF CHARACTERS (in order of appearance)
JOJO, a black man, 54
CRAZY HORSE, a Native American man, 35
NAT TURNER, a black man, 31
ANDY, a white man, 50s
KATIE, a white girl, 15
LUCY, a black woman, 50s
PARAMEDIC (may double with Crazy Horse or Nat Turner)

Death Row, the present. Three adjacent cells. They are divided by walls but these need not be represented literally so long as they are clearly defined. Cell doors, or bars, should be invisible so as not to hinder sight lines.

Andy's chuckle is soft, not a snicker, and often more to himself than to the others. He is good natured, and while his laughing habit may at times seem inappropriate, there is never any intention of cruelty.

SCENE 1

[JOJO sleeps. Suddenly his eyes open.]

JOJO
Hey! I got company. [*He taps on the wall between the cells*] I'm Jojo.
Grew up with Isaiah, he says "Let's go on a adventure ride."
Seen them hitchhikers, one in jean shorts frayed one in black
pants, their car stalled. They ask for a lift to the gas station, we
took 'em the other direction. Raped 'em, strangled 'em. One was
fifteen, one was seventeen. I was twenty-two. I'm fifty-four.

CRAZY HORSE
I'm thirty-five. All rests on the decoys, the timing, when to let
them see us, when to move. They think they're trapping us, if
they suspect otherwise, it's over. I was the decoy leader. Winter
battle, they followed like clockwork like clay we molded the

outcome Fetterman's Soldiers we led them to their deaths a hundred! And Stanley's soldiers under Long Hair Custer, and later, later when I feared all was lost came the Rosebud. I charge, and behind a few fall in, then twice that many behind them, twice that many behind them mighty triangle we form spirit not broken!

NAT TURNER

Crazy Horse!

[JOJO rushes to the other side of his cell. CRAZY HORSE smiles: recognition.]

JOJO

Somebody else! [*No answer*] Hey! Jojo. Rape-murder. Fifty-four.

NAT TURNER

Thirty-one. I drew blood only once, one battle, a woman. Beat her to death. Rest of the war I was the general, organizer, the hands-off orchestrator. The enemy was everything white: "Do not spare age nor sex," I commanded. Men, women, down came the ax, throng of schoolchildren we tossed their headless bodies in a pile, and that's just the abridged version of what we did to them. What they did to us was worse. Nat Turner.

[ANDY enters and, as he speaks, continues crossing the stage to the other side.]

ANDY

[Chuckles to himself]

I remember Nat Turner. [*Sings*] "Unforgettable. . ."

[Exits.]

JOJO

Fellas way down the corridor, but nobody this corner but me, nine years I been monasteryin'. 'Til now. Welcome to the neighborhood.

SCENE 2

[The sound of a clock ticking, second by second. CRAZY HORSE has removed his shirt, socks and shoes. He stands bare-chested, barefoot. JOJO rubs his forearms, cold. NAT does calisthenics to keep warm.]

JOJO

Stud!

[ANDY enters]

ANDY

I ain't gettin' in the game. In Vegas, dealer's the one in charge. [Chuckles]

JOJO

"How the hell you play poker on death row?" you're thinkin'. "The excitement's in the bettin', what we got to bet?" Minutes. One hour every twenty-four we let outa our cells, outside. These sixty minutes is now up for grabs, for every minute you lose you stay inside, tell the C.O., "Sorry, needta crap, gotta stay in my cell 'til I'm done. C.O. say, "Your time, your loss." That you already knew.

ANDY

Hey, Jojo, ain't this a thrill? Other hands beside mine and yours? [Chuckles.]

NAT

Card playing not on my mind, late November chill out. When they turn on the heat?

JOJO

Card playin' somethin' keep your brain off the chill. [No reply. JOJO shrugs.] Kills time.

NAT

Kill that clock! When'd it start?

JOJO

Somethin' in the mechanism went outa whack years ago, dead, who cares? Clock watchin' hardly a popular death row sport. But every few months, no rhyme or reason, suddenly it resurrect: Tick. Tick. Tick. Tick.

ANDY
[Deals to NAT first.]
Crazy got the button. One with the button's the imaginary dealer.

NAT
What's the point? Never be granted more than your daily sixty, so what? you win. Where's the booty?

JOJO
Winnin' the right to do your sixty, the knowledge you get to keep what's yours. If you don't find that precious and rare, you ain't been in long. [Beat] You ain't been in long?

NAT
[Shakes his head no]
And won't be here much longer.

[ANDY has dealt two face-down cards to each and lain one apiece face up outside of the cells. JOJO and CRAZY HORSE have picked up their cards; ANDY and NAT are staring at each other. Then NAT picks up his cards.]

ANDY
Here's what shows: Nat—queen a hearts, Jojo—tray a diamonds, Crazy—ace a spades. Nat first.

[Now ANDY sits outside the cells, staring in.]

JOJO
How soon? Your date.

NAT
Soon. But someone else I know's going down sooner. Five minutes.

ANDY
[Staring at NAT]
And the openin' bet's been placed well I notice a little twitch to his right eye. No, left. And just a moment a clutchin' his cards tighter.

NAT
The cell next to me, this boy, twenty-eight, going to die tomorrow. Gordon.

JOJO

I remember Gordon! Decade ago, when they first bring him here put him right down the hall. Eighteen. Talker!

NAT

When the C.O. throws his dinner at him, Gordon smiles, "Thank you, Mr. Reece." He cleans his plate and is proud of it, tells me. Armed robbery, murder, the two boys he did the deed with usually call him dummy but this day let him play. When the shop owner came running in, screaming, somebody pulled the trigger. Other boys fled. When the police came, Gordon still kneeling, trying to wake the shop owner from his nap.

JOJO

Raise. Ten minutes.

ANDY

Whew! Pushin' the stakes. [Staring at JOJO] Eyelids lifted ever so slightly. The lashes give 'em away. [Chuckles]

NAT

Police ask Gordon if he did it, they've already decided he did. "Yes sir," he says. I ask Gordon if he did it, I don't believe he did. "No sir," he says. Gordon's a good boy. Gordon just aims to please.

JOJO

I remember this about Gordon—one belongin': *One Fish Two Fish Red Fish Blue Fish* by Dr. Seuss which he read every single day like it was the first time.

NAT

In our block I started the loud chanting. "Injustice," "racism," "A.B.A. Resolution 2" which is related to mental incapacity. None of these terms did Gordon understand, he didn't understand we were chanting for him. But he joined in. C.O.s knew I was the fire starter, moved me out. A hundred times, this way and that he's been told his date's tomorrow, going to die tomorrow. In case he's got anything left to do, think about, that information he has a right to. He says "I know" but doesn't. When they take me away, he says he's going to practice, by the time I get back he'll count clear up to twenty, no mistakes.

ANDY
[To CRAZY HORSE]
Mr. Horse! The game's waitin' for you. Hey! [The interjection because he just took a good look at CRAZY HORSE]

CRAZY HORSE
Call.

ANDY
Aintchu cold? [CRAZY HORSE doesn't answer] Hey! He ain't got no shirt on he ain't got no shoes, aintcher nose and toes ice cubed like ours?

NAT
Let him alone.

ANDY
This mornin' in the shower you complainin' cuza the lukewarm quality, you beggin' for steam, now look like you beggin' for pneumonia.

JOJO
Ain't eatin' nothin' neither. Starvin', freezin'. Like he tryn to get the fever.

NAT
Fasting. Which is a universe apart from starving, and the shower complaint wasn't about comfort. He's trying to find higher ground. He's looking for a vision, longs to see. Showers aren't a sweat lodge but through sultrier temps he was hoping for a facsimile. Lukewarm didn't cut it. [To ANDY] Hit the deck.

ANDY
Fourth Street. [Deals another card to each of them]

JOJO
Rape-murder I'm in for, that tend to be a arbitrary thing. But mass killin' usually got some kinda motive.

ANDY
Seven a diamonds to Nat, Jojo got the club deuce, four a spades to Crazy.

NAT

I was the sharp one. Preacher. I could read but that just made me their book-smart nigger, a novelty showpiece, twelve years old they turn me into the fields like everyone else. When I'm twenty-one, country hits a depression so they have a choice: sell us or work us harder, and already we work sunup to sundown. Guess which choice Master Turner makes? Hires a new overseer, new whip, I escape. Fifteen.

ANDY

Cool movin', not even a break in the inflection.

NAT

Month later I return. God gave me the sign: I wasn't yet finished serving my earthly master. Weren't the black people bitter: "You the one s'posed to be so smart?" It wasn't time. But time came.

JOJO

Call.

CRAZY HORSE

Twenty.

ANDY

[Staring at CRAZY HORSE]
Straight face, I catch nothin'. Wait. Twitch a the pinkie?

NAT

Funny thing about Virginia.

ANDY

Fifth Street. [Deals cards]

NAT

North South, considered themselves the benevolent slavers. "We're the good masters," said they, "Look at Alabama, Mississippi." Compared to them, we were treated well, they thought. Not well enough. Thirty.

CRAZY HORSE

Freezing! The whites gave them blankets. Old days, before Indians learned Never Trust 'Em. Thanked them for their generosity, they didn't know the blankets had been infected with smallpox. Whole camps disappeared, *their* disease. [Pause] She was five. [Pause] My only child.

JOJO

Call.

CRAZY HORSE

We called her They Are Afraid Of Her. [Beat] Call.

ANDY

Six Street. [Deals]

JOJO

I got a daughter. Charmaine. She was a baby. Now she's thirty-two, her age is always how long I been inside plus one. Newlyweds with a baby, I married cuz she was pregnant. Lucy and me livin' in the trailer park, a little grass to each house. Lucy was rockin' my screamin' baby when I go out to pull the weeds crowdin' out the back door. Then Isaiah drives by "Jojo! Let's go on a adventure ride."

NAT

Pass.

JOJO

Her name was Katie. I forget the other girl's name, the one Isaiah done it to. Their little light blue car stalled, a basketball sits in the back winda. All through the court proceedin's they's mentioned, how come I can't remember that other gal's name? Maybe I Freud-blocked it.

ANDY

[To NAT and JOJO]

He'll die tonight. Your friend. Gordon. His official date's tomorra so they watchin' the clock now. They like to get it done with, they waitin' for the minute hand to turn midnight. At twelve o' one, it happens.

NAT

Fold. [NAT drops his cards, folding]

ANDY

You can't fold, you just passed, it ain't your turn! [NAT doesn't pick up the cards]

JOJO

Forty.

CRAZY HORSE

Call.

ANDY

Whew! we ain't never flown this high before. Seventh Street: The Wire. [ANDY deals]

NAT

[More to himself]
My mother was a teenager kidnapped from Africa. When I was born a slave on American soil she tried to kill me. The whites saved me. [Laughing] The whites saved me!

ANDY

Thirty-one years together, Jojo, thirty-one years you here, and I started workin' just weeks after you come. All that time, just you and me and the cards. How you know I never cheat? [Chuckles]

JOJO

When I first hear you shufflin', Poker you say, I think Why?
I got nothin' to lose. You got one hour to lose you point out to me, and I ponder that. Cheat me? You gave me, Andy, plenty!
Now I see: I got stuff a value, worth. Hear it?
[Silence except for the ticking of the clock.]

SCENE 3

JOJO
[Closes his eyes]
Come on.

[A blood-curdling scream off. JOJO, eyes open now, slaps his hands together: the sound implies he is slapping someone else.]

JOJO

Scream again, I'll kill ya. [Sound of fast, loud breathing, off]
Be quiet!

KATIE

[Off]

JOJO

I said Shut up, bitch! [KATIE enters, carrying a basketball]
Katie!

KATIE

Didn't think you be callin', look like you got new people to kill
time with.

JOJO

[Guilty]

Almost didn't but . . . I gotta see you.

KATIE

Almost didn't. Ain't you fickle. Tease, the haunted house,
your ol' deserted next-door residences been filled, now guess
your social calendar's too jam-packed for your previous
acquaintances.

JOJO

No! you always with me. Just . . . you never come 'less you
make me remember it first. My bad day, bad hour when I lose
my morality you won't come see me without me livin' it again,
I'm all alone 'less I put it back fresh in my mind: that time, hour
I become a beast. That hour I make you fear and that's the worst:
havin' to hear you fear again hear you tremble, and I done it.

KATIE

Didn't seem to bother you at the time.

JOJO

I know! I know!

KATIE

Think I'm gonna let you forget? You're a losin' motherfucker and
you're gonna burn for it. The chair: how many bodies caught fire
in what was s'posed to be a smooth-sailin' go?

Here we go again.

The gas chamber: you know what death by asphyxiation feels like? I do.

JOJO
I'm sorry!

KATIE
Hey!

JOJO
I take it back!

KATIE
You better. Death by asphyxiation is a long ass death cuz breathin's a habit you been hooked on too long it's a hard one to kick. Just be easier to close your eyes and die but ya can't help it: ya keep tryn and tryn to gasp air, it just keep gettin' harder, harder.

JOJO
I remember it once. Gettin' caught the undertow I accidentally swam beyond the lifeguard recommended boundaries. Alone. Fourteen and dumb, every time I tried to choke the water out, more flowed in. My body tight, it wanna explode and crushin', I feel my face turnin' blue like that water, I know what you're sayin'. I been at that place.

KATIE
Fourteen and dumb? Shit, twenty-two you weren't no smarter. Most rape is separate but equal: white men rape white women, black men rape black women. But you had to go find a white girl, stupid! Nobody goes to jail for rapin' black girls.

JOJO
I wake up, somebody mouth-to-mouthin' me, I see white people, bikinis. Leisure sailboat, if it hadn't happened by I never woulda lived to . . . [Trails off]

KATIE

Remember the old days when you'da hung? And sometimes it went like this: rope snap your neck, your head go flyin' right off your shoulders.

JOJO

The needle.

KATIE

Hah! Hope your veins are easy to find, otherwise they'll poke you like a pincushion. They'll bring in paramedics. Paramedics to kill ya! Whole thing'll seem so sweet and sanitary and they got your best care in mind to the outside world. Before they inject ya they'll alcohol your skin to prevent infection. [Rolls on the floor laughing]

JOJO

Isaiah was twenty-one, year younger 'n me, he got thirty years, I got death. Thirty years was last year, he's out free. They found Isaiah first, he ratted me out. They pronounce us equally guilty, but I die, he serves time and leaves. I ain't resentful. Why should I. He lost everything, family. And how he gonna live? only knows prison, and what they teach him thirty years? Nobody gonna hire someone fifty-two no skills, I ain't bitter, his punishment was severe enough. And continues.

KATIE

[Dribbles]

If I was fifteen now, I mighta had a chance for a b-ball scholarship. Not s'much around then for girls, thirty years back, but things was changin', and they saw my potential, who knows? I was fifth baby a my family, all boys before me. My brothers taught me the game. Think they'd have me shoot like a girl? [Gets into shooting position]

JOJO

Isaiah's the one done in your friend. What was her name?

KATIE

[Stops aiming]

I had potential but someone aborted it, fifteen my life all ahead but someone stopped time.

JOJO

I'm s—! [Stops himself. Pause]

KATIE

Soon?

JOJO

The appeal might come through. [She stares at him] If it don't
. . . soon.

KATIE

So, you think you might die, but there's a slight chance maybe
not. This person you never met before suddenly holdin' your
whole future in his hands, some stranger got the control
whether you live whether you die, you go through all the torture
but you think Please God just don't let him kill me. And he does
anyway. See how it feels. [Pause] How come you always callin'
on me? you know I ain't never got nothin' nice to say.

JOJO

Company.

KATIE

You got neighbors now.

JOJO

Not for long. [Pause]

KATIE

Hey! You think me bein' mean to you means I get my little
revenges you don't got to feel so bad!

JOJO

No!

KATIE

Good! Cuz you stole everything from me, don't think you takin'
my smartassness is comparable repay!

JOJO

I know!

KATIE

It hurts.

[Long pause]

JOJO

Maybe I think you bend the rules once. Let me say it, what I feel. [Pause] Apology.

KATIE

My way. My friend Darla—

JOJO

Darla! She was the other one? Isaiah's?

KATIE

No! I ain't tellin' ya her name, Darla was somebody else, my best friend since second grade 'cept no matter what couldn't say "I'm sorry." She broke the brown crayon, never admit it. She flirt away the guy I told her I liked, she just say, "Well he wasn't your boyfriend." Her stupidity. "I'm sorry" coulda changed her outlook, but 'til you can say it, you never know how good it feels. Relief. That relief I ain't offerin' you. [Pause] You want forgiveness?

JOJO

Thought you wasn't offerin'.

KATIE

I ain't. But wish I could. The best killin' is killin' with kindness, if I acted all sweet and angelic and smiled sad and spoke of divine absolution you'd keel over and die, the guilt. Wish I was cruel enough to be so kind.

JOJO

It ain't forgiveness I want nohow. Not the main thing. Just want you to hear it, hear me say it. I think I owe you that.

KATIE

I can't hear "I'm sorry." "I'm sorry" I'm deaf to. Sorry. [Starts to exit]

JOJO

Not premeditated! [KATIE turns around] Me and him didn't say Let's take these white girls and kill 'em. Not even Let's take 'em and do 'em. I don't know how it became that, rape, it grew into somethin' not planned. And the killin'. . . fear. When we let you go, you took off screamin' and cryin', it hits us: you'll tell. [She stares at him] I ain't sayin' this cuz it makes it okay. Just figured it's information you might be innerested in.

KATIE

Like junior high innermurals, to save time we did all the foul shots the enda the game. But, forty-three—forty-two, us ahead, Blue team, it's up to Tammy Feldman from the Reds to make her foul basket. She never misses. 'Til today. The pressure on, the nervousness, she had that. Like you. That what you mean?

JOJO

No! not like junior high innermurals. [Pause] I am bad.

[Pause]

KATIE

You were.

SCENE 4

[NAT stoops, head bowed, face concealed. CRAZY HORSE stands tense, in thought]

JOJO

We heard it again. The scufflin'. Then holdin' you down, forcin' the medicine down your throat. Feel better?

[No answer. ANDY enters with a tray, sees CRAZY HORSE's face. ANDY is confused, looks from the tray to CRAZY HORSE]

ANDY

This ain't what you ordered? [Shows tray]

CRAZY HORSE

Newly killed game, bear. Or deer. Corn. Sweet potatoes. Ground coffee. Fruit. If they could find it fresh.

[ANDY opens CRAZY HORSE's cell door, hands him the tray: burger and fries.]

Least they charcoaled the burger, I always like that. The dark
stripes acrost.

JOJO
Hey Crazy, you get your vision? The fever?

[CRAZY HORSE sits on the floor cross-legged, the tray on his knees.
Pours hot water from a small pot into a mug, picks up his spoon and
starts dipping out instant coffee. One at a time, he takes out many, many
spoonsful, then stops. Now his head is bowed, face concealed. A long
stillness before he speaks]

CRAZY HORSE
Hungry, Jojo?

JOJO
No! I ain't takin' a man's last meal from him.

CRAZY HORSE
Nat?

NAT
[Who hasn't moved from his position]
Fasting.

CRAZY HORSE
Andy?

[ANDY nervously shakes his head no. CRAZY HORSE can't see him but
senses the answer]

CRAZY HORSE
I DON'T WANT FOOD WASTED! [Silence] For my last request,
I'd like to see this food eaten, I'd like to hear someone enjoy it.
[Beat] In my vision someone enjoyed it.

JOJO
Okay.

[ANDY passes the tray from CRAZY HORSE to JOJO. JOJO stares at the
food in front of him. CRAZY HORSE begins holding his stomach as if he
is in great pain. The OTHERS aren't aware of this.]

Jojo!

[JOJO begins to clink the plate with his fork, making sounds as if he is eating.]

JOJO

Not bad. I like my fries this way. Crispy.

SCENE 5

ANDY

[Stares at his wristwatch]

11:59.

NAT

The rate for imprisonment of black men in America was determined to be five times the rate for imprisonment of black men in South Africa. This was *during* apartheid. All U.S. nuclear testing occurs on Western Shoshone land because there still is Indian land to take and the government is still taking. In 1985 the Philadelphia police department dropped a bomb on a house in a black neighborhood, letting the fire spread to destroy sixty surrounding houses. When the children tried to come out, the police shot them down or sent them running back into the flames. Cain killed Abel, then God put a mark on Cain to protect him from the death penalty—Genesis 4. The Brazilian rainforests are destroyed at the rate of a football field every hour. A popular sport with European colonists in Australia was Lobbing the Distance: burying black children live up to their necks and competing as to how far a white man could kick the child's head off his shoulders, don't forget history, history made today!

ANDY

Midnight.

NAT

[Faster]

Holocaust: One hundred million captured black people died on the slave ships from Africa to America! The only places where children can be sentenced to death today are Saudi Arabia, the Congo, Iran, Pakistan, Yemen, Nigeria and the U.S.! In 1973, after an Indian stole a white's cowboy boots, the FBI declared war on Pine Ridge Reservation, fireworksed the night sky with thousands of bullets, then got surprised when a bullet or two fired back! Then gave one Indian two life sentences! In 1995 Texas a man was proven innocent, then executed anyway! But killing the innocent comes with the territory, ask Christ on the cross about that!

ANDY

Twelve o' one.

NAT
[Cowers]
WHAT'S HAPPENING?

ANDY

They puttin' him up on the gurney. [Pause] Now they strappin' him down, six belts. [Pause] Now they stickin' in the saltwater i.v. [Pause] Now they stickin' in the three needles: one to put him to sleep, one to stop his heart, one to stop his breath. [Pause] Now maybe he's gettin' in a little movement, last word. [Pause] Now he's dead. Takes less than a minute, assumin' all went accordin' to schedule. [Chuckles] But you know how that goes 'round here. [Chuckles]

[A silence]

JOJO

Dr. Baith. Ol' lush, just before he get malpractice-lawsuited the outside they residence him here, three years ago he diagnose a sore throat, too late man find out it's cancer. But execution a different story, pre-execution they always seek out a physician in good standin' so Crazy be healthy and clear-headed for his needle. They got the witnesses comin'.

NAT

A Texas man was involved in a crime but not the trigger puller. He took the rap for his sister. After he was proven innocent, they executed him anyway. 1995. A journalist asked people what they thought about that and the people said this: "Better a few innocent die than a few guilty go free."

SCENE 6

[ANDY stares down at his wristwatch. NAT TURNER's cell is empty. JOJO is screaming while kicking and pounding all sides of the cell. Finally, exhausted, JOJO falls down, panting heavily.]

ANDY
Twelve o' two.

SCENE 7

[JOJO has a worn blanket wrapped around him. Shivers. ANDY enters.]

ANDY
Merry Christmas. [Pulls from his pocket a little wrapped gift]

JOJO
[Stares at it]
Guess best thing 'bout my date's the twentieth is I get my Christmas early.

ANDY
Open it, Jojo.

[JOJO does. It is a brightly colored child's plastic top.]

JOJO
Thank ya!

[JOJO starts spinning the top on the floor. Smiles]

ANDY
They set up the phone call with Lucy. 10 A.M. tomorra.

JOJO
[Looks up from the top]
Lucy comin'?

ANDY

Not tomorra. You wanna talk to her before she come, that's what
you tol' me to tell her, right?

JOJO

Yeah, I gotta ast her bring me a coupla things. But she's comin'?

ANDY

Said she was.

JOJO

Day after tomorra?

ANDY

Thursday.

JOJO
[Taken aback]
Thursday? [ANDY nods] But . . . that's the day.

ANDY

Yeah.

JOJO

Friday's the date but that means minute after Thursday
midnight.

ANDY

Yeah. She'll come earlier in the day.

JOJO

Oh. [Beat. Suddenly] Charmaine be with her?

ANDY
[Beat]
Think she couldn't get off work.

JOJO

Oh.

ANDY

My shift ain't 'til 3 tomorra but don't worry. I'll be in early,
make sure the powers that be don't mess you up, make you
miss that call.

JOJO

Thank you. [Pause]

ANDY

Jojo. I told Lucy about Charmaine's picture. Not a ol' one, right? You wanted it recent?

JOJO

I wanna see what she look like now.

ANDY

That's what I said to Lucy. She said don't getcher hopes up. Charmaine don't like gettin' her picture took, Lucy said she ain't got but one recent snapshot herself, she wanna hold on to that.

JOJO

Charmaine ain't got one to spare? My daughter got a lotta years ahead a her, get more pictures took. I ain't got but days.

ANDY

That's what I said. Lucy said she ast Charmaine, Charmaine said Yeah, but mailin' it, it might not get here on time.

JOJO

What about that overnight mail company? They dependable, quick.

ANDY

That's what I said. Lucy said Charmaine said overnight mail's kinda steep. Ten dollars.

JOJO

Then regular mail. Usually it ain't a disaster, right? We could try—

ANDY

Lucy said Charmaine said no.

[Pause. Then JOJO goes back to playing with the top.]

ANDY

You put in your order for your meal? [JOJO nods] Don't let the recent bureaucratic slipups intimidate ya, mosta the time that room service ain't so shabby.

JOJO

Your family doin' the traditional? Dinner at Ellen's sister's? the holiday?

ANDY

Sure.

JOJO

Ellen make them peanut butter cookies again, the chocolate kiss in the center?

ANDY

First batch already made, I'll bring ya a couple, 'course. [*Pause.*] Cold rain last night. Heard it?

JOJO

Hm. The poundin' wet, and thunder, lightnin': wa'n't that a show.

ANDY

Last night I have to eat my vegetables in shifts. First the mash potatas, then she cleans the pot. Then the corn. She cleans the pot. Then the string beans. Cleans the pot.

JOJO

The pot? When yaw become Bob Cratchit?

ANDY

All the others is use, leaky roof, we got so many damn leaks now . . . [Pause] Fix it when we can afford it.

JOJO

Aintchu up for a end-a-year raise?

ANDY

Freeze on raises. Again. [Pause] While back, I put in a request. Told 'em they need any more strappers, I be willin'. [Pause. JOJO stops the top, doesn't look up] I wouldn't be administerin' the needles, I ain't qualified for that. Just bucklin' the straps. [Pause] Three hundred dollars! They said if a space opens, they keep me in mind. I didn't think you . . . [JOJO starts spinning the top again] They know I could use the money, they think they doin' me a favor. If I turn 'em down, they peg me ungrateful, no tellin' when . . .

[JOJO lets the top spin to a stop. Pause]

JOJO
Might not be so bad. Have a friend with me.

ANDY
I can't, never mind. Don't know why I brought it up forget it, please forget I said it.

[Pause]

JOJO
Three hundred's good money but one fifty ain't bad neither. Split the pot. Send my half to my daughter, her daddy ain't no cheap-o, you write out the check, and a letter. At the top—
To Charmaine Warren
From Joseph Warren
Re: Inheritence

SCENE 8

[JOJO deep in thought. KATIE enters, stares at him. JOJO looks up]

JOJO
Who ast for you?

KATIE
Maybe I ain't always at your beck 'n' call summons. [Pause] I need you to tell me somethin'. I wanna know everything you accomplished the last thirty-one years.

JOJO
[Turns to her]
That's just mean, Katie, plain out. Mostly I live with your shenanigans and smart aleckin' fine, but this . . . [Trails off]

KATIE
Tell me.

[Pause]

JOJO

My place is six foot by ten, and that includes my toilet that
includes my cot, six by ten no windas and they let me have
nothin' else in here. They don't let me out but one hour a day,
now what you think I accomplished? [KATIE stares at him]
NOTHIN'! Okay? It been a waste! life a waste! Fifteen years ago
was a mirror in here, I smash it with my bare hand so I don't got
to look at my ugly face WASTE!

[Pause]

KATIE

We're tied.

JOJO
[Beat]

What?

KATIE

What you took from me, what they took from you: We're even.

JOJO
[Beat]

Ya mean it?

KATIE

I been thinkin' it awhile now. Years. Time to say it.

JOJO

Thank you.

KATIE

Sorry my family won't settle for that though. Not their fault,
they can't see it, never happened to them. Murder. Cuz once
you been through it, you never wish it on nobody else.

[Pause]

JOJO

Talkin' to Lucy tomorra mornin', she's comin' day after. Ain't
visited so often, last time was eighteen years ago, but I ast, she
said okay. Now I'm makin' a list, what I want to take with me.
Underground. My weddin' band, gave that to her 'fore I left.
My football trophy, it ain't too big. And high school diploma,

accomplished that! Snapshot: Fourtha July at my family's,
ten people in the Polaroid, me and Lucy off to the side. And
Charmaine, newborn, Lucy hold her in her baby blanket,
can't even see her face, but she's there! [Pause] I think I have
everything. Think they let me take all that?

KATIE

Your coffin. Long's it all fits.

JOJO

That red and black hanky my mama make for me! God, how'm
I gonna remember all this, tell Lucy?

KATIE

Wait. You want your trophy, diploma, family picture and hanky,
right?

JOJO

And weddin' band.

KATIE

Ring—R, diploma—D, trophy—T, picture—P, hanky—H.
[Thinks] I got it! First change the high school diploma from
diploma—D to school—S, then . . . Ain't Charmaine the
centerpiece a the picture? why you wannit?

JOJO

Yeah.

KATIE

So change picture—P to Charmaine—C. Get it? Charmaine—C,
hanky—H, ring—R, school—S, trophy—T. "Christ!" How could
you forget that? you'll be callin' on him anyway. "Christ" except
for the "I" but you're takin' yourself so the "I" is you.

JOJO

What if I thinka somethin' else?

KATIE

Jojo, you can't take everything—

JOJO

What if I thinka somethin' small?!

Then we'll just have to change "Christ" to a new one. Don't
worry, I'm good at memory devices. [She sits cross-legged in
his cell] Go on. I'll help ya pack.

SCENE 9

[A table, two chairs. LUCY sits. Waits. Sound of the door unlocking.
LUCY stands. JOJO enters, wrists handcuffed in front. ANDY follows,
gently holding JOJO's arm. ANDY shuts the door and steps away from
JOJO. JOJO and LUCY stare at each other from opposite sides of the
room. Finally]

LUCY

Hi Jojo.

JOJO

Hi Lucy.

[More staring. Then JOJO sits. LUCY sits. ANDY tries not to look at them]

LUCY

You took up all the tape on my machine.

JOJO

Sorry, everything's a mess around here, we got no competent
people around here, I complained. Believe me, I said Hey! I got
this appointment, 10 A.M. These screwups done scheduled two
calls for 10, not Andy! Andy done his best to straighten out the
situation but the damage been done and unfortunately the other
10 beats me to the phone. Then all the trouble he has gettin' his
line through, I don't know what the problem is, I keep starin' at
the clock: ten o' seven, 10:10, 10:13, please can'tcha get through
faster? Please wontcha let me do my business, my call scheduled
for 10 A.M., my wife gotta go to work. Andy tol' me her boss
expectin' her at 9 well she got someone to cover the phones 'til
11 but 10:30 she gotta go, lemme talk! They look at me like I'm
from outer space, go back to their business. Finally 10:34 I'm
on the line, one ring. Two rings please God let her still be there.
Three, I move the receiver away from my face, shakin' so hard
receiver bang bang my chin receiver gimme a uppercut, four,

click: machine! I got a lotta stuff, Lucy, a list, I pray tape don't run out I don't wanna forget nothin'! [Pause. They stare at each other] Things. To take with me.

LUCY

I couldn't find nunna them things, Jojo, them things is ol' things.

[Pause]

JOJO

Nothin'? [They stare at each other] Where you live, aintchu got a place? Dusty trunk for ol' stuff? You search under the cobwebs?

LUCY

More 'n thirty years, I don't know where that stuff is! I don't know what picture you talkin' about. The five years after you left I moved three times, how I keep up?

JOJO

Weddin' band? [LUCY glances away. Quiet] How much you get? Hockin'.

LUCY

Sixty yours. Seventy-five mine. [Pause] You was here a long time 'fore I done that, twenty years, and blizzard comin', if again I'da put nothin' toward that overdue heat they'da cut us off.

[Pause]

JOJO

Last time I seen you Charmaine was fourteen. Now she thirty-two. What she been up to?

LUCY

Fourteen she had a singular solitary issue, all her energy absorbed in the solution to the acne problem. Fifteen she know she the only girl on earth don't got a boyfriend. Eighteen she get the graduation award: science.

JOJO

Science!

                              LUCY
Eighteen and a half she in Chester Community.

                              JOJO
College?!

                              LUCY
Twenty she transfer to Canton State, zoology.

                              JOJO
Vet'rinarian?

                              LUCY
Headed toward it, she love them animals. But she graduate, say
she work awhile, year, save up for vet school. So she work in this
bank. Ain't never left. Ten years.

                              JOJO
She like it? Fingerin' that green all day.

                              LUCY
Calls it her life sentence. The chain gang, calls her boss Massa
Rollins and know that don't even make sense for Miz Rollins.
Give her a nice apartment though, if ya don't count the dog
stink, cat hair. Loves them damn animals. [Beat] She gets the
blues. "I hate my job, hate my life," broken record, I ignore it.
But once I call three days, no answer, worried to death I march
over. She just sittin' in the dark, starin' at the TV. Ain't switched
the channel, ain't moved from the couch *three days*. [Shrugs] Life.

[Pause]

                              JOJO
How she wear her hair? She like it wavy?

                              LUCY
Cut it all off recently, like a boy. So she don't gotta fool with it—

                              JOJO
She ain't really that, low, she don't spend her days wishin' she
weren't born. SHE OUT THERE! Nothin' to be blue, she got the
WORLD!

[Silence]

JOJO

Short hair. That's practical. [Chuckles]

LUCY

I gotta go, Jojo. I don't mean to rush I'm havin' a nice time
I just . . . I gotta go.

JOJO

That nail polish color. What you call it?

LUCY

[Shrugs]

Peach. Somethin'.

JOJO

It match you. Your skin or . . . eyes.

[LUCY nods. Pause]

LUCY

See ya, Jojo. [Stands and turns to leave]

JOJO

[Quiet] Search her. [LUCY is now at the door] Search her!

ANDY

Huh?

JOJO

'At's your job she coulda took anything offa me!

ANDY

That ain't my job—

JOJO

Is!

ANDY

My job's to search *you*—

JOJO

Search her!

LUCY

I ain't took nothin' off you, Jojo—

JOJO

I don't know that!

LUCY

Do know that! We had a nice time—

JOJO

Search her.

LUCY

Why you gotta end our nice time rotten?

JOJO

SEARCH HER!

[LUCY, keeping her eyes on JOJO, raises her arms, outstretched to the sides. ANDY reluctantly begins gently patting her down.]

ANDY

[Quiet] Turn around. [She does, facing the door now, her back to JOJO. ANDY pats again]

JOJO

She could walk away with a gran' piana the way you doin', *feel her!*

[ANDY rubs LUCY a little harder and more rapidly, then abruptly stops]

ANDY

She's clean, Jojo.

[LUCY rushes out without turning back around. The door closes]

JOJO

[Eyes on the door]

Just a caution. Can't be too careful with my valuables.

[JOJO chuckles. ANDY does not chuckle]

JOJO

Hey Andy. Can I smell your hands?

[ANDY holds his hands out. JOJO comes to him, takes ANDY's hands. Inhales deeply]

JOJO

I remember this! Fall on my pilla every night, journeyin' to dreams but first I have this. And this I take with me.

SCENE 10

[ANDY enters, looks at JOJO for several seconds. JOJO doesn't notice.]

ANDY

Okay, Jojo.

JOJO
[A hesitation, then]
Hey. Hey, they owe me my last meal! They ain't cheatin' me!

ANDY

Pork chops and bake beans, you cleaned the plate. Remember?

JOJO
[Hesitation]
That preacher! Somethin' I forgot to tell him!

ANDY

He hung with ya a hour, Jojo, he said you didn't have nothin' to say.

JOJO

I just thought of it! [ANDY looks away. Silence] We have time to practice the breathin' exercises first?

ANDY

Sure.

JOJO

Wait! What I got to take with me? Someone dig me up, think I was some worthless bum, whole life no possessions.

ANDY

Take your Christmas present.

JOJO

Okay. [Beat] Okay.

[JOJO picks up the top. ANDY opens the cell. They start to walk]

ANDY

Breathe in deep. [ANDY does, JOJO follows] Now let it out, short and fast.

[ANDY expels the air many times quickly. JOJO takes his lead]

ANDY

In deep. [ANDY does, then JOJO] Out fast. [ANDY, then JOJO] In deep. [ANDY does, JOJO doesn't] In deep.

JOJO

I done it, Andy.

ANDY

Thought you wanted to practice.

JOJO

I got the hang of it, I know how to die faster. Hey. What if I wanna linger on? Breathe in fast and hard and out slow?

ANDY

Don't say that, Jojo, you confuse yourself. [Pause] You don't wanna linger on.

JOJO
[Beat]

In deep.

[He does. Then expels the air properly. Now the gurney is visible. JOJO stops deep-breathing. Silence]

ANDY

Ready?

[JOJO nods. ANDY leads him to the gurney and starts strapping him down. JOJO begins nervously heavy breathing; his rhythm is fast and incorrect. When ANDY has completed his task—JOJO is immobile—ANDY speaks]

ANDY

In deep.

[ANDY demonstrates. JOJO attempts this but, in the midst of the inhale, begins gagging. ANDY quickly searches for something for JOJO to vomit in: nothing. ANDY offers his cupped hand; it touches JOJO's cheek. JOJO recovers. ANDY looks at his wristwatch]

ANDY

Well. I better go.

[ANDY stares at JOJO in silence for several seconds. JOJO, looking straight up at the ceiling, now seems unaware of ANDY. Finally ANDY quietly turns to leave. Just before he is gone, JOJO suddenly speaks]

JOJO

I'm by myself. [Pause] I'M BY MYSELF! WHERE'S THE PARAMEDICS? WHERE'S THE PARAMEDICS? [ANDY quickly moves over to stand next to JOJO]

ANDY

It's midnight, Jojo. They'll be here in a minute.

JOJO
[Still stares at the ceiling]

I DON'T WANNA BE ALONE FOR A MINUTE! NOT A SECOND!

ANDY

Okay! Okay.

[Another lengthy silence]

JOJO
[Big smile]

Andy, you always lied about your age, said between us you was the younger. Come on. How old are ya? Really?

ANDY

Fif—

[Before ANDY can utter it, JOJO laughs hard, drowning out ANDY's reply]

JOJO

I knew it!

[The PARAMEDIC enters, pushing ANDY out of the way]

PARAMEDIC
[To ANDY]

Okay.

[ANDY exits. The PARAMEDIC does his job quickly. As he does, KATIE enters with her basketball. The PARAMEDIC does not see her]

JOJO
[Calm, but pleasantly surprised]

Katie.

KATIE

I heardja say you didn't wanna be alone for a second. You got a few a those left. [The PARAMEDIC exits] I know you're tired. Go ahead, you can close your eyes. I won't be insulted. [He does. KATIE dribbles, fake shoots] The bonus long shot disappeared with the American Basketball League, 1930s. The notion a bringin' it back was still a few years away the time you done me, but I had the vision. I saw it comin'. I'm a long shooter, you know how many times I shoulda had three points but they only counted two?

JOJO
Hey, Katie, what was the name a that other girl? your buddy. All the time they mention her name in court, you think I remember. [He dies]

KATIE
The game against Frederick we lost fifty-two/forty-seven. But I always keep mental tabs a my would-be three-pointers to calculate later, seven of 'em. Seven extra points! woulda put us over the top. 'Course we'd already been eliminated from the finals, this was just the consolation game. Still, dontcha hate that, Jojo? Scoreboard says ya lost. When, this time, you shoulda won.

I wake up early in the morning. That's when all the noisemakers have fallen asleep. Guys who incessantly engage in pointless arguments and banal babble: "If a gorilla and a grizzly had a fight who would win?" Shit like that. They make a racket during the day and well into the night, shouting over each other at insane decibels as if that would leapfrog their train wreck of logic to the forefront of the bedlam. Chaos is their escapism, a way to muffle the real noise in their heads, a way to avoid, if only temporarily, having to deal with the wretched reality of being on death row. It's their routine.

Two hours before dawn it's real quiet. I can think. Get some work done. I pace back and forth in my cell as an alternative to meditation. It's much more effective in setting the tone of my mental focus. I have a cup of coffee. I don't eat breakfast. I stopped years ago when I found part of a rat in my oatmeal. That screwed up my taste buds for a while. I wash my face, brush my teeth, rake my fingers over my hair. I stretch while listening to classical music, then exercise for an hour: calisthenics, pushups, shadowboxing, running in place, triceps on the toilet, and curls with a towel slid through the bars. Statistically speaking, California death row prisoners are more apt to die from poor health or a drug overdose than be executed. I think it's important to stay in shape. I'm manic about it. I don't miss a day.

After my exercise routine I take a birdbath in the sink if it isn't my day to walk to the shower, something we get to do three days a week. It's 6:30 A.M. when I look out the window across from my cell. I try to gauge the weather conditions. That's my barometer for whether or not I'll go to the yard—on rainy and cold days I stay in. San Quentin prison sits on a peninsula overlooking the San Francisco Bay. During the winter months the prison can get covered in fog. We're put on lockdown. No one gets to go out in fog.

The windows are behind the gunrail. A guard, cradling a mini-14 assault rifle and wearing a holstered 38 revolver on his side like a cowboy, watches the tiers. He rarely sits down. He rarely looks out the window. He eats standing up. For eight hours he walks the entire length of the gunrail, about a quarter mile, back and forth. If the alarm goes off, he runs up and down the gunrail, looking for the trouble. He doesn't have to give a warning shot. He could kill without saying a word. That's his routine.

Any time I leave my cell I am searched. Anything I take with me is searched. A guard will examine every piece of clothing, every sheet of paper, and every cavity of my body. I have learned to disassociate myself from the procedure. I stare straight ahead, right through him, as I lift up my scrotum. I am numb when I spread my cheeks and cough. I don't feel anything. Not anger. Not frustration. Not humiliation. There is a cold primal exactitude coursing through my veins, like a predator waiting for one precious moment. There are days when the cells are searched. What meager possessions I own get tossed about and ramshackled. I don't take it personal. Afterwards I methodically return everything to its place. It doesn't matter how long it takes me. I do it. This is prison. This is the routine.

Alone. That's how I processed the news of over a dozen people dying in my family. It is the only emotional arc that can stir up feelings of vulnerability. Each loss makes me acutely aware of my isolation—twenty-four years. Each death gave me a precise sense of my own physical impermanence. I live with an intense sense of immediacy. I engage every day like a man on fire. From a single visit I can absorb a lifetime. In a single letter I could, in vivid detail, translate all the passion of an imprisoned man's heart. I have become stoic, knowing any time I call home there could be another death. There was. My only blood brother died in a foreign country where he didn't even speak the language. He was alone. With his thoughts. His ghost. His regrets. I have watched my hair turn grey. Watched my youth dissolve with the pendulum-like swing of each day. Fear does not keep me company. I am ready to meet my fate. Birth. Decay. Death. This is life's routine.

State level appeal. Denied. Death sentence upheld. Incompetent attorneys. Same old story. For twenty-four years I have moved through the judicial maze like digested food slowly making its way to the final solution. I was the 107th person to join the exclusive group referred to as Dead Men in California. I may leave them soon. As the number climbs toward seven hundred, each face brings with it a reflection of what is wrong with the system. Each face is wrought with an impression of what is wrong in society. But what I am most struck by is the sharp contrast between race, class, who gets death, and how it is all so accepted as routine.

I have long ago come to terms with the possibility of dying here. I'm not overly philosophical about it. If it happens I will have the luxury of knowing exactly when, where, and how I will die. No surprises. This insight has had an effect on me. But my self-transformation is of my own making. I have not had a personal experience with any god. My transcendental experience came the moment I realized that the last routine of my life may occur in this sequence:

Four guards in black fatigues will escort me from the death cell to the chamber. A spiritual advisor, if I want one, can accompany me. Once I'm in what used to be the gas chamber, the guards strap me onto a gurney. The executioner locates a vein and sticks in an IV. When he's finished he'll look at the warden for a signal at which point the warden will ask me if I have any last words. Since I'm not big on monologue I'll shake my head no. The warden then nods to the executioner who releases 5 grams of sodium pentathol via a 60 cc syringe into my bloodstream. In no more than sixty seconds this knocks me out cold. The IV is then flushed with saline and 50 cc of pancuronium bromide is sent through the line. This drug will paralyze every muscle in my body except for the heart. My breathing slows as the muscles controlling the rib cage and diaphragm begin to freeze up. The IV is again flushed with saline, and the final poisonous chemical, 50 cc of potassium chloride, is pumped into my body. This blocks the electrical impulses to the heart, stopping it from beating. The results—my lungs are imploding, my organs are writhing, and my brain is gasping for oxygen. The outward appearance will look uneventful but, internally, all hell is breaking loose. Death comes in less than fifteen minutes. There will be nothing peaceful about it. The warden will announce the time of my demise. But I tell you now, don't dare accept the claim that my murder was routine.

3 Voices and Bodies in Resistance

I had only anger towards the man who murdered my mother, and thought about what his punishment should be if he were ever caught. It seemed to me that he should suffer and die in the same horrible way he forced my mother to. I had to rethink the death penalty when I became a mother myself. I realized that if I had a child who grew up to be a murderer, I would never stop loving him. The degree of love I felt would be the same as the first day I held him. With this realization I found complete forgiveness. I also knew my mother would never want someone killed in her name, as I don't want anyone murdered in mine. The insanity of the death penalty has to end and I oppose it under any circumstance.

—Suzy Klassen, whose mother, Helen Bohn Klassen,
   was murdered when Suzy was eleven years old.

From 1999–2001, Jacques Derrida delivered twenty separate two- to three-hour lectures on the death penalty at the École des Hautes Études in Sciences Sociales.[1] Derrida focused on themes such as sovereignty and exception, the onto-theologico-political implications of the death penalty, cruelty, the theatre of capital punishment, rational calculation of equivalency between crime and punishment, the relation of the death penalty to finitude and infinitude, the abolition of the death penalty, the relation of the death penalty to sexuality, and on the following principal authors: Plato, Immanuel Kant, Friedrich Nietzsche, Theodore Reik, Sigmund Freud, William Schabas, Victor Hugo, Karl Marx, Charles Baudelaire, Robert Badinter, Sister Helen Prejean, Cesare di Beccaria, Jean-Jacques Rousseau. Derrida also cited the Bible, in particular Exodus and Leviticus.

Derrida's library had books by legal scholars like Austin Sarat and Hugo Adam Bedau, and two of his lectures are largely devoted to Schabas's work. While his lectures are thoroughly informed by this reading, Derrida often takes literary authors, like Jean Genet or Franz Kafka, as his inspiration for dismantling the death penalty scaffolds. At one point in the lectures, reflecting on the status of his own discourse, he postulates,

> When one wants to avoid having one's seminar on the death penalty be merely a seminar on the death penalty; when one wants to avoid its being just one more discourse, and a discourse of good conscience to boot, among people who, like us, basically will never be, or believe they never will be, executioners executing a sentence nor legally condemned to death sentences, nor be the lawyers or district attorneys of those who are condemned to death, nor the governors or heads of state having the power of clemency, then, in that case, one must do everything to get as close as possible, in one's own body, to those for whom the death penalty is really the death penalty, in a real, concrete, undeniably and cruelly threatening way, in the absolute imminence of execution.[2]

In this lecture, the vehicle thanks to which he gets close to being inside the space of the death penalty is the telephone. Nietzsche's telephone.[3] It is impossible nowadays, Derrida adds, to imagine the death penalty without the accessory of the telephone (linking the warden to the governor, for example, or the condemned to the outside). In the context of his lecture, the telephone figures as literature as well. In other words, it is a device for being as if present or proximate to a situation while being absent or distant from it. Neither directly involved in the execution of the death penalty nor wanting merely to discourse about it, Derrida aims to approach as closely as possible the death penalty; to do so he must pass through the "telephone," through literature. While referring to legal scholars, philosophers, contemporary politics, and abolitionists, Derrida invokes literary authors for reasons essential to his argument. He does not restrict himself to literary representations, any more than to legal studies or philosophy, but finds it incumbent to splice together modes of discourse, with the literary taken as seriously as any other, and not as just a sort of illustrative discourse but rather as one that thinks through the situation it describes at least as much as philosophical or legal discourses.

This grafting of discourses is perhaps most deft in the death penalty lectures in which Derrida appends Kafka to Kant. Derrida selects Kant's defense of the death penalty ("On the Right to Punish and to Grant Clemency")[4] for special examination because Kant is the foremost philosophical advocate of the death penalty. In the twenty lectures, or roughly seven hundred typed pages, Derrida's interpretation of Kant forms three or four full lectures, or about seventy pages. Kant is the only philosopher whose philosophical and philosophically legal argument on the death penalty is showcased by Derrida as the rational, the noumenal, the properly philosophical pro–death-penalty argument. Derrida brings out how Kant admits numerous exceptions to, contradictions in, or unstable foundations of, the death penalty. In short, Derrida shows a simultaneous deconstruction of philosophy and of the death penalty at work in Kant. The most rational pro–death-penalty argument may be, in fact, its own practical interdiction. After a discussion of this approach to Kant, I spotlight the roughly twenty pages Derrida devotes to Kafka, the Czech Jewish author, because the deconstruction Derrida teases out of Kant is perhaps most brilliantly staged by Kafka's The Trial.

In the death penalty seminar, Derrida finds the term and the notion of "death penalty" to be untenable, inarticulate. No synthesis is possible of the two nouns. He dwells at length on the word "penalty." Derrida works in French, and the word is not the English "penalty," but the French peine: Peine de mort. Peine means "pain," "penalty," or "punishment" — "sentence." Derrida explains to his audience that working on the computer, in order to find quickly his lecture files, he gave them the title "À peine de mort." By using the letter "À," he was sure that all the files would be placed at the alphabetical top of his classifying tree. Afterwards, this struck him as more significant than the title of so many books that in French would be La peine de mort, or The Death Penalty. By using à peine de mort, Derrida gave an idiomatic and untranslatable title. This title, à peine de mort, has the sense of "on the pain of death," as one would say that something is done at the risk of the pain of death. There is also the sense, in the French, of "we are all destined to the pain of death"; à peine de mort names the dead end: we are all heading to the pain of death, à the preposition meaning "to," "toward." But "à peine" in French is also an adverb: it means "scarcely" or "hardly," "barely." In that case, the course title meant "death but barely," or "almost not death."

A French person listening to Derrida use the word peine is never entirely sure if he means "sentence," "penalty," "pain," "sadness." For a translator the problem is roughly the same, but unlike Derrida writing in French, who can let his French have its inherent undecidability, a translator has to make an often painful choice. Because the word peine can mean the penalty, the punishment, as well as the pain, it can be difficult to hold them separate from each other when one is discussing the distinction, say, between a legal punishment (poena forensis) and what, because it is merely natural, is an act of revenge, as in the poena naturalis (when a group of people lynch someone). Derrida grew up in Algeria at a time when such things were done and was familiar with lynching in the American South. In such a case, there is pain but there is not really punishment.

One might say that Derrida scrambles our ready-made or automatic operating reception system that thinks it identifies unproblematically what "death penalty" means, not only because (differing from Foucault here) Derrida covers a historical period and geographical breadth from the Bible and Plato to the most recent international human rights legislation, and not only because Derrida will complicate the word "death" (in the eighteenth lecture, Derrida describes how his "angel" says to him that all of deconstruction has been nothing but a deconstruction of the word "death," and thereby an overcoming of it, or at least a transfer from its path, which meant re-thinking "life"), but also because he'll bring out different senses of pain, punishment, penalty that all simultaneously fracture what we think we know under the words peine de mort or death penalty, capital punishment, pain of death.

Some pains are psychic, some are physical; some punishments are natural, some are non-natural, that is, legal, and still others are counter-natural although not legal. Thus, Derrida writes: "What is a penalty (une peine)? Is this question worth the trouble, the pain, of being asked?"[5] Why does Derrida spotlight these aporias, and why does he entertain hypotheses according to which the syntagm "the-death-penalty" would be untenable and obliged to fly apart? Is it to eradicate, to destroy, the death penalty, death, penalty? Derrida specifies that everything he sketches out, hypothesizes, and all the aporias he catches Kant out in, do not have the purpose or function of reversing oppositions (a life pleasure/reward in the place of a death pain/penalty); their aim is not to substitute other oppositions but rather to "suspend, to mark or to recall the necessity of suspending our naive confidence, that of common sense and the conscious belief in distinctions or oppositions such as inside/outside, natural and interior versus non-natural and exterior (poena naturalis/poena forensis), auto- and hetero-, self and other, auto-punishment et hetero-punishment, execution and murder or suicide."[6] We will see, when Derrida reads Kafka next to Kant, how—symbolically—a legal execution can also be a vile murder and an act of suicide.

Over the course of two years of lectures, Derrida writes several exegeses of Kant's general remark entitled, "On the Right to Punish and to Grant Clemency." In his theory of law, Kant responds to Thomas Hobbes, John Locke, and others, regarding the distinction between the state of nature and the state of legal society. Locke had, in The Second Treatise, identified the punishment of death as the very definition of political power: "Political power, then, I take to be a right of making laws with penalties of death."[7] Locke opposed such punishments by individuals in a state of nature to punishments in and by a political, legal system of state. For Kant, in order to rule out vengeance from humanity, in order to make the human properly human as such, it is crucial to sharpen the distinction between so-called natural punishments that are pre- or extra-legal, and state-sanctioned punishments that are the law, and consequently to expunge natural or animalistic punishment from court-organized punishment. Kant posits the difference between punishments handed out by a court (Richterliche Strafe, poena forensis) and punishments that are natural (poena naturalis). Court punishments are, by law, the law, whereas natural punishments are basically illegal because outside the law. They are examples of personal vengeance, when one takes "the law" into "one's own hands."

The law of punishment, and punishment by law, is a categorical imperative. Were someone not to be punished, the entire society would be brought to ruin. Kant quotes the Pharisaical saying, "It is better for one man to die than for the whole people to be ruined."[8] It is better to kill one person by the death penalty than not to do so and thereby kill humanity itself. If justice is not exacted and executed, human life on earth becomes worthless; the worth, the value, the dignity, of human life is granted by the law being observed. Moreover, the law can never be valued or justified as a means to some other end, such as economic profit or utilitarianism. For Kant, just as the death penalty must contain nothing of vengeance, so also it has no justification as a means to dissuade human beings from crime. In addition, the law and the death penalty can never be sold or exchanged for the sake of a supposedly higher social benefit. For example, if we were to take murderers condemned to death and make use of them in medical experiments for the advance of science instead of killing them, this scientific advantage gleaned from nonexecution of the death penalty would only mean that justice and law would themselves come to an end, would be put to death. Law can never be sold at any price. There is no equivalent for the law, because the law, its execution, is never a means to an end, but rather always the end in itself.

The key term in Kant's categorical imperative of death for death is "honor" (and/or "dignity"). The natural life of the wrongdoer must be put to death, but the cultural or spiritual life of the culprit must be saved. The death penalty is the affirmation of the dignity and the honor of humanity, starting with that of the criminal; it is the triumph of a philosophical idea of humanity. Kant gives the example of the Scottish revolution of 1745, which tried to bring back the House of Stuart. Kant imagines that among the participants were those who acted out of a sense of obligation to restore the House, and those who acted in the private intention of receiving personal gain. Kant says, suppose that the judgment of the highest court was that all the condemned would have the freedom to choose between death and convict labor. Kant predicts that the honorable man would choose death, but the rogue (Schelm) would choose convict labor. The honorable man, Kant says, "knows something that he values more highly than life itself: namely, honor."[9] The rogue considers a scandal-beflecked, a shameful life, better than none at all. Death is the punishment that is most like the perpetrator in both cases: the honorable man does not suffer very much, because he keeps his honor, whereas the rogue suffers very much because he is too sensitive to the loss of life. Life imprisonment and convict labor would be too severe a crime for the honorable man, and not enough for the rogue.

The death penalty is the "best equalizer" because it is based on the idea that there is something higher than life. No philosophy could be based on life as the highest principle, since that would only be the affirmation of the state of nature. Philosophy as such is the step out of the state of nature and into the state of the legal state.

Kant says "death must get death," but his text is rifled by exceptions, and it is not surprising since the right to punish is joined with the right to grant clemency. The necessity with which exceptions impose themselves indicate that the categorical imperative, the principle of likeness, is co-originary with another "principle," this necessity or imperative for a category of exception in the category for likeness. Just as Derrida wedges apart the categorical imperative in Kant by showing that there is a historical gap between what we objectively ought to do and what we subjectively do do, so that the categorical imperative exists to make us aware of an ideal until we will have reached it in reality whereupon it will cease to exist, so, too, does Derrida take the all-too-apparently-self-evident notion of the "death penalty" and dislodge it from itself so that afterwards we are left asking: How did anyone ever come up with such a concept as the death penalty?

> What is it, this thing, the death penalty [la peine de mort]? Is it a penalty, a punishment [une peine]? Is there something that, in truth, answers to this name? This name, these nouns [penalty and death, peine et mort], this nominal syntagm, the-death-penalty or capital punishment, is it a conceivable whole or else an articulated syntagm to the point of being dis-articulatable? And what if the death penalty [la peine de mort] were an untenable artifact, a pseudo-concept, such that the two terms, penalty [peine] and death, punishment [peine] and capital, did not let themselves be joined, like an out of joint syntagm, and such that it would be necessary to choose between the penalty and death without one being able to justify its logical grammar, except by unjustifiable violence, so much so that it would be necessary to choose between the penalty and death?[10]

For Derrida, to put "penalty" (punishment, pain) and "death" together is a monstrous hybrid. Either one chooses "penalty," in which case one lets go of death: the convict does not get put to death; or one chooses death, which is not a punishment, a pain, or a penalty, since all of those presuppose life, continued life. The "death penalty" is impossible, an impossible concept, the existence of which and the legal theory of which, are both based on an "unjustifiable violence," a forcing together of law and nature, as if this were possible.

In the fourteenth lecture, Derrida turns to the writings of Franz Kafka. In Kafka, Derrida finds the theme of presidency or sovereignty (there is no death penalty without a sovereign who could grant clemency), of theatre and literature (his seminar begins with a consideration of the novels and theatre of Jean Genet that often travesty death penalty verdicts in courts), and, for the connection with Kant, of honor and shame as the condemned person embodies them. The last chapter of Kafka's novel *Amerika*, entitled "The Theatre of Oklahoma," represented an empty President's booth in a theatre, which is indissociable from the actual theatre stage itself (an allusion to Lincoln's assassination). Derrida notes that the protagonist, Karl Rossman, although innocent, is just like the protagonist Joseph K. of Kafka's novel *The Trial*, in which K., who is guilty, is condemned to death and executed. Kafka in his notebooks had written: "Rossman and K., the innocent and the guilty, finally both are killed without any difference according to the punishment of death [*strafweise . . . umgebracht*]."[11] Each receives the same fate, each is identical before the law of the death penalty. As Derrida remarks in passing, "in the a priori judicial error, the death penalty is radically unjust, unequal and disproportionate."[12]

This link of the innocent, and thus honorable, figure of Rossmann and the guilty figure of K. sends Derrida to the ending of *The Trial* and to the hyperconfirmation of Kant's categorical imperative of the death penalty, and indeed the implosion upon itself of Kant's categorical imperative. When, in the last chapter, K. is visited one night by two men dressed in black, K. sees what is happening to him—he is already dressed in black, and waiting for the visit—as a scene in a theatre. "Old, second-rate actors," K. says to himself, "they send old, second-rate actors to get me." K. looks at them again, to convince himself, and then confronts them: "What theatre do you play in?" The men play dumb, play non-theatre, as one says, "Theatre?" and looks to the other for advice.[13]

The two pages of the chapter describe how K. is escorted with rigid force by these two men, but also how K. goes along with them and even helps them. Although Derrida does not comment upon this image, in the very formal way he is escorted ("They kept their shoulders tightly behind his, and instead of crooking their elbows, wound their arms round his at full length, holding K.'s hands with a school-measured, much-practiced and irresistible grip. K. walked rigidly [*straff*; rigid, but sounding and looking like Straf, "punishment" in Kant and Kafka] between them, they formed now all three of them such a unity, that, if one would have knocked one of them down, all of them would have been knocked down. It was such a unity as almost only something lifeless can form"[14]), it is hard not to identify the many representations in journalism, novels, and movies of the last steps of the condemned person tightly accompanied and then tied down by the execution team. What Derrida does explicitly say is that Kafka stages the failure of the oneness of condemned and executioner, of the guilty and the innocent, which Kant's philosophy wanted to promote.

Kafka, or K., does it with his unique mixture of humor and humility, thinking to himself that "[p]erhaps they are tenors"[15] on account of their heavy double chins, deciding to resist by refusing to move, but then, when he sees what might be his neighbor, Miss Buerstner, becomes aware that his resistance is "worthless" (Wertlosigkeit), and even decides that there was nothing heroic in resisting, nothing heroic in trying to enjoy the last appearance of life, and thus he starts again walking and the relief shown by his warders actually spreads to himself.[16] Between the warders themselves, and between K. and them, numerous forms of "politeness" (Höflich-keiten, court-manners, formality) are exchanged.[17] Like so many representations of death row condemned men on their way to death, K. says to himself that "the only thing I can now do . . . is keep my calm orderly understanding unto the end. I had always wanted to snatch at the world with twenty hands, and not for a very laudable motive. That was not right [unrichtig]. Should I now show that nothing in this yearlong process has taught me anything? Should I go out as a man with no conceptuality? Shall people say afterwards of me that I began this whole trial wanting to end it, but at its end just wanted to get it started again? . . . I am thankful that these half-dumb, senseless men were sent to accompany me."[18] The condemned man interiorizing the "rationality" of the process follows perfectly the script that, since Kant, dictates that the homo noumenon, the rational man, emerge from the homo phaenomenon (the criminal), thereby in a sense relieving the law of doing anything because the homo noumenon realizes what he himself, as object of the law, must do to himself as subject to the law.

A form of suicide. In many respects, K. decides to help the warders, accepts that what is to be done is to be done. One can point to testimonies in which even innocent people condemned to die cooperate fully and help the process be carried out, largely to prove their own dignity and honor, while greatly relieving the wardens.

Derrida jumps straight from the identification of the warders as theatrical actors to the final scene, noting how so many endings in Kafka ("The Judgment," "The Metamorphosis," "The Hunger-Artist") stage a kind of suicide. After stopping their procession beside a loose rock and undressing the torso of K., the two men in black hold a long, thin, butcher's knife sharpened on both edges over K.'s head, passing it back and forth over his head between themselves: "K. knew now exactly that it would have been his duty, to grab himself the knife, as it swung from hand to hand over him, and plunge it into himself. But he did not do that."[19] This "duty" (*Pflicht*) is straight out of Kant, of course. It is the *Pflicht* of obeying the law, of finding the condemnation to death absolutely right, the categorical imperative. But K. does not do it.

K. turns his neck and looks up to the top floor of a nearby building where he sees a weak and thin man, faraway and high up, leaning out the window, his arms outstretched. K. wonders, "Who was it? A friend? A good man? A participant? One who wanted to help? Were there arguments against all this that he had forgotten? Certainly there were. The logic [of Kant's categorical imperative] was unshakeable, but to a man who wants to live, that logic does not resist. Where was the Judge he had never seen? Where was the high Court, he had never been to?"[20] Derrida skips these lines, but many of the threads of the death penalty tapestry are crisscrossing: the logic of killing oneself according to the categorical imperative; the irrefutable logic of logic that Kant's defense of the death penalty represents, according to Derrida, in the history of philosophy and the philosophy of philosophy (philosophy, like the death penalty, is based on something above life, honor, and duty, such that life is not the supreme value—if it were, there'd be no philosophy or law); the participation of society and whether society is on the side of the execution or the condemned person— is that evanescent man wanting to help K. or to help the executioners?; is the participation of society merely the spectatorship of a society—real or sheerly virtual—without which the death penalty could not be effective?; life or nature as that which cannot accept the law of death, and death as the unalterable law, regardless of the shame that goes with such liveliness. Remember that philosophy is defined as knowing how to die, and we have Heidegger to remind us of that.

Derrida moves directly to the ending to retrieve the rogue (*Schelm*) and the shame (*Beschämung*) from Kant's worthless would-be survivors. Here is the ending of *The Trial*: "But the hands of one of the men laid themselves upon K.'s throat, while the other stabbed the knife deep into his heart and turned it twice. With collapsing eyes, K. still saw, how the men, close in front of his face, cheek leaning against the other's cheek, observed the decision [*Ent-scheidung*, de-cide, sui-cide, homo-cide]. 'Like a dog!' he said, it was as if the shame must outlive him [*überleben*]."[21]

According to Derrida, the shame is the shame of being an animal, more exactly of being treated like an animal, either of returning to animality or being a dog because not even attaining, or failing to attain even, the minimum level of humanity. A suicide would have conferred a meaning, as attested by all the questions without answers or with contradictory non-answers. K. had the freedom to realize his freedom and it would have been manifest in his de-cision (Ent-scheidung) to sui-cide, to kill himself (sich selbst scheiden). If he is guilty of an intentionally committed crime, then he must rationally approve punishment, and in truth (bewähren) apply the pain to himself. As Derrida, reading the palimpsest of Kant between the lines of Kafka, puts it, and I paraphrase: If there is rationality, a rationality of the death penalty, and if humans are capable of the freedom Kant says they are, then the rational man—criminal—must not only understand the penalty but approve of it and even demand it (Gary Gilmore, for example), and feel guilty or ashamed if he doesn't. He ought even to lend a hand to what is in truth the truth of a suicide. A suicide: I have to kill myself, I approve of it and I even—symbolically—do it. The Kantian logic of universal and absolute rationality and of the categorical imperative of the death penalty requires that, from a logical point of view, the execution be a suicide. (This is the self-gratifying operation of the machine in so many accounts.) Not to decide suicide is to be ashamed. Be it K., or the wardens, who are ashamed at being so willing and ready (beschämt durch ihre Bereitwilligkeit).[22]

The dominant feeling of this execution, of this missed suicide, is an ineffaceable shame that survives the death of the innocents and the guilty and is incommensurable with good or with evil, with law and human justice. Such shame attaches itself to the humanity of the human and to the theatre of law.

At this point, Derrida delivers something of what belongs to the structure, the logic, of the verdict of the death penalty. Because the logic of the verdict assumes that the law is in reason, in juridical rationality that is imagined to be universally shared, the guilty person found to be guilty must concede that his judges and his executioners are right, and from that point onwards he concedes reason to the law, he accepts that the law is right, and as soon as he accepts that the law is right, it is as if he killed himself, as if he executed himself. He approves of the sentence and therefore condemns himself to death. The condemned executes the sentence by which he condemns himself. Once he accepts the verdict, he turns the execution into a suicide. The executioners are then only external agents of his internal will.

Derrida points out that as soon as the condemned person accepts that his judges and his executioners are right, are in the right, he transforms symbolically the hetero-punishment (the punishment carried out by an other on himself) into an auto-punishment (the punishment has his full approval and is even ordered by himself). As of that moment, he no longer believes in the reality of a death in which he remains the master of ceremonies. He gives himself this punishment, which might even be a reward and therefore it is not something inflicted upon himself.

The condemned person who usurps the control of the orchestration can therefore believe in it without believing in it. What Derrida is after here is how the fact of turning the execution into a suicide, turning the violence inflicted by a machine into a performance which one operates, gives rise to the feeling of a fictional or theatrical unreality, to a literary or performance aspect. One is not far here from Jean Genet's scenes in which executions are carried out in the imaginations of condemned people who turn what might eventually happen to them into highly symbolic and even campy representations. If any execution, by this logic of rationality whereby the convict becomes his own judge (exactly what Kant stated) dictating his own protocol of execution, turns into a symbolic suicide, then the death becomes a representation, a performance. It is glorified, theatricalized, and made less real. However, this distancing occurs in any death. By representing it to myself, I put it into a theatre. And, as Derrida adds, we never know if death is something that happens to us or something we do to ourselves.[23]

The possibility that I turn a condemnation into a self-inflicted putting-to-death but thereby also turn the putting-to-death into something phantasmic (no matter how real in the end) raises for Derrida the question of what it means for us to believe in death. As he adds, death is always so little natural, so very much cultural, that we are always condemned, always receiving a verdict in the form of a court punishment, and not merely receiving a natural punishment, a "natural death" as it is sometimes put. If death is always a kind of court punishment, a punishment happening to us from some kind of decision or official verdict, as for example when I receive the death sentence of a cancer diagnosis from a doctor, then being condemned to death like a criminal and being condemned to die like any mortal have something in common: they have in common that the supposedly purely "natural punishment" always has something cultural and symbolic to it.

Finally, in this reading emanating from Kafka, Derrida concludes by noting that if execution is always a quasi-suicide, and if hetero-punishment (punishment by the other) is always inculcated as self-punishment (I supplant the other in order to do it to myself), then that confirms the Kantian logic according to which the condemnation to death as the categorical imperative of pure reason must be accepted, approved, and universally taken upon oneself by any rational being, including the person condemned to death who condemns himself to death and even carries out—even if by substitutes or prostheses—the punishment himself upon himself. But, going farther, this hyperconfirmation of Kantian logic, of Kantian rationality, destroys or deconstructs itself. If hetero-punishment (punishment by the Law) reveals itself or is averred to be self-punishment (I do it myself), then one will no longer be able to distinguish between the strict law of a Court Law and the natural punishment. Coming back to Kant, Derrida finds in K.'s dwelling on whether he ought to kill himself, instead of letting the executioners do it to him, the precise thing which is the basis of Kant's categorical imperative and of Kant's Law—that is, the *homo noumenon* in all of us *homo phaenomenae* which makes it possible for the latter to give in to the former—and that this very thing deprives both law and the death penalty of any juridical rationality: again, if I can do it myself, with no need of any legal apparatus, then law comes tumbling down, and we can return to a state of nature or, more precisely, a nature of nature.

Derrida's summary of his reading of Kafka as the implicitly present subtext in Kant is as follows: "I do not know if what I say there is clear enough but you intuit that there is there a veritable self-explosive bomb, a power of implosive deconstruction at the very center of the rationality of law, of the right to punish and, at the center or at the summit of the right to punish, of the law of the death penalty. Once again, Kafka will have helped us, more powerfully than so many other [legal scholars and abolitionists], to follow the thread of what there is here to think, starting from what one so tranquilly calls literature. Or theatre."[24]

The point upon which I'll conclude and upon which deconstruction rests its case is the point of a restlessness, what Derrida often calls an earthquake: that is to say, an event that can always happen, because no structure or opposition is ultimately safe from a solicitation, from a shaking of its foundations. This earthquake in our thinking and in our concepts is deconstruction, and it is what Derrida's work tries to attest, to register, the signs of which his work listens for. Or, as he puts it: "It is the trembling of these boundaries (inside/outside, hetero-punishment/auto-punishment, etc.), their permeability also, their undecidability that is important to me here, and not the re-installing of other reassuring oppositional distinctions, that would permit one to say: yes, there, that is a for sure suicide; here, this is a for sure execution and/or murder. Or, there, there was execution or murder and definitely not a suicide, but here, this was certainly a suicide and not its opposite."[25] This is a very clear statement of what Derrida's lifelong work was devoted to: neither being content with the common sense that has been cast upon us before we can think for ourselves, nor reversing that common sense as if we were being somehow original thinkers or rebels. His thinking is interested in the trembling of the distinctions, the permeability between the distinctions, and their undecidability: not knowing, and not imagining I know, not hiding that I don't know, what hetero-punishment and auto-punishment ultimately are, what literal and figurative ultimately are, what the law and what nature ultimately are. This undecidability is crucial for understanding Derrida's sense of a responsibility to oppose the death penalty and the phantasm of sovereignty that is its basis.

Notes

1. These lectures, currently being edited for publication by Thomas Dutoit, Marc Crépon, and Geoffrey Bennington, will appear in French in January 2012 (Galilée), and in English in March 2012 (Univ. of Chicago Press). In what follows, the English translations of quotations from the typescript are my own, referenced by lecture and page number.

2. Lecture 6, February 2, 2000, 1.

3. "A mouthpiece of the 'in itself' of things, a telephone of the beyond." Friedrich Nietzsche, *On the Genealogy of Morals*, trans. Maudemarie Clark and Alan J. Swensen (Cambridge: Hackett, 1998), 72. The argument is that there is no access to things in themselves, save through metaphor. This condition alters the status of metaphor and of so-called nonmetaphorical discourses.

4. Immanuel Kant, *The Metaphysics of Morals*, trans. Mary Gregor (Cambridge: Cambridge Univ. Press, 1991), 140–45. [331–37 Akademie Ausgabe.] Translations sometimes modified.

5. Lecture 13, December 13, 2000, 2.

6. Lecture 15, January 31, 2000, 3.

7. John Locke, *Political Writings*, ed. David Wootton (Cambridge: Hackett, 2003), 262.

8. Kant, *Metaphysics*, 141.

9. Ibid., 142.

10. Lecture 13, 2–3.

11. Franz Kafka, "September 30, 1915," *Tagebücher 1910–1923*, ed. Max Brod (Frankfurt am Main: Fischer, 1973), 299. My translation.

12. Lecture 15, 9.

13. Franz Kafka, *Der Prozess* (Frankfurt am Main: Fischer, 1979), 190. My translations. In Franz Kafka, *The Trial*, trans. Willa and Edwin Muir (New York: Knopf, 1970), 224.

14. Ibid., 190–91, 224 English translation.

15. Ibid., 191; 224 English.

16. Ibid., 191; 225 English.

17. Ibid., 193; 227 English.

18. Ibid., 192; 225–26 English.

19. Ibid., 194; 228 English.

20. Ibid., 194; 228 English.

21. Ibid., 194; 228–29 English.

22. Ibid., 192; 226 English.

23. When Derrida, some fourteen months after having been diagnosed with pancreatic cancer, said, in an interview with Jean Birnbaum, that he was "at war with himself," he also referred, among other things, to his battle with cancer: the cancerous cells were in his body, were his body, were him, like the blood clot that did kill him came from him, from his body. Jacques Derrida, *Apprendre à vivre enfin: entretien avec Jean Birnbaum* (Paris: Galilée/Le Monde, 2005).

24. Lecture 14, 13.

25. Lecture 15, 3.

I prepare the last meal
for the Indian man to be executed

but this killer doesn't want much:
baked potato, salad, tall glass of ice water.

(I am not a witness)

It's mostly the dark ones
who are forced to sit in the chair

especially when white people die.
It's true, you can look it up

and this Indian killer pushed
his fist all the way down

a white man's throat, just to win a bet
about the size of his heart.

Those Indians are always gambling.
Still, I season this last meal

with all I have. I don't have much
but I send it down the line

with the handsome guard
who has fallen in love

with the Indian killer.
I don't care who loves whom.

(I am not a witness)

When it's the warden's stew I don't care
if I add too much salt or pepper.

For the boss I just cook.
He can eat what I put in front of him

but for the Indian man to be executed
I cook just right.

The temperature is the thing.
I once heard a story

about a black man who was electrocuted
in that chair and lived to tell about it

before the court decided to sit him back down
an hour later and kill him all over again.

I have an extra sandwich hidden away
in the back of the refrigerator

in case this Indian killer survives
that first slow flip of the switch

and gets hungry while he waits
for the engineers to debate the flaws.

(I am not a witness)

I prepare the last meal for free
just like I signed up for the last war.

I learned how to cook
by lasting longer than any of the others.

Tonight, I'm just the last one left
after the handsome guard takes the meal away.

I turn off the kitchen lights
and sit alone in the dark

because the whole damn prison dims
when the chair is switched on.

You can watch a light bulb flicker
on a night like this

and remember it too clearly
like it was your first kiss

or the first hard kick to your groin.
It's all the same

when I am huddled down here
trying not to look at the clock

look at the clock, no, don't
look at the clock, when all of it stops

making sense: a salad, a potato
a drink of water all taste like heat.

(I am not a witness)

I want you to know I tasted a little
of that last meal before I sent it away.

It's the cook's job, to make sure
and I was sure I ate from the same plate

and ate with the same fork and spoon
that the Indian killer used later

in his cell. Maybe a little piece of me
lodged in his mouth, wedged between

his front teeth, his incisors, his molars
when he chewed down on the bit

and his body arced like modern art
curving organically, smoke rising

from his joints, wispy flames decorating
the crown of his head, the balls of his feet.

(I am not a witness)

I sit here in the dark kitchen
when they do it, meaning

when they kill him, kill
and add another definition of the word

to the dictionary. America fills
its dictionary. We write down kill and everybody

in the audience shouts out exactly how
they spell it, what it means to them

and all of the answers are taken down
by the pollsters and secretaries

who keep track of the small details:
time of death, pulse rate, press release.

I heard a story once about some reporters
at a hanging who wanted the hood removed

from the condemned's head, so they could look
into his eyes and tell their readers

what they saw there. What did they expect?
All of the stories should be simple.

1 death + 1 death = 2 deaths.
But we throw the killers in one grave

and victims in another. We form sides
and have two separate feasts.

(I am not a witness)

I prepared the last meal
for the Indian man who was executed

and have learned this: If any of us
stood for days on top of a barren hill

during an electrical storm
then lightning would eventually strike us

and we'd have no idea for which of our sins
we were reduced to headlines and ash.

Lynching, Embodiment, and Post-1960 African American Poetry

DAVID KIERAN

"Capital punishment." "The death penalty." "Executions." In U.S. culture, these words generally conjure an action by the state, but the long history of lynching is a reminder that the death penalty has frequently been imposed without a trial and outside of the jurisdiction (though often with the implicit cooperation) of law enforcement and judicial officials. Amy Wood demonstrates that nineteenth-century public executions "were legal versions of the spectacle lynchings that took place in this same period," while the practice of public executions defined both the social mores and the actual violence that subsequently dominated lynchings.[1] Given this imbricated history, the study of the cultural responses to capital punishment must take a broad view of the death penalty's location and significance. Similarly, the reality that categories of inequality, particularly race and class, significantly shape the likelihood that an individual will face capital punishment, legal or otherwise, encourages consideration of how anti–death-penalty work intersects with activism related to other forms of injustice.[2]

Lynching continues to occupy a forceful place in American culture and memory because, as Wood argues, "it came to stand as the primary representation of racial injustice and oppression as a whole."[3] These spectacle murders provided a means for white Southerners to maintain social control in an increasingly unstable society, impressing upon black Americans their proper place.[4] Narratives and images of lynchings circulated in the media, in photographs, and on postcards.[5] This circulation had multiple effects; on the one hand, it "rendered the violence of a lynching visible and accessible to a wider audience"; it also "helped govern and standardize the practice of lynching" into what Grace Hale calls "a well-known structure, a sequence and pace of events that Southerners came to understand as standard."[6] This structure included hanging and burning as well as other forms of bodily violence, such as amputating digits and genitals, shattering skulls, shooting, and gouging out eyes.[7]

Exemplary is this account of a 1904 lynching of a married couple, the Holberts, in Doddsville, Mississippi. "'The blacks were forced to hold out their hands while one finger at a time was chopped off. The fingers were distributed as souvenirs. The ears of the murderers were cut off. [One] was beaten severely, his skull fractured and one of his eyes, knocked out with a stick, hung by a shred from the socket.'"[8] Similar descriptions dominate accounts of Emmett Till's lynching. An editorial in *The Crisis* described Till's "water-swollen body, with one side of his face beaten to a pulp, a bullet hole in his head"; *Jet* magazine published a picture of Till's mutilated body with the caption, "Savage lynchers crushed boy's skull, shot him, mutilated his face."[9] Mamie Till-Mobley's 2003 description of seeing her son's body is nearly identical: "There was an eyeball hanging down, resting on that cheek. . . . Right away, I looked to the other eye. But it wasn't there. . . . The back of his head was loose from the front part of his face."[10] These atrocities had been reproduced in countless lynchings and were, as Kevin Mumford argues, frequently referenced by critics of 1960s police brutality against African Americans.[11]

By the mid-1960s, dismemberment, castration, skull crushing, gunshot wounds, and eye destruction, as well as the public performance of violence, were established as the dominant signifiers of lynching. While spectacle lynchings had largely ceased by the mid-twentieth century, the act remains, as Carol Henderson observes, "a subtext that underwrites the cultural narrative of black male identity."[12] In ways that have gone unremarked or received only passing mention, several African American poets have mobilized these images and this legacy in work that critiques violence during the 1960s and into the 1980s. Dudley Randall, Larry Neal, Etheridge Knight, Michael Harper, and Sonia Sanchez deploy images of the lynching victim's mutilated body to comment upon other realities, such as the 1967 riots in Newark and Detroit, the assassination of Dr. Martin Luther King Jr., the 1985 bombing of MOVE in Philadelphia, and the effects of institutionalized antiblack violence. Neal and Randall, poets who helped to theorize black nationalism and promote a nationalist aesthetic, published poems that explicitly reference lynching's history before describing contemporary violence and calling for violent revolution. Knight, Sanchez, and Harper evoke the lynched body more subtly to assess U.S. culture's lack of progress on matters of racial equality.

The Nationalist Poetry of Dudley Randall, Larry Neal, and Etheridge Knight

Although the notion of a single, coherent Black Arts Movement is problematic, it is possible to identify a set of theoretical, ideological, and aesthetic debates and the figures central to them.[13] In different ways, Larry Neal and Dudley Randall were two such figures. By the late 1960s, Randall "increasingly adopted a nationalist tone in his comments about the goals of Broadside Press," which he had founded, while simultaneously crafting poems "inspired by the Black Arts Movement."[14] Neal was the coeditor (with Amiri Baraka) of the foundational anthology Black Fire and was associated with the journal Liberator. This journal was, James Edward Smethurst writes, "crucial in defining the ideological field of the Black Power and Black Arts movements in the Northeast."[15] Many poems of this period represent the African American body affirmatively; as Michael Bibby argues, "the body is foregrounded as the terrain for the signification of a racially assertive and empowered subjectivity."[16] In contrast, poems by Randall and Neal respond to continued violence against African Americans by invoking signifiers that establish the contemporary African American body as having been effectively lynched.

Randall first published "Roses and Revolutions" in 1948, almost a decade and a half before the idea of a Black Arts Movement emerged and would receive its greatest attention after it appeared in Randall's 1968 collection Cities Burning.[17] Melba Joyce Boyd explains that "because the poem became prominent during the 1960s, the imagery is associated with the many race riots of that decade. . . . [A] more accurate historical association would be the 1943 Detroit race riot and the lynchings that occurred in the south after WW II."[18] By using signifiers of the lynched body to describe the plight of urban African Americans, the poem merges historical contexts and establishes contemporary oppression of the North as equivalent to earlier violence of the South.[19]

Randall constructs the victim of racial and economic oppression endemic to the urban North as the victim of a lynching, but he does so only after he invokes the history of lynching in its traditional Southern context: "I saw the Negro lying in the swamp with his face blown off." Readers encountering the poem in the 1960s would likely have recalled the particulars of Till's murder, which contextualize the next two lines: "and in northern cities with his manhood maligned and felt the writhing / of his viscera like that of a hare hunted down or a bear at bay." The suggestion of lynching allows the words "manhood maligned" to take on additional meanings, relying on the multiple connotations of "manhood" to move from one symbolic register to another, from psychological emasculation to physical castration.

The next line likewise recalls lynching imagery. Wood remarks that "the image of white men posed next to their black victim bears an uncanny re-semblance to the familiar snapshot of a hunter with his prey." This long as-sociation of hunting and masculinity in Southern culture "underscores the ways in which lynching photographs bore with them both white suprema-cist ideology and the gendered elements of that ideology."[20] Randall's com-parison of northern African Americans to hunted animals recalls this prac-tice and reinforces the emasculating effects of contemporary oppression. The notion of spectacle is significant as well; these acts of violence are spectacles "[seen]" and "felt" by the poem's speaker.

These signifiers transform lynching's trauma into the psychological trauma and attendant physical distress suffered by oppressed, disempow-ered men. Images of emasculation—psychological castration—recur as the speaker describes "men working and taking no joy in their work / and embracing the hard-eyed whore with joyless excitement / and lying with wives and virgins in impotence." The structural oppression and economic exploitation of African Americans is an extension of the physical violence of lynching, and the desire to overcome produces the speaker's vision of "the blood-red flower of revolution."

Larry Neal more explicitly connects the history of lynching in the South with the specific violence of the 1967 Newark riots. The riots began in July after Newark police officers, whose brutality African American leaders had already criticized, arrested an African American taxi driver on dubi-ous charges. The driver suffered injuries during his arrest and jailing. The subsequent riots lasted for several days, as African American resis-tance (including reports of snipers firing on white officials from housing projects) led to the deployment of not only Newark police officers but also the New Jersey State Police and the National Guard.[21] In his history of Newark, Mumford notes that "only a week before the riots, Newark police made several highly controversial arrests of Black Muslims" and that one of those arrested suffered "a fractured skull."[22] He also reports that dur-ing the riots "central command sent patrols into the stairwells of public housing projects," which became the site of repeated police shootings.[23] Ron Porambo's journalistic account describes several children being shot by National Guardsmen as well as police assaults on housing projects: "they would empty three hundred rounds into the entire apartment build-ing, shooting from the first floor to the fifth or sixth floors."[24] Porambo describes numerous accounts of African Americans having received sig-nificant head wounds at the hands of white authorities.[25] After the riots,

Life magazine's cover photograph showed a child "apparently unconscious as the result of injuries from stray bullets of law enforcement."[26]

"Commemoration," the second section of Neal's "Orishas," was published in his 1974 collection *Hoodoo Hollerin' Bebop Ghosts*.[27] The speaker asks, "Who are the dead?" and then:

> Whose eyes are these, gouged out
> mucus smeared in the red earth?
> Whose figure hanging tarred about the lynch fire?
> What bodies are there crushed, maimed, brains
>   kicked out on the piss pavements of these cities?
> (Neal, "*Orishas*," 39, 46–50)

Like Randall, Neal begins with a reference to lynchings in the South — "red earth" — and to injuries familiar from its remembrance — "eyes . . . gouged out" and a "hanging," immolated body. As in Randall's poem, the first three lines provide a context that structures the interpretation of the next image, which recalls the shattered skull and brings lynching into an urban context. The poem's more specific question, "whose children shot to pieces in Newark tenements?" evokes excessive gunshot wounds and dismemberment (51). The poem connects the riots to the long history of antiblack violence by describing the very real violence perpetrated by the police and the National Guard in terms that evoke the mutilated, lynched black body.[28] This linkage contextualizes critiques of racial progress made in the riots' aftermath and foregrounds Neal's call for African Americans to "accept nothing less than the death of your enemies" (79).[29]

One of the best-known poems associated with the Black Arts Movement, Etheridge Knight's 1968 "Hard Rock Returns to Prison from the Hospital for the Criminal Insane," offers a critique of racist violence inside U.S. prisons through a similar mobilization of images.[30] The speaker describes the lobotomy of a prisoner, Hard Rock, who had been one of the most vigorous opponents of the racism of white guards and inmates; the doctors "bored a hole in his head, / Cut out part of his brain." A reference to Hard Rock as a "freshly gelded stallion" suggests castration, and the description of his eyes as "empty like knot holes in a fence" constructs them as absent and recalls gouged-out eyes.

Hard Rock's lobotomy produces the same ideological effects as a lynching. Hard Rock's injuries, John F. Callahan argues, are inflicted partly to enable greater control over all incarcerated African Americans.[31] That control is achieved by making Hard Rock visible to his fellow inmates who "waited and watched, like a herd of sheep, / to see if the WORD was true." Although they initially celebrate Hard Rock's resistance, Hard Rock's post-treatment body/person is on display. His only response is to "just grin and look silly." Such a reference replicates the language used to describe African Americans in a host of late nineteenth- and early twentieth-century cultural productions, particularly minstrelsy. As in spectacle lynching, where the public display of the mutilated black body served to warn and control the larger African American community, it is the spectacle of Hard Rock's mutilation that destroys the prisoners' capacity for resistance. Upon seeing what has been done to his body, the prisoners "[turn] away, [their] eyes on the ground. Crushed."

These poems, each written by a poet who contributed to Black Arts literature and ideology, recall the lynched body to address ongoing violence without diluting the specificity of past violations or contemporary instances of violence and oppression. In the 1970s and 1980s Michael Harper and Sonia Sanchez continued this use of signifiers drawn from lynching's memory to draw attention to the enduring oppression that African Americans face at the hands of whites.

The Memory of Lynching in Poems by Michael Harper and Sonia Sanchez

Harper has not traditionally been associated with Black Nationalist poetry or been located under the umbrella of the Black Arts Movement. His career, beginning with publication of *Dear John, Dear Coltrane* in 1970, has largely occurred after the decline of nationalist politics and the aesthetic debates that occurred in relation to them.[32] However, Harper's "Martin's Blues" (1972) and "A Mother Speaks" (1970) borrow from the same cultural archive, remembering well-known incidents of violence through lynching imagery.

"Martin's Blues," Harper's response to the assassination of Dr. Martin Luther King Jr., and published in *History Is Your Own Heartbeat*, recalls the murder in these terms: "He came apart in the open, / the slow motion cameras / falling quickly."[33] Harper transforms his death from a shooting into dismemberment—King "[comes] apart"—and presents the trauma as a spectacle; the "slow motion cameras" produce a graphic, widely disseminated image of the murder that recalls the still photographs on lynching postcards.

Despite a formidable antilynching movement, lynching worked to quash

African American challenges to white-dominated power structures.[34] In Harper's poem, King's death truncates not only his life but also his promise of equality. King's assertion that "[w]e shall overcome" is reduced to "a pruned echo," hinting that King's message will not endure his passing. Such language makes problematic any literal reading of the final line: *"Yes we did!"* Given the destruction of King's body and the establishment of that violence within the history of lynching, this line can only be read as grimly ironic or, more troubling, the "we" becomes a nation in which white supremacist ideas have "overcome" the African American quest for civil rights. Thus, while "Martin's Blues" rejects, or perhaps suggests the futility of, the revolution called for by Randall and Neal, it similarly presents King's death as a spectacle lynching and confirms that such violence, and the white supremacy that it enables, endures in spite of the emergence of King's leadership and the civil rights gains of the 1960s.

Harper's poem "A Mother Speaks: The Algiers Motel Incident, Detroit," included in *Dear John, Dear Coltrane*, remembers a high-profile account of white-on-black violence during the 1960s.[35] This poem imagines the experience of Rebecca Pollard, whose son Aubrey Pollard was killed during a police raid on the Algiers Motel during the Detroit riots—what Harper refers to as the "occupation of Detroit, 1967."[36] The Detroit riots began on July 23, 1967, following a police raid on an unlicensed nightclub. In the five days that followed, local police and the National Guard occupied the city, several black-owned businesses were burned, and numerous arrests and incidents of police violence occurred.[37] On July 26, 1967, three African American young men were killed by white police officers. As Suzanne Smith notes, "conflicting testimony and cover-ups shrouded the murders. Law enforcement officials circulated rumors that the three victims were snipers, who were shot by unknown assailants. Witnesses and leaders in the black community argued that three Detroit police officers . . . [had perpetrated] another vicious episode of police brutality."[38]

The events were documented by John Hersey in his 1967 book, *The Algiers Motel Incident*, and the title of Harper's poem reflects Hersey's title and the subtitle of the section in which Hersey interviews Rebecca Pollard. As well, several lines of the poem are drawn from that interview. Harper makes the connection with lynching evident by reiterating the injuries that Pollard, through Hersey, described and by crafting a poem in which the victim's mother recounts not what happened to her son but rather her experience of seeing his embalmed body. The change of context from Hersey's interview, which emphasizes the mother's outrage at the police, to an account that describes her viewing of Aubrey Pollard's body in a funeral parlor is particularly significant. In choosing this setting, Harper emphasizes not only the mutilated body's function as a spectacle but also the degree to which Rebecca Pollard's account of her son's injuries parallels Mamie Till-Mobley's account of seeing Emmet Till's body.

Cataloging the mortician's extensive reconstructive work, the mother indicates that her son's body has been brutally dismembered:

> the undertaker
> pushed his body
> back into place
> with plastic and gum

These early lines transform the victim's particular wounds into a generalized mutilation that requires extensive reconstruction. "Back into place" takes on multiple meanings, recalling both lynching's historically disciplinary function and Harper's consistent evocation of a culture in which white authorities desire to obliterate "transgressive" African Americans. Moreover, the speaker's catalog of her son's injuries relies upon the language of lynching:

> They tied the eye
> torn out
> by shotgun
> into place
> and his shattered
> arm cut away

The description of the injuries is more specific than Hersey's. The son's eye is "torn out," and the arm is not only "shattered" but, recalling dismemberment, "cut away."

The poem concentrates on the postmortem display of the body rather than on the violent act itself. The mother's witnessing is strategically managed: she is made to realize that those who killed him are capable of destroying black identity, but she is forbidden from interrogating how that obliteration is achieved:

> When I looked for marks
> or lineament
> or fine stitching
> I was led away

without seeing
this plastic
face they'd built
that was not my son's

Because her access to the corpse is limited, in the end she can only testify that white authorities have the power to kill her son and to transform his body into something alien. The reconstructive embalming is destructive rather than restorative. Hale maintains that lynching showed that "the very bodies of African Americans were subject to invasion by whites" and that an African American was "someone who could be publicly tortured and killed, prevented even from being a person."[39] In Harper's poem, the mutilated body's visibility affirms racist social structures by demonstrating white license to destroy black personhood while silencing witnesses' critiques of violence and the ideology that it buttresses.[40] In the end, the mother can only know that white authorities are able to kill African Americans violently, indiscriminately, and with impunity.

Quoting Mrs. Pollard's account of the last words of the victim, the speaker reports:

My son's gone
by white hands
though he said
to his last word—
"Oh I'm so sorry,
officer, I broke your gun."

Harper terms this confession a "victim's plea for his life."[41] These words affirm the victim's innocence and the baseless brutality of the crime, and recall lynching's use of "torture to extract confessions."[42] In *The Algiers Motel Incident*, Pollard states "the man was beating him over the head and his face so that he tore off his face and half his eye was hanging out his head . . . and Aubrey said, 'Oh, I'm so sorry I broke your gun.' . . . And then after he broke his gun, he shot half his arm off."[43] Although obviously unreliable, such confessions are used retroactively to validate torture.[44] An admission of having destroyed white property and having challenged white institutional authority would establish, according to lynching rituals, this man as a criminal and justify his death.[45]

Significantly, Harper added the word "officer" to the line that otherwise directly quotes Hersey; in doing so, he expands upon the initial claim of violence caused by "white hands" to emphasize that this continued brutality toward African Americans is not only public but also officially sanctioned and perpetrated by the criminal justice system. His poetry, like Knight's "Hard Rock" and Neal's "Commemoration," invokes the cultural memory of lynching to critique the violence with which law enforcement authorities persecute African Americans. These poems challenge assertions of African American criminality as well as narratives that treat contemporary racial politics as substantively different from earlier eras.

Sonia Sanchez mobilizes these images as well in her 1987 poem, "Elegy (For MOVE and Philadelphia)."[46] Sanchez had initially been associated with black nationalist ideologies and Black Arts aesthetics, but as Smethurst notes she was among those who subsequently "sought some other sort of activist politics at odds with their earlier positions."[47] The subject of "Elegy" is the bombing of the MOVE headquarters by Philadelphia police on May 13, 1985.[48] The raid on the row house occupied by MOVE, an Afrocentric group, followed months of complaints to the city about unsanitary conditions and disruptive protests.[49] The police raid, and the fire that it produced, killed eleven people, five of them children, and decimated the neighborhood. The bombing of MOVE received considerable attention in the Philadelphia press. Although several articles were unsympathetic toward MOVE, the police received the most substantial criticism, particularly in the Inquirer's report that "for weeks, and possibly months, the police department quietly and secretly tested explosive substances . . . on lumber structures in preparation for the siege on MOVE."[50]

Sanchez, like Neal, Knight, and Harper, positions the police not as defenders of freedom but as those who seek to truncate African American rights and self-determination, "combing the city for lifeliberty and / the pursuit of happiness" (Sanchez, "Elegy (For MOVE and Philadelphia)," 4:10– 11). Yet, it is the general public that receives the most severe criticism in this poem. The speaker refers to Philadelphia as a "disguised Southern city," a comment that Joyce Pettis notes "evokes the atmosphere of a lynching to illustrate the insistent, murderous power of those who possess it" (1:2).[51] Joyce Ann Joyce notes that Sanchez "castigates the political components of racial oppression through hard-hitting sarcasm," and the poem sardonically establishes the entire city as the audience of a spectacle lynching by deploying now familiar language.[52] The speaker declares, "c'mon girl hurry down to osage st / they're roasting in the fire / smell the dreadlocks and the blk/skins" (2:1–4). Descriptions of other injuries similarly rely on lynching imagery: "over there, one eye / escaping from its skin / and our heartbeats slow down to a drawl" (4:3–5). The word "drawl" reinforces the Southern temperament, suggesting that witnesses are being *made* Southern and thus are complicit in the oppression by virtue of their gaze. That the bombing's aftermath has become a public spectacle is reinforced by the speaker's exhortation "c'mon newsmen and tvmen / hurryondown to osage st," lines reflecting the media's broad dissemination of images from the bombing and their role in stoking the public's morbid curiosity (2:5–6).

More significantly, the victims' bodies, clearly established as "black," are described as having been lynched. Again we see gouged-out eyes, and the verb "roasting" recalls the use of "barbeque" to describe lynchings.[53] Notably, the *Philadelphia Inquirer*'s intense coverage of the MOVE raid contained no references to such images. Most often, the event was described as a "war," and several articles referenced Vietnam.[54] The only smell described was "the acrid smell of tear gas."[55] Though articles noted that several bodies had been found "in parts," they provided no details regarding specific injuries.[56] Thus, Sanchez, like Harper and Neal, responds to an actual event by insistently imagining the bodies of those who died as suffering the same violence as lynching victims.

The poem's references to the public and the media eagerly witnessing the event likely respond to *Inquirer* articles that emphasized the degree to which the raid, the fire, and devastation became a spectacle. One report recalled accounts of crowds gathering to watch a lynching or to view its aftermath: "Lured perhaps by morbid fascination or just plain curiosity, people had come to see it happen. Lining the streets long before dawn, standing in the rain at times, they had come to witness the spectacle. . . . Some of them drank wine, some drank beer. Some talked about game plans, as if they were discussing baseball strategy."[57] The next weekend, an article reported on the influx of suburban visitors who had come to take photographs of the scene: "The BMWs and Fiats came out yesterday. And the Minoltas and the Pentaxes. On the first weekend showing since the bomb was dropped, attendance was excellent on Osage Avenue."[58] The response to the reporter's quandary—"What might a person do with a photograph of a street that used to be?"—met with a response that could have been applied to the circulation of lynching photographs: " 'Just keep it.' "[59]

Sanchez's poem is a lament "for MOVE and Philadelphia." Like Harper, Sanchez does not present this violence as evidence of the need for violent revolution. Rather, as Pettis suggests, "the poem does not end with reconciliation but with the idea that somewhere beyond the city's ordinary façade of activity, honor and peace lie in wait."[60] That change, however, requires activism, and Joyce asserts that "the end of the poem manifests the poet's persistence in attacking the societal maladies that destroy human lives and stifle the human spirit."[61] The speaker inveighs, "exile us from our laughter / give us this day our rest from seduction / peeling us down to our veins" (6:3–5). Here, the metaphoric wound from which the speaker seeks relief recalls the image of flayed skin and posits the "seduction" of participation in passive, unsympathetic witnessing as the source of such pain. This observation resonates with critiques made by antilynching rhetoric in the 1930s and 1940s, which "posited white society and the white psyche to be the primary victims of lynching."[62] Again, the mobilization of terms and images from the cultural memory of lynching contextualizes the brutal oppression that African Americans continue to suffer in the urban north.

Conclusion

The cultural memory of the lynched body has been persistent in poetic critiques of public violence that African Americans continue to endure, most frequently under the auspices of the law enforcement or correctional systems. Whether imagining fictional accounts of racist violence or poetically representing actual incidents of police violence, Neal, Randall, Knight, Harper, and Sanchez respond to the rise of "legal lynching" by mobilizing the imagery of the lynched body to assert that the violence suffered by contemporary African Americans is an extension of the violence that their ancestors experienced at the hands of Southern mobs.[63]

These poems challenge dominant understandings of the relationship between embodiment and violence in African American poetry and suggest avenues for broadening the study of the history of capital punishment. The majority of the essays in this collection examine literature that specifically addresses the death penalty. Certainly, I do not question the validity or importance of such analyses. And yet, this poetry contributes to the work of scholars arguing for histories of capital punishment that look beyond state-sanctioned violence. The persistent significance of lynching's memory in this literature indicates the need to more fully interrogate the historical, cultural, and literary links between capital punishment and other forms of historical and contemporary violence. As well, the use of this discourse of memory fundamentally troubles the argument that the government adheres to the highest legal, ethical, and medical standards in that it emphasizes continuing structural inequality, oppression, and violence. Finally, the imagery of lynching in these poems compels us to question how, for example, the history of the death penalty and the attendant issues of race and class have been significant in literary responses to forms of racial and economic oppression that exist outside of prison walls. Pursuing these questions will provide a more complete understanding of the death penalty's location within American culture, the ways it has been promoted and opposed, and the means through which social change can be achieved.

Notes

1. Amy Louise Wood, *Lynching and Spectacle: Witnessing Racial Violence in America, 1890–1940* (Charlotte: Univ. of North Carolina Press, 2009), 29, 24. More generally, see Wood 24–40. In her analysis of the literature of capital punishment, Kristin Boudreau has wisely not differentiated between lynchings and killings perpetrated by the state; see *The Spectacle of Death: Populist Literary Responses to American Capital Cases* (New York, Prometheus Books, 2006).

2. Apel writes, "the legacies of segregation, racial stereotypes, and the sexualization of politics continue to haunt American society" and that "long imprisonments and 'legal lynchings' began to replace lynchings so that the persecution of black men continued unabated." *Imagery of Lynching* (New Brunswick, NJ: Rutgers Univ. Press, 2009), 15, 45. See Wood, *Lynching*, 26.

3. Wood, *Lynching*, 1.

4. Wood, *Lynching*, 13–14; Grace Elizabeth Hale, *Making Whiteness: The Culture of Segregation in the South, 1890–1940* (New York: Vintage, 1998), 203, 205, and 228–29; and Leon Litwack, *Trouble in Mind: Black Southerners in the Age of Jim Crow* (New York: Alfred A. Knopf, 1998), 308–9.

5. Wood, *Lynching*, 11–12. For the visual imagery of lynching, see Apel, *Imagery*; Hale, *Making Whiteness*; and Jerry Bryant, *Victims and Heroes: Racial Violence in the African-American Novel* (Amherst: Univ. of Massachusetts Press, 1997), 76.

6. Wood, *Lynching*, 80, 9; Hale, *Making Whiteness*, 203. See also Apel, *Imagery*, 44.

7. Bryant, *Victims and Heroes*, 76–77; Hale, *Making Whiteness*, 204–5; and Litwack, *Trouble in Mind*, 281–92.

8. Quoted in Litwack, *Trouble in Mind*, 289.

9. Editorial, "Mississippi Barbarism," *Crisis* 62 (1955), 480; "Will Mississippi Whitewash the Emmett Till Slaying?" *Jet*, September 22, 1955, 9.

10. Mamie Till-Mobley and Christopher Benson, *Death of Innocence: The Story of the Hate Crime that Changed America* (New York: Random House, 2003), 135–36.

11. Kevin Mumford, *Newark: A History of Race, Rights, and Riots in America* (New York: New York University Press, 2007), 117–18.

12. Carol E. Henderson, *Scarring the Black Body: Race and Representation in African-American Literature* (Columbia: Univ. of Missouri Press, 2002), 143. On lynching's "gradual decline," see Wood, *Lynching*, 261.

13. On periodizing the Black Arts Movement, see James Edward Smethurst, *The Black Arts Movement: Literary Nationalism in the 1960s and 1970s* (Chapel Hill: Univ. of North Carolina Press, 2005), 2–3; 57. For the unifying aims of those who could be subsumed under the umbrella of Black Arts, see Smethurst, *The Black Arts Movement*, 15.

14. Ibid., 227; 232.

15. Ibid., 150; on the significance of *Black Fire*, see Ibid., 152. For Neal's endeavors to promote African-American cultural production, see Ibid., 92–93 and 132.

16. Michael Bibby, *Hearts and Minds: Bodies, Poetry, and Resistance in the Vietnam Era* (New Brunswick, NJ: Rutgers Univ. Press, 1996), 57.

17. Melba Joyce Boyd, "Introduction," in *Roses and Revolutions: The Selected Writings of Dudley Randall*, ed. Melba Joyce Boyd (Detroit: Wayne State University Press, 2009), 4; Boyd, *Wrestling with the Muse: Dudley Randall and the Broadside Press* (New York: Columbia Univ. Press, 2003), 80, 197; on its interpretation in documentary film, see Boyd, *Wrestling with the Muse*, 397. Dudley Randall, "Roses and Revolutions" in *Trouble the Water: 250 Years of African-American Poetry*, ed. Jerry W. Ward Jr. (New York: Penguin, 1997), 208.

18. Boyd, *Wrestling*, 80.

19. Smethurst's analysis of Randall's "The Southern Road" makes a similar observation, noting the lynching imagery and arguing that Randall is "thematically making a connection between African-American experience North and South" (*The Black Arts Movement*, 232).

20. Wood, *Violence and Spectacle*, 95; 95–97.

21. Mumford, *Newark*, 98. For a general account, see Mumford, *Newark* 98–169 and Ron Porambo, *No Cause for Indictment: An Autopsy of Newark* (New York: Holt, Rinehart, and Winston, 1971).

22. Mumford, *Newark*, 110.

23. Mumford, *Newark*, 110; 142–43.

24. Porambo, *No Cause for Indictment*, 22.

25. Ibid., 18; 48–49; 97–99.

26. Mumford, *Newark*, 153.

27. Larry Neal, "Orishas," in *Hoodoo Hollerin' Bebop Ghosts* (Washington: Howard Univ. Press, 1974), 26–28.

28. See note 11.

29. Mumford, *Newark*, 138.

30. Etheridge Knight, "Hard Rock Returns to Prison from the Hospital for the Criminal Insane," in *Trouble the Water*, 259–60.

31. John Callahan, "Hearing Is Believing: The Landscape of Believing in Ernest Gaines's *Bloodline*," *Callaloo* 7:1 (1984), 102.

32. See Robert B. Stepto, "Let's Call Your Mama and Other Lies about Michael S. Harper," *Callaloo* 13:4 (1990), 802; Bibby includes Harper's "Debridement" in his analysis of "Black Liberationist" anti-Vietnam poetry (*Hearts and Minds*, 66–69).

33. Michael Harper, "Martin's Blues," in *Songlines in Michaeltree: New and Collected Poems* (Urbana: Univ. of Illinois Press, 2000), 38.

34. Hale, *Making Whiteness*, 208–9; 239. See Litwack, *Trouble*, 308–9.

35. Harper, "A Mother Speaks: The Algiers Motel Incident, Detroit," in *Dear John, Dear Coltrane* (Pittsburgh: Univ. of Pittsburgh Press, 1970), 76.

36. Harper, *Songlines in Michaeltree*, 376.

37. For a brief account of the riots, see Suzanne E. Smith, *Dancing in the Street: Motown and the Cultural Politics of Detroit* (Cambridge: Harvard Univ. Press, 1999), 193–205, as well as Heather Bachman, Sharon Stanford, and Teresa Kimble, eds., *Eyes on Fire: Witnesses to the Detroit Riot of 1967* (Detroit: Aquarius Press, 2007).

38. Smith, *Dancing in the Street*, 200–201.

39. Hale, *Making Whiteness*, 229.

40. My analysis draws upon Elaine Scarry, *The Body in Pain: The Making and Unmaking of the World* (New York: Oxford Univ. Press, 1985), 27.

41. Harper, *Songlines in Michaeltree*, 377.

42. Hale, *Making Whiteness*, 204; Wood, *Lynching*, 61.

43. John Hersey, *The Algiers Motel Incident* (New York: Knopf, 1968), 330.

44. Scarry, *The Body in Pain*, 41–42; Wood, *Lynching*, 62.

45. Wood, *Lynching*, 62.

46. Sonia Sanchez, "Elegy *(For MOVE and Philadelphia)*," in *Trouble the Water: 250 Years of African-American Poetry*, ed. Jerry W. Ward Jr. (New York: Penguin, 1997), 294–96.

47. Smethurst, *The Black Arts Movement*, 3.

48. For an overview see "The MOVE Siege: A Chronology of Events," *Philadelphia Inquirer*, May 14, 1985, 12A; Matthew J. Countryman, *Up South: Civil Rights and Black Power in Philadelphia* (Philadelphia: Univ. of Pennsylvania Press, 2006), 325–26; and John Anderson and Hillary Hevenor, *Burning Down the House: MOVE and the Tragedy of Philadelphia* (New York: W. W. Norton, 1987).

49. Countryman, *Up South*, 325.

50. Ron Wolf et al., "How the Bomb Decision Was Made," *Philadelphia Inquirer*, May 17, 1985.

51. Joyce Pettis, *African-American Poets: Lives, Works, Sources* (Westport, CT: Greenwood Press, 2002), 297.

52. Joyce Ann Joyce, *Ijala: Sonia Sanchez and the African Poetic Tradition* (Chicago: Third World Press, 1996), 137.

53. See Apel, 32–33.

54. See, for example, Margaret Del Giudice et al., "Battlefield; 'I'm at Home Seeing War,' Says Neighborhood Man," *Philadelphia Inquirer*, May 14, 1985; Frank Rossi, "At the Barriers: Seeking Sense," *Philadelphia Inquirer*, May 14, 1985; and Dorothy Storek, "In This Case, Everyone Lost," *Philadelphia Inquirer*, May 14, 1985.

55. Storek, "In this Case, Everyone Lost."

56. "Six Bodies, 2 of Children, Taken from MOVE Rubble," *Philadelphia Inquirer*, May 15, 1985; Larry Eichel and Robin Clark, "MOVE Death Toll Reaches 11," *Philadelphia Inquirer*, May 16, 1985.

57. Janice McMillan, "Watching, but Scarcely Believing, in West Philadelphia," *Philadelphia Inquirer*, May 14, 1985.

58. Steve Lopez, "Osage Avenue the Stage, Devastation the Attraction," *Philadelphia Inquirer*, May 19, 1985.

59. Ibid.

60. Pettis, *African-American Poets*, 297.

61. Joyce, *Ijala*, 138.

62. Wood, *Lynching*, 226.

63. Apel, *Imagery*, 45.

State Killing, the Stage of Innocence, and *The Exonerated*

KATY RYAN

Jessica Blank and Erik Jensen's documentary play *The Exonerated* brings to the stage the experiences of six people who spent between two and twenty-two years on death row for crimes they did not commit. Drawn from interviews and developed with Allan Buchman, director of the Culture Project, *The Exonerated* was first performed by the Actor's Gang in Los Angeles on April 19, 2002. The play moved to Off-Broadway six months later, directed by Bob Balaban, and has been performed across the country, in Europe, and at the United Nations. Often staged as readers' theater with a minimal set and high-profile actors, *The Exonerated* has won numerous awards, including the Outer Critics Circle Award for Best Off-Broadway Play. It appeared on lists of the top ten plays for 2002 in the *New York Times* and *Time* magazine and was made into a movie by Court TV in 2005. Writing for the *Telegraph*, Charles Spencer "approached *The Exonerated* with a certain degree of dread" — "There are few spectacles more ridiculous than Hollywood stars in one of their periodic fits of morality" — but he found the play moving and important. Ben Brantley in the *New York Times* called it "intense and deeply affecting."[1]

Through a popular merger of first-hand testimony, star power, and sentimental address, *The Exonerated* elicits sympathy for former death row prisoners. The hallmark signs of sentimentality are abundant: human connectedness, shared pain, broken ties, compassion in brutalized contexts, and redemptive suffering. Brantley writes that the clear goal of *The Exonerated* is "to edify." By focusing on innocence, Blank and Jensen hoped to "sidestep much of the polarized ethical debate that so often bogs down conversations about the death penalty and get right to the human issues involved."[2] Balaban describes the work as less polemical than pedagogical.[3]

As a celebrated example of political theater, *The Exonerated* also provides a critical forum for conversations about state killing. The script may not sidestep a debate as much as inscribe key cultural dynamics. In part, *The Exonerated* promotes reform by substituting universal vulnerability for a more accurate assessment of imprisonment and judicial murder. Although hardly uncontroversial, the play does generate a deceptive sense of shared agreement—after all, few people argue that innocent people should be poisoned or electrocuted. (William Rehnquist and Antonin Scalia have come close.)[4] In its steady tone and narrow focus, the play cedes to sentimentalism's "generic wish for an unconflicted world, one where structural inequities, not emotions and intimacies, are epiphenomenal."[5] Beneath the play's sentimental structure lie the murderous realities of the justice system.

A few years ago at an orientation session for teachers at a federal prison in West Virginia, I was given a handout of things not to do with inmates. Top on the list of don'ts was this requirement: "Don't overidentify." We were warned about the cunning of prisoners, their capacity to play on visitors' sympathy. We were given detailed instructions on what to do in a hostage situation. The warden made clear that in the case of an attempted escape, he is trained to kill—and it doesn't matter if he's aiming at a man or a woman, or if the woman is a mother, as most women in prison are. To sympathize with people held captive under such conditions is a needed, ethical response, and *The Exonerated* moves in this direction. I realize my analysis may seem wearily skeptical (What are the bad consequences of this good literary work?), but the need to reflect on what we talk about when we talk about the U.S. prison system is especially urgent.

Starting the Conversation

Blank and Jensen interviewed on the phone forty people who had been wrongfully convicted of capital crimes and selected twenty to meet in person. For the play, they whittled the twenty down to twelve, and the twelve down to the following six cases. In the early 1970s, Delbert Tibbs was convicted of the murder of a white man and the rape of a sixteen-year-old white woman in Florida. The evidence against him consisted of the eyewitness account of the rape victim. "Now, initially," Tibbs explains, "the girl who survived the thing described the murderer as a black man about five six, very dark complexion, with pockmarked skin and a bush Afro. [*Beat.*] Now that don't fit me no matter how you draw it—except racially. . . . We're both black men" (E, 23). On appeal, the original conviction was overturned and Tibbs was released in January 1977. In 1991 in Mississippi, Robert Hayes was convicted of the rape and murder of a white woman. Hayes recalls, "[I]n my first trial, I *knew* I was going to prison—I had eleven whites and one black on that jury" (E, 12). The Florida Supreme Court overturned his conviction in 1995, and he was acquitted in a retrial in 1997. David Keaton, a black teenager, confessed under torture to the murder of a police officer in 1971. "I didn't know the rules," Keaton says, "and they were threatenin' me, and all that. And I was afraid. I mean they could go in there and beat you up, mess you up, hang you up, nobody'd ever hear nothin' else about you. And so I say, okay, to prevent that, I'm gonna go ahead and confess to the crime" (E, 20). He trusted that witnesses would verify that he was not at the scene of the murder. Keaton was convicted and sentenced to death in Florida. In 1973, the state supreme court reversed the conviction and ordered a new trial. Keaton was released after another man was convicted for the murder.

The remaining three cases involve white defendants. In 1993, Gary Gauger was convicted of killing his parents in Illinois. During an all-night interrogation, Gauger was encouraged to provide police with a "vision statement," describing how, hypothetically, he would have committed the crime. This statement, full of factual errors, was used to convict Gauger. His death sentence was overturned in 1996, and in 2002 former governor George Ryan extended a full pardon to Gauger. Neither of the two final cases resulted in a legal exoneration, a factual discrepancy with the play's title that has not been lost on pro–death-penalty reviewers.[6] In 1976, Sonia Jacobs was convicted of killing a police officer and Canadian constable. From prison a few years later, Walter Rhodes claimed that he had been the actual shooter. In 1981, the Supreme Court commuted Jacobs's sentence to life. Jacobs later took the Alford plea and was released in 1992. Lastly, Kerry Max Cook was arrested in 1977 for the murder of a white woman in Texas. Cook was working at a gay bar at the time of his arrest and was assumed to be gay. In closing remarks, the prosecution urged the jury not "to give this pervert his butcher knife back" and to "let all the freaks and perverts and murderous homosexuals of the world know what we do with them in a court of justice" (E, 42). During his twenty-two years in prison, Cook saw 141 people go to the death chamber. After four separate trials, he also took the Alford plea and was released.

The playwrights wove these experiences into a compelling narrative of arrest, prosecution, imprisonment, and release. The result has had clear impacts. The Exonerated has been seen by magistrates from London and district attorneys from New Jersey as well as attorneys general and Supreme Court justices.[7] Former attorney general Janet Reno argued that it would "'do more to promote justice than any literary effort I have seen.'" A production for the American Bar Association in Texas raised $100,000 for DNA testing and resulted in a lead prosecutor publicly apologizing to Cook.[8] Mary Jo White, a federal prosecutor from Manhattan, acknowledged the play's accuracy, noting that the "degree to which [the zealousness of cops] permeates the American justice system, I fear, is not insignificant."[9]

The script contains a conversion story as well. Sandra Cook, who met and married Kerry Max Cook after his release, admits that she initially assumed that he must have been guilty of something: "I'm ashamed to have had this thought—What did he do to get himself in that situation? That's how I looked at it . . .'cause you know, I was very conservative . . . [Beat.] and also very stupid" (ellipses in original, E, 69). At some performances, there have been talkbacks, panel discussions, abolitionist and other social justice organizations in the lobby. Although the people featured were not extended copyright protection, financial contributions from audience members amounted to more than $800,000 for the six participants.[10]

On December 17, 2002, in Chicago, George Ryan, his top staff, and members of the general assembly attended a special performance. The evening had been arranged by a coalition of groups—the Center on Wrongful Convictions, the Illinois Coalition against the Death Penalty, and Murder Victims' Families for Reconciliation—as part of a strategy to compel the governor to grant commutations to Illinois death row prisoners. A Republican and long-time supporter of the death penalty, Ryan had issued a moratorium on the death penalty two years earlier: twelve people had been executed and thirteen people exonerated in the state since 1976. As Ryan explained, "I'm a pharmacist. If I got 50 percent of my prescriptions back because they were filled wrong I wouldn't be in business."[11] Also at the performance were individuals portrayed in the play. Cook described it as " 'the most important night of my life. . . . This honestly transcends the day I was freed. Through Richard Dreyfuss, I was getting the chance to talk to Governor Ryan.' "[12]

Approximately three weeks later, and three days before leaving office, Ryan granted a mass commutation. Balaban was told that the play had influenced his decision,[13] and Louise Kennedy began her article in the Boston Globe, "Before outgoing Illinois Governor George Ryan decided to commute the sentences of all the prisoners on that state's death row last weekend, he watched a play."[14] The playwrights' hopes had been exceeded: "The power of these people and their stories translated—we hadn't gotten in the way. We'd done our job" (L, 275).

The death penalty abolition movement has gained significant traction because of the number and visibility of cases of "actual innocence," a phrase meant to distinguish exonerations based on factual innocence from those resulting from due-process or legal errors. Since 1973, 138 people have been exonerated of capital crimes in the United States.[15] Bryan Stevenson, director of the Equal Justice Initiative, often points out that a defendant in a capital case is better off being rich and guilty than poor and innocent.[16] The Supreme Court's decision in *Herrera v. Collins* (1993) provided little reassurance. William Rehnquist argued that "errors of fact" discovered after a constitutionally fair trial do not require judicial remedy, citing *Patterson v. New York* (1977): "'[D]ue process does not require that every conceivable step be taken, at whatever cost, to eliminate the possibility of convicting an innocent person.'"[17] The petitioner, Leonel Herrera, was executed in 1993. Three years later, Bill Clinton introduced and Congress passed the Anti-terrorism and Effective Death Penalty Act, reducing the federal appeals process. In June 2009, Scalia wrote in a dissent in Troy Davis's case that "this court has *never* held that the Constitution forbids the execution of a convicted defendant who has had a full and fair trial but is later able to convince a habeas court that he is 'actually' innocent."[18]

Yet some abolitionists, including attorney David Dow, founder of the Texas Innocence Network, believe that the innocence argument is a tactical and moral mistake. Most people on death row are, Dow emphasizes, guilty. Having seen many of his clients put to death, he insists, "[I]t is the humanity of the inmates—of my clients—that is the critical moral fact. I remain convinced that the obsessive attention to innocence distracts from that fact."[19] Penal history is filled with theories and practices that promise reform and transformation but deliver more convictions and more prisons. This is, Michel Foucault argues, the point of prison/reform. If we do not confront the intentional aim of capital punishment, we open the door, Dow attests, to reform, not abolition. And reform was the route taken by most state legislatures after *Furman v. Georgia* (1972). For Dow, concentrating on flaws in the administration of the death penalty only encourages governments to tinker and "design a better mousetrap."[20]

Crafting Reform

Programs, reviews, and the Court TV version emphasize the fact-based character of *The Exonerated*. "With a few exceptions," the playwrights stress, "each word spoken in this play comes from the public record—legal documents, court transcripts, letters—or from an interview with the exonerated person" (E, xiii). Blank and Jensen chose cases that they thought were "most representative" in terms of race, gender, geography, personality, and life experience (L, 225). Once the playwrights had chosen the initial subjects, and actors had begun reading the script, they "took a big Magic

Marker and crossed out the boring parts, the awkward parts, the parts that didn't translate. Our interviews were beginning—just beginning—to look a little bit like stories" (L, 186). Balaban recalls, "I immediately threw it on its feet with a bunch of movie stars. . . . In the course of five years we cut it down. I was the director at this point so I helped organize this and helped bring in more material so this could feel more like drama."[21] Blank and Jensen explain that had they "not been willing to chip away at [the manuscript] ruthlessly, we would have been left with rough edges, undefined lines, coarse masses of words" (L, 226). In this documentary paradox— between staying out of the way and ruthlessly cutting—*The Exonerated* was composed.

Among the people interviewed who did not become part of the performance is Darby Tillis, who was suspicious of the playwrights' motives. The playwrights acknowledge in their memoir that Tillis educated them about the need to clarify their intentions and address compensation up front. Tillis told them that plays make money—" '[T]hat's what you're doing this for; don't tell me any different' "—and refused to be tape-recorded (L, 60). Tillis does not appear in the play because, according to Blank and Jensen, he did not want to be. Lost in the performance are his telling historical objections to ceding his voice.

Blank and Jensen also spoke with Henry Drake but knew ten minutes into the conversation that he could not be in the play: "As we sat talking with Henry [Drake], we knew there was no way his story could make it into the play. We were fashioning a play based on people's own words, and Henry's weren't cohesive enough for an audience to understand" (L, 115). People with mental disabilities confess far more often to crimes they did not commit than people with average IQ scores.[22] Since 1976, more than forty people with IQs under seventy have been executed, and it was not until *Atkins v. Georgia* (2002) that the Supreme Court declared the execution of mentally retarded people unconstitutional. The death penalty extends, write Jensen and Blank in their memoir, to "the most defenseless, most vulnerable members of our society" (L, 116). Rather than grapple with the challenges Drake would present to the form of the play, they cut his story, admitting they "were unhappy with that" (L, 237).

Carol Martin points out that documentary theater generally claims that "everything presented is part of the archive. But equally important is the fact that not everything in the archive is part of the documentary."[23] The selection process resulted in hurt feelings among some whose stories were eliminated after the first productions. Blank and Jensen apologize to these unnamed individuals in *Living Justice* and add, "If it's any consolation, we learned something from our mistake and have tried to evolve from the experience" (227). The performance joins a tradition of enfranchised people speaking for formerly captive people and benefiting from the publication or recording.[24] Like oral histories of American Indians, slaves, and prisoners, contemporary documentary work often draws attention to patterns of privilege. The inevitably subjective criteria at work in the crafting of *The Exonerated*—with whom could the playwrights relate? who wanted to work with them? which cases were more easy to convey?—resulted less in a representative group than a broadly familiar narrative. Prison reform efforts have similarly focused on the most "accessible" or "sympathetic" victim, often to avoid facing the antiblack engine of the criminal justice system.[25]

The second sentence of the introduction tells us that the people with whom Blank and Jensen spoke "were from vastly different ethnic, religious and educational backgrounds. . . . The only thing they held in common was that they had each been sentenced to die" (E, xi). This description, repeated in program notes, is perplexing. Most of the people exonerated from death row in the United States—and most of the people the playwrights chose to feature—have at least three things in common: poverty, a conviction in the South, and a case involving a white victim. The overwhelming number of defendants in capital trials cannot afford a private attorney, and in Alabama, more than 80 percent of those on death row were represented by defense attorneys whose costs were capped at $1,000.[26] Of post–1976 executions, 80 percent have occurred in the South, and cases in two states, Florida and Illinois, account for 43 of the total 138 exonerations. (Three of *The Exonerated*'s six cases were prosecuted in Florida.) Finally, the murder of white people more often results in capital convictions than the murder of black people. The majority (79 percent) of those on death row were convicted of killing a white person,[27] even though, according to the U.S. Bureau of Justice Statistics, black Americans constitute more than half of all murder victims—52 percent from 1976 to 2005.[28] And though you cannot learn this from the play, all the victims in these cases were white. Still, we are told the only common ground between the wrongfully convicted is the sentence of death.[29]

Of the people featured in *The Exonerated*, three are black and three are white. Unless contextualized by the racial makeup of the United States, this "balanced" presentation risks obscuring the disproportionate impact of mass incarceration, wrongful convictions, and capital sentencing on African American, American Indian, and Latina/o individuals, families, and communities. While anyone may wind up in prison for a crime he or she did not commit, the person most likely to be in this position has historically been, and continues to be, a black man with little or no money. Black men and boys are more likely to be innocent, and more assumed to be guilty, than their white counterparts.[30] Cook points out in *The Exonerated*, "I wasn't trash, I came from a good family—if it happened to me, man, it can happen to anyone" (E, 48). Jacobs describes her shock at the indictment: "I'm one of those peace-and-love people. I'm a *vegetarian*. How could you possibly think I would kill someone?" (E, 43). These moments contrast sharply with Hayes's response: "I *knew* I was going to prison."

Given racism, fear of violent crime, and dehumanizing accounts of prisoners, stressing that anyone could end up on death row might seem to make strategic sense. But this decision masks one of the strongest legal arguments against the death penalty—unequal protection based on race[31]—and forecloses reflection on the workings of the criminal justice system. U.S. reform movements have disappointed repeatedly, most notably those that have grappled insufficiently with racial and economic injustice.

Although the race of the victim is the most telling contemporary indicator of unequal sentencing, the race of the defendant remains salient. Almost 42 percent of people on state death rows, and 59 percent of those on federal death rows, are black, overwhelmingly male. These percentages, higher at the time of *The Exonerated*'s composition, need to be contrasted with the percentage of the population who are black men—approximately 6 percent. The combined percentage of racial minorities on state death rows is over 55 percent; this number goes up to 75 percent on federal death row.[32] These numbers can be dismissed as precisely the kind of academic or "nonhuman" approach to the death penalty that the playwrights wanted to sidestep. Certainly the individual voices are the play's great strength, and statistical studies can never convey the scope of suffering caused by the death penalty.

Still, I find it useful to contrast the interview-based form of much contemporary documentary theater with the form of the Federal Theater Project's "Living Newspapers." Stage directions for *The Exonerated* warn against "stapling newspaper headlines to the back wall or throwing electric chairs all over the stage" (E, 8). By using narrators and projections to convey statistics and factual information, Living Newspapers aimed to elicit a critical and emotional response. For instance, in Arthur Arent's *One-Third of a Nation* (1938), the depression housing crisis is captured by rolling out a carpet to represent a plot of real estate in Manhattan. More and more people purchase lots and crowd onto the carpet until there is, literally, no remaining room. Meanwhile, we see the owners getting richer and richer.

A similar presentational style could serve in the case of death rows, allowing audiences to see the historical color of prisons. Instead, *The Exonerated* confines white supremacy to overtly racist Southern sheriffs and zealous prosecutors, a few bad apples. The audience can feel sympathy for the wrongfully convicted and anger at those directly responsible without having to confront either the racist history of the death penalty or race-based support for executions.[33] Similarly unexplored are grassroots efforts that have galvanized legal interventions, like the Committee to Free Delbert Tibbs. By isolating Gauger, Tibbs, Jacobs, Cook, Hayes, and Keaton from the cultural context of prisons and from each other (Tibbs is the only one who can respond to others onstage), *The Exonerated* risks leaving in place what David Garland calls the "easy intelligibility" of crime policy.[34]

Directing Empathy

Toward the end of *The Exonerated*, Jacobs asks audience members to imagine their lives during her captivity: "1976 to 1992, just remove that entire chunk from your life, and that's what happened. [*Long pause, the length of a count to six.*]" (E, 66). Audience members are encouraged to step into Jacobs's experience and consider, then erase, sixteen years of their lives. This dramatic invitation goes to the heart of empathic operations: Can you, will you, imagine my pain? Lauren Berlant observes that sentimentality requires you to "imagine yourself with someone else's stress, pain, or humiliated identity. The possibility that through the identification with alterity you will never be the same remains the radical threat and the great promise of this affective aesthetic."[35] She recognizes that this threat has rarely been realized in the U.S. history of sentimental writing.

The Exonerated puts personal losses on center stage and presses into consciousness the particular tragedy of convictions based on error or malfeasance. Jacobs's mother and father died during her imprisonment, her children grew up without her, and her partner, Jesse Tafero, was killed in a botched execution in Florida. Jacobs recalls in the play, "It took *thirteen and a half* minutes for Jesse to die. Three jolts of electricity that lasted fifty-five seconds each. Almost a minute. *Each*. Until finally flames shot out from his head, and smoke came from his ears, and the people that came to see the execution, on behalf of the press, are still writing about it. *Ten years afterward*" (E, 74). Gauger mourned his parents while being prosecuted and imprisoned for their murder. Keaton lost a spiritual connection that he had felt with God since he was a child. While in prison, three men raped Cook and carved an epithet into his buttocks. His older brother began to drink, lost a good job, and separated from his wife and children: "He put himself right on death row with me," Cook explains. One night outside a bar, his brother was shot and killed. Cook says, "I know it's going to sound corny there, but—and I mean it—every day that goes by I wish I could tell him how much I love him" (E, 60).

Blank and Jensen warn actors against "over-emotionalizing" and emphasize that the events described happened a long time ago (E, xvi). They explain in their memoir: "Whenever emotion runs the show, whether it's in the form of a desire for vengeance, a deeply felt need for a quick resolution or 'closure,' a real fear of further violence, or a prosecutor's personal desire to get ahead at all costs, it inevitably obscures the truth and leads to wrong decisions—often with tragic consequences" (L, 283). Yet, The Exonerated is an emotional play, and many reviewers describe audience members crying. At the conclusion of an early version of the play in Los Angeles, attorney Larry Marshall introduced the people whose stories had been staged. The playwrights describe the moment:

> The audience jumped to their feet and roared. The actors—totally shocked to find out that their alter-egos were in the audience—started weeping. The exonerated folks joined the actors onstage; the audience went on applauding at top volume for what seemed like five minutes.
>
> Neither of us expected how that moment would feel. We knew it would be powerful, but we had no idea how intense it would be to see everything come together like that: art and life, the play we'd put together and the real people it was based on. We clenched each other's hands as chills ripped through us. We both had goose bumps; tears streamed down our faces. It was the highest moment of either of our lives. (L, 217)

This bodily response—chills, goose bumps, tears—suggests the sentimental energy of the play, its capacity to evoke a feeling, to compel identification, and perhaps to elicit action.

Langston Hughes reflects on tears in a poem from 1938. Spoken from the perspective of Clarence Norris, the only Scottsboro defendant still sentenced to be killed, the poem asks if you would like to "see a black boy die. / Would you like to come and cry? / Maybe tears politely shed / Help the dead. / Or better still, they may help you— / For if you let the 'law' kill me, / Are you free?"[36] Hughes names the ongoing spectacle of executions ("Would you like to come and cry?") and exposes the empty sentimentalism of "tears politely shed." The quotations around "law" make clear that lethal actions, and actors, are hidden behind abstractions. Tears do not help the dead but might help those on the outside see our complicity and unfreedom.

Scholars continue to debate the character and import of empathy's tears. Joanne Dobson affirms the political power of sentimental values, insisting on the relevance of "a body of literature giving primacy to affectional connections and responsibilities."[37] Unfavorable critiques of sentimentalism emphasize its suggestion that feeling deeply constitutes moral character, its preference for personal remedies over structural ones, and its aversion to complexity. Glenn Hendler finds sentimental politics summarized in a moment from *Uncle Tom's Cabin* when Harriet Beecher Stowe answers her own inquiry, "'But, what can any individual do?' with her most famous injunction: 'they can see to it that *they feel right.*'" Hendler asks the necessary follow-up, "What does it mean to 'feel right' about slavery in particular, or about other forms of physical and emotional suffering?"[38] Does it mean *doing* anything? Saidiya Hartman also warns against "the dangers of a too-easy intimacy" and "the violence of identification."[39]

Abolitionists often urged white people to sympathize with the enslaved, but given the insensitivity of the white majority to black suffering this effort was strained. Hartman maintains that the white body had to "be positioned in the place of the black body in order to make this suffering visible and intelligible." She cites a letter John Rankin wrote to his proslavery brother. To portray the cruelty of slavery, Rankin describes himself, his wife, and his child as slaves. Hartman scrutinizes the implications of this strategy of replacing black bodies with white ones; such empathy "fails to expand the space of the other but merely places the self in its stead."[40] Rankin's substitution arguably reinforces the heightened regard for white life that is supposedly critiqued by his imaginative act.

The overt dynamic in *The Exonerated* is not white bodies replacing black ones—though this replacement does obtain in subtle ways, as I've suggested—but rather the free and the famous replacing the exonerated and the unknown. The performance relies on a rotation of Hollywood stars: Danny Glover, Susan Sarandon, Vanessa Redgrave, Brian Dennehy, Marlo Thomas, Tim Robbins, Robert Vaughn, Mia Farrow, Kathleen Turner, Parker Posey, Blair Brown, Stockard Channing, Aidan Quinn, Robin Williams, Brooke Shields, Steve Earle, and Debra Winger, among many others. The faces we know and the sentimental appeal we expect bring in the larger audience but also lessen the imaginative ethical work required for the abolition of the death penalty and the transformation of the prison system.

Tibbs functions as a choral figure, creating a second order of mediation and transitioning between stories while telling his own. He speaks the opening lines:

This is not the place for thought that does not end in concreteness;
it is not easy to be open or too curious.
It is dangerous to dwell too much on things:
to wonder who or why or when, to wonder how, is dangerous.
How do we, the people, get outta this hole, what's the way to fight,
might I do what Richard and Ralph and Langston'n them did?
It is not easy to be a poet here. Yet I sing.
I sing. (E, 8)

Situating himself within a tradition of black writers, Tibbs revises these lines in the play's conclusion, suggesting that this is the place (the prison, the theater, the poem) "for thoughts that do not end in concreteness." Wondering "why / and how and when" is exactly how we get out of the hole (E, 76).

The performance text does not wonder about the murders that led to these convictions. Based on individual accounts—and only Jacobs was present at the scene of the crime—the play does not include information that would demand more than the single direction of empathy. In trials and the media, murders are accounted in gruesome detail, and the prosecution frequently argues that it is seeking death on behalf of murder victims and their families. Judge Alex Kozinski explains that his support for capital punishment was solidified when he worked as a law clerk: "Whatever qualms I had about the efficacy or the morality of the death penalty were drowned out by the pitiful cries of the victims screaming from between the lines of dry legal prose." Kozinski struggles with the capital system but affirms his position, ending his argument with "the tortured voices of the victims crying out to me for vindication."[41] The script of The Exonerated changes only the person in the position of victim, leaving unchallenged rehearsed understandings of guilt and innocence. James Baldwin feared exactly this: that sentimental renderings of injustices shield an audience from the most difficult and needed reflections on personal and social responsibility.

Activating the Audience

The final lines of *The Exonerated* are forceful and quite beautiful. Gauger speculates about light beams and wonders if DNA may well be a miraculous presence in our lives. Jacobs says that she harbors no bitterness about her imprisonment and wants to be a living monument to Tafero. She has never been to his grave because she does not believe that is where he is. "My life is my monument," she explains (E, 76). Tibbs cites Gandhi's belief that the discovery of God relieves human beings of fear, and he expresses the need to work for justice. In the final gesture of the play, Keaton is able, in contrast to an earlier moment, to stop the rain with his faith.

While the play acknowledges the impediments to a free life postrelease—the difficulty of getting work, the accusations that persist in everyday life, the assault on the spirit and scars on the body—in interviews Blank and Jensen rightly compare the exonerated to returning veterans [42]—the play yields to substantial uplift in its concluding lines and staging choices. With these moves, suffering may become, to borrow from Toni Morrison, domesticated. Morrison argues that slaves in nineteenth-century white-authored literature serve as "surrogate selves," a way to reflect on questions of liberty and freedom, "to contemplate limitation, suffering, rebellion, and to speculate on fate and destiny." [43] The imprisoned play a related role in movies, plays, and film—a subject of fascination, contempt, horror, occasional sympathy. After a post-9/11 crisis of faith in the play (Blank and Jensen live in New York City), the playwrights discovered a new relevance to the work: "[T]he exonerated people had something to teach us about facing darkness—even death—and coming out the other side. . . . [T]he exonerated people had something to teach us about survival, endurance, and hope. That was the heart of the play" (L, 254). The applicability of the script to other lives revives meaning, and abstractions become its "heart," not murders in homes, on streets, in execution chambers.

In contrast to the ending of *The Exonerated*, Gauger describes in *Surviving Justice* his ongoing stress and anxiety: "I have very vivid memories of the injustice that I went through. Sometimes I'm out in the fields driving the tractor where nobody can hear me, and all of a sudden I'll get a memory and I'll just scream." [44] *The Exonerated*'s accent on freedom is especially pronounced when the wrongfully convicted people are invited onstage at the end of performances. Spencer writes that "the most emotional moment of a deeply affecting show" occurred when Jacobs—"tiny and indomitable Sunny herself"—came onstage after the play was over. Retta Blaney had a similar response: "Then in what was possibly the most dramatic moment in

an afternoon filled with them . . . in walked several of the real-life exonerated, Kerry Max Cook among them. He held a toddler with curly blond hair
and rosy cheeks who smiled and waved at someone in the audience." Another reviewer recalls, "For me, it is one of those transcendent moments.
Before us are people who had the courage to stand strong and unbroken
through unspeakable horrors."[45] The audience has been well prepared for
this moment in which the exonerated step into the role reserved for them.

By deploying sentimental conventions, including a carefully mediated,
empathetic subject, a focus on private experience, and a movement toward
redemption, the play crafts and directs sympathy while averting our gaze
from the still-imprisoned and the dead. The Court TV version of *The Exonerated* ends with Lyle Lovett singing "Amazing Grace" as a shot of each
actor fades into his or her real-life counterpart who addresses the audience. Their comments, under thirty seconds each, are positive and uplift-
ing—except for Robert Hayes, who does not say anything. With the sixth
actor, we are segued to a photograph of Hayes, and a subtitle explains that
he is in jail on an unrelated charge and again has an innocence claim. No
voice attends this still photograph, and the documentary lens moves on
quickly.[46] In 2004, Hayes pleaded guilty to arson and manslaughter that
occurred in 1987 and is now serving 15–45 years. With the photograph, the
line dividing the free and innocent from the trapped and guilty dissolves,
and nothing in the script has prepared us to understand or sympathize with
the twenty-year-old Hayes, who may have, with drugs raging through him,
killed another person.

Illinois abolished the death penalty in 2011, citing concerns over wrongful convictions and a severe budget crisis. The abolition of the death penalty
and the current criminal justice and prison system will result from a range
of strategies and struggles, including efforts to raise consciousness about
wrongful capital convictions—yet even this phrasing seems to posit right-
ful ones and to bypass reflection on the goals and methods of retributive
justice. The history of *The Exonerated* reminds me that nothing short of a
direct confrontation with the violence of the social order will get us fully
out of this hole, will uproot the antipathies and allegiances that build death
houses, isolation chambers, innumerable cells.

Notes

1. Charles Spencer, "These Real-Life Stories of Life on Death Row Are Gripping,
Harrowing—but Never Depressing," Telegraph.co.UK, February 28, 2006, www
.telegraph.co.uk/arts/main.jhtml?xml=/arts/2006/02/28/btexon28.xml; Ben Brant-

ley, "Someone Else Committed Their Crimes," *New York Times*, October 11, 2002, www.nytimes.com/2002/10/11/movies/theater-review-someone-else-committed-their-crimes.html.

2. Jessica Blank and Erik Jensen, *Living Justice: Love, Freedom, and the Making of "The Exonerated"* (New York: Atria, 2005), 9. Further references to this text will be cited parenthetically in the text as L.

3. See Sally Cragin, "Mistrial by Jury: Bob Balaban Defends *The Exonerated*," Boston *Phoenix* [no date], www.bostonphoenix.com/boston/arts/theater/documents/02653598.htm.

4. I cite William Rehnquist later in the essay. According to Antonin Scalia, "One cannot have a system of criminal punishment without accepting the possibility that someone will be punished mistakenly. That is a truism, not a revelation" ("Consensus on Counting the Innocent: We Can't," *New York Times*, March 25, 2008). Also see Ernest van den Haag, "The Ultimate Punishment: A Defense," *Harvard Law Review* 99 (May 1986): 1662–69; Lola Vollen and Dave Eggers, eds., *Surviving Justice: America's Wrongfully Convicted and Exonerated* (San Francisco: McSweeney's, 2005), 352.

5. Lauren Berlant, "Poor Eliza," *American Literature* 70 (September 1998): 646.

6. See Joshua Marquis, "The Myth of Innocence: Don't Believe Everything You See on Court TV," *National Review*, January 27, 2005, www.nationalreview.com/comment/marquis200501270742.asp.

7. Blank and Jensen, interview with Rachel Kramer Bussel, "Jessica Blank and Erik Jensen, Playwrights, The Exonerated, Authors, Living Justice," *Gothamist*, April 11, 2005, gothamist.com/2005/04/11/jessica_blank_and_erik_jensen_playwrights_the_exonerated_authors_living_justice.php.

8. Julia C. Mead, "THEATER; A Star of His Own Life Story," *New York Times*, August 17, 2003, www.nytimes.com/2003/08/17/nyregion/theater-a-star-of-his-own-life-story.html.

9. Adam Liptak, "The Death Penalty: A Witness for the Prosecution," *New York Times*, February 15, 2003, www.nytimes.com/2003/02/15/theater/the-death-penalty-a-witness-for-the-prosecution.html.

10. Blank and Jensen, "Playwrights of the Exonerated," *New York University Steinhardt Podcast*, January 15, 2008, http://odeo.com/episodes/17623703.

11. Michael Sneed, Abdon M. Pallasch, Annie Sweeney, and Carlos Sadovi, "Ryan to Commute All Death Sentences," *Chicago Sun-Times*, January 11, 2003, 4.

12. Chris Jones, "'Exonerated' an Enlightening Evening for Ryan," *Chicago Tribune*, December 18, 2002.

13. Mead, "THEATER."

14. Louise Kennedy, "Enter Policy, Stage Right: Theaters Now Dramatize, Debate the Hot Issues," *Boston Globe*, January 19, 2003.

15. "Innocence Cases, 2004–present," *Death Penalty Information Center*, www
.deathpenaltyinfo.org. See Michael L. Radelet, Hugo Adam Bedau, and Constance E. Putnam, *In Spite of Innocence: Erroneous Convictions in Capital Cases* (Boston:
Northeastern Univ. Press, 1992).

16. See Bryan Stevenson, "Crime, Punishment, and Executions in the Twenty-
First Century," *Proceedings of the American Philosophical Society* 147 (March 2003): 27.

17. *Herrera v. Collins* (91-7328), 506 U.S. 390 (1993), www.law.cornell.edu/supct/
html/91-7328.ZC1.html.

18. *Supreme Court of the United States in Re Troy Davis on Petition for Writ of Habeas
Corpus* (08-1443), August 17, 2009, www.supremecourt.gov/opinions/08pdf/08-14
43scalia.pdf.

19. David R. Dow and Alan Hirsch, "Needle in a Haystack: Is Innocence the Best
Argument for Ending the Death Penalty?" *Texas Observer*, February 23, 2007, 25.

20. Dow and Hirsch, "Needle," 13.

21. Bob Balaban, interview with Josh Horowitz, "Bob Balaban Gets Exonerated,"
Movie Poop Shoot, December 3, 2003, www.asitecalledfred.com/interviews/30.html.

22. Morgan Cloud and George Shepherd, "Low I.Q. and the Death Penalty," *New
York Times*, February 20, 2002, www.nytimes.com/2002/02/20/opinion/low-iq-and-
the-death-penalty.html.

23. Carol Martin, "Bodies of Evidence," *TDR* 50 (Fall 2006): 9.

24. Kate Taylor reports that *The Exonerated* "turned [Blank and Jensen], seem-
ingly overnight, into playwrights of national stature as well as experts on the death
penalty, wrongful convictions and documentary theater." The pair received funding
from the Ford Foundation for their next play, *Aftermath* ("Wedded to Docudrama,
and Each Other," *New York Times*, August 26, 2009, www.nytimes.com/2009/08/30/
theater/30tayl.html). See Ryan Tracy, "After 'Aftermath,'" *Countercritic*, October 20–
21, 2009, countercritic.com/2009/10/20/after-aftermath.

25. See David Oshinsky, *"Worse than Slavery": Parchman Farm and the Ordeal of Jim
Crow Justice* (New York: Free Press, 1996), 74–75; Emily S. Sanford, "The Propriety
and Constitutionality of Chain Gangs," *Georgia State University Law Review* 13 (1997):
1155–92; and Yale Glazer, "The Chains May Be Heavy, But They Are Not Cruel
and Unusual: Examining the Constitutionality of the Reintroduced Chain Gang,"
HOFSTRA Law Review 24, no. 4 (1996): 1195–224.

26. Bryan Stevenson, "Close to Death: Reflections on Race and Capital Punish-
ment in America," in *Debating the Death Penalty: Should America Have Capital Punishment?
The Experts on Both Sides Make Their Best Case*, ed. Hugo Adam Bedau and Paul G. Cassell
(New York: Oxford University Press, 2004), 94.

27. See "National Statistics on the Death Penalty and Race," *Death Penalty Information Center*, www.deathpenaltyinfo.org/race-death-row-inmates-executed-1976.

28. "Racial Differentials Exist, with Blacks Disproportionately Represented among Homicide Victims and Offenders," *Bureau of Justice Statistics*, bjs.ojp.usdoj. gov/content/homicide/race.cfm. Of those exonerated, 71 are black, 53 white, 12 Latino, and 2 "other" (*Death Penalty Information Center*, www.deathpenaltyinfo.org/ innocence-and-death-penalty#race).

29. The playwrights offer more accurate descriptions in later interviews and in *Living Justice*. See, for instance, Ann Freeman, "Critically Acclaimed Play by U Alum Examines the Death Penalty," *UM News* (Summer 2004), www1.umn.edu/news/ features/2004/UR_11287_REGION1.html; and L, 55.

30. Karen Parker, Marí DeWees, and Michael Radelet, "Race, the Death Penalty, and Wrongful Convictions," *Criminal Justice Magazine* 18.1 (2003). Barry Scheck, Peter Neufeld, and Jim Dwyer report that the most common factors that lead to wrongful convictions "are more pronounced in the conviction of innocent black men" (*Actual Innocence: Five Days to Execution and Other Dispatches from the Wrongly Convicted* [New York: Doubleday, 2000], 246).

31. See "CD" and Lee Bernstein, "'. . . Give Me Death': Capital Punishment and the Limits of American Citizenship," in *States of Confinement: Policing, Detention, and Prisons*, ed. Joy James (New York: St. Martin's, 2000), 10–21.

32. *Bureau of Justice Statistics*, "Capital Punishment Statistics," www.ojp.usdoj .gov/bjs/cp.htm.

33. See James D. Unnever and Francis T. Cullen, "The Racial Divide in Support for the Death Penalty: Does White Racism Matter?" *Social Forces* 85 (March 2007): 1281–301; and Joe Soss, Laura Langbein, and Alan R. Metelko, "Why Do White Americans Support the Death Penalty?" *Journal of Politics* 65 (May 2003): 397–421.

34. David Garland, *The Culture of Control: Crime and Social Order in Contemporary Society* (Chicago: Univ. of Chicago Press, 2001), 1.

35. Berlant, "Poor Eliza," 648.

36. Langston Hughes, *The Collected Works of Langston Hughes*, ed. Arnold Rampersad (New York: Knopf, 1994), 204–05.

37. Joanne Dobson, "Reclaiming American Sentimentalism," *American Literature* 69 (June 1997), 280.

38. Glenn Hendler, "The Structure of Sentimental Experience," *Yale Journal of Criticism* 12 (Spring 1999), 146.

39. Saidiya Hartman, *Scenes of Subjection: Terror, Slavery, and Self-Making in Nineteenth-Century America* (New York: Oxford Univ. Press, 1997), 19, 20.

40. Ibid.

41. Alex Kozinski, "Tinkering with Death," *Debating the Death Penalty*, 2.

42. See Hugh Hart, "Life after Death Row," *Los Angeles Times*, April 7, 2002,

articles.latimes.com/2002/apr/07/entertainment/ca-hart7; Blank and Jensen, "Playwrights of the Exonerated."

43. Toni Morrison, *Playing in the Dark: Whiteness and the Literary Imagination* (New York: Vintage, 1993), 53.

44. Vollen and Eggers, *Surviving Justice*, 111.

45. Spencer, "Real Life"; Retta Blaney, "Listening to the Exonerated: Powerful Play Tells the Stories of the Innocent Freed from Death Row," *National Catholic Reporter*, October 25, 2002, natcath.org/NCR_Online/archives2/2002d/102502/102 502m.htm; C.J., "The Exonerated: The Theater of Life and Death," *Revolutionary Worker*, November 13, 2000, rwor.org/a/v22/1070-79/1078/exoner.htm.

46. *The Exonerated*, directed by Bob Balaban, aired January 27, 2005 (Court TV).

Rap Sheet of Capitol Crimes Music, Murder, and Aesthetic States of Terror

MATTHEW STRATTON

> One can argue about the effectiveness of the death penalty generally. But when it comes to terrorism, national security concerns should be paramount.
> —Jessica Stern[1]

U.S. Attorney General John Ashcroft famously denied Timothy Mc-Veigh's request to have his own execution broadcast on national television while simultaneously suspending Bureau of Prison regulations so that more family members of victims could watch the lethal injection on closed-circuit television. Declaring that eight witnesses would be "plainly inadequate," Ashcroft justified his decision by enumerating McVeigh's crime: "This brutal act of terrorism killed 168 innocent people, including 19 children, and injured hundreds more. Its savagery stole parents from 219 children and made 30 children orphans in a single act."[2]

Ashcroft's rhetorical calculations resonate with most serious considerations of capital punishment, which are built upon statistical information: as of 2011, for example, thirty-four states and the federal government had statutes providing for capital punishment, and 1247 people had been executed in the twenty-three years since the Supreme Court affirmed the constitutionality of the death penalty. Is it arguing about "the death penalty generally" to note that, from 1973 to 1999, an average of 3.1 people per year were exonerated and released from death row and that the "South accounted for 80 percent of the nation's executions—449 out of 562"?[3] Just how general would a discussion have to be to exclude the fact that African Americans comprise "roughly 11 percent of the U.S. population," but "have constituted 50 percent of all individuals executed from 1800 to the present," or the fact that those convicted of killing "white victims . . . were more than 3.5 times as likely to receive a death sentence as those who killed a black or a Hispanic individual"?[4]

If the mere existence of such data calls into question the possibility of discussing "the death penalty generally"—that is, as an abstract moral or political problem—the information itself raises an odd question: just how "specific" are numbers? Phrased differently, what specific kinds of information do spreadsheets necessarily omit, and what kinds of knowledge do they thereby produce or foreclose when they are the only game in town? Since 1936, after all, executions in the United States have been "public" affairs conducted outside of the view of anything resembling a public.[5] If mainstream media sanitize images of war—acts of violence that, like executions, are defined as a *res publica* and legitimized by the legitimacy of states—executions are "public" acts that are scrupulously sequestered from public experience. Journalists may be present as witnesses for the public, but any larger public is excluded from chambers that resemble a private sphere limited to family members of victims or of the executed.

It is perhaps there, in the chamber, that conceptual resemblances between acts of terrorism and executions become legible as operations within the related spheres of law and myth. The liminal blend of the private and the public in terms of law is, after all, what partially defines both acts of terrorism (nonstate actors committing illegal acts of violence to produce spectacular public effects) and capital punishment (state actors committing legal, publicly invisible acts of violence against individuals). Furthermore, the specific rationality of statistics putatively justifies rendering those acts visible or invisible, legitimate or illegitimate; as Tom McCall has argued, "Law is inscribed violence, myth the act of its inscription," and in capital punishment the ostensibly inscribed division between "myth" and "law" is attenuated to the point of convergence.[6] Legal and mythic violence is "more visible in the law of the death penalty than in other laws, where the show of violence gets hidden behind or is camouflaged within another show that upstages . . . myth: the show of the rational system of measured crimes and corresponding punishments."[7] Capital punishment operates generally and specifically according to a logic that is homologous with the logic of terrorism, the function of which is to produce spectacular disciplinary narratives. With respect to the death penalty, statistics serve to obscure the unquantifiable effects of a paradoxically invisible spectacle.

In other words, although statistics delineate capital punishment in terms of its frequency and demographic distribution, such data also limit the conversation to a sort of "specific generality" because each number simultaneously refers to an individual while erasing information about that individual.[8] If ethical judgments about the political, corporeal, and psychological effects of violence require thicker forms of information than numbers, then the most effective medium for critique of capital punishment may well not be calculation, but aesthetic representation. However "staggering" the numbers may be, it is the language of aesthetics—representation, perception, sensation—that effectively illuminates how various forms of violence necessarily operate as legible or illegible, visible or invisible, legal or illegal.

While writers such as Walter Benjamin and Frantz Fanon are canonical figures in political and philosophical analyses of violence in its statist and antistatist forms, I want to position in conversation with them a different kind of aesthetic critique of capital punishment and its relationship to violence, which offers an unnerving synthesis of philosophy, politics, and entertainment: the seminal 1992 gangsta rap album entitled *Guerillas in tha Mist*. Released by Da Lench Mob just five months after the acquittal of four police officers for beating Rodney King, the album entered a socio-critical and rhetorical context that framed violent rap as either strictly mimetic (the idea that rap "tells it how it really is")[9] or as commercially instrumental (violent songs as merely a "cynical move to spark record sales through the time honored play of controversy").[10] Although such simplistic dualities about rap have been corrected in more recent criticism, something remains to be said about the complex political work performed by albums such as *Guerillas in tha Mist*: the album identifies how, rhetorically, capital punishment serves as a key mythologem to obscure the terroristic logic of states.[11] Martin A. Miller observes that the positioning of "terrorism" as specifically "antistate" makes us "less willing to accept the notion that virtually all states engage in forms of enforcement, deprivation, neglect, and harm that operate as everyday realities," a notion the album insists we take seriously.[12]

Guerillas in tha Mist violently reintroduces the spectacle of capital punishment into a popular imaginary and reminds listeners that discussing the death penalty "generally" not only occludes past, present, and future victims of perpetual terror, but also obscures other, more systemic, forms of violence that undergird liberal society. A re-examination of the album today, nearly twenty years after its debut, reveals a potent critique of doggedly persistent discourses about the political roles played by the police and the justice system: the album specifically illuminates how the death penalty functions in relation to the concepts of law, justice, and violence itself.[13] McCall rightly insists that while "violent spectacles [such] as war, genocide, or capital punishment qualify as hyperbolic instances of mythical violence," they are "most in need of criticism, for the manifest violence we can measure proceeds from a violence we cannot."[14] Far more than simply narrating or measuring particular acts of violence, Da Lench Mob offers a critique of violence, illuminating the ways in which representations of violence are understood and disseminated not merely as representations, but as *representative*: not merely illustrative or evidentiary, but iconic and metonymic. Austin Sarat emphasizes that "law is violent in many ways—in the ways it uses language and in its representational practices, in the silencing of perspectives and the denial of experience, and in its objectifying epistemology. It arises from the fact that the linguistic, representational violence of the law is inseparable from its literal, physical violence."[15] It is in the act of de-objectifying legal epistemology and re-emphasizing the human experience of capital punishment that the album suggests that the pragmatic function of the death penalty is not to deter or punish acts of violence, but to affirm the legitimacy of state violence both pragmatically and ontologically.[16] Listeners are served much more than a judgment against the death penalty; they receive a staging of the very problem of judgment under systemic conditions of violence, of which the death penalty is only one symptom. Neither specific narratives—case studies, as it were—nor statistics suffice, the album powerfully suggests. To discuss the death penalty seriously, either generally or specifically, requires a consideration of aesthetic violence more broadly.

On or Around April 29, 1992

Two months after the Rodney King Uprising/Los Angeles Riots, *The Ron Paul Political Report* analyzed the violent response to the acquittal of police officers who had beaten Rodney King, asserting that "most white Americans . . . are going to have difficulty avoiding the belief that our country is being destroyed by a group of actual and potential terrorists—and [that] they can be identified by the color of their skin."[17] A year later, the president of the National Association of Chiefs of Police published an essay, "The Music of Murder," in a prominent law journal; while denouncing rap as "primitive music," he lamented the degraded state of American culture, claiming that the founders could never have foreseen "a day when music would become a tool to destabilize a democratic society by provoking civil unrest, violence and murder."[18] (Lest one imagine that social anxiety surrounding rap music's representation of violence is a quaint relic from the first Bush administration, in 2009 a Florida rapper frustrated by police harassment was sentenced to two years in prison for posting a song called "Kill Me a Cop" on his MySpace page.)[19] Indeed, the curious, persistent, and supposedly causal relationship among one popular art form's representations of murder, the actual taking of human life, and how these actions might be characterized as "terror," still sheds light on the function of violent discourse almost twenty years after the riots.[20]

Perhaps the uprising/riots require little rehearsal, at least partially because particular images linger in one version of popular memory: a 2007 *Time* magazine article revisiting the riots, for example, profiled fifteen "key figures" in the events, five of whom were directly related to the attack on white truck driver Reginald Denny; there was no profile of the ten people shot to death by the police and National Guard.[21] That National Guard troops were brought onto the streets of Los Angeles to supplement an already militarized LAPD should also be understood in light of a more global view of 1992. As Giorgio Agamben remarks, "One of the least ambiguous lessons learned from the Gulf War is that the concept of sovereignty has been finally introduced into the figure of the police."[22] Indeed, the declaration that African Americans should literally be viewed as a potential terroristic threat to America may be rhetorically shocking, but it is wholly congruent with broader policing efforts. As Jeff Chang recounts, California Governor George Deukmejian in 1988 signed the "Street Enforcement and Prevention Act" into law, which criminalized street gangs while creating massive databases about young urban people of color, regardless of their relationship to gangs; moreover, "what united the sweep laws of the early 1990s was a new logic of erasing youths—particularly youths of color—from public space."[23] Federal models of intervention were simultaneously developed when in 1992 the Bush administration "created the Violence Initiative, a series of federally funded studies that sought behavioral and biological markers for predicting a propensity for violence in young males."[24]

Shortly thereafter, Congress passed the "Violent Crime Control and Law Enforcement Act of 1994," which expanded "the Federal death penalty to cover about 60 offenses, including terrorist homicides, murder of a Federal law enforcement officer, large-scale drug trafficking, drive-by-shootings resulting in death and carjackings resulting in death."[25] Ironically, then, as the Rodney King tape made police violence against African Americans newly visible to millions of Americans, state and federal governments were working to identify invisible and supposedly natural causes for acts of non-state violence, to render young people of color invisible to a general public, and to increase the number of acts that are punishable by death.[26] Yet surely nobody is surprised by the fact that the iconic image of violence from these years remains young black men dragging a white driver from his truck and stomping him with a cinder block.

Illegal Violence and the Violence of Law

If music is a resolutely aural medium, the rhetorical action of *Guerillas in tha Mist* also commences visually, with the album title and art. The album's homophonically punning title is central to understanding its political aims, since it is a parodic transformation of racist epithet (gorilla) into violent political agent (guerilla). The pun is elaborated by the album cover, where the name of the group is visually reinforced by a noose prominently slung across one member's shoulder.[27] In yet another visual pun, two of the men wear black makeup, simultaneously invoking both a racist minstrel tradition and military camouflage, iconography reinforced on the inner sleeve, which shows them in undergrowth wearing black stocking masks (Fig. 3). In their study of the discursive construction of "terrorism" as a sociopolitical phenomenon, anthropologists Joseba Zulaika and William Douglass note, "If there is an emblematic stereotype of guerrillas or terrorists in action, it is of the masked men/women. It is not their weapons but rather their masked facelessness that is the perfect icon for their expatriation from society. . . . Withdrawal of a human face that will take direct responsibility for a victim's fate is ultimate terror."[28] Da Lench Mob's album cover presents the group as "a cross between the Black Panthers and the Zapatistas,"[29] and the guerrilla persona depends upon the juxtaposition of the concealing mask with "the real face, its commanding proximity, [which] proves to be more compelling than any fiction, allegory, ritual, or narrative."[30] As Angela Davis observed with some ambivalence, in the early 1990s the "image of the armed Black man" was "considered the 'essence' of revolutionary commitment today."[31]

Perhaps the characterization of "revolutionary commitment" seems too strong for the majority of the album's tracks, as they occasionally seem to rehearse conventional narratives of police harassment or urban gun play (and occasionally of homophobia and misogyny). But Da Lench Mob's album cover and its guerilla personae visually frame the narrative episodes in the album, demanding recognition (as a song from the group's second album emphasizes) that "Guerillas Ain't Gangstas."[32] Furthermore, the sternly "real" faces—adorned with camouflage paint and black stocking caps, wreathed with an iconographically overdetermined noose—openly inflect the narrative strategies promoted by more canonical theorists of guerilla warfare: the Brazilian revolutionary Carlos Marighella and his manifesto "Mini-Manual for the Urban Guerilla"; Frantz Fanon's "Concerning Violence"; and the CIA author, pseudonymously known as "Taya-

3. *(Top)* The cover of Da Lench Mob's *Guerillas in tha Mist*, 1992.
(Bottom) Inner sleeve of *Guerillas in tha Mist*.

cán," who wrote and distributed an instructional pamphlet for the U.S.-backed Contras in Nicaragua.

Voltaire famously remarked that killing a man is murder, unless one kills a lot of men to the sound of trumpets. While there are few trumpets on *Guerillas in tha Mist*, there is certainly a lot of killing: cop killing, vigilante killing, and "killin' 47 million civilians."[33] As Marighella asserts, "the urban guerrilla's reason for existence, the basic condition in which he acts and survives, is to shoot."[34] In "Freedom Got an AK"—a song that "typifies the fears of rap's detractors," according to one reviewer[35]—Da Lench Mob directly links the violent possibilities of the automatic weapon with the possibilities of resistance, but does so with an explicit observation about the sublime impossibility of numerical accounts: "The AK talks / and bullshit runs / I wish I had time / to count all my guns." The line is accompanied by the sounds of automatic gunfire and a paraphrase of a leader of the Black Panther party: "H. Rap [Brown] said / freedom got a strap." In an act of historical fantasy, the speaker wishes that such violent means had been utilized by activists in the American South toward the inarguably justified ends of civil rights, for "I wish I was in Dixie / A-K, A-K / and shit wouldn't have been bad in the sixties / no way, no way."

Invoking the history of political struggle and asserting that confronting Southern "lynch mobs" with a Californian "Lench Mob" would have changed the nature of that history and historiography, the songs reinterpret and repurpose accounts of mere "social" violence as acts of militant political violence. This is particularly true when, in songs like "Who Ya Gonna Shoot Wit That," lyrics call for an end to the financially motivated crime of robbery in favor of targeting counterrevolutionary agents such as drug dealers, police, and the KKK. In a short skit introducing one song, Da Lench Mob engages in their own extra-statist policing by confronting a drug dealer and demanding he stop "robbin' black folks of they checks." The drug dealer (played by Ice Cube) responds with his own economic logic: "So what should I do? / Work for $3.22? / 'Welcome to McDonald's may I please help you?' / I don't think so."[36] The temporality of the group's threats flows both ways as they justify violence historically with reference to the Middle Passage: "Keep your boys cause we got big toys / with the one mile scope, takin' whitey's throat / Why? 'Cause he made me ride a boat / A lot of us died afloat."[37] Political assassination is similarly recounted when a speaker exclaims, "I'm glad that Lincoln got bucked in the face / we shoulda been free in the first place,"[38] demythologizing a hero model of history and pointing out that supposedly transformative proclamations of emancipation remain unrealized. The dictates of peaceful civil disobedience and of New Testament notions of forgiveness no longer obtain in 1992 Los Angeles when the album warns that "this week / we don't turn the other cheek." Similarly, political action through existing legislative channels is dismissed with "don't come to me with no petition / fool, come to me with ammunition."

While the power of the weapon's presence is acknowledged, the simple notion of politically effective gun battles is qualified by Tayacán, the CIA theorist of insurgent guerilla violence: "Implicit terror always accompanies weapons," he writes, "since the people are internally 'aware' that they can be used against them, but as long as explicit coercion is avoided, positive attitudes can be achieved with respect to the presence of armed guerrillas within the population."[39] In terms of Da Lench Mob's positioning armed guerillas by way of this album, "explicit coercion" is avoided by virtue of the likelihood that the listener confronts a stereo system rather than a gun-toting outlaw. More significantly, the album avoids the "explicit terror" warned against by Tayacán when "Freedom Got an AK" admits the discursive construction of its own threats and the intended terror that results: "shoot 'em up, shoot 'em up oh yeah / talking like that I have them all scared." Here it is emphatically the "talk" that results in fear, provided that it is speech of a certain caliber that intersects with dominant narratives about ghetto violence; furthermore, "these ritualized threats [that] are backed up with real force"[40] are closely intertwined with dominant narratives of the death penalty, including the fact that "whitey can't wait to see yo' ass in the hot seat."[41]

Chief Dennis Martin observed in his early nineties screed, "Society is now finding that it cannot ridicule the enforcers of the law on one hand and build respect for the law on the other."[42] Assuming that he wasn't thinking of Woody Guthrie (author of popular cop-killing ballad "Pretty Boy Floyd") or Johnny Cash (who claimed to have "shot a man in Reno just to watch him die"), the objection seems to be directed at narrative scenes such as the one where J-Dee stabs a prison guard with his "ink pen" or fights "motherfuckin' deputies / tryin' to do the same thing that they did to Rodney King,"[43] or where Ice Cube attacks "the fuckin' cop with the flat-top / standin' over niggaz face down on the blacktop / That shit's gotta stop, so I kick the hip-hop / Pop that devil in his ass and make him flip-flop."[44]

Before dismissing Martin's objections as mere conservative handwring-
ing, one should recall that Frantz Fanon had observed forty years earlier
that "aesthetic expressions of respect for the established order serve to create around the exploited person an atmosphere of submission and of in-
hibition which lightens the task of policing considerably."[45] Indeed, those
who disagree about whether such representations are laudable or lamen-
table seem to agree that certain forms of disrespect make the task of policing the "exploited person" more difficult. As Marighella writes, the urban
guerrilla must "use the assault for propaganda purposes, at the very moment it is taking place, and later distribute material, leaflets, every possible
means of explaining the objectives and the principles of the urban guerrilla as expropriator of the government, the ruling classes, and imperialism."[46] This is to say that while freedom may well have an AK, and while the
opposite of freedom may well have lethal injections, violent acts must be
rhetorically framed so that they are understood to be revolutionary or conservative rather than random or pathological. Thus, when Ice Cube writes
about emptying a clip from his AK, it is because "That's how you got filthy
rich / I know the game / so I'm gonna do the same / you don't like when I
play the same way."[47] Ice Cube emphasizes that the accumulation and preservation of American wealth relied upon the very violence that is now either
dismissed as "terroristic" or understood as retributive, defensive, and constructive—but certainly not "senseless."

In what may be the most compelling episode of the entire album, "Ankle
Blues" first appears to be a story about executing vigilante justice against
a drug dealer, and then is revealed as the dream of a sleeping narrator.
What finally emerges is a narrative rumination upon the problem of justice, violence, capital punishment, and signification itself. The song's first
episode sees the narrator "sittin' at the pad watching cops / Trippin' off
the pigs keepin' niggaz off the block / But don't let a nigga get caught out
the ghetto / cause you know gettin' caught out the ghetto / is a motherfuckin' no-no." In response to the police behavior of "keepin' niggaz outta
Crackerville / they do it and they love it," the group suggests that one "vice
verse the kicks / and put Da Lench Mob crew / on the other end of the
stick," and thereby replace police violence with their own violence. Describing their response to "a 911 call on another fuckin' peckerwood," they
chase and execute a white man who "looked like he was trying to sell some
fuckin' dope" by asserting that "we ain't goin' out like that / that's when I
let his ass have it with a gat / shot him in his back / stopped in his tracks /
he would never sell dope to another fuckin' black." Against this diegesis, a

background vocalist quietly enters the narrative: "He is the epitome of anti-disestablishmentarism" (sounding very much like "antidisestablishmen-terrorism"), raising the question of just which character is counterrevo-lutionary. Is it the drug dealer? Or is it the narrator who has just executed someone for "looking" like he was a drug dealer, and thereby reproducing the violent logic of police who act as sovereigns within a putative democ-racy?

As the narrators move on to their next execution, it becomes even more clear that they are enacting a parody of capital punishment as law enforce-ment, and the action is revealed as explicit fantasy within the fiction of the album as a whole. When the narrator recalls that "we hung him by his neck 'til it snapped / that's when my homie woke me up out my nap / waking back up to the signs of reality / tripping off the shit that we watching on TV," he redirects the listener toward an ethical judgment of the hanging by a "Lench Mob" whose imagination has been almost entirely constituted by media images of the cops and television shows, such as the homonymic *Cops* the narrators are watching at the beginning of the song. The judg-ment of the listener is not structured as an either/or proposition (either the means of the fantasy hanging *was* justified by the ends of a safer neighbor-hood or it was *not*), but rather through a recognition that such judgments of justice "in reality" remain stubbornly elusive: the informational precon-ditions for such evaluation are already based not on "reality," but precisely on "signs of reality" produced and distributed by the same media conglom-erates (such as Time Warner) that, in the wake of the Los Angeles Riots, censored rap with descriptions of crime against whites or authority figures, but allowed descriptions of black-on-black violence to remain for broad-cast.[48] The "signs of reality" produced by the song call into question the adequacy of mimesis and diegesis to represent conditions wherein law is either violated or upheld, justice either achieved or deferred, violence either produced or reproduced. In the liberal tradition, deontological ethics have depended at least partially on the faculty of sympathy. As Kant writes, "Na-ture has already implanted in human beings receptivity to . . . sensible feel-ings of pleasure or displeasure (which are therefore to be called 'aesthetic') at another's state of joy or pain feelings,"[49] an account that has driven the assumptions of political reform literature since at least the nineteenth cen-tury. "Ankle Blues" suggests that neither reform nor revolution will rely upon an illusion of sympathy with other people's illusive reality, but upon the staging of the inadequacy of modern imagination.

Capital Punishment inside tha Head of a Black Man

Critics have ignored the opening cut on *Guerillas in tha Mist*, "Capital Punishment in America." The song is essentially a descriptive litany of statistics about the history of executions in the United States, related with newscaster intonation in standard American English with occasional interjections of the words "Lench Mob":

> The methods America has used to execute its criminals have changed over the years: from burning, to drawing and quartering, to hanging. Criminals have been axed, crucified, buried alive, pressed with weights, stoned, impaled, starved, decapitated, and gibbeted. Gibbeting is the hanging of a condemned man by chains to rot. Death often takes weeks to occur. (Lench Mob) Today the breakdown of execution looks like this . . .

The narrator proceeds to give specific, accurate, state-by-state statistics about the number of criminals who, "as of 1987," awaited execution, and the number of states employing hanging, lethal injection, and firing squad to execute criminals.

On the one hand, the historical data would seem to fall directly within the strategic purview of the urban guerrilla as Enlightenment citizen: as Marighella writes in *The Mini-Manual for the Urban Guerrilla*, "Careful reading of the press with particular attention to the organs of mass communication, the investigation of accumulated data, the transmission of news and everything of note, a persistence in being informed and in informing others, all this makes up the intricate and immensely complicated question of information which gives the urban guerrilla a decisive advantage."[50] For Marighella, such information is to be used to engrave the guerilla's memory with the historical forces that keep people servile, and which can be used as a motivation for the guerrilla and as a tactical advantage when immediate decisions must be made in an urban combat situation.

Unlike data compiled and distributed by the Department of Justice, however, Da Lench Mob delivers this information over a drum beat combined with the sounds of glass breaking and the tortured screams of men and women embodying these statistics. That is to say, Da Lench Mob renders this information aesthetically, suggesting the inadequacy of mere statistics to represent capital punishment. Furthermore, in the movement from historically recognizable forms of American execution (e.g., hanging) to forms of execution with a history that more explicitly generates mythology (e.g., crucifixion), Da Lench Mob subtly focuses attention on the ways in which methods of execution can serve as foundational moments in national, as well as theological, mythologies. In a genre that values verbal facility, the opening of aesthetic space between the materially historical "facts" about American capital punishment and the presymbolic screams of its victims depends upon the very *inarticulation* of the tortured. As Elaine Scarry showed, such intense pain destroys not only language, but consciousness itself: during torture, "in the most literal way possible, the created world of thought and feeling, all the psychological and mental content that constitutes both one's self and one's world, and that gives rise to and is in turn made possible by language, ceases to exist."[51] Da Lench Mob's simulacra of torturous executions serves as a terrifying form of negation: the dry statistics about the number of people executed in the U.S. resonate with the screams, each inflected by the other, with no comment on their dialectical juxtaposition; the space in between is left to be filled by the subsequent narrative episodes on the album and by the imagination of the listener.

The nature of this statistical information changes further when the litany of data gives way to the story of the public hanging of Rainey Bethea, the last public execution in the United States: "In the United States, public execution occasionally led to violence in the crowd, and senseless tragedy for a few unfortunate witnesses," the narrator recounts. "The last public execution in America was on August 14, 1936. Nearly 20,000 people showed up to watch the hanging death of Rainey Bethea, a black man accused of raping a white woman." A presumably white southern voice is heard describing the entertaining event at which lemonade was sold, and "of course the saloons did a bumper business, and everybody had a good time, but the mob was just totally unruly, mob was totally unruly, mob was totally unruly." Historians confirm that "hot dog and drink vendors set up near the gallows" at the execution that "ended the practice of public hanging in the United States."[52] But it is the use of the man's proper name—Rainey Bethea—amongst the anonymous statistics that sharply relocates the scope of the historical information from the numerical data of state-sanctioned killing (capital punishment) onto a named and hanged body, and onto the invisible spectators. Fanon says that the anticolonial fighter knows that "[f]rom birth it is clear to him that this narrow world, strewn with prohibitions, can only be called in question by absolute violence."[53] In this song the "mob" that became "unruly" whilst watching the state-sanctioned killing—that is, the crowd whose presence calls into question the distinction between the "legitimate" violence of the state and the "illegitimate" violence of lynching—becomes metonymically associated with a differently unruly "Lench Mob," who will narrate absolutely violent acts to call these prohibitions and categorical distinctions into question.

Throughout the album, fatal violence is recognized as central to the constitution of a social and political imaginary, and songs often focus on the glorification of illegal acts and the stark difference between what Walter Benjamin terms "sanctioned" and "unsanctioned" violence.[54] Yet, as Zulaika and Douglass note, "Arbitrary terroristic killings make no claim of legality; indeed, they are extralegal statements questioning the legitimacy of the constituted legal order. When the constitutional forces of that order resort to similar tactics, there is the need to justify them in the name of 'lawful killing.'"[55] It is precisely upon the law's relationship to legitimacy and violence that Da Lench Mob insists that listeners reflect. The historical information in "Capital Punishment in America" may be necessary but insufficient for understanding the violence of the album as "extralegal" rather than "illegal," but in an historical moment and location in which the law fails to apply equally, undermining an absolutist theological injunction against killing *qua* killing radically changes the status of acts that might be dismissed as "merely" criminal: thus these narratives of fictional violence call into question the just authority of law itself.

In Benjamin's formulation, "law demands of all violence a proof of its historical origin, which under certain conditions is declared legal, sanctioned."[56] For Benjamin, Da Lench Mob's repurposing of violent acts would reflect a cultural intervention wherein nonstate actors refuse to "give up their violence for the sake of the state."[57] Here, extralegal violence of the streets threatens state law "not by the ends that it may pursue but by its mere existence outside the law."[58] These songs distinguish themselves from acts of what Benjamin calls "predatory violence," and the murders they depict are figured as executions that would never be sanctioned under a corrupt state. It is thus that these narratives become potentially active, in Benjamin's words, "as a basis for, or a modification to, relatively stable conditions."[59] The outrage of legislators and police chiefs at violent rap may be understood not only as a familiar conservative objection to profanity, but as opposition to "the threat of declaring a new law."[60]

In this analysis, representatives of the state (and its attendant ideological apparatus) express fear not because "Capital Punishment in America" condemns racially biased jurisprudence, but because the depictions of violence acknowledge the historical roots of law in life-death violence. As Benjamin argues, the purpose of the death penalty itself "is not to punish the infringement of law but to establish new law. For in the exercise of violence over life and death more than in any other legal act, law reaffirms itself."[61] This is because, as Werner Hamacher describes, "As long as a legal institution does not rule out recourse to violence, its violence is one which *serves* that institution—if only to perpetuate it—and which, therefore, cannot be taken as a form of liberty, mediacy, or justice."[62] The question is no longer whether one should abjure violence for the goal of a relatively peaceful state, but whether or not the fundamental violence of the state renders anything resembling "nonviolence" a coherent proposition in the first instance.

The final song on the album is "Inside tha Head of a Black Man" and is identical to "Capital Punishment in America," with one key exception: the historical statistics about capital punishment are absent, leaving only the beat, minimal music, and the screams of the executed. This maneuver flies in the face of classically liberal theories of political transformation, wherein information is distributed to more-or-less rational actors in a public sphere, who can then adjudicate among various courses of action to be mimetically reflected by their political representatives. Instead, guerilla politics lie precisely within the interplay of narrative and psychology, statistics and sounds of pain inflicted in the name of and by the state (rather than social-scientific data both tallying and erasing that pain). Coming at the end of the album, the track underscores and rhetorically repositions the historical data and fictional narratives preceding it. Indeed, the structural framing of the album, with the two versions of "Capital Punishment in America" bookending intermediary tracks, is as crucial to the ideological work of the album as the visual frame provided by the album title and cover.

If the consciousness of the listener has been re-formed through the structural and rhetorical machinations of the album, the consciousness of "tha Black Man" in the final track has experienced no such progressive reformation. This central figure of the album remains in the painful realm of the continually breaking-down, expressed via the presymbolic cries of pain that continue to accompany material conditions of oppression. The violent narratives that constitute the rest of the album emerge not as mere urban sociopathologies outside of the law, but as spectacular violence calling for new law and new relationships between states of consciousness and the consciousness of states. Benjamin's political theory challenges a notion of politics based on "the production of social life and its presentation in the 'moral organism' of the state" and instead suggests a politics as "that which subverts the imperative of production and self-production, which evades the institutions of its implementation and suspends the paradigm of social self-production—the law, the law-positing and law-preserving speech act."[63] In these terms, the dual frame of *Guerillas in tha Mist* via the spectacle of public execution and litany of statistics, on the one hand, and the evacuation of those significations "Inside tha Head of a Black Man," in favor of what Benjamin might call the "ghostly, all-pervading presence" of tortured executions is what "suspends the paradigm of social self-production." This frame calls into question the various forms of failed violence in the diegetic narratives of the album's tracks: when, for example, the narrator recounts entering "tha system" because of failure to pay a ticket, then "shanking a guard" and being thrust deeper into incarceration, until finally being released with the recognition that social conditions outside of the visible prison walls are no less carceral: "the day I got out, man I was wishin' / but I'm back on the streets, still lost in tha system."[64] These are the ineluctable interpretive conditions for the social conditions narrated by the other songs, illuminating how local instances of violence are constituted by the explicitly mythical—and all-too-real—violence of the state.

While Benjamin's critique is "informed by Kant's fundamental distinction between morality and legality in that he too sought to define the morality of an action by disengaging it from the judicial system," Benjamin "purported to surpass the correlation between justified means and just ends that still informed Kant's moral philosophy."[65] This surpassing of the means/ends connection is also staged by Da Lench Mob's songs. The crucial question is no longer whether the goal of ending violence against African Americans "justifies" the violent means of antipolice violence, but whether such a calculus were ever possible in the first instance. "Benjamin's critique doesn't arrive at a criterion for judging which violence is just and which is not; it arrives at an aporia where the very possibility of human judgment is no longer secure,"[66] Benjamin Morgan writes. It is precisely this aporia that is produced by Da Lench Mob's framing of violent narratives within the overarching, mythic violence of capital punishment. Furthermore, Da Lench Mob has ironically followed none other than the CIA's suggestions on how to resist and destabilize the reigning government, giving "ideological training, mixing these instructions with folkloric songs"[67] and "popular words and expressions, i.e., the language of the people"[68]—in this case, the popular idiom of gangsta rap. Da Lench Mob's album is not finally a collection of tracks that glorify or condemn violence as such but a sustained critique of violence as the philosophical, material, and legal basis of liberal "democratic" society. The formal frame of "Capital Punishment in America" and "Inside tha Head of a Black Man" radically alters the stories of violence, revealing the impossibility of adequate judgment within the ultimate violence of capital punishment: neither the utilitarian calculation of means, ends, and collective good, nor a Kantian metaphysical judgment whereby capital punishment is necessary in order to keep the "scales of justice" proportionally balanced.

A calculus based on historical and sociological research tells us that executions in the United States account for an infinitesimal number of deaths, and that they always have: "The death penalty has never been a common or standard penalty for even the most terrible crimes in the United States," anti–death-penalty researchers write. "Of the thousands of murders committed each year, only a minute fraction see the murderer charged with a capital offense (and, of course, only a fraction of those are sentenced to death, and only a fraction of those are actually executed)."[69] In light of this information, we have to take seriously Da Lench Mob's implicit question: if capital punishment in America is only one aspect of deep systemic violence—and a relatively infrequent one at that—what are the ethical, political, and rhetorical grounds for focusing so much attention upon it, and what kind of knowledge is either illuminated or obscured by such a focus? The question of what is to be done about the death penalty is thereby expanded to subsume a different duty: not simply to collect and analyze further statistics about whom the state puts to death and whom it does not, but to ask what kind of ethics are at work when one promotes the figurative death of life imprisonment as ethically preferable to death itself, or when one focuses attention on the problem of capital punishment at the expense of the pervasive violence that it enables and perpetuates. Listeners are invited to imagine a politics explicitly beyond the scope of rational calculus: whether that calculus is understood as a utilitarian argument against genocide, as a liberal-humanist logic of "reducing" instances of cruelty, or as the explicitly mathematical language of social "equality."

Notes

1. See Jessica Stern, "Execute Terrorists at Our Own Risk," *New York Times*, February 28, 2001, A19.

2. "Okla. Families Can Watch McVeigh Execution on TV," CNN, April 12, 2001, http://archives.cnn.com/2001/LAW/04/12/ashcroft.mcveigh.02.

3. Lawrence Meir Friedman, *American Law in the 20th Century* (New Haven: Yale Univ. Press, 2004), 220.

4. Frank R. Baumgartner, Suzanna de Boef, Amber E. Boydstun, eds., *The Decline of the Death Penalty and the Discovery of Innocence* (Cambridge: Cambridge Univ. Press, 2008), 33–35.

5. Kristin Boudreau describes public execution and its relationship to classical republicanism. Before public opinion turned against collective witnessing of executions, "the rituals of execution day in colonial America guaranteed an immense public spectacle, one that began on the Sunday before the execution with a church service and a sermon aimed at interpreting the event and generating public interest." Kristin Boudreau, *The Spectacle of Death: Populist Literary Responses to American Capital Cases* (New York: Prometheus Books, 2006), 23.

6. Tom McCall, "Momentary Violence," in *Walter Benjamin: Theoretical Questions*, ed. David S. Ferris (Stanford: Stanford Univ. Press, 1996), 199.

7. Tom McCall, "Momentary Violence," 202.

8. Perhaps more important, emphasis on the death penalty as a unique form of violence—even among its opponents—may be used to justify a broader project of policing an already disciplined populace: when calculating the financial data about capital punishment, "the additional cost of having the death penalty is equivalent to thousands of police officers nationwide." Baumgartner et al., *Death Penalty*, 45.

9. Jimmie L. Briggs Jr., "Where They're Calling From: Cultural Roots of Rap," *William & Mary Bill of Rights Journal* 2:1 (Spring 1993), 152.

10. Chris Heim, "The Rage of Rap," *Chicago Tribune*, February 12, 1993, 1.

11. As Tricia Rose writes, "many critics of hip hop tend to interpret lyrics literally and as a direct reflection of the artist who performs them. They equate rappers with thugs, see rappers as a threat to the larger society, and then use this 'causal analysis' (that hip hop causes violence) to justify a variety of agendas: more police in black communities, more prisons to accommodate larger numbers of black and brown young people, and more censorship of expression. For these critics, hip hop is criminal propaganda. This literal approach, which extends beyond the individual to characterize an entire racial and class group, is rarely applied to violence-oriented mediums produced by whites." Tricia Rose, *The Hip Hop Wars: What We Talk about When We Talk about Hip Hop–and Why It Matters* (New York: Basic Civitas, 2008), 37.

12. Martin A. Miller, "Ordinary Terrorism in Historical Perspective," *Journal for the Study of Radicalism* 2.1 (2008), 128. In addition to the recognized acts of terrorism such as the "lynching" of roughly four thousand African Americans, Miller describes other American acts of what he calls "ordinary terrorism" performed by and in collusion with the state, such as "the brutal expropriation and expulsion of blacks living in towns that were declared for whites only. . . . These less noticed acts of terrorism, involving local officials as well as organized groups of white citizens,

accompanied the more sensational acts of violence against African Americans, particularly in the decades before and after the First World War." Miller, *Ordinary Terrorism*, 137–38.

13. A number of music and social critics have remarked on *Guerillas in tha Mist*, focusing on the ways that Da Lench Mob claims for itself a "guerilla" aesthetic. One early critic, Russell Potter, offers this take on the album's titular pun: "Against this hegemonic metonym [the connotative signifieds of 'black man' and 'gorilla'] and its deployment in the service of brutally repressive violence, hip-hop shifts the connotative signified along a radical pole suggested and enabled by homonymic indifference." Russell A. Potter, *Spectacular Vernaculars: Hip-Hop and the Politics of Postmodernism* (Albany: State Univ. of New York, 1995), 78.

14. McCall, "Momentary Violence," 186.

15. Austin Sarat, ed., *The Killing State: Capital Punishment in Law, Politics, and Culture* (New York: Oxford Univ. Press, 1999), 6.

16. Julie Skurski and Fernando Coronil emphasize the possibility of praxis within such conditions: "While hegemonic rhetorical violence has the effect of rendering visible some forms of violence and obscuring others, political violence has the potential to upset the stability of dominant narratives and to bring to the surface their underlying assumptions." Julie Skurski and Fernando Coronil, "Introduction: States of Violence and the Violence of States," in *States of Violence*, Julie Skurski and Fernando Coronil, eds. (Ann Arbor: Univ. of Michigan Press, 2006), 7.

17. See James Kirchick, "Angry White Man: The Bigoted Past of Ron Paul," *New Republic*, January 8, 2008, http://www.tnr.com/politics/story.html?id=e2f15397-a3 c7-4720-ac15-4532a7da84ca. The essay from *The Ron Paul Political Report* was preserved by The Nizkor Project, a group that catalogs hate speech: http://www.nizkor .org/ftp.cgi/people/g/ftp.py?people/g/gannon.dan/1992/gannon.0793.

18. Dennis R. Martin, "The Music of Murder," *William & Mary Bill of Rights Journal* 2.1 (Spring 1993), 161.

19. José Patiño Girona, "Rapper's Rant against Police Brings Poetic Justice," *Tampa Tribune*, July 30, 2009, http://www2.tbo.com/content/2009/jul/30/rappers-rant-against-police-brings-prison-time/news-breaking/.

20. Tricia Rose points out that there are "increasing attempts among far-right commentators to connect hip hop to Islamic terrorism and nonwhite hostility to Western society" which is to "reiterate a legacy linking fear of infiltration, decline of society, and economic insecurity to black culture." Rose, *Hip Hop Wars*, 99.

21. Madison Gray, "The L.A. Riots: Fifteen Years after Rodney King," CNN, http:// www.time.com/time/specials/2007/la_riot/article/0,28804,1614117_1614084,00 .html. For people who died during the riots, see Jim Crogan, "The L.A. 53," *LA Weekly*, April 24, 2002, http://www.laweekly.com/2002-05-02/news/the-l-a-53/.

22. Giorgio Agamben, "Sovereign Police," *Means without End: Notes on Politics*, trans. Vincenzo Binetti and Cesare Casarino (Minneapolis: Univ. of Minnesota Press, 2000), 103. One of the ways that nonstate actors began to mobilize politically in the wake of the riots was a historical truce by the Crips and Bloods, only to be intentionally derailed by the Los Angeles Police Department. Agamben reminds readers that "the police—contrary to public opinion—are not merely an administrative function of law enforcement; rather, the police are perhaps the place where the proximity and the almost constitutive exchange between violence and right that characterizes the figure of the sovereign is shown more nakedly and clearly than anywhere else." Ibid., 104. For an account of the LAPD's role in derailing these movements, see especially Jeff Chang, *Can't Stop, Won't Stop: A History of the Hip Hop Generation* (New York: St. Martin's Press, 2005), 357–79, 385–88.

23. Chang, *Can't Stop*, 389. Eithne Quinn recounts how the media focused on the chaotic rioting but not on the more recognizably political effects: "The televised King incident (followed by the astonishing acquittal) and the urban rioting led to a concentrating of political minds and a radicalization of message" about ways to respond to violence of the police and the state. Eithne Quinn, *Nuthin' but a "G" Thang: The Culture and Commerce of Gangsta Rap* (New York: Columbia Univ. Press, 2004), 109. Da Lench Mob's rhetoric must be understood in the context of that "radicalization of message."

24. Kitwana Bakari, *The Hip Hop Generation: Young Blacks and the Crisis in African American Culture* (New York: Basic Civitas Books, 2003), 15.

25. "The US Department of Justice Fact Sheet," National Criminal Justice Reference Service, last modified October 24, 1994, http://www.ncjrs.gov/txtfiles/billfs.txt.

26. The state of California performed its first execution in twenty-five years when Robert Alton Harris was executed in the gas chamber of San Quentin Prison on April 21, 1992, just one week before South Central Los Angeles reacted to the King verdict.

27. Russell Potter provided a useful early analysis of the album's title. After hitting Rodney King forty-five times with his baton, Officer Larry Powell spoke about a call he had received prior to the drunk-driver incident involving King and described a black family in a domestic incident as being "straight out of *Gorillas in the Mist*." Powell's own words become a running theme throughout the album, using the persecution of the African mountain gorilla as a metaphor for police harassment of African Americans.

28. Joseba Zulaika and William A. Douglass, *Terror and Taboo: The Follies, Fables, and Faces of Terrorism* (New York: Routledge, 1996), 204.

29. Chris Woodstra and John Bush, *Old School Rap and Hip-Hop: All Music Guide Required Listening 2* (New York: Backbeat, 2008), 50.

30. Zulaika and Douglass, *Terror and Taboo*, 220.

31. Chang, *Can't Stop*, 334.

32. Quinn observes, "In 'Guerillas in tha Mist,' Lench Mob invokes the southern past, contemporary South Central, the racist status quo, and the African jungle. The notion of a concrete jungle populated by urban guerrillas engaged in mortal combat with predatory policing foes explicitly links contemporary black life to the destructive legacy of imperialism and racial oppression." Quinn, *"G" Thang*, 105.

33. Da Lench Mob, "Freedom Got an AK," *Guerillas in tha Mist*, Street Knowledge Records 7 92296-2, Atlantic Recording Corp., 1992.

34. Carlos Marighella, "Minimanual of the Urban Guerrilla," *Urban Guerrilla Warfare*, ed. Robert Moss (London: International Institute for Strategic Studies, 1971), 23.

35. Larry Flick, "DA LENCH MOB: Freedom Got an AK," *Billboard*, December 19, 1992, 71.

36. Da Lench Mob, "All on My Nut Sac," *Guerillas in tha Mist*.

37. Da Lench Mob, "Buck Tha Devil," *Guerillas in tha Mist*.

38. Da Lench Mob, "You & Your Heroes," *Guerillas in tha Mist*.

39. Tayacán, *Psychological Operations in Guerrilla Warfare* (Castro Valley, CA: Combat Arms, 1995), 3.

40. Da Lench Mob, "Guerillas in tha Mist," *Guerillas in tha Mist*.

41. Da Lench Mob, "All on My Nut Sac," *Guerillas in tha Mist*.

42. Martin, "The Music of Murder," 163.

43. Da Lench Mob, "Lost in Tha System," *Guerillas in tha Mist*.

44. Da Lench Mob, "Buck Tha Devil," *Guerillas in tha Mist*.

45. Frantz Fanon, "Concerning Violence," *The Wretched of the Earth*, trans. Constance Farrington (New York: Grove Press, 1968), 38.

46. Marighella, "Minimanual," 31.

47. Da Lench Mob, "Freedom Got an AK," *Guerillas in tha Mist*.

48. Quinn, *"G" Thang*, 110.

49. Immanuel Kant, *The Metaphysics of Morals*, trans. and ed. Mary Gregory (Cambridge: Cambridge Univ. Press, 1996), 204.

50. Marighella, "Minimanual," 29.

51. Elaine Scarry, *The Body in Pain: The Making and Unmaking of the World* (New York: Oxford Univ. Press, 1985), 30.

52. Stuart Banner, *The Death Penalty: An American History* (Cambridge: Harvard Univ. Press, 2002), 156.

53. Fanon, "Concerning Violence," 37.

54. Walter Benjamin, "Critique of Violence," in *Reflections: Essays, Aphorisms, Auto-biographical Writings*, trans. Edmund Jephcott (New York: Schocken Books, 1978), 279.

55. Zulaika and Douglass, *Terror and Taboo*, 159.

56. Benjamin, "Critique of Violence," 280. Imani Perry has analyzed the way in which "narratives about the law, and narrative critiques of the law, within hip hop go hand in hand with the work of critical race, law, and literature scholars who appeal to narrative to critique legal institutions." Imani Perry, "The Glorious Outlaw: Hip Hop Narratives, American Law, and the Court of Public Opinion," in *Prophets of the Hood* (Durham: Duke Univ. Press, 2004), 111.

57. Benjamin, "Critique of Violence," 278.

58. Ibid., 281.

59. Ibid., 282.

60. Ibid., 286.

61. Ibid., 286.

62. Werner Hamacher, "Affirmative, Strike: Benjamin's 'Critique of Violence,'" trans. Dana Hollander, in *Walter Benjamin's Philosophy: Destruction and Experience*, ed. Andrew Benjamin and Peter Osborne (London: Routledge, 1994), 113.

63. Hamacher, "Affirmative, Strike," 125.

64. Da Lench Mob, "Lost in Tha System," *Guerillas in tha Mist*.

65. Beatrice Hanssen, "On the Politics of Pure Means: Benjamin, Arendt, Foucault," *Critique of Violence: Between Poststructuralism and Critical Theory* (London: Routledge, 2000), 20.

66. Benjamin Morgan, "Undoing Legal Violence: Walter Benjamin's and Giorgio Agamben's Aesthetics of Pure Means," *Journal of Law and Society* 34:1 (March 2007), 52.

67. Tayacán, *Psychological Operations*, 21.

68. Ibid., 19.

69. Baumgartner et al., *Death Penalty*, 26.

A Poem for No Reason

These songs are usually born for some reason

A thought that one thinks immortal or ought
To be

Or to help brothers and sisters see
Something curious or something seldom seen
The intense green of the Earth
The awe and wonder at the birth of a child and death
Things we want to share with our kindred
But a poem for no reason?
I did meet a sweet little woman named season

But she is not the reason for this song—once
Long, long ago, I heard some sounds and some silences
That sparked a fire in me and no form that I know could contain
It and even Leonardo or Donnie Ray Carter
could never frame it
So terrible it was

Reason alone could never explain it and I have been on it ever
Since always

For Gary Graham, a.k.a. Shaka Sankofa

Gary, this is written some hours before your scheduled execution; you say murder and you know best; well, brother, I say these words to your spirit which obviously is not on lockdown; a locked spirit could not have touched these thousands of hearts as you have and we have fought for you. I too have been near to where you are but our kinship is greater than what the Death machine can make and those who know not the sacred thing called life may break and destroy the physical body but your warrior spirit will never Die; you are a part of the One who made the Sun and the Stars and the laughter of children and love—I don't tell you to be strong. Because I know you are—nor do I say don't cry or fret because at times even strong men do that; but I do believe that what is is and what ain't is not; likewise I believe that the judge will be judged, the governor will be governed; the executioner will be executed and I believe that One who is totally righteous will Come and judge and restore all things and I believe you, Gary, will be a witness.

DEATH LAW

THE GOVERNOR FOR PENNSYLVANIA
SIGNED MUMIA'S "DEATH WARRANT"
TODAY IS WHAT MY SISTER IN THE
MOVEMENT SAY SPEAKING TO ME ON
THE CELLULAR PHONE
A RENEWED PROTEST IS ON, PLEASE
COME
I THINK TO MYSELF—THE BASTARDS
SIGNED IT WHEN HE WAS BORN
A BLACK MAN IN THIS WILDERNESS OF
NORTH AMERICA
THEN THEY SIGNED IT AGAIN WHEN HE
DECIDED TO STAND AND AS A MAN WITH
BLACK PANTHER PARTY—THO ONLY
SIXTEEN YRS OLD

THEY SIGNED IT AGAIN BEFORE THE
ASHES WERE COLD AT THE HOUSE
ON OSAGE AVE. WHERE THE MOVE WAS
BURNED DOWN
                              BECAUSE
                              HE WENT TO
                              GROUND
AND SPOKE THE TRUTH
              ABOUT THE POLICE AND THE
CHIEF

RUNNING DOG NIGGER

NIGGER WHO GAVE THE ORDER TO BURN
JOHN AFRIKA AND HIS CHILDREN ALIVE

YEH, I WAS THINKING, THEY ALWAYS

SIGNING DEATH OR OTHER KINDA
WARRANTS FOR THE LIKE OF MUMIA AND
ME
                              CAUSE WE
BE FREE IN SPIRIT
IN MIND AND HEART
              AND NO MATTER WHAT
                              WE GO

ON AND ON
'CAUSE WE STRONG
              STRONGER THAN STRONG
                              YEH.

I SAID TO MYSELF
WE STRONGER THAN STRONG

I Need a Poem

I need a poem, need a poem, a master poem, once and for all,
I need a poem to destroy poetry

And break these iron bars

A poem to make the stars weep

I need a poem to trouble the sleep of the chained, some words
and strikes of magic to be heard through all the worlds

Power sounds to hurl all wrong to appropriate places, a poem to
make spaces for feeling and being

An easy but invincible poem

For the sick and the lame and the maimed in mind, for the blind
with eyes, for the deaf with ears, a poem of peace in war years.

And a poem of war when war is Holy

For the unborn and the dead, a poem to be read when all books
are blank pages, a poem for judgment day and

A poem for the ages and epochs and eras

My poem, your poem, our poem

For all and it is

Contributors

Sherman Alexie is the author of over twenty books of poetry and fiction, and the recipient of many literary awards, including the 1999 O. Henry Award, the Poetry of America's 2001 Shelley Memorial Award, and the 2000 PEN Short Story Award.

John Cyril Barton is director of graduate studies and assistant professor of English at the University of Missouri–Kansas City. He has published essays that examine capital punishment in the writings of Theodore Dreiser, William Gilmore Simms, and Lydia Maria Child. He is writing a book on the death penalty in nineteenth-century U.S. law and literature.

Steve Champion (now Adisa Akanni Kamara) is a death row prisoner at San Quentin State Prison. A former Crips member, he grew up in South Central Los Angeles and has been incarcerated for twenty-five years. He is self-taught and conversant in African history, philosophy, political science, and comparative religion. In 2010 he published a memoir, *From Dead to Deliverance*. In 1995 he was awarded honorary mention in the short fiction category of the PEN Prison Writing Contest, and in 2004 he won first place in nonfiction. He is coauthor of two works: *Afterlife* and *The Sacred Eye of the Falcon: Lessons in Life from Death Row*.

Kia Corthron's other plays, including *Breath, Boom, A Cool Dip in the Barren Saharan Crick* and *The Venus de Milo Is Armed*, have been produced by Playwrights Horizons, Ensemble Studio Theatre, Actors Theatre of Louisville, London's Royal Court Theatre, New York Theatre Workshop, Minneapolis Children's Theatre, Mark Taper Forum, Alabama Shakespeare Festival, Yale Rep, Huntington Theatre, Atlantic Theater Company, New York Stage and Film, Baltimore's CenterStage, London's Donmar Warehouse, Goodman Theatre, Manhattan Theatre Club, Hartford Stage, and elsewhere. Awards include Bellagio Residency (Italy), McKnight National Residency, Wachtmeister Award, Daryl Roth Creative Spirit Award, National Endowment for the Arts Award, and Writers Guild Outstanding Drama Series Award for *The Wire*.

Thomas Dutoit is a professor of English literature at the University of Tours, Paris 7, and Lille, and the author of *A Rose, A Ghost, in Edith Wharton*. Dutoit has translated and edited works by Derrida, including *Aporias, On the Name*, and Derrida's twenty lectures on the death penalty (to be published in French and English in 2012). Dutoit has published articles on sexuality in Quentin Tarantino's *Pulp Fiction*, on sovereignty in Frank Zappa's art, and on the death penalty in Norman Mailer's writing.

Cultural historian **H. Bruce Franklin** is the author or editor of nineteen books, including *War Stars: The Superweapon in the American Imagination*, *M.I.A. or Mythmaking in America*, *Prison Writing in 20th-Century America*, and *Vietnam and Other American Fantasies*. He has been publishing on Herman Melville since 1961. Currently the John Cotton Dana Professor of English and American Studies at Rutgers University in Newark, he can be reached through his home page: http://andromeda.rutgers.edu/~hbf.

Tom Kerr is an associate professor of writing and rhetoric in the Department of Writing at Ithaca College, where he teaches courses on the essay, academic and scholarly writing, and composition theory. His writing on prison and prisoners has appeared in *San Francisco Bay View*, *counterpunch.org*, and *Writing on the Edge*. He edited Steve Champion's memoir *From Dead to Deliverance*, and edited and published *The Sacred Eye of the Falcon: Lessons in Life from Death Row* by Steve Champion, Anthony Ross, and the late Stanley Tookie Williams.

David Kieran is a postdoctoral fellow in the American Culture Studies Program at Washington University. His work focuses on cultural memory and representations of violence and conflict in contemporary U.S. culture. Kieran is the cofounder of the War and Peace Studies Caucus of the American Studies Association, and his writing has appeared, among other places, in *M/MLA: The Journal of the Midwestern Modern Language Association* and *American Studies International*.

Jennifer Leigh Lieberman is a National Science Foundation postdoctoral fellow in the Department of Science and Technology Studies at Cornell University, where she also teaches in Auburn Prison (home of the first electric chair) through the Cornell Prison Education Program. She received her Ph.D. in English from the University of Illinois at Urbana-Champaign, and was a research fellow at the Illinois Program for Research in the Humanities, the Smithsonian Institution's Dibner Library, and the Bakken Library and Museum.

Jill McDonough's poems have appeared in *Threepenny Review*, *Poetry*, *New Republic*, and *Slate*. She has been teaching with Boston University's Prison Education Program since 1998. Her awards include a Pushcart Prize and fellowships from the NEA, the Fine Arts Work Center, Stanford's Stegner Program, and the Cullman Center for Scholars and Writers. Her first book of poems, *Habeas Corpus*, was published in 2008.

Anthony Ross (now Ajani Addae Kamara) was raised in South Central Los Angeles. A former gang member with the Crips, Ross has been incarcerated for twenty-four years. While in isolation, he began to study metaphysics, psychology, mythology, African and Asian history, and follow a spiritual path. After ten years in San Quentin's Adjustment Center, he is now a writer and mentor. In 1995 he won the PEN Prison Writing Award for best short fiction: "Walker's Requiem," an account of a young man's last day before being executed. Ross is coauthor of *The Sacred Eye of the Falcon: Lessons in Life from Death Row* and has been published in several books and periodicals. His work appears in the anthology *Children of the Dream: Growing Up Black in America*. He is completing his memoir, *The Road to Purgatory*.

Katy Ryan, an associate professor of English at West Virginia University, founded the Appalachian Prison Book Project in 2004 (http://aprisonbookproject. wordpress.com). Her essays appear in *American Literature*, *African American Review*, *Philosophy and Literature*, *Studies in the Novel*, and *Texas Studies in Literature and Language*. In 2008–2009, she was a research fellow at the Tanner Humanities Center at the University of Utah and at the Harry Ransom Center at the University of Texas–Austin.

Elizabeth Ann Stein, a former political reporter for United Press International, is an independent writer and filmmaker living in Houston. She is also producer of the Houston radio program *Execution Watch*.

Rick Stetter served as director of Southern Illinois University Press, Texas A&M University Press, University of Nevada Press, and Museum of Northern Arizona Press. He is currently an officer with the Brazos County, Texas, Sheriff's Department, and has worked as a correctional officer with the Texas Department of Criminal Justice.

Matthew Stratton is an assistant professor of English at the University of California–Davis. He has published articles in *Arizona Quarterly* and *Twentieth Century Literature*, and is at work on a book manuscript about the politics and aesthetics of irony in twentieth-century American literature and literary culture.

Jason Stupp is a doctoral candidate in English at West Virginia University. His dissertation focuses on activist voices in post–civil rights era American literature. He teaches a prison studies composition course with a civic engagement component.

Delbert L. Tibbs is a writer, poet, activist, and musician. Exonerated from death row in 1977, Tibbs is featured in the documentary play *The Exonerated* and in Studs Terkel's book *Will the Circle Be Unbroken?* He is a speaker for the Witness to Innocence Project (http://witnesstoinnocence.org/aboutus.php) and is completing a memoir.

Selected Bibliography

Abramson, Stacy and David Isay, prods. *Witness to an Execution.* 2000. http://
soundportraits.org/on-air/witness_to_an_execution/transcript.php.

Abu-Jamal, Mumia. *All Things Censored.* New York: Seven Stories, 2000.

———. *Live from Death Row.* New York: Harper, 1996.

Alexander, Michelle. *The New Jim Crow: Mass Incarceration in the Age of Colorblindness.*
New York: New Press, 2010.

Alexander, William. *Is William Martinez Not Our Brother? Twenty Years of the Prison
Creative Arts Project.* Ann Arbor: Univ. of Michigan Press, 2010.

Algeo, Ann M. *Courtroom as Forum: Homicide Trials by Dreiser, Wright, Capote, and
Mailer.* New York: Peter Lang, 1996.

Amnesty International. http://www.amnesty.org.

Bair, Asatar P. *Prison Labor in the United States.* New York: Routledge, 2008.

Baker, David V. "American Indian Executions in Historical Context." *Criminal
Justice Studies* 20.4 (2007): 315–73.

Banner, Stuart. *The Death Penalty: An American History.* Cambridge: Harvard Univ.
Press, 2002.

Baumgartner, Frank R., Suzanna De Boef, Amber E. Boydstun, eds. *The Decline
of the Death Penalty and the Discovery of Innocence.* Cambridge: Cambridge Univ.
Press, 2008.

Baus, Janet, Dan Hunt and Reid Williams, dirs. *Cruel and Unusual.* 2006.

Beccaria, Cesare di. *On Crimes and Punishments and Other Writings.* Ed. Richard
Bellamy. Trans. Richard Davies. Cambridge: Cambridge Univ. Press, 1995.

Beck, Elizabeth, et al. *In the Shadow of Death: Restorative Justice and Death Row Families.*
New York: Oxford Univ. Press, 2007.

Becnel, Barbara and Shirley Neal, dirs. *Tribute: Stanley Tookie Williams.* 2008.

Bedau, Hugo Adam. *The Death Penalty in America: Current Controversies.* Oxford:
Oxford Univ. Press, 1997.

Bedau, Hugo Adam and Paul G. Cassel, eds. *Debating the Death Penalty: Should
America Have Capital Punishment? The Experts on Both Sides Make Their Best Case.* New
York: Oxford Univ. Press, 2004.

Bernstein, Lee. *America Is the Prison: Arts and Politics in the Prison in the 1970s.* Durham:
Univ. of North Carolina Press, 2010.

Blackmon, Douglas. *Slavery by Another Name: The Re-enslavement of Black Americans
from the Civil War to World War II.* New York: Doubleday, 2008.

Boudreau, Kristin. *The Spectacle of Death: Populist Literary Responses to American Capital
Cases.* New York: Prometheus Books, 2006.

Bowers, William J., with Glenn L. Pierce and John F. McDevitt. *Legal Homicide: Death as Punishment in America, 1864–1982*. Boston: Northeastern Univ. Press, 1984.

Brown, Michelle. "'Setting the Conditions' for Abu Ghraib: The Prison Nation Abroad," *American Quarterly* 57.3 (2005): 973–97.

Bryant, Jerry. *Victims and Villains: Racial Violence in the African American Novel*. Amherst: Univ. of Massachusetts Press, 1997.

Burton-Rose, Daniel, Dan Pens, and Paul Wright, eds. *The Celling of America: An Inside Look at the U.S. Prison Industry*. Monroe, ME: Common Courage Press, 1998.

Carter, Dan. *Scottsboro: A Tragedy of the American South*. Rev. Ed. Baton Rouge: Louisiana State Univ. Press, 1979.

Caster, Peter. *Prisons, Race, and Masculinity in Twentieth-Century U.S. Literature and Film*. Columbus: Ohio State Univ. Press, 2008.

Champion, Steve. *Dead to Deliverance: A Death Row Memoir*. Vestal, NY: Split Oak Press, 2010.

Chessman, Caryl. *Cell 2455, Death Row: A Condemned Man's Own Story*. New York: Prentice-Hall, 1954.

———. *Trial by Ordeal*. New York: Prentice-Hall, 1955.

Chevigny, Bell Gale, ed. *Doing Time: 25 Years of Prison Writing*. New York: Arcade, 2000.

Cohen, Daniel A. *Pillars of Salt, Monuments of Grace: New England Crime Literature and the Origins of American Pop Culture, 1674–1860*. Amherst: Univ. of Massachusetts Press, 2006.

Conquergood, Dwight. "Lethal Theatre: Performance, Punishment, and the Death Penalty," *Theatre Journal* (2002): 339–67.

Crane, Gregg. *Race, Citizenship, and Law in American Literature*. Cambridge, UK: Cambridge Univ. Press, 2002.

———. "Reasonable Doubts: Crime and Punishment," *American Literary History* 18.4 (2006): 797–813.

Crenshaw, Kimberlé. "Mapping the Margins: Intersectionality, Identity Politics, and Violence against Women of Color," *Stanford Law Review* 43.6 (1991): 1241–99.

Critical Resistance. http://www.criticalresistance.org.

Davis, Angela. *Abolition Democracy: Beyond Empire, Prisons, and Torture*. New York: Seven Stories, 2005.

———. *Are Prisons Obsolete?* New York: Seven Stories Press, 2003.

Davis, David Brion. *From Homicide to Slavery: Studies in American Culture*. Oxford: Oxford Univ. Press, 1986.

Davis, Mary Kemp. *Nat Turner before the Bar of Judgment: Fictional Treatments of the Southampton Slave Insurrection.* Baton Rouge: Louisiana State Univ. Press, 1999.

Dayan, Colin. *The Law is a White Dog: How Legal Rituals Make and Unmake Persons.* Princeton: Princeton Univ. Press, 2011.

———. *The Story of Cruel and Unusual.* Cambridge: MIT Press, 2007.

Death Penalty Information Center. http://www.deathpenaltyinfo.org.

Denno, Deborah W. "When Willie Francis Died: The 'Disturbing' Story behind One of the Eighth Amendment's Most Enduring Standards of Risk," in *Death Penalty Stories.* Eds. John H. Blume and Jordan M. Steiker. New York: Foundation Press, 2009, 17–94.

Dieter, Richard C. "Struck by Lightning: The Continuing Arbitrariness of the Death Penalty Thirty-Five Years after Its Reinstatement in 1976," *Death Penalty Information Center,* July 2011, http://www.deathpenaltyinfo.org/documents/StruckByLightning.pdf.

Dow, David R. *The Autobiography of an Execution.* New York: Twelve, 2010.

Drehle, David Von. *Among the Lowest of the Dead: The Culture of Death Row.* New York: Faucet, 1996.

Du Bois, W. E. B. *Black Reconstruction in America, 1860–1880.* New York: Free Press, 1962.

Durand, Allan, dir. *Willie Francis Must Die Again.* 2006.

Eisenberg, Stephen F. *The Abu Ghraib Effect.* London: Reakton Books, 2007.

Elder, Robert K. *Last Words of the Executed.* Chicago: Univ. of Chicago Press, 2010.

Espy, M. Watt, and John Ortiz Smykla. *Executions in the United States, 1608–1991: The ESPY File* [Computer file], 3rd ed. Ann Arbor, MI: Inter-university Consortium for Political and Social Research, 1994.

Farr, Kathryn Ann. "Defeminizing and Dehumanizing Female Murderers," *Women and Criminal Justice* 11.1 (May 2000): 49–66.

Ferguson, Robert A. *The Trial in American Life.* Chicago: Univ. of Chicago Press, 2007.

Foner, Philip S. *Autobiographies of the Haymarket Anarchists.* New York: Humanities Press, 1969.

Foucault, Michel. *Discipline and Punish: The Birth of the Prison.* Trans. Alan Sheridan. New York: Vintage, 1977.

Frankfurter, Marion Denman and Gardner Jackson, eds. *The Letters of Sacco and Vanzetti.* New York: Penguin, 1997.

Franklin, H. Bruce. "Can the Penitentiary Teach the Academy How to Read?" *PMLA* 123 (May 2004): 643–49.

———. "From Plantation to Penitentiary to the Prison-Industrial Complex:

Literature of the American Prison," *Modern Language Association Conference*, December 2000, http://andromeda.rutgers.edu/~hbf/MLABLACK.htm.

———. "The Inside Stories of the Global American Prison," *Texas Studies in Literature and Language* 50.3 (2008): 235–42.

———. *Prison Literature in America: The Victim as Criminal and Artist*. New York: Oxford Univ. Press, 1989.

———, ed. *Prison Writing in Twentieth-Century America*. New York: Penguin, 1998.

Garbus, Liz, dir. *The Execution of Wanda Jean*. 2002.

Garland, David. *Peculiar Institution: America's Death Penalty in an Age of Abolition*. Cambridge: Harvard Univ. Press, 2010.

Gilmore, Mikal. *Shot in the Heart*. New York: Anchor, 1995.

Gilmore, Ruth Wilson. *Golden Gulag: Prisons, Surplus, Crisis and Opposition in Globalizing California*. Berkeley: Univ. of California Press, 2007.

Goldstein, Richard. "Queer on Death Row," *Village Voice*, March 13, 2001.

Gordon, Avery. "Abu Ghraib: Imprisonment and the War on Terror," *Race and Class* 48.1 (2006): 42–59.

———. "Methodologies of Imprisonment." *PMLA* 123.3 (2008): 651–57.

Gottschalk, Marie. *The Prison and the Gallows*. New York: Cambridge Univ. Press, 2006.

Gray, Ian and Moira Gray, eds. *A Punishment in Search of a Crime: Americans Speak Out against the Death Penalty*. New York: Avon, 1989.

Guest, David. *Sentenced to Death: The American Novel and Capital Punishment*. Jackson: Univ. Press of Mississippi, 1997.

Hamann, Paul, dir. *Fourteen Days in May*. 1988.

Hames-García, Michael. *Fugitive Justice: Prison Movements, Race, and the Meaning of Justice*. Minneapolis: Univ. of Minnesota Press, 2004.

Hamm, Theo. *Rebel and a Cause: Caryl Chessman and the Politics of the Death Penalty in Postwar California, 1948–1974*. Berkeley: Univ. of California Press, 2001.

Hartnett, Stephen John, ed. *Incarceration Nation: Investigative Prison Poems of Hope and Terror*. Lanham, MD: AltaMira Press, 2003.

Hartnett, Stephen John, et al., "Fighting the Prison-Industrial Complex: A Call for Communication Scholars to Change the World," *Communication and Critical/Cultural Studies* 4 (2007): 402–20.

Haslam, Jason. *Fitting Sentences: Identity in Nineteenth- and Twentieth-Century Prison Narratives*. Toronto: Univ. of Toronto Press, 2005.

Herivel, Tara and Paul Wright, eds. *Prison Nation: The Warehousing of America's Poor*. New York: Routledge, 2003.

Holland, Sharon Patricia. *Raising the Dead: Readings of Death and (Black) Subjectivity*. Durham: Duke Univ. Press, 2000.

Jackson, Bruce. *Wake Up the Dead Man: Hard Labor and Southern Blues.* Athens: Univ. of Georgia Press, 1999.

James, Joy. *Resisting State Violence: Radicalism, Gender, and Race.* Minneapolis: Univ. of Minnesota Press, 2007.

———, ed. *The New Abolitionists: (Neo)Slave Narratives and Contemporary Prison Writings.* Albany: SUNY Press, 2005.

———, ed. *Warfare in the American Homeland: Policing and Prison in a Penal Democracy.* Durham, NC: Duke Univ. Press, 2007.

Jones, Paul Christian. *Against the Gallows: Antebellum American Writers and the Movement to Abolish Capital Punishment.* Iowa City: Univ. of Iowa Press, 2011.

———. "'I put my fingers around my throat and squeezed it, to know how it feels': Antigallows Sentimentalism and E.D.E.N. Southworth's *The Hidden Hand*," *Legacy* 25.1 (2008): 41–61.

King, Gilbert. *The Execution of Willie Francis: Race, Murder, and the Search for Justice in the American South.* New York: Basic Civitas Books, 2008.

King, Rachel. *Capital Consequences: Families of the Condemned Tell Their Stories.* New Brunswick, NJ: Rutgers Univ. Press, 2004.

———. *Don't Kill in My Name: Families of Murder Victims Speak Out against the Death Penalty.* New Brunswick, NJ: Rutgers Univ. Press, 2003.

Kudlac, Christopher S. *Public Executions: The Death Penalty and the Media.* Westport, CT: Praeger, 2007.

Kupers, Terry. *Prison Madness: The Mental Health Crisis behind Bars and What We Must Do about It.* San Francisco: Jossey-Bass, 1999.

Lamb, Wally, ed. *Couldn't Keep It to Myself: Testimonies from Our Imprisoned Sisters.* New York: Harper, 2003.

Lawson, John Howard and Wesley Robert Wells. *Letters from the Death House.* Los Angeles: Civil Rights Congress, 1953.

Lawston, Jodie Michelle and Ashley E. Lucas, eds. *Razor Wire Women: Prisoners, Activists, Scholars, and Artists.* Albany: SUNY Press, 2011.

Lewis, Reginald Sinclair. *Leaving Death Row.* Lewis, 2000.

———. *Where I'm Writing From.* Lewis, 2005.

López, Ernie and Rafael Pérez-Torres. *To Alcatraz, Death Row, and Back.* Austin: Univ. of Texas Press, 2005.

Lyon, Danny. *Conversations with the Dead.* New York: Henry Holt, 1971.

Mackey, Philip English. *Hanging in the Balance: The Anti–Capital Punishment Movement in New York State, 1776–1861.* New York: Garland, 1982.

———, ed. *Voices against Death: American Opposition to Capital Punishment, 1787–1975.* New York: Burt Franklin & Co., 1976.

MacQuarrie, Brian. *The Ride: A Shocking Murder and a Bereaved Father's Journey from Rage to Redemption*. Cambridge, MA: Da Capo Press, 2009.

Marable, Manning. *The Great Wells of Democracy: The Meaning of Race in American Life*. New York: Basic Civitas Books, 2002.

Markowitz, Jonathan. *Legacies of Lynching: Racial Violence and Memory*. Minneapolis: Univ. of Minnesota Press, 2005.

Masters, Jarvis Jay. *Finding Freedom: Writings from Death Row*. Junction City, CA: Padma, 1997.

————. *That Bird Has My Wings: The Autobiography of an Innocent Man on Death Row*. New York: HarperOne, 2009.

Masur, Louis P. *Rites of Execution: Capital Punishment and the Transformation of American Culture, 1776–1865*. New York: Oxford Univ. Press, 1991.

Mauer, Marc. *Race to Incarcerate*. New York: New Press, 1999.

McAllister, Pam. *Death Defying: Dismantling the Execution Machinery in 21st Century U.S.A.* New York: Continuum, 2003.

McFeeley, William S. *Proximity to Death*. New York: W. W. Norton, 1999.

Meeropol, Michael, ed. *The Rosenberg Letters*. New York: Routledge, 1994.

Miller, Arthur S. and Jeffrey H. Bowman. *Death by Installments: The Ordeal of Willie Francis*. Westport, Conn.: Greenwood Press, 1988.

Miller, D. Quentin, ed. *Prose and Cons: Essays on Prison Literature in the United States*. Jefferson, NC: McFarland, 2005.

Miller, James A. *Remembering Scottsboro: The Legacy of an Infamous Trial*. Princeton: Princeton Univ. Press, 2009.

Miller, Jerome G. *Search and Destroy: African-American Males in the Criminal Justice System*. Cambridge, UK: Cambridge Univ. Press, 1996.

Mitford, Jessica. *Kind and Unusual Punishment*. New York: Vintage, 1974.

Morris, Errol, dir. *Thin Blue Line*. 1988.

Mulvey-Roberts, Marie, ed. *Writing for Their Lives: Death Row U.S.A.* Urbana: Univ. of Illinois Press, 2007.

Murder Victims Families for Human Rights. http://www.mvfhr.org.

Murder Victims Families for Reconciliation. http://www.mvfr.org.

Norris, Clarence and Sybil D. Washington, *The Last of the Scottsboro Boys: An Autobiography*. New York: G.P. Putnam's Sons, 1979.

Ogletree, Jr., Charles J. "Black Man's Burden: Race and the Death Penalty in America." *Oregon Law Review* 81.1 (Spring 2002): 15–38.

O'Shea, Kathleen. *Women and the Death Penalty, 1900–1998*. Westport, CT: Greenwood, 1999.

Oshinsky, David M. *"Worse than Slavery": Parchman Farm and the Ordeal of Jim Crow Justice*. New York: Free Press, 1997.

Palmer, Jr., Louis J. *The Encyclopedia of Capital Punishment in the United States*. New York: McFarland, 2001.

Patterson, Haywood and Earl Conrad. *Scottsboro Boy*. Garden City, NY: Doubleday, 1950.

Pfeifer, Michael J. *Rough Justice: Lynching and American Society, 1874–1947*. Urbana: Univ. of Illinois Press, 2004.

Pizer, Donald. "Crime and Punishment in Dreiser's An American Tragedy," *Studies in the Novel* 41.4 (Winter 2009): 435–50.

Prejean, Sr. Helen. *Dead Man Walking: An Eyewitness Account of the Death Penalty in the United States*. New York: Vintage, 1994.

———. *The Death of Innocents: An Eyewitness Account of Wrongful Convictions*. New York: Random House, 2004.

Radelet, Michael, ed. *Facing the Death Penalty: Essays on a Cruel and Unusual Punishment*. Philadelphia: Temple Univ. Press, 1990.

Radelet, Michael L., Hugo Bedau, and Constance L. Putnam. *In Spite of Innocence: Erroneous Convictions in Capital Cases*. Boston: Northeastern Univ. Press, 1992.

Rappaport, Elizabeth. "The Death Penalty and Gender Discrimination," *Law and Society Review* 25.2 (June 1991): 367–83.

———. "Staying Alive: Equal Protection, Re-election, and the Execution of Women," *Buffalo Criminal Law Review* 4.2 (2001): 967–1007.

"Ray" and S. O'Riain. *Condemned: Letters from Death Row*. Dublin, UK: Liberties, 2008.

Rideau, Wilbert. *In the Place of Justice: A Story of Punishment and Deliverance*. New York: Knopf, 2010.

Rodriguez, Dylan. *Forced Passages: Imprisoned Radical Intellectuals and the U.S. Prison Regime*. Minneapolis: Univ. of Minnesota Press, 2006.

Rosenblatt, Elihu, ed. *Criminal Injustice: Confronting the Prison Crisis*. Boston: South End Press, 1999.

Sarat, Austin. *When the State Kills: Capital Punishment and the American Condition*. Princeton: Princeton Univ. Press, 2001.

———, ed. *The Killing State: Capital Punishment in Law, Politics, and Culture*. New York: Oxford Univ. Press, 1999.

Scheck, Barry, Peter Neufeld, and Jim Dwyer. *Actual Innocence: Five Days to Execution and Other Dispatches from the Wrongly Convicted*. New York: Random House, 2000.

Sharpe, Susan F. *Hidden Victims: The Effects of the Death Penalty on the Families of the Accused*. New Brunswick, NJ: Rutgers Univ. Press, 2005.

Shortnacy, Michael B. "Sexual Minorities, Criminal Justice, and the Death Penalty." *Fordham Urban Law Journal* 32 (2005).

Smith, Caleb. *The Prison and the American Imagination*. New Haven: Yale Univ. Press, 2009.

Solinger, Rickie, et al., eds. *Interrupted Life: Experiences of Incarcerated Women in the United States*. Berkeley: Univ. of California Press, 2010.

Streib, Victor L. "Death Penalty for Lesbians," *National Journal of Sexual Orientation Law* 1.1 (1995): 105–26.

———. *The Fairer Death: Executing Women in Ohio*. Athens: Ohio Univ. Press, 2006.

Sweeney, Megan. "Legal Brutality: Prisons and Punishment, the American Way," *American Literary History* 22.3 (Fall 2010): 704.

———. *Reading Is My Window: Books and the Art of Reading in Women's Prisons*. Durham: Univ. of North Carolina Press, 2010.

Till-Mobley, Mamie and Christopher Benson. *Death of Innocence: The Story of the Hate Crime That Changed America*. New York: Random House, 2003.

Trounstine, Jean. *Shakespeare behind Bars: The Power of Drama in a Woman's Prison*. New York: St. Martin's Press, 2001.

Useem, Bert and Peter Kimball. *States of Siege: U.S. Prison Riots, 1971–1986*. Oxford: Oxford Univ. Press, 1991.

Vandiver, Margaret. *Lethal Punishment: Lynching and Legal Execution in the South*. New Brunswick, NJ: Rutgers Univ. Press, 2006.

Whitmer, Benjamin. "'Torture Chambers and Rape Rooms': What Abu Ghraib Can Tell Us about the American Carceral System," *New Centennial Review* 6.1 (2006): 171–94.

Wideman, John. *Brothers and Keepers*. New York: Vintage, 1995.

Williams, Gary. *Siege in Lucasville*. Bloomington, IN: Rooftop, 2006.

Wood, Amy Louise. *Lynching and Spectacle: Witnessing Racial Violence in America, 1890–1940*. Durham: Univ. of North Carolina Press, 2009.

Zehr, Howard. *Changing Lenses: A New Focus for Crime and Justice*. Scottdale, PA: Herald Press, 1990.

Zimring, Franklin E. *The Contradictions of Capital Punishment*. Oxford: Oxford Univ. Press, 2003.

Index